Art Today

AN INTRODUCTION

TO THE FINE AND FUNCTIONAL ARTS

REVISED EDITION

Art Today

AN INTRODUCTION

TO THE FINE AND FUNCTIONAL ARTS

REVISED EDITION

RAY FAULKNER
Stanford University

EDWIN ZIEGFELD
Teachers College, Columbia University

GERALD HILL
General College, University of Minnesota

HENRY HOLT AND COMPANY · NEW YORK

Contents

Contents

Part IV. PAINTING, SCULPTURE, AND ARCHITECTURE

Illustrations

Chapter 3. ART IN RELIGION   *pages 91-98*

Chapter 4. ART IN INDUSTRY   *pages 115-122*

Chapter 5. ART IN COMMERCE

Chapter 6. TWO AIMS OF ORGANIZATION   *pages 165-168*

Chapter 7. THE PLASTIC ELEMENTS   *pages 185-192*

Chapter 8. THE PLASTIC ELEMENTS: *Continued* *pages 209-212*

Chapter 9. PRINCIPLES OF DESIGN *pages 229-236*

Chapter 10. THE THREE VIRTUOSI   *pages 269-276*

Chapter 11. CERAMICS AND GLASS   *pages 293-300*

Chapter 12. TEXTILES

Illustrations

Preface to Revised Edition

MANY events of greatest historical importance have transpired since the printing of the first edition of *Art Today* in 1941. Although it might have been thought that a war would have seriously curtailed development of an interest in the arts, such was not the case. True, some artists were forced to forsake temporarily their creative work, but many others made good use of their creativity and skill: painters and photographers recorded major military events; industrial designers gave new form and efficiency to military equipment; architects planned housing units, military camps, hangars, and laboratories; and city planners developed the site plans for such buildings. Under emergency pressure, some new materials, processes, and approaches came into use.

Art museums and galleries greeted record crowds, proving beyond doubt that art fills a deep need even under conditions of great strain. Perhaps this continuance of interest in art was to be expected because we were fighting for freedom and no field offers greater opportunities for the free development of an individual or of a culture. Men and women found in the art of the present and the past not merely an escape but a goal in their search for order, rightness, freedom, and inspiration.

With the cessation of hostilities and the return to normal pursuits, the interest in art has maintained itself, for men still cherish the spiritual satisfaction which it offers. And there are also favorable economic factors. A period of prosperity has produced new patrons of the arts ranging from the purchasers of washing machines and percolators and paintings to the builders of homes and factories.

This has seemed to be a logical time to prepare a revised edition of *Art Today*. A great deal has happened in the last few years and the authors felt that the content of the book should be consistent with its title. Primarily, the task of the revision has been a matter of bringing the book up to date. Many sections which appeared in the first edition have been deleted, inadequately developed ones have been enlarged, new ones have been added. As with the first edition, this is largely written around the illustrations. They, too, have been revised. Some of the plates remain, but many new ones have been included and the total number has been increased.

A major change has been made in the organization of the book. Whereas the first edition consisted of three sections only—the first concerned with human needs, the second with organization, the third with materials—the revision has four. The three original sections remain, but the chapters on Painting and Sculpture have been taken from Section I and Architecture from Section III and after extensive revision, now constitute a section by themselves. By bringing them together, the treatment of each has been made more adequate, yet their relation to the basic problems of human needs, organization, and materials remains clear.

Since it was first printed, this text has been used in many colleges and universities throughout the country. The authors have appreciated the many kind comments and helpful suggestions that have been proffered by teachers and students, for they have been invaluable in guiding and directing the revision of the book.

The authors are indebted to many organizations and individuals for help and assistance. The staffs at the Museum of Modern Art and the Metropolitan Museum of Art were especially helpful in providing illustrative material. Artists, galleries, and commercial and industrial concerns were generous in providing information and materials. Many individuals gave of their time, their ideas, and their energies: Professors Edward Farmer, Victor Thompson, and Arthur Young aided in the preparation of sections of the manuscript through their critical and helpful suggestions. Sarah Faulkner and Beatrice Harrison carefully edited portions of the text; Anna Lacovara, Fred Triplett, Boris Ilyn, and Charles Olsen aided greatly in the final preparation of the manuscript. To these and to many others the authors are indeed grateful.

Stanford, California	R. F.
New York, New York	E. Z.
Minneapolis, Minnesota	G. H.

November 23, 1948

Preface to the First Edition

THE last few decades have seen a phenomenal increase in art interests in the United States. Painting and sculpture, of the past and present, have been brought forcibly to the attention of a wider public through new and often startling experiments, through excellently printed books and reproductions, and through expanding programs of museums and educational organizations. Our architecture, influenced by new ways of building and living, is rapidly changing in structure and appearance. Nearly all of the useful products of daily life have been redesigned by industrial designers, and the containers in which they are packaged have been given new consideration. During the present century college courses in art have increased rapidly, and art in the public schools, once regarded as a frill, is now seen to be an integral part of the educational program. This increased interest, however, has not always been matched by an increased understanding of how the arts do, and can, improve contemporary living.

This book, written for laymen and students alike, is an introduction to those arts of form and color with which we come in contact every day. Sometimes they are referred to as the Fine and Industrial Arts, the Fine and Applied (or Allied) Arts, or the Plastic and Graphic Arts. Whatever the name, the field comprises city planning, architecture (including the furnishing of interiors), painting, printing and the graphic arts, sculpture, and the arts of industry and commerce. The title *Art Today* has been chosen not because the book deals only with contemporary manifestations, but because emphasis is placed on the many ways in which modern and historic art products influence present-day living and thinking. The book is a direct outgrowth of the experiments in general education, undertaken at the General College of the University of Minnesota, to make various fields of human endeavor meaningful and vital in contemporary society. The point of view presented in this book was outlined in a sylla-

Preface to the First Edition

bus published in 1935 at the University of Minnesota. This was subsequently revised and enlarged after its use with different interest and age groups.

In preparing the materials for this book, the authors have drawn on sources far too numerous to list in detail. Many persons have contributed, knowingly or otherwise, to the development of this approach to art, and the authors are indebted to all. To Dr. Malcolm S. MacLean, the authors owe a great debt for his constant encouragement of and critical interest in the art program from which this book has developed. Miss Lucille Fisher contributed in many ways toward planning and making effective this program. In preparing the manuscript for publication, the authors have had invaluable assistance from Dr. Helen R. Haggerty, Miss Sarah Key, and Mr. Eugene E. Myers. Miss Josephine Lutz and Mr. William Saltzman prepared the series of studies in the analysis and organization of the still-life painting used in Chapter 15. Professor Arthur Young gave many helpful suggestions in the chapter on Printing and the Graphic Processes, and Mr. J. Sheldon Carey aided in the preparation of the chapter on Ceramics. To these and the many others not mentioned here the authors express their gratitude.

New York, New York
Minneapolis, Minnesota

R. F.
E. Z.
G. H.

March 18, 1941

For the Reader

NEEDING shelter and protection, we build houses and wear clothes; finding it necessary to move easily from one place to another, we develop rapid means of transportation; producing goods, we advertise them to attract buyers. Man, being an intelligent animal, sets about to meet and satisfy his needs, to adjust himself to his environment. But the houses we build are more than shells to keep out the wind and rain, automobiles are more than seats on self-propelled frames, advertisements are more than dull recitals of the merits of products. We demand in these and in all the other objects we use a visual appeal and beauty that goes beyond that which results from merely meeting functional requirements. Houses, kitchen utensils, automobiles best fulfill their purposes when fashioned in accordance with basic principles of design.

But human needs are not only for such practical things. Frequent, certainly, are the desires for experiences other than eating, working, sleeping, or traveling. It is no feeble urge that compels us to seek ways to express and communicate our thoughts and ideas, feelings and aspirations, through paintings, drawings, etchings, photographs, ceramics, sculpture, textiles and a host of other products. There are paintings arising from the desire to communicate religious ecstasy. There are vases that result from and satisfy someone's urge to make something, to create objects "right" in color, inviting to the sense of touch, strong in the feeling of the clay from which they are made. There is sculpture expressing the ideals and aspirations not alone of individuals but of communities of people living together.

All of these belong to the field of art—for art touches our lives at every point, is integral with all our activities. To limit the field of art to painting, sculpture and architecture, as not a few academicians do, is to obscure the constant impact of art on all our actions. Art, interpreted broadly, refers not only to a group of specialized products, but also describes the manner in which any activity can be performed. There can be artistry in gardening and woodworking, in furniture arrangement and table setting, quite as much as in the so-called "Fine Arts." The distinction between the "Fine" and "Applied Arts" is hardly defensible, for as someone has remarked, if a product is not "fine," it is not art. Keeping in mind that anything which man does may have art value protects us from a snobbishly narrow concept of art.

The primary purpose of this book is to help make art more effective in daily living. Each person is faced with the necessity of selecting such articles of common use as clothing and furniture, and the pleasure enjoyed from such things depends to a large extent on how wisely they are chosen. Another everyday art problem is combining and arranging such things as furniture in a room, pictures on a wall, or plants in a garden for maximum comfort and pleasure. Then, too, we all have opportunities to appreciate public buildings, great paintings and sculpture, rare vases and textiles. Because these activities are part and parcel of our existence, we like to talk about them. All of them offer genuine possibilities for expressing one's own personality, for coming to understand the experiences of others, in short, for richer individual and social living.

To make art more effective in daily living this book presents a way of looking at art products, art processes and art problems. Art, in spite of the haze which often obscures its nature, is no mysterious activity to be understood only by a few. It is one of several fields of human activity in which all men use their powers and abilities to communicate their experiences to fellow men and to transform the materials of the natural world for human use.

Art always arises out of human needs, and these demand first study. But when a human need arises which can be met by art, the effort to meet it raises two questions: What shape or form will the solution take? How, and of what materials, will it be made? Hence, the first three parts of the book are:

PART I. THE PROBLEM OF HUMAN NEEDS
The art problems in each life area, such as the home, the community and religion, and the expressions arising from meeting these needs and solving these problems.

PART II. THE PROBLEM OF ORGANIZATION
The principles of organization which influence the development and form of art objects, the selection and arrangement of parts, the choice of shapes, colors, textures and spaces.

Part III. THE PROBLEM OF MATERIALS AND PROCESSES

The possibilities and limitations of materials—clay, stone, wood, etc. —and the processes by which they are transformed into art objects.

Each of these problems is intimately related to the other two. For example, an art problem of the home, involving the satisfaction of human needs, requires materials for its solution as well as attention to organization. Thus in the selection and arrangement of furniture for a living room a consideration of the possible uses of every piece of furniture, the relation of each article to the others in terms of function and design, and the use of appropriate materials are interwoven aspects of a single problem.

Because of the continuous importance of painting, sculpture, and architecture chapters on these three arts form the fourth part of the book.

Part IV. PAINTING, SCULPTURE, AND ARCHITECTURE

The ways in which painters, sculptors, and architects transform raw materials into works of art.

Art is a many-sided subject, and can be approached in a variety of ways. You can read about it, talk about it, see it, appreciate it, or produce it. Each of these activities can contribute something to the depth and breadth of your art understanding. Art appreciation is far more than knowing the names and dates of important artists and their works. It involves attitudes, feelings, emotions, preferences and personal tastes, for these to a large extent determine the manner in which you dress and furnish your living quarters as well as your reactions to the buildings, paintings and sculpture that you see. This book can only be a stimulus to action, a guide and a catalytic agent in helping you to react intelligently and emotionally to the visual richness that surrounds you.

"He doesn't know anything except facts."
(Courtesy of James Thurber and the *New Yorker*.)

PART I

The Problem of Human Needs

CHAPTER 1

Art in the Home

E̲VER since there were not caves enough to go around and the winter winds coming down off the ice-age glaciers grew too cold, the problems of comfortable shelter have beset man. Ice, straw, mud, wood, stone, steel and glass have been used as materials for shelter. Individual pioneers have built with their own hands houses from stones and logs. Pioneering governments, employing housing experts, have planned and built housing groups covering acres of land. New materials have been introduced and old materials discarded, architectural styles have been born and have died, but this basic human problem—*comfortable shelter*—is as fresh today as in the days of the Pharaohs. It is one of your concerns. In this chapter are examples of rooms and houses well planned for comfortable living. They call attention to how alive and close-knit are our daily habits, our homes and art. The discussion is first of contemporary problems and solutions, then of historic ones.

A ONE-ROOM APARTMENT

Many young persons live in small apartments. Because it is often the first home of their own, it is no trifling matter. They need space for living, space in which to express their own tastes and preferences; because man is a gregarious animal, they want a home to which their friends will enjoy coming. In most instances this must all be achieved with limited funds. And it can be done if thought is given to the problem. Figures 1 and 2 illustrate a one-room apartment planned to provide efficient and attractive living conditions at small cost.*

The needs of such young persons have been carefully considered. They

---

* This room was furnished as a demonstration project by the home-furnishing experts of *McCall's Magazine.*

need a room in which they can sit comfortably and read, listen to the radio, entertain a few friends, write letters, eat and sleep. Books, magazines, and ashtrays should be within easy reach; lights should be planned for reading or pleasant conversation groups; and storage space for clothes and accessories, necessarily limited in a one-room apartment, should be convenient. Although their eating and sleeping must be done in this room, they will not want it to look like a dining room or a bedroom. Essentially it is a living room and, in spite of its many uses, must not look like a catch-all.

For sitting there are two studio couches and a rattan chair, both well lighted, and within easy reach of several small tables. They invite one to sit down and read or converse. For eating, there is a simple, sturdy table. Working and letter writing can be done at the desk near the window. Storage space is provided by two chests of drawers. For sleeping there are studio couches which solve many problems for those living in a small space. Compact as the room is, it provides for a surprising number of activities because it is planned on a basis of function, on how the people who live there are going to use it. Nothing that should be within reach is beyond reach. Seats and tables are well arranged, lights are well placed. No outworn rule of style or fashion interferes with straightforward usefulness.

But appearance must be considered as well as efficiency. In addition to functioning well the room should be attractive. As the illustrations show, there is a fundamental idea from which each part of the room has grown, a fundamental idea of straightforward functional simplicity. Plain surfaces and well-related forms give the room a solid, architectural quality. Varied textures of rugs, Venetian blinds, curtains, upholstery, wood, and glass give enough interest so that little decoration is necessary. No "sour" objects intrude. No frilled curtains, no flowered scatter rugs, no highly carved "imitation antiques" detract from this basic unity.

There are four major furniture groups, two showing in each photograph: (1) the studio couches plus the small tables, lamps and picture, form the dominant group because of importance, size and the contrast of the dark couches against the light walls; (2) the second group—the dining table and wall decorations—is well related to the first by the heights of the tables; (3) the desk, chairs, and plants at the window end of the room are unified by the Venetian blind which repeats and emphasizes the horizontal lines of the furniture; and (4) the two chests, pushed close together to save space and increase the horizontal effect, achieve promi-

One room apartment, functional in arrangement, attractive in appearance, inexpensive in cost.

1. (*Upper*) Two related furniture groups against one wall, one for eating and the other for sitting and sleeping.

2. (*Lower*) Chests and mirror provide space for storing clothes and facilities for dressing, desk in corner for writing or studying.

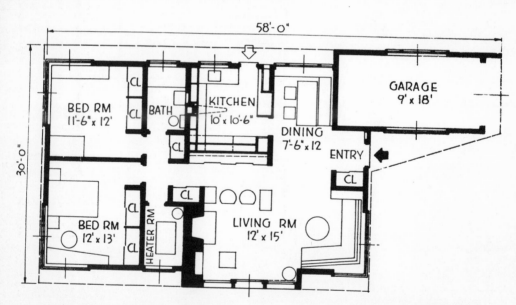

A Model House, modest in size and unpretentious in character, designed for comfortable, efficient living on one floor. Walter W. W. Jones, architect.

3. (*Upper*) Roof extending from garage gives shelter over entrance, terrace extending from living room increases spaciousness.

4. (*Lower*) Plan shows compact, segregated areas for living and eating, sleeping, work and utilities.

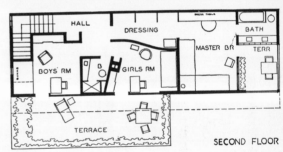

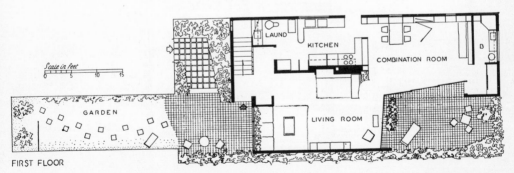

The House of Ideas, larger than the Model House and two stories high, shows what can be accomplished with more space. Edward D. Stone, architect.

5. (*Upper*) Exterior shows several spaces for outdoor living, well-spaced windows, and redwood siding used horizontally and vertically.

6. (*Lower*) Plans show first floor arranged for varied activities, second floor with three bedrooms and two baths.

Living room in House of Ideas illustrates orderly yet informal placing of comfortable, sturdy furniture and vistas increasing apparent size of room.

7. (*Upper*) Entrance end shows built-in couch as center of furniture group.

8. (*Lower*) Fireplace wall with views of terrace and combination room.

Combination room in House of Ideas may be used for eating, dancing, projecting movies, study or reading, and as a guest room.

9. (*Upper*) Note dining table which folds into wall, pass-through bar to kitchen.

10. (*Lower*) Study-guest end can be separated by panels folding out from wall.

9

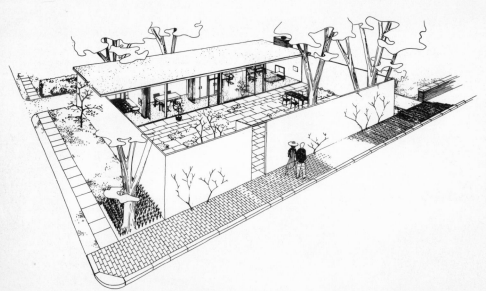

The Johnson house, Cambridge, Massachusetts, is notable for its precise regularity and formality. Philip Johnson, architect.

11. (*Upper*) Living room exemplifies great simplicity and restraint, reduction to essentials.

12. (*Lower*) Drawing shows rectangularity of design, continuous glass wall on garden side.

The Johnson house gains a remarkable sense of spaciousness and freedom through its simple furniture, absence of applied ornament, and floor-to-ceiling glass wall.

13. (*Upper*) The winter sun brings warmth and cheerfulness, reduces heating costs.

14. (*Lower*) In summer the garden is an extension of the living room.

Three examples of historic, traditional architecture from three continents.

15. Interior of Japanese house shows use of panels, simple furniture, and natural materials similar to contemporary trends in the United States.

16. Anne Hathaway's cottage, Stratford-on-Avon, England, illustrates the straight-forward, functional use of forms and materials characteristic of Elizabethan England.

17. The Travis house, Williamsburg, Virginia, is another house deeply expressive of the time and place in which it was built.

Interiors of Williamsburg houses exemplify good traditional design.

18. (*Upper*) The Travis house dining room has vigorous, functional table and chairs, well-designed fireplace and doors.

19. (*Lower*) The Raleigh Tavern Parlor shows judicious use of ornament.

13

Designed by Thomas Church, the Carpenter garden in Palo Alto, California, encourages varied outdoor activities in limited space.

20. Seen through the sliding glass doors of the living room, the garden is literally an extension of that area. There is ample pleasant space for eating, entertaining, or relaxing.

21. Seen from above, the garden shows an ingenious pattern of paved area, lawn, planting areas, and sandbox. The raised planting beds bring flowers nearer eye level, make maintenance less fatiguing, give good places to sit down.

22. The apparent size of the garden is greatly increased by the judicious use of diagonal lines and unexpected shapes. Planting, concentrated around the edges, frames and encloses the much-used paved and lawn areas.

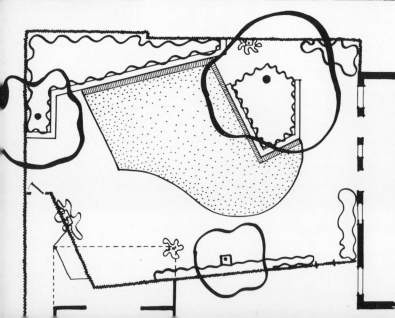

14

nence with the mirror and candles. Each group consists of furniture, accessories, and objects such as pictures, mirrors, plants or decorative molds, on the wall. This is an example of good organization in art.

The colors used in this one-room apartment are as fresh and interesting as the furniture. The walls are white to increase the apparent size and lightness of the room; a twelve-inch band of light blue framing the window brings stimulating contrast. The furniture is shellacked and waxed to preserve the natural beauty of the wood color and grain. The curtains are absinthe green, and the pillows on the couches are bright red. Pottery, metal and glass introduce other colors and textures.

Most persons living in such apartments must limit their expenditures and plan carefully in furnishing their living quarters. This room was inexpensively furnished, yet it is both comfortable and attractive. It has been developed out of basic, human, everyday needs, just as all works of art, from one-room apartments to movie stars' palaces, and from kitchen chairs to propaganda murals, are developed out of human needs and interests. Art is successful only when these needs are faced, studied and met in a straightforward manner.

THREE CONTEMPORARY HOUSES

A TWO-BEDROOM HOUSE

Planning a house is similar in many respects to furnishing a room. In both activities the basic problem is identical: organizing space for comfortable living. In furnishing a room, areas for different purposes are indicated by furniture arrangement, whereas in planning a house the walls, floors, ceilings, and openings—as well as the furniture—are designed and arranged.

In Figures 3 and 4 we see what can be accomplished in designing a small, yet attractive and livable, house. The simple, compact plan provides areas for the diverse activities of living, eating and cooking, sleeping and bathing through its ample living-dining room, compact kitchen-laundry unit, two bedrooms, and centrally located bathroom. The living room gains in apparent size because of its irregular shape, large windows, and view into the dining space. The efficiently planned kitchen is but a few steps from the dining table and only a few more from the front door.

The bedrooms each have two closets, and windows on two exposures. The intelligent use of corner windows in bedrooms and living room does much to increase the apparent size of the rooms, for placing windows in the corner calls attention to the diagonal, the longest dimension of a room, and keeps the larger wall surfaces unbroken.

The exterior is a straightforward expression of informal, pleasant living. The horizontal mass, the low-pitched roof and projecting eaves, the horizontal lines in the corner windows and the siding, the stone flower bed and the terrace give the house a secure, ground-hugging quality, a quality which is emphasized and relieved by the strong verticals of the sturdy chimney and the adjacent vertical windows. It is a house that fits into its surroundings as though it belonged there. Such a house costs no more than the ugly ones we know so well, but it can be achieved only through thoughtful planning. Compare this house for livability and appearance with houses of similar size in your community.

A MEDIUM-SIZE HOUSE

To get a deeper understanding of art in the home as well as of architecture in general, we turn now to a house planned specifically to meet the needs of a contemporary family. The example selected, appropriately called the "House of Ideas," was designed and constructed to demonstrate what is possible in contemporary domestic architecture.*

Much careful thinking and clear planning are necessary background for building a house which is easy and desirable to live in, and the first step in this direction is an understanding of the conditions which make living in a house pleasant. Look carefully at the compact flexible plan of the House of Ideas (Figure 6), the smartly designed interiors (Figures 7, 8, 9, 10), the straightforward exterior (Figure 5), and then consider the house in the light of the following interrelated problems which form a basis for thinking about or planning a house.

Functional Problems

Houses are built for people to live in. In the light of this simple statement it seems obvious that the needs of a family, both physical and psychological, should determine the forms and materials of a house.

---

* This house was designed by Edward D. Stone; the interiors were done by Dan Cooper in collaboration with Mr. Stone. It was sponsored by *Collier's Magazine* and was built as a project of the Rockefeller Home Center.

1. Shelter, Safety, Lighting, and Ventilation. Prime requisites of a house are that it gives its occupants and their possessions protection from cold and heat, wind and dust, rain and snow, flies and mosquitoes and, of course, burglars. Walls, roofs, and floors provide this physical shelter and at the same time give a comforting sense of enclosure and privacy in varying degrees. Today it is possible to build relatively thin walls which none the less have amazing insulating qualities. Of this development, the House of Ideas takes full advantage. Here insulated walls and windows with two sheets of glass add materially to the efficiency of the forced-draft, hot air heating system.

A good house not only gives shelter, but also provides sufficient light and fresh air for healthful, pleasant living. In the House of Ideas many new concepts of window planning and spacing are illustrated. First, a large pane of fixed plate glass forms one wall in the living room, and glass building blocks are used for one wall in the upstairs bathroom. Second, large concentrated areas of glass take the place of many smaller openings, giving greater unity to the exterior, a greater sense of spaciousness in the interior. Third, doors and windows extend to the ceiling, again to give an increased feeling of expansiveness. Fourth, windows face the garden rather than the street or the neighbors, and are more numerous on the east and south—generally favorable directions—than on the north and west. And in spite of the large amount of window space, the heat loss from that source has been conspicuously reduced through the use of double-glazed windows.

2. Functional Areas. Civilized living requires areas carefully planned for the uses to which they are to be put, and this organization of functional areas—the plan—is the most important single aspect of designing a house. The typical house of the past century achieved this segregation of areas by making each room a box or cell more or less completely separated from adjacent rooms, giving what is called a *closed plan.* Before the advent of central heating, it was highly desirable to be able to shut off each room from the others. Today, however, with improved heating and insulating devices, this is no longer necessary. Because it gives a greater sense of spaciousness and permits a more flexible use of the available space, the *open plan,* exemplified by the House of Ideas and the Johnson house (Figures 11 through 14), is rapidly gaining favor.

The *entrance* area need not be large. It serves as an introduction to the house, provides access to the other important areas, and has a closet

17

for coats and hats. In the House of Ideas the entrance area (Figure 7) is only partially separated from the living area by a clothes closet which does not reach the ceiling—thereby increasing the sense of free space. *Relaxation* and *entertainment* suggest large spaces and furniture planned for many uses. The living room (Figure 8) offers opportunity to group furniture around the fireplace, the built-in seat, or the large window, and is suitable for small or large groups of persons. The combination room offers still wider possibilities: the end near the living room and kitchen (Figure 9) is used for dining, work, or cards, while the farther end (Figure 10) separated by an ingenious movable partition which can be folded back into the wall (as indicated on plan) suggests reading, talking or a nap. With the partition open and the dining table folded up into the wall, the combination room is large enough for dancing or games. In mild weather two of the three large windows open to make the terrace an integral part of the room, extending further its size and possible uses.

Cooking demands a specially ventilated area near a space for eating. Observe the compactly designed kitchen (in plan and photograph) separated from the combination room by a counter, with a rolling panel above, that becomes either a serving buffet or a breakfast counter. This opening has the additional advantage of permitting a person in the kitchen to watch children playing in the combination room.

Sleeping necessitates privacy, good ventilation, and freedom from excess noise within and without the house. Often, as in this house, a separate floor is designed for sleeping, but here the bedrooms are planned not merely as sleeping rooms, but also as work rooms, studies, or retreats. The typically wasteful guest room has been eliminated, and in its place the end of the combination room, when separated by the folding partition, forms an attractive unit with a closet and bath.

Bathing, washing and *toilet needs* require the customary bathrooms and washrooms, generously provided for in this house. *Laundering* clothes demands space with water, tubs, drains, dryers, ironing boards and the like. As shown in the plan, the laundry is at one end of the kitchen, a pleasant and convenient location.

Storing things is a major concern of most people, and the problem has only recently been given the attention it deserves. Functionally designed wardrobes with sliding doors are far more efficient than the customary dark hole-in-the-wall closets; cupboards designed for specific purposes are more useful than attics. Notice that one entire wall of the combination room is built, honeycomb fashion, of cellular closets and cupboards with the doors treated as sections of a paneled wall.

Finally, *outdoor activities*—gardening, watering the lawn, or just plain sitting—suggest areas giving reasonable privacy, close contact with nature and with the house. The garden at the front, the brick-paved terrace off the living and combination room, and the two terraces on the second floor allow the occupants of this house really to enjoy the out-of-doors.

3. *Circulation*. There should be short, desirable routes from one part of the house to the others; excess space given to halls is a genuine waste in initial construction cost, upkeep, and occupants' energies. The House of Ideas disposes of this problem beautifully. Look at the plan and notice (1) that you can get from the front door to the living room, kitchen or upstairs without going through other rooms; (2) that there is a close relationship between the kitchen and the dining area and terrace; (3) that all of the bedrooms and one of the bathrooms can be reached from the small central hallway upstairs, with the passageway in the master bedroom efficiently used for closets and dressing space; and (4) that little space has been given to circulation alone. The house is planned to save space and steps.

4. *Furniture and Equipment*. The furniture and accessories in a home should bear a definite relationship to the building and should be designed functionally for their special uses. A good example of this is seen in many of the new kitchens and bathrooms where the fixtures have been carefully designed and built to be used and at the same time to be attractive. Other rooms in houses have often been much less functional because the furniture has been chosen and the pictures hung with more regard for ornamentation than for the character of the activities to be carried on in them. In the House of Ideas the manner in which cupboards and closets, shelves, plant boxes, built-in seats, as well as the chairs, tables, beds, and lamps, take their places as part of the house distinguish it as eminently practical and beautiful. From the many possible illustrations we mention but one: the chairs in Figure 7 have structurally sound and esthetically pleasing wood frames, seats and backs woven of tan leather, and cushions of airfoam rubber. They are comfortable, durable and attractive.

In summary, a house is designed primarily to provide shelter and protection, so that the activities of a family may be carried on comfortably, conveniently, and pleasantly. Thus the first criterion of domestic architecture becomes: The building should meet the human needs for which it was designed.

The Problem of Human Needs

Geographical Problems

We all know that Eskimos sometimes live in igloos of ice, African Negroes in grass huts, southwest American Indians and Mexicans in adobe houses. Each group uses a native product and builds a characteristic form of dwelling directly suited to its mode of living and to its geographical setting. More sophisticated peoples have likewise developed their architectural forms out of local conditions. Thus the houses in Scandinavia have steep roofs to shed snow and have a cold, northern look about them; those along the French Riviera have flatter roofs, are sprawling rather than compact, and appear warm, southern, and friendly. The Colonial houses in Massachusetts were built in a compact manner with rooms shut off from each other because there was no central heating system to give warmth to the house as a whole. Colonial houses in Georgia on the other hand were likely to have large rooms with high ceilings for coolness in summer, with many open spaces, with cross-ventilation and with large living porches to take advantage of the milder climate.

In the past, methods of transportation and communication were so poorly developed that only local materials and to some extent only regional architectural concepts were available to the builders. As a result the architecture of different regions developed much local flavor. The forests in New England gave rise to the early Colonial frame houses. Where wood was not so plentiful, stone was used as a building material or native clay was fired as brick.

Today industry has produced an almost uncounted number of new building materials, and the vast network of modern transportation lines has made it possible to ship both native and processed materials far from their original sources. Thus local builders are not restricted to local materials and contemporary architecture has not the regional quality it once had.

This fact is admirably illustrated in the House of Ideas. It is suitable to most areas in the United States. The building material—California Redwood—is eminently practical. The insulated walls and double windows protect against too great cold in winter and against excessive heat absorption in summer. The compact plan allows for easy heating in winter, the many windows for enjoying the spring and summer breezes. A more open plan with greater provision for cross-ventilation and with higher ceilings would be appropriate for localities in Florida, Arizona and Southern

California. But with the exception of the extreme northern and southern sections the house could be built almost anywhere in the United States.

The building site also conditions the type of house which is to be built. Is the land flat or rolling? Are there trees, or a lake or pond? Are there views? Which point of the compass should the house face? The orientation of a house should take into consideration light, air, and outlook so that the windows in important rooms face the best views and the sun and breezes are used to good advantage. If, for example, afternoon sun is wanted in living rooms, a house built on one side of a street will have a different floor plan and consequently a different exterior from a house across the street.

The House of Ideas was designed for a conventional, narrow city lot fronting on the street to the west. Since northwest winter winds are cold and the afternoon sun is hot, windows are generally most desirable on southern and eastern exposures. Study of the illustrations shows that windows and outdoor living areas, both upstairs and downstairs, are concentrated on the south and east. There are few windows on the north, except in the kitchen, and appropriately enough that side of the house is given over to the stairway, to storage cupboards on the first floor, and to closets on the second. This is especially desirable inasmuch as the house would be built as close as possible to the northwest corner of the property leaving maximum space to the south and east for lawn and gardens, views of which could be enjoyed from windows and terraces. The usual planning of houses, on the contrary, gives about the same number of windows on every side resulting in higher heating bills, less comfort in summer, and views in all directions whether or not they are worth looking at. How much better it is to place windows so that they give full advantage to light, air and attractive outlooks! This is a fundamental, common-sense solution of an art problem. Art is, in a large part, good common-sense, enlivened by touches of imagination.

From this discussion emerges the second criterion: The house should be related to its geographical location. It should take advantage of desirable views, be suited to the climate, and look as though it belonged to its setting.

Community Problems

Because the house is a part of the community, it becomes more than an individual shelter. Except in occasional situations it is one of many in a group of houses. Building ordinances prescribe certain features such as the amount of window space and the general location on the lot as an aid to healthful buildings. Some districts and subdivisions have restrictions which dictate not only the minimum cost and size of the house or the materials to be used but the general style as well. However, in the majority of instances there are no such restrictions, and each man chooses freely the kind of house he will build. Quite often he gives some attention to the general character of the community, although herein lies a difficulty: his community, unlike those to be discussed in the next chapter, may have no unified character. It may be a confused jumble of houses, and there is little a new homeowner can do toward clearing up the condition. In many of our residential sections Colonial houses jostle uneasily with Tudor imitations, and the vertical lines of a French provincial fight against the horizontals of a contemporary house. Even more numerous are those American creations built without benefit of architect which lack any distinguishing features: every city has block after block of houses of this type.

The House of Ideas demonstrates an intelligent solution of the problem of relating a new house, expressing the interests of its owners, to the group of houses in which it might be placed. Although it is contemporary in every respect it would not be out of place in the typical American city or town. The basic forms are as straightforward and functional as those of the earliest New England house or the most modern furniture. The material, wood, is one of the oldest known building materials; the exterior redwood is oiled rather than painted to give it a natural effect which blends well with the surroundings. The simple sloping roof is the least expensive type to build, and probably has a wider appeal than a flat roof (although a house such as this might very well have a flat roof). The windows, placed where needed, produce an interesting pattern.

It will become increasingly evident that every art product belongs to a particular time and place, a particular social order, and that significant art expresses its period without hesitancy or flamboyancy. From the discussion of the relation of a house to the community comes a third criterion: The house should express the community of which it is a part, and the period in which it was built.

Individual Problems

In addition to fulfilling the functions of a house in a given climate and a particular community, the building should be related to the needs and interests of those who are to occupy it. The house and its furniture should live up to the people for whom it is home. The people should not be required to live up (or down) to it, for a family should certainly feel at home in its own house. The relation of the house to the individual family involves several factors.

In the first place, the size of the house is in part determined by the size of the family. But the financial, professional, and social position are also to be considered. Some few families need large spaces for entertaining of a very formal kind, but most, operating on limited budgets and preferring simple ways of life, entertain informally and require no space other than that used by the family every day.

Beyond these practical requirements, every homemaker—woman and man—has a right to a home expressing in some way his own personality. Individual interests and hobbies demand as much consideration as the pocketbook will permit. The photographer needs his dark room, the woodworker his bench and tool racks, the person interested in reading his quiet book-lined study. The fisherman needs space for his tackle, the hunter for his guns; the musician, amateur or professional, wants a location for his radio-phonograph quite as much as the gardener wants a garden.

From the redwood exterior, the plywood walls, the light and informal furniture, one can tell a good deal about the kind of persons for whom the House of Ideas has been designed. The whole spirit of the house suggests lively occupants who entertain easily and informally and who have a number of interests. The downstairs bathroom is so equipped that it may readily be turned into a photographic darkroom; a projection screen is concealed above the guest couch; and projection equipment is stored in a tall cupboard beside the breakfast counter. The many persons who today are interested in photography are justified in taking this common hobby into consideration in designing their house.

In a well-planned house the actual appearance of the occupants, their manner of dress, their patterns of behavior help determine the character of the house. Does this mean that each house must be so individual that it can be lived in by only one family? Not at all. Within groups of families of similar size, income, and social status there are many which are much alike. A house may be suited to the interests, activities, and dispositions of from ten to a thousand different families and yet have desirable individuality. The primary consideration is that the general character of the house be adaptable to the needs of those who are to live in it. Thus the

23

fourth criterion is: The house and its furnishings should express and contribute to the personalities of its occupants. It should have an interesting,
individual character.

Appearance

Does the problem of appearance really come last? Is that not the first
consideration of the artist? You might well ask such questions because
much recent "Revival Art" has placed looks foremost, function and expression hindmost. We know that the history of art gives ample evidence
that art objects develop out of human needs, are fashioned to meet these
needs directly, and that the final appearance is largely a result of such
processes. The same is true today. Consider the way in which the House
of Ideas was developed. First, a careful study of the needs of contemporary
families was made. After that came preliminary sketches of room arrangements, rough sketches of the exteriors, and constant consideration of the
materials from which it would be built. The choice of the materials was
one of the earlier definite steps, and the materials, of course, were chosen
for their durability, beauty, and suitability. Last came a process of refining and further developing these ideas to produce greater efficiency and
beauty.

Consider the specific ways and means used to make the house attractive.
The exterior achieves distinction from the interesting basic shape, from
the effective concentration of large areas of smooth glass and textured
wood, and from the patterns created by using the redwood siding vertically
and horizontally. The open terraces, the sloping roof, the walls at an
angle relieve the house of any boxy quality, and add variety in lights and
shade. The rich brown-red of the wood is emphasized by the narrow white
frames of the windows and the greens of trees, shrubs and vines. The
simple, functional forms, plus the beauty of oiled redwood, make this
exterior attractive in form and color.

The interior is equally, if not more, distinguished. The living room
walls (Figure 8) are paneled with oak plywood, waxed and laid in squares
to form an interesting panel pattern; the ceiling is also of plywood without
emphasis on the panels; and the floor is of the "blox-on-end" type, laid to
form an interesting pattern. The simple brick-lined fireplace, temporarily
filled with plants for summer decoration, has a cream marble face below
a narrow shelf on which are a small bronze statuette and clear crystal
vases filled with flowers. An unusual effect results from the use of a redwood trellis, rather than the more customary wall, to separate living

from combination room. Here again are growing plants in cream-colored pots decoratively arranged on the trellis. The east end of the living room is a wall of clear glass, extending from floor to ceiling, which makes living room and terrace seem to be one unit. The opposite end of the living room shown in Figure 7 has high windows facing the street, the coat closet, a long box for growing plants and an extra long, soft davenport upholstered in rich brown machine-loomed cotton fabric. The vertical poles along the stairway echo the trellis. Small pictures are effectively hung against the paneled walls. The color scheme is that of natural woods —oak, walnut, pine, and mahogany—as a background for the green of the plants and the red-oranges and yellows in the upholstery.

The combination room (Figure 10) shows a beautiful relationship of couch, chairs, built-in shelves, table, lamp and small sculpture. Here the walls are of ribbed plywood, and the floor is of large squares of red and black composition flooring covered with a grass matting rug. As in the living room, the large windows bring views of the garden, adding immeasurably to the interest of the room and making unnecessary much pattern or decoration. With the exception of the printed textiles on the pillows, the patterns in this room are structural rather than applied: the texture in the rug and chair backs results naturally from the process by which they were made; the grain of plywood and the functional panels add further interest; and the adjustable bookshelves with their books and other objects give a three-dimensional, architectural setting for the furniture.

The importance of paintings in making a house a pleasant place for living is illustrated here just as it was in the one-room apartment. Since earliest times, man has shown interest in enriching his living quarters with drawings and paintings which express worthwhile human experience. So universal is this human need that it would be difficult to find a home without pictures of some sort on the walls, and it is precisely because this need is basic that painting has always occupied a place of major importance. Today there are painters and print makers whose interest is in producing pictures for use in homes. Their work is often so inexpensive that nearly everyone today can afford original paintings or prints of one sort or another if he wishes them. In addition to these, excellent color reproductions, well worth a place on walls, are available from many sources: magazines, art museums and print dealers. Selecting and hanging paintings in one's home goes beyond merely relieving the bareness of walls. It is one way in which a person expresses his interests and tastes for his own and his friends' pleasure. The paintings and the sculpture in the House of Ideas express convictions about the use of such art objects in domestic interiors.

The problem of the appearance of a house is no mere afterthought: it is one of the several basic problems of designing satisfying shelter. Thus the fifth criterion becomes: The house should be pleasing in appearance, both inside and out.

Designed around the needs of the occupants, the House of Ideas functions well as a shelter for contemporary living. It is called "modern" because it meets existing needs directly, takes advantage of technological progress, and has not borrowed (or stolen) ornament or forms belonging to historic periods and ill-suited to this century. Consequently, it is a forthright expression of life today. The plan is open, the space can be used as the occasion demands, and the beauty comes from the sensitive design of form and the colors and textures of materials. It is important to note that it was *designed from the inside out;* the exterior was developed from the interior. This stands as one of the basic principles in architectural design.

Diametrically opposed to this concept of functional planning is the common practice of beginning the design of a house by choosing a "style" —Early American, Georgian, English, French, or Spanish—on the basis of appearance. Having decided prematurely what shape, ornamentation, and fenestration the house will have, the architect and owner then compromise the space behind this façade as best they can for contemporary living. To refer to such houses as "traditional" betrays a basic misunder standing of the history of architecture, a history marked by continuous development of new forms to meet contemporaneous needs. The magnificent achievements of historic architecture—houses, temples, churches, public buildings—deserve our highest admiration as works of art expressing their cultures. If we truly appreciate and esteem them, we can only be embarrassed to see them imitated and burlesqued in climates and geographical locations where they are not at home, executed in unsuitable materials, ornamented with detail lacking refinement, conviction, and spirit.

The analysis of the manner in which the House of Ideas developed naturally from the conditions of family life today exemplifies the approach followed in the design of true architecture as distinguished from masquerades of false fronts concealing, rather than expressing, their func tion and period. In houses as in people, honesty and sincerity are esteemed qualities because they express a fundamental integrity of character.

ANOTHER MODERN HOUSE

Do you like houses as sleek as a plane, as simple (and beautiful) as a mathematical formula, as logically conceived as a philosophical discourse, and yet designed with great sensitivity to relationships of space and mass? Look at the house architect Philip Johnson designed for himself in Cambridge, Massachusetts (Figures 11, 12, 13, 14). The owner-designer has long been an enthusiast for the type of modern architecture that takes full advantage of machine production, that gains an exciting twentieth-century beauty from broad, free treatment of space. As the drawing shows, the basic character of the house is simple and rectangular, the dominant theme is the continuous glass wall along the east side. Almost the entire property is enclosed by a wall, part of the enclosed space has a roof and a glass wall and a few partitions, and the remainder is paved for outdoor living. No curves or diagonals interrupt the restful, austere straight lines.

No ordinary house, this one resembles an apartment efficiently yet generously planned for a bachelor. A spacious living room freely opens into space for dining from which it can be separated by a curtain. Beyond the dining space is the bedroom and bath. A compact kitchen completes the house. The living room (Figure 11) is extremely formal. One wall of rich wood paneling has a chaste fireplace in the exact center, the other two walls are plastered, and one is enlivened by a large abstract tapestry. The furniture, simple to the point of austerity, completes the regularity of the room. Figure 13 shows the glass wall continuous along the east side of the house which literally opens the house into the enclosed garden, a summer view of which is shown in Figure 14.

The garden deserves a word, for here is one designed for living. High walls give privacy and protection from wind; solid pavement gives firm, dry footing. Straightforward furniture, only part of which is shown in the photograph, invites relaxation. Plants are reduced to a minimum with a few varieties in neat beds contrasting splendidly with the mathematical regularity of the house and wall. This is no garden for a horticulturist, but it demands a minimum of upkeep and lends itself to a variety of uses.

The Philip Johnson house represents a phase of contemporary architecture often referred to as the INTERNATIONAL STYLE of which it is the best domestic example in the United States. A study of this house and other examples—the New Bauhaus in Germany (Figure 80) and the Tugendhat house in Czechoslovakia (Figure 121)—reveal that this style, in common with all significant modern architecture, places emphasis on *volume* and *space* (rather than on mass), *openness, flexibility,* and *continuity.* The qualities that differentiate it from the characteristic work of such architects as Edward Stone and Frank Lloyd Wright (see Figures 145 and 289) are its greater emphasis on *regularity, smoothness,* and *precision.* As its name implies, it is not an architecture growing out of local conditions but is nonregional or international in character. It grows far less out of its geographical setting and local traditions than it does out of twentieth-century technology and ideals. It is "world architecture" aiming toward the coordination of basic, generalized, human needs and the techniques of standardized industrial production.

Simplicity has been achieved through standardization, repetition, and the elimination of everything unnecessary. Interest is achieved through uninterrupted surfaces, rich textures, and a few—a very few—decorative objects such as textiles, prints, and plants. The architect made no attempt to produce the informality and hospitable charm inherent in the design and furnishing of the House of Ideas. But he achieved what he wanted— a clean-cut, formal precision. Which do you prefer? Both are worth study and admiration; each demonstrates a trend in contemporary house design.

OTHER HOUSES

To broaden our horizons and to increase our understanding of art in the home, we may study examples of dwellings from widely varying cultures: from Japan, Elizabethan England, and Colonial America.

A JAPANESE HOUSE

When one looks at the interior of the Japanese house (Figure 15), the clean-cut simplicity, the sensitive spacing of objects, the delightful use of materials are at once apparent. Although we might expect a Japanese house to have little relation to the contemporary homes discussed above, there are many points of similarity. Panels, not unlike those suggested for prefabrication, or the sheets of plywood in the living room of the House of Ideas, are seen on the walls and floors. Also, like many contemporary American homes, the Japanese house gives a feeling of extensiveness and free space. The furniture is simple. A few art objects displayed with meticulous care give charm and individuality. This house, too, is "modern" because it grew out of a way of living.

ANNE HATHAWAY'S COTTAGE

Since conditions in Elizabethan England were quite different from those in Japan, we expect Anne Hathaway's cottage at Shottery, England (Figure 16), to be radically different in appearance. It is. As opposed to the lightness and flexibility of the Japanese house, Anne Hathaway's cottage is heavy and solid.

According to present-day standards it is dark, poorly ventilated and difficult to heat, yet it functioned efficiently when judged by sixteenth-century standards of living. It stands in the same relation to contemporary American houses as Elizabethan stagecoaches to our latest automobiles.

The cottage is consistently charming. The irregularities of the roof, walls, and chimney lend it a naturalness which the use of the materials has emphasized. Stone quarried nearby and laid horizontally in both house and garden wall gives a rugged texture, a play of color. In contrast, part of the masonry wall has been plastered to a flat smoothness. The brick texture is midway between the plaster and stone in smoothness and regularity. The straw thatch makes a fitting roof. Notice, too, the patterns made by the timbers, structural members which are also decorative. The dooryard cottage garden is as delightful as the house, and forms an admirable transition from man-made architecture to nature. Could any house be a better, more sincere expression of the sixteenth century in rural England?

HOUSES FROM COLONIAL WILLIAMSBURG

From 1699 to 1779 Williamsburg was the center of the governmental, economic, religious and social activities of the Colony of Virginia. Its decline began during the Revolutionary War with the removal of the capital to Richmond, and from that time to the present Williamsburg has continued as a quiet college town and as the seat of the county government. Attracting little attention until recently, it is now world-famous because of the extensive restoration program carried on so that "the

29

present may learn from the past." Today Williamsburg stands as a museum giving a vivid picture of an eighteenth-century American capital.

How do the homes of Williamsburg, built approximately two centuries ago, differ from contemporary homes? Are there similarities? They, too, were built as shelters for family life and, in their eminently successful answer to the problem of designing a house for existing needs, they stand in the history of architecture as some of the best "modern" houses of the past. But life in those days was not what it is today. Once this is understood we will have made strides toward defining the basis of art in terms of the sources from which it grows.

Figure 17 is a photograph of the Travis house, a handsome example of a Colonial home built eleven years before the Revolution. The house has an unadorned, dignified charm developing from the simple straightforward masses, the well-proportioned, well-spaced windows, the white picket fence relating the house to the grounds. Although not the type of Colonial most widely imitated today, it is representative of the period. The comely doorway commands first attention for its simple detail. The dark shutters contrast effectively with the white clapboard siding, and afford the protection needed at the time from cold or breakage. The materials—clapboards, shingles and bricks—emphasize the structure of the building, and their variety provides surface interest. Small-paned and shuttered, the windows of the Travis house reflect the prohibitive cost in the eighteenth century of large panes of glass, and the need for additional protection against cold and against breakage.

The dining room from the Travis house (Figure 18) bears out the general character of the exterior. Although somewhat uncomfortable according to present standards, the chairs are straightforward, honest, and simply ornamented at important points. The table, much cruder than the sideboard, looks as sturdy as the wide planked floor. The fireplace and two doors, designed as a single unit, mark a focal point for the portrait. The wainscoting, window-high, and the heavy wood cornice, act as unifying elements. The tableware and glassware are in harmony with the room; the decorative draperies add variety. The room attains harmony and distinction because the furnishings are consistent in simple design and frank use of good materials: wide floorboards; smooth, fine-grained wood in the furniture; rush seats on the chairs; metal and glass on the table. As with the exterior, there is little need for applied ornament and decoration when the basic forms and materials are sensitively handled.

Another example from Williamsburg, the parlor from Raleigh Tavern (Figure 19), belongs to the same period, but expresses greater refinement and elegance, more interest in decorative pattern, less emphasis on materials. The woodwork has more complex moldings and is painted rather than stained and waxed. The design of the furniture shows more detail in shapes and carving. It is a room designed for genial, sophisticated living. In spite of minor differences, the rooms from the Raleigh Tavern and the Travis house have much in common just as the furniture and houses at Williamsburg belong together. In the Raleigh Tavern as well as in the Travis house there is no break in continuity from interior to exterior, from function to form.

Such integrity and singleness of purpose come when art products grow naturally from integrated social conditions. The Colonial builder was never troubled by the problem of what "style" to build in—he built in Colonial *style* because he was building a house for Colonial family life. From each great period of history has come a period of art, important because it has expressed something deeply characteristic of that age. Architects, painters, designers and consumers who look forward do not condemn original examples of historic styles, however much they many deprecate imitations of them. They are the first to recognize the magnificent beauty of the Parthenon and Gothic cathedrals, the more intimate beauty and charm of Cape Cod cottages and the graciousness of the Williamsburg houses. And they are the first to recognize the inherent fallacy of trying to reproduce them. Although the buildings of past ages seem to have little in common, they all share this: they are direct, sincere expressions of life of the times. They stand as memorials to their designers—builders who worked and thought in the spirit of their age.

FURNISHING THE HOME

Selection and arrangement of furniture and accessories have been discussed in relation to the apartment, House of Ideas, Johnson house, and the houses at Williamsburg. In essence, this problem is strikingly similar to that of planning a house. Perhaps now is a good time to set down a few thoughts in this important area of art.

Furnishing a home is basically simple if notions of "periods," fads, and tricks are swept away. While we are sweeping the cobwebs away, we might as well also rid ourselves of a misconception inherent in the phrase "interior decoration." Because of the antics of many "interior decorators" with their frills and furbelows, this phrase now seems more applicable to Christmas trees and wedding cakes than to homes. The problem is to *furnish*, not to *decorate*, space for living. It is a problem for which there is no one sure-fire, readymade solution, but one in which common sense, imagination, and ingenuity play their part along with sensitivity to human needs, to form, and to color.

Here is one approach. First, decide what activities will normally take place in the room and what equipment you will need for them; in other words, give thought to the room's functions. Read again the paragraphs about the ways in which the needs of the occupants of the One-Room Apartment and the House of Ideas have been analyzed and met. What will you want to do in the room? Relax? Read? Converse? Listen to music? Study? Each of these activities makes its special demands. The more comprehensive and detailed you make this analysis, the better the chance of getting a functional room.

Second, decide on the basic character or personality that you want the room to have. Should it be formal or informal, joyful or subdued, exciting or serene, in order to meet your needs? What are your needs—and your wishes? Do you want a room with quality similar to the Raleigh Tavern parlor, to the House of Ideas, or to the Philip Johnson house? This is the time for self-analysis and realism. Your dreams and visions may call up Romeo and Juliet scenes of great halls, balconies, rich brocades, and massive furniture; or they may take you to an interior of glass, plastics, and metals. Remember that such backgrounds, suited to your personality as they may be, cannot be achieved in a typical apartment or the little suburban house. Keep your dreams but give them a practical base.

Having established the room's character, your third step is to select the more important (in size, color, cost, interest), then the less important, items to carry out this idea in form and color. Should your furnishings be predominantly rough or smooth, delicate or massive, plain or ornamented? How well will the various items go together? If you know exactly where you are going to live for the next twenty years, or even for the next five, select each object with that space in mind. If you do not know, think carefully about furniture that can be used in many places, even for various uses. Then there is color. Should it be rich or pale, contrasting or harmonious, intense or grayed? Such factors are discussed in Chapters 7 and 8.

All along, of course, you should have been thinking about arranging the furniture and accessories for maximum comfort, convenience, and attractiveness, for this is your fourth consideration. In planning your furniture arrangement, you will want to think of the importance to you of each piece. For example, if you like music and play your radio and phonograph frequently, they should be readily accessible. The same holds true for the equipment needed for any other special interest. It is the problem of human need again. And in all this arrangement, you will be thinking of balancing the pieces, of placing them so that they relate rhythmically to each other, and of giving due emphasis to the more important objects. For specific help on this phase of the problem you will want to study Chapter 9.

Did we say that this problem is basically simple? Well, *basically* it is. To be sure, you cannot become a master by reading a few pages in a book, but as you proceed further with your study of this and other books, you will learn more about which forms, colors, and textures lead to desired effects. As you analyze each room you see to determine what produces its pleasantness, or lack thereof, you will begin building your working vocabulary of home furnishing ideas. Finally, as you try your hand at arranging what furniture you now have and observe or ascertain your friends' reactions to the results, you will learn by experience, still the best teacher. Do not be afraid to experiment. Begin now—it is none too early.

The several problems central in designing a house, as analyzed in the section on the House of Ideas, are also encountered in varying degrees of importance in furnishing the house. The *functional problem* retains its first-rank importance for obvious reasons. The *geographical problem* drops to secondary importance because of the standardization of furniture and accessories and the control of climate within the house. The *community problem* is also less important because the community by and large is less concerned with house interiors than with house exteriors. The *individual problems* and those of *appearance*, however, retain their paramount significance, for certainly everyone wishes his home to have an individual, attractive character. It is the one area above all others where individuals have control over their own surroundings; the one place where it is essential that the occupants feel literally "at home." For many people this is the most important area of art today.

DESIGNING THE GARDEN

The Philip Johnson garden (Figure 14) is a rectangular space, mostly paved, but with some planting beds for trees and shrubs, screened from the street by a high wall but separated from the house only by a glass wall. It is as simple and precise as is the house. Planned for relaxed outdoor living, it requires minimum upkeep. In contrast, the garden around Anne Hathaway's cottage (Figure 16) is irregular and picturesque, harmonizing nicely with the thatch-roofed, half-timbered house. A profusion of flowering plants give a color pattern variegated as a patchwork quilt. Clearly, it is a garden for a climate in which flowers prosper and for persons who enjoy horticultural pursuits. Contrasting to both of the above, the Garden of the Governor's Palace at Williamsburg (Figure 25) is notable for its elaborate, geometrical symmetry. It is a garden to be admired from the Palace windows, to be walked through, and to be laboriously maintained. These three gardens only hint at the diverse paths open to the garden designer: the Egyptians, Greeks, Romans, and Spaniards extended their houses into the garden as true outdoor living rooms, living space enclosed by house, wall, and arcade and enlivened with pools, fountains, sculpture, furniture, and plants; medieval Europeans protected their beds of roses and herbs and their arbored or arcaded walks with the strong walls of castle and monastery; the artists of the Italian Renaissance opened their gardens to nature with broad walks and shady groves, yet related them to architecture with walls, balustrades, fountains, pools, seats, and garden pavilions; the Japanese with consummate artistry produced subtle effects with picturesque trees and shrubs, rocky waterfalls and pools, stone lanterns, and gaily ornamented bridges and tea houses; the English who "jumped the fence and discovered that all nature was a garden" gave us the naturalistic type based on the theory that "nature abhors a straight line." The rich history of gardens is the story of man's delight in nature and of his achievements in adapting nature to his needs.

Because the garden is literally an extension of the house, all of the principles of house design and furnishing are applicable. Figures 20, 21, and 22 show the plan and views of the Thomas Carpenter's California garden designed by Thomas D. Church. Considerations of function and human need, first as always, led to a garden directly accessible from kitchen and living room with paved areas ample for outdoor eating, playing, or just plain sitting. A service yard and work space have been located at the rear adjacent to the garage. Visible from both kitchen and living room is a raised sandbox which can later be easily transformed into a flower bed. The raised flower beds supported by weathered redwood planks have distinct advantages: they make the care and enjoyment of flowers easier and give the garden an architectural character which relates it to the house, while the broad ledges provide seating space for many persons. Fences of redwood stakes and planting (which had not attained its full growth at the time these pictures were taken) give comfortable privacy.

The plan is ingenious. The general diagonal direction gives a feeling of greater spaciousness and minimizes the boxy feeling common in small backyard gardens. The contrast of curved line against right angles and diagonals introduces a variety that makes each visit to the garden a new and rewarding experience; yet one feels the unity resulting from the dominating continuous paved area, the single interestingly shaped patch of lawn, the concentration of flowers where growing conditions are best, and the enclosing seat height and eye-level redwood walls. It is a garden which has grown out of the needs of its owners, harmonious with its geographical and community setting, individual in character, and attractive in appearance.

In designing a garden as in furnishing a home, it is wise to analyze one's needs, decide on the character one wishes, and then proceed to selecting and arranging all items to achieve the desired goals. In this process keep in mind that a garden should be designed for human use, not for the benefit of plants. Do not forget, too, that adequate enclosure increases its usefulness. Plan your garden as you do your house, for it is part and parcel of the home.

The topic of art in the home is so large that no one could hope to exhaust the material on it, and this chapter can do little more than act as an introduction to activities which can be carried on in the future of which the following are suggestive:

First, observe sharply and discriminatingly the houses that you see every day, the furniture sold in your local stores, the houses, furniture and accessories discussed and advertised in magazines and newspapers. Think of them in terms of home life today, and apply to each the criteria stated in this chapter.

Second, look in the following sections of this book for further ideas about color, design and materials which apply to the home. This chapter, with its emphasis on the human problems, serves as a foundation for the study of the effects and uses of color; the design principles of balance, rhythm and emphasis; and the intelligent understanding of materials. See how many direct applications to your own home you can make of the facts and principles in Parts II and III.

Third, read some of the many stimulating books on this subject to broaden and deepen your understanding, to sharpen your discrimination. For general background:

A. F. Bemis and J. Burchard: *The Evolving House* (Technology Press, Mass. Inst. of Technology, 1933-36) for its scholarly analysis of the problems of historical and contemporary shelter.

Suzanne La Follette: *Art in America* (Harper, 1929) for its clear description of the development of art in America.

Richard Tallmadge: *The Story of Architecture in America* (W. W. Norton, 1936) for the same reason.

Frank Lloyd Wright: *An Autobiography* (Duell, Sloan and Pearce, 1943) for a genuinely fascinating account of the development of a new American architecture by its most brilliant exponent.

For more specific help in solving your own problems:

Dan Cooper: *Inside Your Home* (Farrar, Straus, 1946) for a book showing that house design and decoration are one and the same thing.

James and Katherine Ford: *Design of Modern Interiors* (Architectural Book Publishing Company, 1942) for an excellent presentation of contemporary interior design.

James and Katherine Ford: *The Modern House in America* (Architectural Book Publishing Company, 1940) for a good survey of contemporary houses in this country.

Margaret O. Goldsmith: *Designs for Outdoor Living* (Stewart, 1941) for a good introduction to garden design.

H. and V. Goldstein: *Art in Everyday Life* (Macmillan, 1940) for a sound discussion of design principles applied to home decoration.

B. K. Johnstone and Associates: *Building or Buying a House* (Whittlesey House, 1945) for a realistic guide to wise investment in houses.

Elizabeth Mock: *So You Want to Build a House* (Museum of Modern Art, 1946) for an intelligent—and entertaining—discussion of factors to consider in home planning and the suitability of contemporary forms for contemporary problems.

George Nelson and Henry Wright: *Tomorrow's House* (Simon and Schuster, 1945) for an exciting presentation of present and future possibilities in house design.

Christopher Tunnard: *Gardens in the Modern Landscape* (Architectural Press, 1938) for the best discussion of the modern garden.

Roger Stewart Tyler: *Plan Your House to Suit Yourself* (Scribner, 1938) for its clear and thorough analysis of house planning written so that it is of value to the layman or professional architect.

Richardson Wright (ed.): *House and Garden's Guide to Interior Decoration* (Simon and Schuster, 1947) for a beautifully illustrated presentation of a variety of trends in interior design.

F. R. S. Yorke: *The Modern House* (Architectural Press, 1935) for its survey of contemporary houses in different countries.

CHAPTER 2 *Art in the Community*

A COMMUNITY is a body of people living together and having a common organization and common interests. In some cases it may consist of a single family living in isolation in a small group of buildings on productive land, with a simple blacksmith shop in one corner of the barn, a root cellar for the storage of fruits and vegetables raised on the land, a house for the family to live in. Here the members of this little community meet to thresh out their simple problems of government. Here are, as the need arises, the barber shop, hospital, bakery, and tailor shop. Occasionally there are journeys to town to exchange surplus produce for a bag of salt, simple tools, and a few knick-knacks. Otherwise the community exists by and for itself.

In striking contrast is New York City, a gathering of nearly eight million people. If independence characterizes the small community described above, interdependence is the rule here; in place of simplicity, here is complexity. To get from home to work a New Yorker is dependent on subways, busses, trains, ferries and elevators. He depends on the milkman to bring cream for his morning coffee, the gas or electric company to provide fuel for cooking, the telephone to permit him to talk to his business associates. Each person—the tailor, the barber, the busman, the milkman—renders his own specialized service. A single hitch in this vast complexity, such as failure of electric power for even a few minutes, the shutting off of water, an interruption of the subway schedule, strongly affects thousands of individuals who have surrendered a large part of their independence for the gains (often dubious) of living closely packed with several million of their fellow men.

Between the extremes of the one-family community and the metropolis are communities of many sizes. These may be villages or cities, that is, complete units in terms of their governmental organization, or they may be sections or areas within a town or city, communities within a community, the members of which are held together by common interests and

38

ideals. Of primary importance to us is the fact that the many different kinds and sizes of communities that exist are real units in a society, and as such they have their own customs, laws, languages and mores, and *their own ideals to express.* These last may take form as community arts—city plans, public buildings, parks, painting and sculpture of a civic nature —and in a democratic society they are expressive of the ideas and ideals, not of a few people, but of the group.

WILLIAMSBURG AGAIN: THE COMMUNITY

Williamsburg, Virginia, was one of the most important cities in the original American Colonies. In it were centered the governmental as well as the educational, social, religious, and economic activities of the Colony of Virginia. Restored recently for the purpose of a closer study of historic community life, it stands today as a great outdoor museum.

When Colonial Williamsburg served as the capital, it covered about a square mile of ground, with approximately 300 houses, and a resident population of around 3000. When the assemblies and courts were in session, as many as 4000 more came to the city to stay in the taverns, inns, and public houses; many came for the business of government; others came to see the newest fashions from London and to be amused by the fairs and horse races, the lotteries, the cock fights and other diversions. Merchants and planters came to transact business and craftsmen brought products to the market. During such times Colonel Spotswood boasted that his supper guests at the palace numbered 400, and Governor William Gooch said: "The gentlemen and ladies here are perfectly well bred, not an ill dancer in my government."

Out of the busy life of eighteenth-century America came the community of Williamsburg. Common interests and common goals banded the citizens together and produced a group which in appearance was a natural and unaffected expression of themselves, their actions, their philosophies and ideals. The beauty which developed in Williamsburg came from the frank and honest way the people solved the problems of their community when they built their houses, schools, palaces and inns. The question of which architectural style or styles to use never existed. There was no bitter dispute over the Governor's Palace—whether or not it should be a copy of a Greek temple or a French château. Home builders did not imitate Normandy cottages or Swiss chalets. The builders of Williamsburg had brought with them the traditions of the English Renaissance, and since neither their way of living nor the geographical conditions were radically different from those in England, they made few changes. The entire community was built in the style of the period, the style that the inhabitants of Williamsburg had helped develop and that expressed their mode of living.

THE PLAN OF WILLIAMSBURG

In Williamsburg (Figure 23) the main artery of the city is Duke of Gloucester Street, a noble thoroughfare ninety-nine feet wide and almost

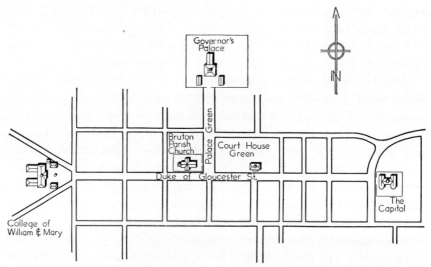

23. Plan of Williamsburg, Virginia. The Governor's Palace and Garden at Williamsburg, Virginia, are a direct expression of eighteenth-century ideals of formality and elegance.

a mile long, which forks at the west end into the main roads to Richmond and to Jamestown. At this important intersection stands the College of William and Mary. At the other end stands the Capitol, the major building in Colonial Williamsburg and consequently in the most important position. Between these two public buildings, this major thoroughfare is lined with other community buildings, shops, and important residences. Parallel to Duke of Gloucester Street are several narrower streets for residences. Beyond these, at one time, were the farms providing food for the community. Exactly halfway between the College and the Capitol on Duke of Gloucester Street is Palace Green, a broad lawn extending two blocks north to the Governor's Palace and providing a dignified approach to the residence of the Colony's most important political personage.

The plan of Williamsburg is thus very simple. In the right angle relationship of the streets it resembles the gridiron pattern of most American cities. These are important differences, however, that set Williamsburg apart and give it a distinctive character which most cities lack: the width of the streets varies according to their importance; the blocks are not all the same size; and the chief buildings are placed at the ends of streets. Compare the effect of walking down Duke of Gloucester Street or Palace Green, where well-designed buildings terminate the view, with the effect of walking along the main streets of most towns which, having no terminal feature, seem to stretch from nothing to nowhere. This is indicative of the manner in which Williamsburg was designed. The streets in this Colonial capital were not merely traffic arteries but played their part in giving the city a simple grandeur essential to eighteenth-century living. For its purpose and its time, it was an excellent plan. During the nineteenth and early twentieth centuries, most of this was forgotten, and the monotonous gridiron was repeated almost without variation from one ocean to the other. Williamsburg was planned for living; the typical nineteenth-century city was planned to produce salable parcels of land. Such differences in the approach to planning lead to significant differences in appearance.

The Governor's Palace

The Governor's Palace (Figure 24) is orderly, dignified, and consistent. Its symmetrical façade and crowning cupola, the curving wall, the imposing entrance gate, and the two flanking buildings make it easy and pleasant to look at. The appearance of the building indicates that it is more than a simple home, that it is the dwelling of the chief dignitary of the Colony, the Governor. It looks like a place to serve several hundred royal guests. The designer succeeded in making it visually as well as functionally the official center of government and hospitality for the Colony of Virginia.

This has been achieved in a variety of ways, not the least important of which is the location of the building at the end of Palace Green. Its size also accounts for some of its imposing appearance, for it is larger than any other home in Williamsburg. But the design of the building, apart from its location and size, commands respect. The symmetrical layout contributes in a large measure to this impression. The two small identical buildings flanking the main structure have a real function in emphasizing through contrast in size the importance of the large one. They throw into relief its actual size and give it strength and stability by extending it visually as well as by locking it securely in place.

The main building is a masterpiece of refined design. Symmetrical like the general layout, it is saved from monotony by the rightness of its proportions and the subtlety of its detail. The building is a simple rectangular solid, its greater horizontal dimension giving the effect of stability and repose. The rectangular mass is capped by a truncated pyramid which acts as a transition between the lower portion and the cupola. The verticality of the windows, the chimneys, and the cupola contrasts pleasantly with the horizontality of the main mass of the building. Subtleties in the design can be observed in the gradually diminishing size of the windows from the first floor to the third (the interior of the building being expressed on the exterior), and in the increasing size of the masonry areas between the windows from the center to the edges. This latter gives the appearance of strength by reinforcing the ends of the building (important in masonry construction) and also directs interest to the central doorway, window, and balcony. The detail is restrained and judiciously placed.

The design of the building suggests a comparison with musical practices of the period. Eighteenth-century European composers were fond of displaying their technical powers of musical composition, and one of their favorite forms was the Theme and Variations. They would begin their composition with a simple tune of their own, or some popular song or hymn known to everybody, and then without disturbing a hair in their powdered wigs proceed to treat the original tune in many varied ways. Williamsburg architects were also fond of showing off their meticulous style and control of their art. Notice how many times the designer of the Governor's Palace repeated or varied the truncated pyramid form of the main roof in the structure he gave to the roofs of several of the flanking buildings, to those of the dormers, and to the tops of the chimneys. Echoing and varying an important shape in this way bestows importance on the basic shape and helps to unify the design.

Just as the conversation in the glittering drawing rooms was characterized by gracefully turned phrases, delicately poised innuendoes, correctly balanced sentences, so too was the architecture characterized by gracious proportions, delicately molded ornaments, exquisitely carved brackets, beautifully curved balustrades, and airy, almost lacy cupolas. Throughout all Williamsburg the graceful design and the shrewd use of ornament are so effective that today, as we look at the community, we are transported across the centuries to that age of aristocracy, royal display, and delicate precision.

The Governor's Garden

The garden of the Palace (Figure 25), restored according to the best available information on the original gardens, continues in further variations the fundamental ideas expressed in the house itself. There is the same precision, the same elegance, the same formality. Possibly too formal for the present day tastes of many people, it reflects, as does the Palace, the eighteenth-century love of ordered surroundings. People who wore powdered wigs and lacy jabots did not appreciate free-growing shrubs and hedges. The love of natural beauty as we know it today was rare. The age of intellectualism demanded that plants, as well as building materials, be altered for human use. Notice that the designer has continued his theme and variations into the garden. The diagonally placed hedges in the beds are reminiscent of the roof lines, and the plants at the corners recall the cupola in shape.

The effect of the whole garden must have been breath-taking, back in the days when Williamsburg was alive, standing in such startling contrast to the wild forests only a few miles away. We wonder how the Indian Chief felt when he walked its formal paths. We wonder how the wilderness-worn traveler felt when—with a memory full of tangled forest and jagged rock—he first looked upon the mathematical precision of the clipped shrubs. The garden belonged not only to the Governor and his family, but to Williamsburg, to the Colony of Virginia, to Colonial America: it served home needs, it impressed the local visitor, it refreshed the traveler, it reminded the citizens of their homeland, it convinced the Indians that the pale-faces were no fools. It was truly a community garden.

The community of Williamsburg needed other public buildings: the Capitol and the Courthouse among them. Each of these was erected with the same fundamental idea that molded the Governor's Palace. Since the community was a highly integrated one, the several public buildings of Williamsburg shared many architectural details in common: the basic rectangular shape, the cupola, the small paned windows, the sensitive proportions, and the building materials of wood and brick.

43

The Problem of Human Needs

The graceful architecture of the eighteenth century is one of our priceless heritages of the past. However, there is something wrong, almost sacrilegious, in the copying of the forms of the eighteenth century in buildings of the twentieth. Certainly it is incongruous for a Williamsburg house to stand upon a street in Colorado, or to serve as the offices of an aviation landing field, or as the shelter for a filling station. We would laugh at the sight of a gas station attendant stepping out in a copy of the afternoon clothes of old Colonel Spotswood who went to his grave two hundred years ago!

As we now look upon restored Williamsburg, we find the simplicity of it beautiful. But yesterday cannot be lived over again. Today is here always; and today, the present, we must express if we are to achieve communities of lasting distinction, of real meaning, or of maximum use and benefit. Williamsburg did all that when it was built. It still has distinction —but its meaning is of the eighteenth century, not of the twentieth; its functional arrangements are suited to Colonial life, not ours.

A CONTEMPORARY COMMUNITY: GREENBELT, MARYLAND

That one-third of this nation is ill housed comes as a shock to many. So interested have we become in the dizzy heights of our skyscrapers, the speed and beauty of our automobiles, that the everyday matter of providing decent living conditions for citizens has been overlooked. Men and women, crowded into poorly lighted, unsanitary, badly ventilated and heated cells try, in the face of tremendous odds, to raise families and enjoy life. Conditions such as are shown in the photograph (Figure 26) exist in the United States in appalling numbers. Tremendous increases in urban population, lack of planning and control, unpredictable expansion, greed and exploitation, and the continued development of industrialization are only a few of the many factors that have resulted in cities out of joint with the needs they are supposed to serve. The problems of community planning are infinitely more complex now than in the days of Colonial Williamsburg and they cannot be solved by allowing our towns and cities to grow as they will, for that process has been shown to be wasteful and inefficient, and productive of cities which are ugly and unhealthy. Our national and individual welfare is interrelated with the problem of providing decent living conditions for all people, an issue we cannot escape.

In the 1930s the Resettlement Administration of the Federal Government was one of the many public and private agencies to attack the problem of housing. Realizing the inadequacy of housing in many of our large cities, it has built as demonstrations of possible solutions three communities: Greenbelt, Maryland, about five miles from Washington, D. C., Greenhills, Ohio, near Cincinnati, and Greendale, Wisconsin, near Milwaukee. Here city planners, landscape architects, architects, engineers, painters, sculptors, furniture designers, educators, and sociologists cooperated on new cities to meet present-day needs. The following statement indicates the functions of the new communities.

> The new communities will be "greenbelt" towns, so called because each of them will be surrounded by a broad girdle of park and farm land. A greenbelt town is simply a community built on raw land, in which every acre is put to its best use, and in which the traditional lines between town and country are broken down. To the city worker it offers a home in healthful country surroundings, yet within easy reach of his job. To the small farmer living in the greenbelt area, it offers better facilities and a steady market within a few hundred yards of his own fields. For both of them, it combines the conveniences and cultural advantages of a city with many advantages of life on the land. Such a union of town and country has been made possible by technology, transportation improvements and a host of other factors. We need only to make use of the tools which are lying at hand.*

Because these communities represent thoughtful planning in advance, in terms of group as well as of individual and family needs, they are of special interest to us. The three of them are similar, but this discussion will be concerned with Greenbelt, located at Berwyn, Maryland.

What problems does the contemporary city planner face on such projects? Were he to list them he would discover that he had to provide:

A Community Plan which will:

Keep at a minimum interference of one phase of life in the community with any other, such as the blighting effect of industrial or commercial developments on residential areas.

---

* From *Greenbelt Towns*, Resettlement Administration, Washington, D. C.

Keep at a minimum the costs. One of the best ways to do this is to reduce the amount of street area.

Insure safety of the pedestrians from dangerous and fast-moving automobile traffic.

Provide sufficient and accessible space for recreation.

Provide adequate settings for important community buildings in accordance with the position of importance which they occupy.

Buildings which are:

Good-looking comfortable homes providing the essentials for happy healthful living.

Designed for the government of the community and for recreation.

Planned for commercial and industrial enterprises.

A *Whole Community* which is:

Suited to present-day needs and therefore expressive of the twentieth century.

Attractive in appearance and engendering civic pride in the people living in it.

How do these problems compare with those faced by the designers of Williamsburg? Basically, the problems are the same, but new conditions demand new solutions. Automobiles, for example, have brought with their speed and efficiency new concepts of community plans; factories have raised the necessity for zoning laws and protective greenbelts. Thus, even though many of the problems remain relatively constant, the solutions to them can never merely repeat the past. If a community meets contemporary needs squarely, it will sincerely express the period in which it was built and necessarily differ from any built before. There are new types of equipment, such as electric lights, automobiles, radios, and motion pictures, and there are new types of service, such as improved sanitation and community heating plants. Then, too, there is always a contemporary "spirit of the times," changing ideals of the good life, new concepts of beauty. Such changes may or may not mark progress, but they inevitably stamp the art expression of each period.

Throughout the discussion on Greenbelt keep the above points in mind: observe how the designers have approached these community problems and decide whether or not you think they have been well solved. It is possible that you will not like the type of architecture or some other

24. (*Upper*) The symmetrical exterior of the Governor's Palace is enlivened by the sensitive spacing of the windows, the delicacy of detail in the cornices and cupola, and the gracefully curving wall of the forecourt. The rich red brick, white trim, and gray slate roof contrast harmoniously with the colors of sky and foliage.

25. (*Lower*) The formality of the garden behind the Governor's Palace is in perfect harmony with the architecture, repeating and echoing the geometric shapes of the building. Both Palace and Garden have a clear-cut yet gracious regularity.

47

Contrasts in living conditions can be found in all parts of the world.

26. (*Upper*) Slum conditions in which healthful living is impossible.

27. (*Lower*) The entire community of Greenbelt, Maryland, has been planned to meet contemporary needs. Unlike the typical gridiron plan, the design is organically related to the topography and to the lives of the people.

The buildings at Greenbelt, Maryland, are simple, dignified structures set in park-like surroundings.

28. (*Upper*) The row houses are simple in mass. Bands of dark brick unify the patterns of windows.

29. (*Lower*) Dwellings are located in super-blocks to minimize noise and danger of automobile traffic. All houses face parks and are near woodland. *49*

The buildings of the Tennessee Valley Authority express with monumental grandeur man's attempt to control a wayward river.

30. (*Upper*) The Hiwassee Dam and Powerhouse are as dynamic as the river they harness.

31. (*Lower*) The Pickwick Powerhouse shows the sculptural beauty of precise geometry which often develops when forms are genuinely functional.

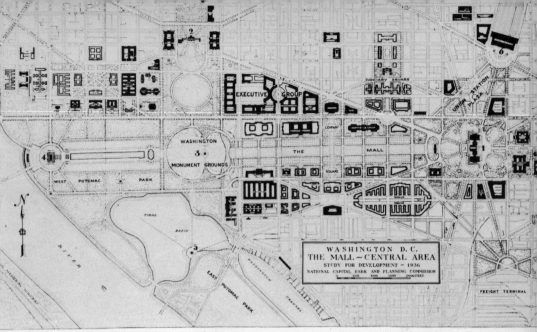

Three contrasting city plans.

32. (*Upper*) The plan of Washington, D. C., provides designed open spaces surrounding major public buildings. The Capitol (1), the Washington Monument (3), and the Lincoln Memorial (4) are on the major axis. The White House (2), the Washington Monument (3), and the Jefferson Memorial (5) form a secondary axis.

33. (*Lower*) Existing (*left*) and proposed (*right*) plans for Queens. The proposed plan reduces street area, increases public open space, provides through traffic arteries and dead-end streets for residential sections.

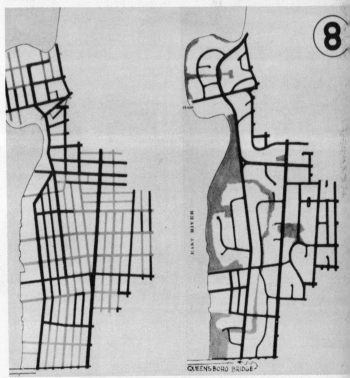

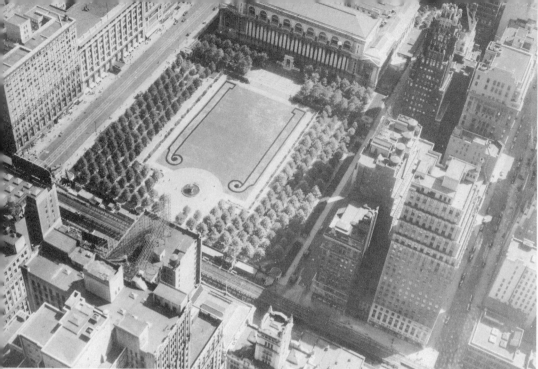

Parks and parkways in a community as extensive as New York are varied.

34. (*Upper*) Bryant Park is a small city park, axially related to the Public Library, in a congested commercial section.

35. (*Lower*) Central Park offers extensive breathing space near the city's center.

36. Grand Central Parkway provides a four-lane highway well separated from lesser roads. Notice the sports area and gridiron subdivision in the foreground.

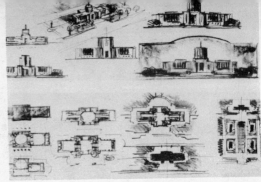

The sketches and model of the State Capitol at Salem, Oregon, show the manner in which architects Trowbridge, Livingston, and Kealy developed their ideas for a public building.

37. (*Upper left*) First sketches showing varied ideas tried by architects.

38. (*Upper right*) Further development and variations of surviving ideas.

39. (*Left*) Refinement in advanced stages of the solution of the problem.

40. Model of the final design.

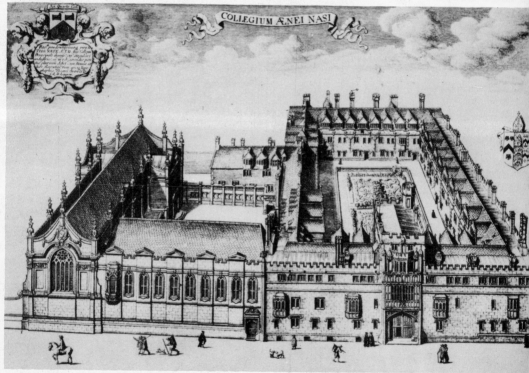

Two public buildings, one eclectic and the other traditional.

41. (*Upper*) The Public Library in Boston, Massachusetts, is an example of the nineteenth-century classic revival. McKim, Mead, and White, architects.

42. (*Lower*) Brasenose College, Oxford University, in Oxford, England. The building on the left is of a later period and consequently a different style from the quadrangle on the right, yet the two are harmonious.

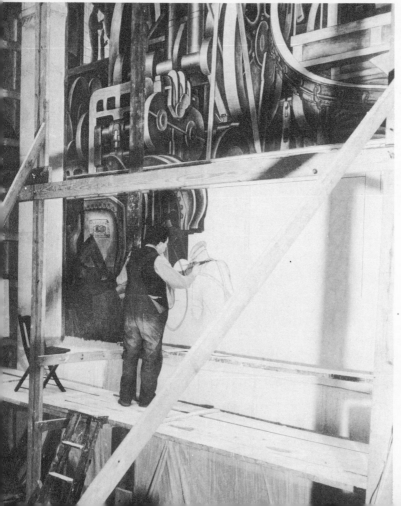

Diego Rivera's mural "The Making of an Automobile" in the Garden Court of the Detroit Institute of Arts.

43. (*Upper*) The heroic figures and hands at the top symbolize the significance of manpower in manufacturing. The next panel shows iron, coal, lime, and sand. The bottom panel shows men and machines transforming natural materials into automobiles.

44. (*Lower*) Detail showing Rivera at work putting color on fresh plaster in true fresco technique.

56

Anton Refregier's
mural in the Rin-
con Annex Post
Office, San Fran-
cisco, California,
graphically tells
the story of the
state's history.

45. (*Upper*) A sec-
tion of the panel
called "Fire, 1906"
shows a major ca-
tastrophe painted
with grandness
and dignity.

46. (*Lower*) A de-
tail of the panel
conveys the grief
of a child over the
loss of her mother.
All details in the
painting are treat-
ed in an architec-
tural manner
relating them to
the walls of which
they are a part.

47. Carl Milles' Peace Memorial in the City Hall, St. Paul, Minnesota, is one of the most powerful examples of contemporary sculpture done on large scale. The heroic expression of peace is worthy subject matter for community art.

feature of the development because it is too new or too different from what you have seen and known. But do not let external appearances lead you astray, for planning a community goes far deeper than merely designing pretty fronts for houses and taking photographs when the lilacs are in bloom.

Greenbelt grew from a fundamental idea which was carefully studied from all angles. First came the thoughtful study of housing conditions in the city of Washington. Was there a sufficient number of adequate houses for the citizens of that important city? The answer was no. Then followed an investigation of the available land—land which was near enough so that workers could commute easily. The planners did not want a small parcel of ground to be cut into just another typical subdivision with wasteful streets and narrow lots and houses only a foot or two apart; they wished sufficient acreage so that the community could be surrounded by a green belt of farms and woodland. It was also to be protected against the invasion of industry or overcrowding.

Years ago an Englishman named Ebenezer Howard pioneered the "Garden City" movement. Distressed by the conditions in which he found English factory workers living and rearing children, he advocated smaller communities planned from the beginning for a limited number of industries and a limited number of dwellings. Growth was not to proceed unchecked, since that always led to the congestion common to ill-planned cities. Each garden city was planned to grow to a healthy size, and then, if necessary, a new one separated from the original by farm or woodlands would be started. Greenbelt would delight Ebenezer Howard, were he still living, because it incorporates many of his ideas, especially the surrounding belt of farm lands.

At Greenbelt the rural space provides for the National Agricultural Research Center, one of the world's greatest farm laboratories. Here the government scientists develop new crops and new farming methods which are making millions of dollars for the American farmer. Farm experts carry out demonstrations in forestry and soil conservation. Use for every foot of the original 16,000 acres has been planned by these experts to form the community of Greenbelt. For the first time since Maryland was settled, the soil is being used scientifically, so that its fertility will be saved instead of wasted.*

---

* The material in this and some of the following paragraphs has been taken from a folder, *Greenbelt*, published by the Resettlement Administration.

The Problem of Human Needs

The drawing (Figure 27) showing the community as seen from the air demonstrates clearly the general plan. Notice that the town was laid out in curving lines because the topography suggested that roads in this pattern could be built more efficiently than in the customary checkerboard pattern. In addition, the curved streets would tend to discourage fast driving, add interest, and would give a pleasant domestic character to the residential sections. Observe also that the residential sections are arranged in a horseshoe shape around the community center which is thus given a position of importance and convenience.

The first rough drafts of Greenbelt called for sixty-six miles of streets; the final plan includes the same number of houses but only six miles of streets. Good art is not an expensive luxury; it can make real money savings. This striking saving was effected by the development of "super blocks." As is clearly shown in Figure 29 these are many times the size of ordinary city blocks. Instead of having twenty to thirty houses in a block, there are two hundred. In super blocks a small amount of pavement will serve many houses. Streets are costly to build, expensive to maintain, and dangerous to cross, and the typical gridiron plan with its large proportion of area devoted to streets (fifteen to twenty percent and frequently more) thus imposes a tremendous burden on the taxpayers. Excess areas in streets and roadways can better be used in parks, as Greenbelt shows.

The advantages of the super block go far beyond dollars-and-cents economy because this plan provides opportunities for infinitely pleasanter living sites. In Greenbelt many of the groups of houses are served by cul-de-sacs (dead-end streets with a turn-around at the end). Such streets will never have heavy traffic in contrast to those in gridiron plans, which are all potential if not actual traffic thoroughfares. *All houses in Greenbelt face on parks* traversed only by footpaths. That is a luxury enjoyed only by a few urban dwellers. It should be remembered, too, that Greenbelt was planned for people of below-average income, not for the well-to-do. Garages are grouped around courts off the roadways and near the houses they serve. Although it is not possible to drive a car up to all the individual homes, the small amount of walking that one must do from the garage court is indeed a small price to pay for the privilege of having one's house face on broad green lawns both front and back. The photograph shown here (Figure 29) was taken while the plants in the parks were being set out. This somewhat barren look was relieved after several years of plant growth.

In going from a house to the school or shops in the community center, it is never necessary to cross a busy thoroughfare. At the few points where footpaths and highways intersect underpasses have been built. The nearby Baltimore-Washington highway carries heavy traffic around, not through, the town. Thus we have an organization of residential and business areas, streets and parks which were carefully planned before one street was built. Nothing has been left to chance or whimsy or purely commercial interests. Greenbelt stands as an important milestone along the road to sensibly planned communities, and contrasts vigorously with the typical, unplanned development with which we are all too familiar.

The architects solved their problems as ably as did the city planners. In the photograph (Figure 28) of a typical group of row houses, notice the simple, attractive exterior. Contrasting bands of dark brick have been used to unify the windows, and the doorways have been accentuated by functional projecting shelters. The interior room arrangements, of which the exterior is a direct expression, are planned for maximum convenience. Living and dining areas are simple, kitchens are relatively small. Detail around window and door openings is reduced to a minimum. Today, there seems to be no money for decoration as elaborate as at Williamsburg, nor is there need for it in the contemporary scene. In the midst of economic and political complexity, architectural simplicity is welcome.

Just as the furniture in the Williamsburg buildings was harmonious with the architecture, so it is at Greenbelt. Architects, home economists, and technical experts worked to produce furniture adapted to modern living. It is simple, straightforward, and comfortable. Best of all, the basic furniture for a family of four costs only a few hundred dollars.

The homes in Greenbelt include a type not found in Williamsburg: the multiple dwelling—structures serving as living quarters for more than one family. This is a type that has become increasingly common because of economies of construction, materials, and land usage. In addition, certain service functions are more easily met if homes are multiple rather than single. The single dwelling unit, however, is still the desirable standard for most situations.

The commercial center of Greenbelt is approximately in the center of the residential areas and includes shops and a theater. The school is nearby. No helter-skelter mixture, the stores are grouped neatly and efficiently around an open paved and planted court which affords splendid views of the lake beyond. The school building is planned not according

61

to Gothic or Renaissance or Colonial needs, but on the basis of the needs of youngsters and teachers of Greenbelt, Maryland. Naturally, it is of the same general character as the other buildings.

Other features were instituted at Greenbelt to insure well-rounded community living. A local newspaper was established, a community health insurance plan was set in operation, and a school program differing from the typical in its emphasis on cooperative living was carefully worked out. A visit to a Greenbelt school would show children drawing and painting scenes of their own town, studying the development of cities, and the advantages of good planning. Here are all the elements of full integrated living.

Greenbelt is a courageous and exciting attempt to remedy many of the ills that have beset our towns and cities, inadequately planned as they were to meet new conditions. Practically no community in the country has escaped the blighting effects that are caused by expansion, sudden shifts in population, unplanned-for industrial developments, unpredictable commercial growths, speculation and over-development. The growth of American cities for almost a century proceeded on the assumption that there is an unlimited supply of people and a limited amount of land. Both appear to be ill-founded. Greenbelt is designed for families of a particular economic group and only they will live there. It cannot grow beyond a certain size for it cannot penetrate its surrounding greenbelt of farm lands and woods. Its maintenance as a residential community is thus insured.

Two generalizations can be drawn from the study of Williamsburg and Greenbelt. The first is the emphasis in both developments on the community as a whole rather than on the individual units. Relationships, not elements, are stressed. Second, both communities have a strong definite character which resulted from planning in terms of the needs to be served at the time they were built. Williamsburg is an eighteenth-century answer to community living, Greenbelt a twentieth-century. Neither could have occurred at any other time and yet be the sincere direct expression that it now is. Both communities abound in remarkable features which we would do well to heed in guiding the future developments of our cities.

TENNESSEE VALLEY AUTHORITY

The Hiwassee Dam and Powerhouse (Figure 30) offer a great change of scene from the comparatively small and simple communities of Williamsburg and Greenbelt to the largest, most intensively and comprehensively planned development in the United States. The Tennessee River whose valley lies in the seven states of North Carolina, Virginia, Georgia, Alabama, Mississippi, Kentucky, and Tennessee has been transformed from an uncontrolled and frequently destructive force into a chain of lakes reaching from the Southern Applachians 700 miles to the Ohio River. Twenty-one dams hold spring floods in great reservoirs to develop electricity as needed and create a series of navigable channels to permit inexpensive transportation of goods. To accomplish this end, 113 million cubic yards of concrete, rock fill, and earth—38 times the cubage of the Pyramid of Khufu (pages 95 and 445)—have been put in place. Its most apparent results are the massive dams and powerhouses from which copper power lines carry electricity over the countryside in one great unified system; but these are only symbols of the impact this development has had on the community.

The purpose of the TVA is simple: to put a river to work for the people. Its astoundingly varied results include new houses, and fresh paint on old ones; electric water pumps in backyards, and community refrigerators; new private industries, and the revival of some gone into decay; less tax delinquency, and more money in the people's hands; new public library service, more hospitals, and better schools; improved methods of farming and reforestation of valleys. In sum, it has resulted in a new release of human and natural energy.

Important as all this is, the TVA would not find its place in an art book were it not for the fact that city and regional planners, architects, and other artists cooperated with specialists in every branch of technology to produce natural and structural forms worthily expressing the concept of a river working for people. The Hiwassee Dam and Powerhouse and the Pickwick Powerhouse Generator Room (Figure 31) testify that the TVA artist rose to the challenge. As one sees the dam from miles away it appears as placid and self-assured as an Egyptian pyramid; but as one gets nearer, the Herculean thrust of steel and concrete against a wall of water has the

63

dynamism, at an enormous scale, of Gothic cathedrals. This photograph, taken on the roof of the powerhouse, shows the clean, strong sweep of the spillway above which towers the massive crane, or gantry. The circular form is the generator cover which can be removed to permit maintenance and repair work. Only slowly does a visitor find his scale as he sees nicely detailed doors and windows or the rich imprint of the wood forms on the concrete slabs. TVA architecture is not "decoration of engineering"; it is not naked, accidental, or unrefined. It is rather truly monumental, forthright expression of the massive forces harnessed for the benefit of this expansive community.

Although the dams and powerhouses communicate most emphatically the spirit and purposes of TVA, many other features acquaint the visitors with the underlying unity of the development. The houses, many of which are prefabricated, are pleasantly domestic and contemporary in style. The schools and community buildings are friendly, informal structures well related to their geographical settings. The highways speed the traveler to his destination, the parks invite relaxation. Do not think for a moment that all TVA architecture is as monumental as the dams. Each type, each example, is suited to its specific purpose. The designers of land and buildings have given the citizens freshly conceived, functional space for their activities. Appropriately, they have enriched this space with photomurals, painting, and sculpture, but they have always remembered that over-all planning is fundamental in community art.

The Generator Room of the Pickwick Powerhouse (Figure 31) shows what Tennessee Valley Authority designers have done to make industrial interiors good places in which to work. The mighty and impersonal generators dominate the room, as well they might, for they are among the most believable symbols of power that this age has produced. Their sculptural cylindrical forms make known the whirling motion within and give such impact that the observer is at first aware of nothing else—just great generators in a long, high room. Light flooding in from high windows pleasantly illumines the French gray tile floor, the blue-green tile wainscot, the lighter blue-green wall above, and the band of sulphur yellow near the ceiling. Spots of metal, notably in the well-designed railings and wall lights, give a sense of human scale. Gone is the eye-tiring, nerve-fatiguing confusion of the earlier generator rooms in which a multiplicity of shapes and colors distracted the attendants. Here is a room designed by men who know engineering, art, and psychology and who have controlled the visual effect as skillfully as they have impounded the river.

64

CITY PLANS AND CITY PLANNING

The idea that a city plan is anything more than laying out streets at right angles to one another is not new, but the twentieth century has brought renewed sensitivity to advantages of planning intelligently the ground on which cities are built. A good city plan meets many requirements. From the functional point of view it provides a street system that permits easy, economical, rapid and pleasant transportation; segregates areas for different purposes and plans each for maximum efficiency; and permits all inhabitants to get a maximum of air and light. From the social point of view, a good city plan is adapted to the social organization of the community; provides housing developments suited to all groups; segregates industrial areas so that the health and well-being of all residents are insured; and provides readily accessible parks and playgrounds. From the geographical and climatic points of view, the efficient city plan takes the greatest possible advantage of the natural topography: streets are laid out to follow the natural contours; street grades are adapted to climatic conditions; and worthwhile natural features are preserved. From the esthetic point of view, a good plan gives the citizens a sense of order and provides adequate locations and settings not only for the major public buildings and monuments, but for all structures in the city.

The basic problem in city planning is organizing land and buildings for group living. City planning is thus a gigantic social art serving both the group and the individual and, as with all art forms, it not only expresses our culture but very markedly influences the thinking and living of people. Dwelling in slums, we have found, tends to develop many undesirable human characteristics; well-planned communities bring out more acceptable behavior patterns. City planning, although a highly technical field, has its roots in fundamental human needs. When cities were small and grew or declined slowly, they developed in an orderly, organic way: related activities became segregated almost naturally and transportation was a minor problem. But with the industrialization of society and the startling increase in population during the past two centuries, simplicity vanished, and the growth of cities became almost malignant. It is pertinent to note that the population of Europe increased threefold during the nineteenth century although it had remained more or less static (at approximately 180,000,000) for the preceding twelve centuries. The population of our country also increased tremendously. The demand for industrial labor brought multitudes of people into cities which were quite unplanned for satisfactory living: industry was poorly located in relation to residential areas; residential areas were not planned to provide adequate light and air; and new means of transportation placed an increasing burden upon street systems designed for horses and buggies. Traffic jams are as characteristic of the twentieth century as radio. The overcrowding, tangled transportation, and general inefficiency resulting from this uncontrolled expansion are widespread. Until recently, there was no art or science of city planning developed in relation to present-day problems and needs.

In organizing land and buildings for group living, the need for four types of areas—*industrial, commercial, residential,* and *recreational*—becomes clear. Ways and means must be found to plan each of these areas functionally and to relate them one to another with efficient *transportation*. In addition to such obvious factors as size and location, the city planner must also consider geography, topography, natural resources, and industrial and agricultural production possibilities. Sometimes military and political considerations are important. City planning is clearly no small problem.

Industry requires areas large enough to provide for related types of manufacturing; it should be convenient not only to the areas in which the workers live but to the means of transportation. It should also be so located that prevailing winds do not carry smoke and fumes into residential developments. Commercial areas should be of sufficient size to provide diversified shopping facilities but not so large that crippling traffic congestion results. Residential areas should be convenient to recreational space as well as to industrial and commercial centers but should be sufficiently separated from the latter two so that noise, smoke, and traffic do not intrude. Recreation facilities should be available to all members of the community without undue travel.

In solving these problems, two general types of plans have developed: the *centric* and the *ribbon* (Figure 48). The centric plan, as the name implies, places emphasis on a center from which all developments radiate and on which they also converge. Most of our cities, from the small New England village centered around its Common to the vast metropolis centered around its industrial and commercial districts, are of this type. Both Williamsburg and Greenbelt fall into this category. It is a logical plan as long as the community remains moderate in size, especially if it is small enough to permit most travel to be done on foot. Each new block, however, multiplies the difficulties at the city's center. As the city increases in size, more and more space, time, and money are devoted to making the frequent and necessary trips from one section to another.

The ribbon or linear plan, developed from the one-street villages, are found in many parts of the world. Stores, shops, and houses line both sides of the street; behind them extend gardens and then fields. As early as 1882 the Spanish writer Soria y Mata suggested that cities expand

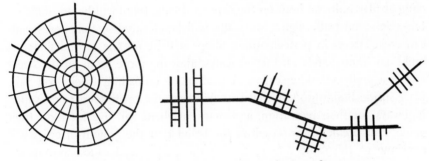

48. Centric and ribbon types of city plans.

along transportation routes so that, for example, Cadiz might be at one end and St. Petersburg at the other. As a matter of fact, this type of growth has been developing naturally in many parts of this country as can be seen along highways leading out of large cities. Unfortunately, however, the lack of planning makes them extremely unattractive. Communities along highways, formerly separated, are stretching out until they merge. Such developments can also spread out in fan-shaped patterns. The ribbon plan has many advantages: by establishing new centers, expansion can proceed almost indefinitely while each unit remains an identity limited in size; much of the movement from residential to industrial, commercial, or recreational areas can be accomplished on foot; open space for farms and gardens and for light and air are adjacent to more densely settled sections.

Few possibilities have so captured the imagination of architects and designers as the planning of the city of the future, and the descriptions of tomorrow's metropolis vary with the outlook held by the writer. Let us look at four proposals, the first two of which are of the centric type, the latter two of the ribbon.

67

The Problem of Human Needs

One group of planners sees the future city as an intensification of the present pattern. There will be more and more skyscrapers, greater concentration of activity near the center, and, of necessity, vastly more efficient means of transportation. The skyscrapers will be planned in relation to one another and to open spaces so that all may receive some of the benefits of sunshine and fresh air. Such an actual example is seen in the Rockefeller Center group. But the visionaries see far beyond our single-level traffic arteries: streets will be built on different levels with underpasses and overpasses at each intersection; streets will be segregated for express and local traffic, all traffic going more than ten or so blocks traveling at fifty miles an hour on the express streets; there will be no traffic intersections, no traffic lights; sidewalks will be elevated so that pedestrians can cross streets in perfect safety. Shops will be on the second floors of buildings immediately off the sidewalks, allowing more room on the street level for traffic. Parking cars and loading or unloading trucks will take place inside buildings. City dwellers will seek the open country on superhighways for their recreation, and many of them will live far from their work. This prediction is based on the belief that the growth of cities will continue at the same rate as during the past few decades, and makes no radical break with the city of today. It is merely more of it in more concentrated form.

A second concept of the city of tomorrow is provided by Le Corbusier, a French architect who, more through his writings and ideas than through his constructed buildings, has exerted tremendous influence on contemporary art. He suggested, in his most extreme proposal for the community of the future, that all business will be carried on in a few, enormous, isolated skyscrapers seven hundred feet high and a quarter of a mile apart. The ground covered by buildings will be limited to fifteen percent, in place of the thirty to sixty percent averages at present, and the remaining eighty-five percent will be given over to parks and boulevards. Traffic arteries will be wide, direct and unimpeded. Housing will be of two sorts: great apartment buildings at least one hundred and ten feet (twelve stories) high surrounded by parks, and garden cities outside the city limits for those who prefer single dwellings. Between the city and the suburbs is a protective boundary of woods and fields, a fresh air preserve not unlike the "greenbelts" around Greenbelt. The principles on which his plan is based are: (1) the centers of our cities must be de-congested; (2) the population must be concentrated in tall, widely spaced apartment buildings; (3) the means of getting about must be improved; (4) parks and open spaces must be increased. Obviously, large skyscrapers surrounded by open spaces are Le Corbusier's answer.

Unlike the first proposal, this plan differs sharply from present practices, and if put into effect, would mean demolishing and rebuilding our present cities. The advantages, however, would be conspicuous: large park areas; clean, fresh air and excellent outlooks from all buildings; concentration of similar activities for convenience and efficiency. The disadvantages are that very tall buildings are exceedingly costly not only to build but to operate, and that the proposal demands the planning of a whole city— buildings as well as streets—by one designer or one group of designers. In many ways the latter is not a disadvantage, but makes difficult the carry- ing through of such a plan. It is interesting to note that Le Corbusier's most recent proposals are greatly modified, but his earlier propositions are worth consideration as an extreme but impracticable plea for centraliza- tion, standardization, and mechanization. They represent in their purest form an approach to city planning.

A third vision—Frank Lloyd Wright's "Broadacre City"—is entirely different from the other two. Wright for many years has favored decentral- ization, has believed that large cities are on the decline, has declared that overcrowding has robbed many people of their natural birthright of sun, air, and land. He believes that decentralization should be hastened through building small communities around one or several industries similar to the garden cities described above. It is true that decentralization is made possible by modern transportation, particularly the motor car; modern communication, such as the telephone, radio, television; and standardized methods of production and distribution.

For purposes of demonstration, Wright has made a plan for the develop- ment of a plot of ground four miles square. In this area provision has been made for 1400 families, or about 6000 persons, to live under health- ful conditions. A family is provided with at least one acre of land on which to build its home and on which to raise fruits, vegetables, flowers, and perhaps some livestock. The families will neither own nor rent the land, but will hold it as long as they use and improve it. By establishing this close contact with nature and by raising some of its own food, each family will achieve a degree of self-sufficiency and independence almost unknown in present-day cities of any size. Most of the dwellings will be of the single-family type, but unlike the houses in typical cities will be de- signed to be in harmony with one another. Some areas will be designated for apartment houses which will be architecturally related to the single dwellings. Large areas will be intensively developed for sports and recreations of all sorts. The few industries will be carefully isolated by trees and open spaces from residential sections.

With most families living in single houses and raising some food on acre plots, there would not be the congested living conditions that are now all too prevalent. Communities would be connected by arterial lines consisting of railways and of many lanes for high-speed cars and trucks. The highways are elevated, and the space under them used for storing raw materials. Wright's plan, based on decentralizing population, is directly opposed to the present widely held concept of urban living.

A fourth group, typified by Hilberseimer, believe in ribbon planning. Hilberseimer proposes individual settlement units, limited in size. Each has all necessary elements separated according to function. The backbone of his system, as in Wright's, is a traffic artery along which stretch four major areas: *industry* lines the leeward side so that smoke and fumes will not blow into the residential and park areas; *commerce, parks,* and *residences* form successive bands on the windward side. The exact design of each area is determined by specific conditions: they can be large or small; linear, point-formed, or fan-like in shape. But the residences would always be within walking distance of commercial and industrial areas, and each area would always remain an identity.

Our best guess is that no one of these visions of the future will entirely supersede the others. In few instances is there opportunity to plan an entire community according to one ideal of what a community should be. It does appear, however, that the tendency toward increased urbanization is checked, and that there is a trend toward decentralization.

STREET LAY-OUTS

One of the most significant phases of city planning is the manner in which streets are laid out; for, being in a sense the skeleton of a city, the streets are a basic structure on which all parts are built.

We have seen that Williamsburg was planned to serve the governmental, commercial, residential, and recreational needs of a small eighteenth-century community. The streets at right angles to each other relate it to the first of four types of street plans—the *gridiron*—although the varied street widths and block sizes and the locations given important buildings distinguish it from the gridiron pattern that characterizes New

York City. In New York (with minor exceptions), each section has blocks of the same size, streets at right angles to each other, and parallel streets of the same width. Because different sections were sometimes planned independently of one another, a series of awkward junctions interferes with, but does not alleviate, the monotony as illustrated in Figure 33. The virtues of the gridiron arrangement are that it is easy to plan and simple to travel, especially if the streets are designated by numbers rather than by names. It is the lazy surveyors' and strangers' delight, but its disadvantages are numerous: it makes no allowance for the lay of the land and is, therefore, suited only to flat topography; the absence of diagonals complicates traffic from one corner to the other; costly and hazardous street area is excessive; dangerous intersections are irritatingly numerous; and it is difficult to segregate through from local traffic.

Washington, D. C. (Figure 32), like Williamsburg, was planned from the beginning as a capital city. Its major characteristics are: it provides splendid settings for government buildings and monuments; it reserves much space for parks, malls, and squares; and it has streets radiating from a number of centers, the important streets connecting with other centers —in other words a *radial* street plan combined with a gridiron. Such a plan tends to make transportation direct, to give impressive settings for monuments and buildings, and to provide interest and variety. Like other eighteenth-century expressions, however, Washington was planned for "show." The circles and traffic centers, handsome as they are, are suited for horse and carriage traffic, not automobile.

The *ring* or *centric* plan (Figure 48) is found in a number of European cities where successive edges of a growing city have been marked by streets or boulevards, much as we find in the annual rings of a tree. In some European cities these rings have been old walls or canals, later turned into avenues; in others, such as Detroit, they were originally laid out as streets. The distinctive characteristic is a series of streets laid out in concentric rings to promote an easy flow of traffic.

Another type of street lay-out, which might be termed *functional* for lack of a more specific term, does not follow any set of rules or predetermined geometric pattern but has streets placed where they are needed. Sometimes these are straight, sometimes curved, or more often a combination of the two. This free approach to street planning permits adaptation to rolling or rough topography, as in Greenbelt, or to special needs as in New York City (Figure 33). The proposed revision for this section greatly reduces the amount of street and clearly distinguishes

71

between thoroughfares and local traffic streets. This reduces cost and traffic hazards, frees more land for productive use, and provides the basic pattern for a pleasant community.

PARKS AND PARKWAYS

Three phases of the problem of planning outdoor areas for the enjoyment of city dwellers are illustrated by parks in and near New York City. Bryant Park (Figure 34), named for the New York editor and poet, William Cullen Bryant, is typical of the best in small city parks. Located at the rear of, and axially related to, the Public Library, the park gives the library a setting commensurate with its size and importance. Although not all such parks are adjacent to imposing edifices, they are likely to be, and thus derive their essential characteristics from this man-made environment. Thus such parks usually partake of the formal qualities of architecture rather than the ruggedness of nature. In Bryant Park the central axis continues the main axis of the building (visible even in the library's roof plan) and divides the park into two identical halves; the trees are planted in geometrical patterns as precise as the lines of the streets; and the flower beds at the sides of the lawn show a decorative, conventionalized use of flowers not unlike the patterns in carpets. Because such parks are usually small and located in densely populated areas, much of the space is paved, for turf would not stand the wear and tear of the large numbers of people. Seats, protected in Bryant Park by the shade of sycamore trees, are decorative and functional elements in the design. Water features, when present, are generally small, regular in outline, and placed in geometric relationship with other features. In such parks the land forms, and even the plants themselves, are consciously shaped for man's intensive use.

Large city (or country) parks, such as Central Park (Figure 35) show a quite different character. Nature rather than man becomes the guiding light, and, consequently, rigid patterns give way to informality. Such parks often include natural features of interest—lakes, hills or rocks—and these, not buildings, are dominant. Paths and roadways meander naturally to follow the ground contours in easy fashion. Lawns and meadows are diversified in shape, are bounded by irregular bays and promontories, as seen in the natural countryside. Masses of many kinds of trees, faced down with low shrubs, are varied in size, outline, color and texture to add interest. The landscape architects who plan such parks hold nature as a model to be approximated as closely as funds and skill permit.

Central Park as it stands at present is the result of almost a hundred years of planning and effort. Initially planned by Frederick Law Olmsted and Calvert Vaux, American pioneers in the naturalistic school of landscape design, the park has been continuously developed with few deviations from the original concept. Much larger than most city parks, Central Park covers 840 acres and has 32 miles of winding footpaths. Although it is atypical in size, its influence on American park design has been profound. Probably no large park in this country has escaped some influence from this early effort to bring rural atmosphere into urban surroundings.

Parkways are as new—and as American—as the movies. The two may well be America's most significant art contributions. It is certainly true that they have much in common. Both are products of a dynamic age, both tend to annihilate space. The constantly changing vistas perceived while speeding along a parkway are remarkably similar to many effects produced by the movies. Parkways (see Figure 36) are simply elongated parks with highways in the middle, but their functions have extended far beyond merely getting people from one place to another. They provide breathing space, pleasant and rapid access to the open country and recreational facilities (notice the athletic fields served by the Grand Central Parkway). But equally important is the visual effect. Seeing nature from a rapidly shifting point of view enlarges the range of esthetic experiences possible to man. Speeding automobiles on super-speedways have called attention to kaleidoscopic views of nature.

They have also introduced a host of new problems. Traffic lanes have to be carefully separated or at least clearly designated. Curves must be long and well banked. Changes in grade must be as slight as is consistent with topography. But the problem which has brought the most dramatic solution is that of highway intersections. Complex over-and-under passes, bridges, clover-leaf intersections, and other devices to prevent traffic snarls are as exciting as contemporary painting and sculpture, with which, in visual design at least, they rightly have much in common.

These three parks and parkways show the major design tendencies prevalent today. Bryant Park and Central Park, only a few blocks from each other, demonstrate clearly the differences between formal and informal landscape design. To say that one is superior to the other is to ignore the basic principles that form should follow function. Of the three examples, the parkway is most dynamic, in concept and in design, and most characteristic of today. These free-flowing forms are, furthermore, beginning to affect the design of smaller park areas.

73

COMMUNITY ARCHITECTURE

Having considered Williamsburg and Greenbelt as integrated communities, and having looked at city plans, parks and parkways, we now turn attention to buildings such as state capitols, libraries, and schools which house communal activities. We saw that in Williamsburg, Greenbelt, and the Tennessee Valley Authority the architecture was an integral part of the total development. Now we look specifically at the manner in which architects designed a modern state capitol; then at the Boston Public Library which exemplifies the eclectic approach to art, an approach in direct contrast to the preceding and following examples; and finally at a college of Oxford University in which change of style, reflecting contemporaneous trends of thought, resulted in satisfying architectural harmony.

SALEM, OREGON: STATE CAPITOL, A.D. 1936

In struggling with art problems of everyday life we often wish for the skill and training of a professional artist. We may rest assured, however, that in spite of his training and experience, such a person may suffer just as acutely as any layman. Indeed with him the procedure may be more prolonged, certainly more intense. No art object springs full-grown from an artist's hands. It is most likely the result of hard thinking, hopeful hunches, many trials and infinite persistence. The next example of community architecture will show how true this is.

A few years ago the state of Oregon conducted a competition for the design of a new capitol building. The winning design has received much criticism, both favorable and derogatory, but whatever your reaction to the building itself, the preliminary sketches reveal much of the architects' thinking. Study the many small sketches (Figures 37, 38 and 39) which led to the final design (Figure 40). Note the many variations tried and discarded before a solution, satisfactory to the architects, was reached. Furthermore, the sketches reproduced here are only a fraction of the total number they prepared.

In an article written by the architects they point out that the problem differed from that of the typical state capitol because the ground space

74

was relatively small, and that it was necessary to keep total cubage and costs down. Two paths were open: to design a domed building along historic lines, or to design a building more expressive of the period that we refer to as modern. Choosing the latter, the architects ruled out a miniature skyscraper because

> such a building might be anything—a financial or insurance or a court house—but it would not be identifiable as the Capitol. We felt that it should be immediately recognized as a Capitol building by the average citizen, who associated such a structure with a dome or some dominating feature similar to a dome. We decided, however, to try to design something that would be distinctive and different so that this Capitol would stand apart from all other Capitols.
>
> From the beginning we also felt that this building should have all the simplicity and fine proportion that is associated with the classic, but that the detail should be related to contemporary life. This thought seemed especially appropriate when we considered the section of the country where the Capitol is to be placed, the progressive Northwest where the newer idea has more fertile soil to grow in.*

Two other ideas profoundly affected the design. First was the elimination of the grandiose flight of steps usually included in civic buildings such as this, a feature which often discourages rather than invites the visitor to enter the building. The function of monumental stairways is open to question. Visually, and for impressiveness, they can serve a definite purpose. In many instances, however, they have a tendency to keep all but the stout-hearted and sturdy-limbed from visiting important public monuments. One might justifiably ask if impressiveness, certainly important in civic buildings, cannot be achieved by means which appeal more to the observer's emotions and less to his muscle. The architects of the Oregon State Capitol felt that as impressive an architectural feature as the great lobby should be easily accessible to all who might want to see it.

The second idea was to create an exterior design that would clearly express the legislative chambers inside the building. Expression of civic and community ideals in a structure has already been discussed, but carrying the principle further it is logical that a building should express the

---

* The material in this paragraph is taken from an article, "The Design That Won," by Trowbridge, Livingston and Kealy in *Pencil Points*, July, 1936.

specific functions which it fulfills, that is, the rooms (the interior) should determine the exterior design. The two most important large elements in the capitol building are the legislative chambers. The plan, as finally developed, placed these two important sections flanking the central entrance hall. The legislative chambers are thus brought to the surface of the building rather than buried in the interior, and the legislators may work in well-lighted chambers. Architecturally, the legislative structure of the state of Oregon has been made visible.

The exterior, composed of a central vertical unit plus two horizontal wings, thus reveals the essential unity of the building. There is little decoration, but what there is has been thoughtfully placed: the door and window grilles, two massive sculptured groups at each side of the entrance, and a figure twenty feet high, symbolizing the Oregon pioneer, at the top of the building. In the interior, murals portray the history of Oregon. Ornament is used to symbolize the state of which the building is a part, rather than merely for ornament's sake.

Naturally, there were hundreds of other problems to be solved: of construction, plumbing, heating and ventilation, materials, and costs. Besides, thousands of citizens had to be satisfied. But dominating the work was the idea that the building belongs to Oregon, not to Italy or France or England.

BOSTON: PUBLIC LIBRARY, A.D. 1888-1895

Libraries and schools are also observable measures of public taste and attitude. Built at the end of the last century, the Boston Public Library (Figure 41) tells us much of its builders. That it is a truly beautiful building few will deny. The design, marked by simplicity, emphasizes the long row of arched windows which identify the reading room, the largest room in the building. This is another example of interior function being expressed on the exterior. The first floor, broken by a few smaller windows, throws the upper floor into contrast. The building throughout shows detail sensitively related to the total design. The interior is finished with rich stone and decorated with mural paintings by Sargent, Chavannes, and Abbey, important artists of the period when it was built.

Although it is not the purpose of this book to trace the sources of art objects nor to discuss their historic development, it is worthwhile noting that the design of the Boston Library follows closely the design of a nineteenth-century library in Paris, an adaptation of the French Renaissance which, in turn, stemmed from the Italian Renaissance. The roots of the design are buried deep in the past, with little nourishment from American ways of living. Is it, then, a good expression of nineteenth-century Boston? Yes and no. In spite of our own glorious heritage of Colonial architecture, such as the beautiful towns of New England and Williamsburg, the Victorian city fathers of Boston felt that culture and its subsidiary, art, must come from Europe. In that aspect the building is an expression of the times. But that concept of art was artificial, for it did not have its roots in what was happening in this country at that time—the rapid expansion, the industrialization, the inventiveness, the hopes, the promise for the future which our country held. Artistically the building looks in one direction only: backwards. As an expression of an imitative, superficially "cultural" aspect of America when it was built, it is successful; as a sincere expression of the time and place, it is a failure. The life cord, connecting the 250-year-old child, American art, with the mother countries, still had to be cut. In its attitude toward art, Boston was still a colony.

ENGLAND: OXFORD UNIVERSITY, BRASENOSE COLLEGE: SIXTEENTH AND SEVENTEENTH CENTURIES

For contrast, let us look at an English university. Entwined with traditions of centuries of English culture, Oxford University stands as a symbol of advanced learning. The picturesque quadrangles have developed and aged along with English history because they are part of it. Brasenose College is an excellent illustration of how an institution can sincerely embody architectural ideas from different periods and yet combine them into a unified product. A glance at the illustration (Figure 42) gives the impression of two quadrangles forming a compact building group. In general effect they are unified, yet closer observation shows them to be products of different cultures. The quadrangle on the right was built in 1509 in the style of the period, late English Gothic. It displays the characteristics of that style: smallness of scale; informal disposition of openings, chimneys and the like; pointed arches over some of the doors and windows; and battlements and turrets.

In contrast to this medieval freedom the quadrangle on the left is characteristic of early Renaissance architecture introduced into England about a century later. Part of the Revival of Learning and stemming from the Roman period, it supplants informality with austerity, irregularity with precision, pointed arches with round. It is interesting to note that combined with the Renaissance elements—the pediments, pilasters, finials, and swags—are details such as tracery, oriole windows, battlements left over from the Gothic period. This fusion marks it as a building of a transitional period, for here are many forms that were later to develop into English Georgian which in turn were modified to produce the architecture of Colonial Williamsburg. But the important thing to observe here is that these structures represent two different approaches to architectural design. Yet the designers of both buildings did not hesitate to express the ideas of the periods in which they were living. Even at the risk of creating buildings unlike their neighbors, they dared to build frankly and sincerely according to contemporaneous trends of thought. The unity which binds the two buildings together is not due to any natural affinity between the styles, for the styles are significantly different, but rather to the skill of the designers in solving their problems. Many persons believe that once the architectural character of a community has been established no variations or developments should be tolerated. Brasenose College is only one example among thousands which illustrate that tradition does not mean conformity.

COMMUNITY PAINTING

The Mexican painter, Diego Rivera, was commissioned to paint murals on the walls of the Detroit Institute of Arts. Murals as large as these are unusual in the United States, but more striking than their size is their subject matter (Figures 43 and 44). They portray the automobile factories which have raised Detroit to a position of world importance. To use such subject matter in paintings today may seem logical, but had the mural been commissioned twenty-five years earlier the chances are that it would have shown goddesses holding olive branches for some automobile magnate who, dressed in a Roman toga, pointed vaguely toward a rosy future. When Rivera sought the character of Detroit, he realized that the subject matter of his painting might well be men making automobiles.

Rivera studied the city's factories and made hundreds of sketches. These he used in a dynamic composition, not a scene in one particular factory but a generalized expression of many. He painted the spirit of mass production. Individual men and machines take their place in a design as rich as Flemish tapestry. In the upper panel are monumental figures and hands giving just importance to the human element in maufacturing. Directly below one sees the origins of the four basic materials: coal, iron, lime, and sand. In the lower panel workmen are transforming these raw materials into automobiles. Here is community painting that lifts everyday experiences into the realm of monumental art. In the years that have elapsed since Rivera finished his mural, public buildings throughout the country have benefited from a renewed interest in mural painting. Post offices, libraries, schools, and hospitals can be pointed to with justifiable pride as civic architecture enriched with civic painting. Various governmental art projects have hastened the realization that art can be as real and vital to contemporary society as it was to the citizens of Periclean Athens, Renaissance Florence, or Colonial Williamsburg. Inspired by the challenge, American artists rose to the occasion.

Anton Refregier's mural in the Rincon Annex Post Office, San Francisco, California, exemplifies our government's sponsorship of community art. Chosen on the basis of a nationwide competition, Refregier brought a wealth of experience as a mural painter. He had long studied the subtle and complex relationships of mural painting to the archcitecture of which it is a part and to the public who see it. Selecting as his theme the history of California, Refregier portrayed in successive panels the major events in the state's development. Figures 45 and 46 show a section and detail of the panel called "Fire 1906." Against a background of crumbled buildings and wreckage, figures stand or sit in attitudes of terror, grief, and anguish. A tragic content is communicated to the beholder not merely by facial expressions and gestures but by the drawing of every line and form. The raw materials of an actual happening have been transformed into significant art, and the mural has been invested with a monumental grandeur that makes the problems of these people symbolic of grief wherever found. It is a painting "belonging" to San Francisco but also "belonging" in a deeper sense to all the people in the country.

COMMUNITY SCULPTURE

Several years ago the city of St. Paul, Minnesota, erected a new city and county building. At the end of the entrance hall, a dramatic room with a light floor, black marble walls, and a warm-colored metal ceiling,

79

the city decided to erect a statue as a World War I memorial but dedicated to peace. The artist commissioned to create the statue was Carl Milles, a Swedish sculptor living in America.

The statue (Figure 47), over thirty feet in height, represents an Indian chief smoking a pipe of peace. The material is Mexican onyx, slightly translucent and creamy in color, which contrasts dramatically with the black background. Many people on seeing it could not reconcile the Indian war-chief with the idea of peace and it does, at first thought, seem unusual. Milles, in answer to this paradox, stated that one of the sources of this conception was an incident in his early experience when he heard an Indian chieftain in Oklahoma deliver a moving oration on peace to his gathered tribe. Subject matter, of course, is only a part of a basic idea. In this case the idea of peace was the important force back of the making of the statue, and the carving of the figure of an Indian chief happened to be the form which it took. Any number of other subjects might have been used. Milles expressed peace by an intelligent handling of form, color, and texture strikingly emphasized by the background. Movement in the statue is upward to the solemn and calm face—aloof, impassive, detached—by no means warlike, angry or furious. The position of the arms, while expressing direction, also emphasizes poise and dignity. In forceful sculpture, each and every part of it builds into the total pattern. Each form expresses the spirit of the whole. Milles has given an organization of orderly, pacifying, and quieting shapes surmounted by a countenance whose imperturbable expression is a fitting climax to this monumental work.

When the finished work was unveiled in 1936 an intense controversy arose over the appropriateness and beauty of the statue. Citizen groups took sides and passed judgments. The furor reached such proportions that workers were stationed near the statue to jot down the comments of the visitors.

"My! Ain't it big!" "What's the idea of having a warrior stand for peace?" "A waste of taxpayers' money." "It is the most noble statue I've ever seen, and I've been through all the galleries of Europe." "It expresses peace; deep reverence." "The onyx is so warm and inviting that you want to touch it." "I have never seen a statue more perfectly related to its background."

Hundreds of comments like the above were gathered. They indicated almost all possible reactions, from anger and annoyance to almost ecstatic approval. Some people seemed upset because of the fear and distrust of something new. Some were intrigued with the material; others with the statue's size; others with its basic conceptions.

The controversy in St. Paul over the Milles statue is typical of what is likely to happen when any significant piece of community art is unveiled to the public. A work that pleases everyone *immediately* is not likely to be an important work of art. One that is forward-looking, a contribution and milestone in art, is almost bound to meet with antagonism, for it must of necessity be in advance of the taste of most of the people who are to pass judgment on it. Herein lies one of the great paradoxes in community art. It must be an expression of the community, but it must at the same time present some new and satisfying formulation of their community ideals, and these new formulations are likely to be the ones that arouse the most protests. This is not to say that the general public cannot like good art. That snobbish attitude is as untrue as it would be unfortunate. Every citizen in this democratic country has the right to pass judgment on all the community works of art for which he, as a taxpayer, helps pay. There is, therefore, a tendency for art in the community, in an attempt to please as many people as possible, to be dull and without spirit. Such things are never great. Important art of the community, and in other fields as well, should lead and educate and should not be innocuous repetitions of what most people already know and think.

CONCLUSION

How does the art of the community differ from the art of the home? Being the expression of a larger group, it is less individual, less personal. It represents a city, not a family. The buildings house many persons, serve many and complex functions. To express this, the architect makes them impressive in design (Oregon State Capitol), the city planner gives them important locations (Governor's Palace, Williamsburg) and pleasant surroundings (Greenbelt). Since public buildings represent the spirit of the community, they transcend purely utilitarian requirements. Rich materials, paintings, and sculpture embody the ideals and traditions of the community. Future historians, prying into what will then be the past, will use these buildings, this art, as a basis for understanding the present civilization. Will our buildings impress them as original, creative, and vital, or as weak and imitative?

Look at your own community, critically yet appreciatively. When was the city laid out? Is the plan functional? Where could it be improved?

Look at your own public buildings. When were they designed—and by whom? In what "style" were they built? To what extent do they express the community? To what extent do they function efficiently? Is there evidence of a changing attitude?

Then look at housing conditions. Are there slums? If so, what has caused them? Are the new residential sections thoughtfully laid out? Are the apartment houses well designed?

Finally, look at the painting and sculpture which belong to your community. Where is it? Is it appreciated today?

As always, study your own situation, become familiar with all of its aspects, and then see what you can do to improve it. Community art in the United States has suffered because the members of the community have so often failed to face the problems, failed to make decisions.

But there is the future!

Naturally, community art has a long history. Of the many books which have been written about it, the following are suggested:

Catherine Bauer: *Modern Housing* (Houghton Mifflin, 1934). A readable, informative book stating the problems of housing and pointing ways to solve them.

Holger Cahill and Alfred Barr: *Art in America* (Reynal & Hitchcock, 1935). A factual discussion of important American art.

Walter Gropius: *Rebuilding Our Communities* (Paul Theobald, 1945). The need for planning our total environment presented by an eminent architect and designer.

Talbot F. Hamlin: *Architecture Through the Ages* (Putnam, 1940). A book which shows the relation of architecture to social forces.

Ludwig Hilberseimer: *The New City: Principles of Planning* (Theobald, 1945). An excellent discussion of the historical and contemporary aspects of city planning by a man who favors "ribbon" developments.

Suzanne La Follette: *Art in America* (Harper, 1929). Explains why we have what we have in the development of American Art. Well worth reading.

David E. Lilienthal: *TVA: Democracy on the March* (Harper, 1944). A frank account of the problems of progress of one of the country's largest community planning projects.

Lewis Mumford: *City Development* (Harcourt, Brace, 1945). An application of the author's ideas to specific contemporary problems.

Lewis Mumford: *The Culture of Cities* (Harcourt, Brace, 1938). Timely and thorough study of cities, what they are and should be. The best introduction to a genuine understanding of community art.

David Robb and J. J. Garrison: *Art in the Western World* (Harper, 1942). An account of the history and development of the "Fine Arts."

Grace N. Rose: *Williamsburg, Today and Yesterday* (Putnam, 1940). A well-written and beautifully illustrated account of Williamsburg.

Eliel Saarinen: *The City, Its Growth, Its Decay, Its Future* (Reinhold, 1943). A survey of past trends in city planning and proposals for the future.

Jose Luis Sert: *Can Our Cities Survive?* (Harvard University Press, 1942). An extremely good primer of city planning problems.

Thomas Sharp: *Town Planning* (Penguin, 1940). A short but excellent book by an expert who favors "centric" developments.

Nathan Strauss: *Seven Myths of Housing* (Knopf, 1943). A housing authority's answer to the arguments most frequently used against government housing.

CHAPTER 3

Art in Religion

T WO churches in Finland are shown in Figures 49 and 50. Direct, simple, and sincere expressions of religious thoughts and activities, these two churches give sharp insight into the nature of the arts of religion.

Strikingly different, they yet have many points in common: (1) they are in approximately the same geographic region—the climate, the soil conditions, and the scenery are the same; (2) the people who built them are the same blood though not of the same time—these are Finnish churches for Finnish people; (3) the underlying religious creed is the same—they are both Christian churches.

But the times of building are different. One is low and solid and has roofs that are steeply pitched so that the heavy snow and ice will not accumulate and crash through the roof. Every part of it has the rugged picturesqueness which often comes with hand workmanship. The other is tall, graceful, and refined, defying the snow and ice and wind with the materials and methods of construction of the twentieth century. Although the two churches differ markedly in these respects, their basic organization is similar: a tower from which to call the worshipers, an auditorium in which to hold the services.

The materials are different. One is rough, hand-chiseled stone, laid in random patterns. Everywhere the observer is conscious of textures, variations, irregularities. The other is smooth with the sleekness of an automobile or airplane. Textures are concentrated at the top of the tower and in the windows. One has sheet-metal doors, electric lights, and mechanically operated chimes. The other has no artificial lights except for the occasional flicker of tallow candles. Its single, huge bell will sound only when the bell-ringer throws the weight of his whole body against the short length of rope and then leaps into the air with the rope as it slowly sets the huge mass of cast-bronze into ponderous motion.

We have now looked briefly at the churches from two points of view:

first, the problem of form or design; second, the problem of materials. But from the most important viewpoint, that of the human problem, we have not, as yet, made any close observations. Fortunately certain elements in the human problem, the race of people, their religious expression, the geographical location are stationary or in suspension. Not often are comparisons so easy to make—we have here only to understand how these Finns and the interpretation of their religious belief changed in five hundred years. One way of doing this is to imagine the two churches in actual use, each at the time it was built.

Five hundred years ago the population of Finland was predominantly agricultural. Their community needs were simple and for many of them Sunday was the one day of the week when labors of the fields and duties of the farmhouse were forgotten. On Sunday they planned to spend their day near the church, their community center. Early in the morning the entire family arose and put on special Sunday clothes. Then most families walked to church—some rowed across the lakes of which there are so many in Finland, and others, the older people, were drawn to church in stout wagons. They gathered in the churchgrounds, sometimes hours before the services began, and the menfolk talked of weather and crops and their animals. The women exchanged the news of their own families, nodded gravely at the sad tale of a neighbor's sick wife, asked each other about butter and weaving and cooking, and, all the while, watched the children running about the field lest they become too noisy or get into fights. The younger men and women formed groups of their own.

Presently the bell would ring out to remind the distant tardy that the services were about to begin. The people moved towards the doors of the church and the minister stepped out to welcome his parishioners while, at the same time, he glanced down the paths to see how far away the late ones were. But there was no haste; Sunday was the day for rest and meditation.

Today Finland is a fast-moving, complex nation. Although it is still chiefly an agricultural country, there are many industries and an active commerce served by a speedy system of communication and transportation. The church at Rajamäki stands near a paved road. Most of the people arrive at the same time, enter the church directly, and listen to services which are designed to serve only their religious needs.

The comparisons become lively. We can rule out geography and climate, and race and creed: although these are powerful in their effect on man's activities, on his art products and his labors, in this example they remain constant. It is the *time element* that is sharply different. It has changed the entire tempo of the people and their activities; in five hundred years, from a slow, plodding, simple community they have become a swift, direct and energetic one. In five hundred years new materials were discovered and still more materials were literally forced into existence.

Now look again at the two churches. One stands on a hill-top, with many small doors opening to the four directions of the compass. The other has a solid group of doors which can be thrown open to make one large one. To the one church the people slowly walked, coming from all directions along narrow pathways. To the other they come directly, swiftly, at the same time, on well-paved highways. In this respect, each church is beautifully designed. One church is simple, striking, commanding. Its outward form may be grasped in one glance from the windows of a speeding car, plane, or train. The other church is more detailed, calls for closer study, cannot be absorbed unless one almost stands still. Yet each fulfills its specific need completely. The modern one, almost in a flash, impresses you with its fundamental idea: a house for Christian worship. The cross stands dramatically, unmistakably against the sky. The fifteenth-century church tells its story more slowly, almost hides its symbol of the fundamental idea in architectural details: the cross is a part of the ornament on the gable. In the modern church the bell-tower points heavenwards triumphantly, and the cross stands triumphantly against the sky.

These two simple churches show that if mankind uses the power and drive that his religious needs generate, he is equipped to build significant art. He can build an art which belongs to him and to his life because it has grown from what he knows and believes and values. The Sipoo church and the Rajamäki church are not merely shelters for worship because if that had been their only purpose, there would be only four walls and a roof. They are expressions of the religious urges that compelled men to build them. Here again is art springing directly from life.

THE BUILDING OF A CONTEMPORARY CHURCH

The next church shown (Figures 51 and 52) is one that in appearance seems to stand somewhere between the two Finnish churches. It is as contemporary as the church at Rajamäki and yet it is as close to the soil and humble as the one at Sipoo. This church was designed by Rudolf

Schwarz, a German architect who has been mentioned as the true contemporary representative of Catholic church architecture. He believes that nothing in or outside a church building should detract from the service. The interior of the church should provide for the liturgy a background which is so stark, so shorn of ornate, material things that there is nothing in the room but the "divine action and presence." Architect Schwarz believes in building beautiful proportions of monumentality and majesty that will move us just as does the "magic" quality of the pyramids, the Temple of Ammon, the Parthenon, the splendor of Chartres Cathedral. He builds into his churches an austerity that is not insufficiency, frail weakness nor pauperism. His churches are expressions of a strong grasp of the essentials of Catholic belief in holy mysteries which demand preparedness to face eternity, self-denial of personal gain, and a tense will to refuse surrounding distractions.

Look over the pictures of the chapel in Leversbach. It

shows how Schwarz is able to create a sacred place with the simplest local materials and with exclusion of all pseudo-hieratic style elements, without which other modern architects have been unable to make a church distinguishable from a factory or silo. Here is an interesting reaction from the village teacher of Leversbach who watched the peasants during their work: "I was prepared for anything, even to lose my job in the village which I loved so much. So long as we planned, all seemed well, because few people can really understand plans and charts. And everybody was glad that something was being done. . . . They expected something which would somehow be different, although nothing so startling and altogether different as this chapel . . . yet I had never concealed from them our real intentions. I always told them that the chapel would be something strange to them. When the walls rose, there was growing resistance. People from other villages came and ridiculed those walls without windows and pinnacles. In the evenings, half the village stood there with distrusting looks. He who knows people realizes that they are afraid of nothing so much as the unusual, the strange, the new, the different. . . . Many expressed wishes for vaults, a steep roof, steeple, organ loft. We ruled these out easily by pointing to their considerable expense. We told them why we wanted the priest to stand among the people during his confession, why we had the windows at the altar, why only one room with a 'real' sanctuary

87

> in this little chapel. . . . But while we (Architect Schwarz
> and I) saw already the beautiful and noble proportions, the
> touching simplicity, the 'essentiality,' they noticed only the
> crude, the raw, the empty. But in the meantime, however, they
> have lived in the chapel, have worshiped there, and now they
> object if they have to go to another." *

THREE AMERICAN CHURCHES

The Bruton Parish Church (Figure 54) built in Williamsburg, Virginia,
between 1710 and 1715 *belongs* in general character, in basic structure
and detail, and in materials to the community of Williamsburg, discussed
in the preceding chapters. An expression of the thinking and feeling of
Colonial America, this church naturally has much in common with the
homes and public buildings of the period. But anyone can tell at a glance
that it is a church, not a home, school, or courthouse. The steeple, the
tall windows, the cruciform plan all give this structure a specifically religious character while the simple symmetrical masses of red brick ornamented with classical cornices and other details stamp it as emerging from
the same social order that produced the Governor's Palace in the same
community.

The Ranchos de Taos Church (Figure 55), built in Taos, New Mexico,
some time between 1772 and 1816, is also a colonial church in America,
but it belongs to another tradition, another environment and, as one
might expect, is different in character. The land around Taos is semi-
arid and thinly vegetated, the light has unfiltered brilliance, and the scale
of the landscape is tremendous. The Spanish missionaries found the
Pueblo Indians living a sedentary, agricultural life in permanent villages
built of adobe or stone. In attempting to convert the natives to Christianity, one of their first tasks was the erection of religious structures. The
friars were not trained as architects but brought with them some familiar-
ity with religious buildings, especially the fortress-churches of Mexico.
They found no artisans skillful in working stone or wood; in fact, any
kind of labor was scarce, eliminating the possibility of complex or highly
ornamented building.

---

* This quotation as well as the pictures are from the *Architectural Forum*, January,
1939.

The churches of New Mexico with their high blank walls and massive construction are defensive in appearance, for there was need for defense against marauding enemies and against extremes of heat, cold, and light. Literally raised from the earth, the Ranchos de Taos Church is made of sun-dried mud (or adobe) bricks, a building practice common to all semi-arid countries of the world since prehistoric times. The New Mexican churches illustrate to a remarkable degree the manner in which architectural forms are determined: the walls could be no higher than was safe with adobe brick; the building could be no wider than the length of available timbers to support the roof; and the length was determined by the size of the congregation. Adobe bricks, the only feasible building material, give a stable, monolithic appearance and a stable, permanent, well-insulated structure. They do not, however, lend themselves to complex structural devices nor to elaborate ornamentation. Thus, we have the conditions: native Indians and zealous Spanish friars; no skilled artisans and a minimum of labor of any sort; building materials limited to wood, adobe, and field stone; a semi-arid land of intense sunlight and extremes of temperatures. And churches were to be built.

The result was a new style of architecture organically developing from the conditions and fulfilling its functions as admirably as did the Bruton Parish Church. The religious architecture of New Mexico has a beauty of simple masses, strong and decisive, yet with outlines enlivened by subtle handcraft irregularities. Its simplicity is comparable to that of the Tennessee Valley Authority dams, its charm similar to that of handmade pottery.

Among the contemporary religious structures in the United States, the projected design for the Cleveland Park Synagogue (Figure 53) is notable for the manner in which all aspects of the problem were conscientiously studied and imaginatively solved. The forms express their functions, are strategically related to the topography, and are marked by the imaginative freedom and individuality characteristic of architect Eric Mendelsohn's work. In the words of the architect:

> The Cleveland Park Synagogue is, in fact, a community center, sheltering the three activities of a contemporary congregation:
> the house of worship—the House of God,
> the school for the education of the children—the House of the Torah,
> the auditorium for the assembly and recreation of the adult members—the House of the People.

The wedding-chapel close to reception-room and club-rooms, the administration with library and board-room are additional though essential facilities for the proper working of the Center. To combine organically these various functions in accordance with the climate, to create a well-working plan, an economical structure, and a symbolic appearance was the final aim of the architect.

The Site at his disposal—30 acres, hilly and densely wooded—demanded and, at the same time, facilitated a bold approach. Along the small axis of the site and across its highest elevation runs a clear stream in a 20-foot deep ravine forming with its branch a peninsula. This fan-shaped peninsula, clearly visible from the highway—the main approach road, seemed to be predestined to carry the *Temple Area* with assembly, foyer, temple proper, choir-room, chapel, garden-court, and amphitheater which is cantilevered out over the tip of the promontory.

The only available space large enough to carry a *School* for 1000 pupils was across the ravine to the North of the peninsula providing, as it does, the needed North-South exposure for the classroom-wings.

As the *Administration* has to serve both major parts of the building: Temple Area and School Area, a bridgelike structure over the ravine seemed to be the most natural device.

These were the practical considerations, the factual material with which the architect had to work. Facts and ideas, however, are not separated in our art. They start to interact at the moment the building program is studied and the site visited.

For the Building Program discloses the final needs of the client and, at the same time, exerts the intellectual possibilities of the third dimension.

All three dimensions form the architect's field of action on which his creative act has to be performed. This creative act is the integration of what he knows from experience and detailed study of his specific object, and of what he sees in his imagination as tectonic—as total solution of the problem.

And it is only a gradation in substance and mental attitude whether the project to be solved is a residential or industrial, a commercial or a sacred building.

Compare these two Finnish churches built five centuries apart. Both are good examples of religious architecture and show how the art and science of building change to meet new needs and take advantage of new materials and techniques.

49. (*Upper*) The fifteenth-century church at Sipoo, Finland, shows massive forms of rugged stone masonry warmly expressive of a rural handcraft society.

50. (*Lower*) The twentieth-century church at Rajamaki, Finland, designed by Erkki Huttunev, exemplifies an approach to building as characteristic of the Machine Age as it is expressive of Finland.

51. The Chapel at Leversbach, Germany, was designed by Rudolf Schwarz. Built of local materials by local workmen, it "belongs" to its surroundings and parishioners. The interior is marked by a frank exposure of the vigorous construction 92 which is harmonious with the simple dignity of the altar.

52. (*Upper*) The exterior of the Leversbach Chapel has a rural dignity reminiscent of the church at Sipoo. The excellence of the basic shapes and the rich pattern of stonework make ornamentation unnecessary.

53. (*Lower*) The model of the Park Synagogue, Cleveland, Ohio, shows a fluidity of mass in striking contrast with the solid, stable forms of the Leversbach Chapel.

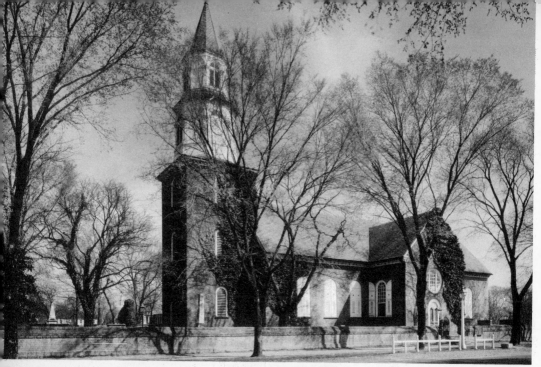

54. (*Upper*) The Bruton Parish Church at Williamsburg is a religious building in harmony with the palace, houses, and gardens of the Colonial community.

55. (*Lower*) The Ranchos de Taos Church at Taos, New Mexico, is typical of the Spanish-American culture of the southwestern United States.

Religious sculpture from Africa marked by a depth of feeling and conviction characteristic of significant religious art.

56. (*Upper*) A Negro statuette from the Ivory Coast of Africa. Although carved from wood and small in size, this figure embodies the magical, mystical feelings of the African Negroes' religion in forms that appear both permanent and monumental.

57. (*Lower*) The Sphinx and the Great Pyramid of Khufu at Gizeh, Egypt, have long stood as symbols of religious mystery and permanence. Heroic in scale, this sculpture and architecture tell us much of the spiritual life of their builders.

Two examples of religious sculpture from Europe give further evidence of the range of expression in religious art.

58. "Hermes" by Praxiteles is characteristic of the humanistic religious art of Greece in the fourth century B.C. The emphasis on physical beauty through softly rounded, well-proportioned forms is lifted above the commonplace by a spiritual idealism.

59. The sculptured portal on the Cathedral at Chartres, France, was done in the twelfth century A.D. The ascetic angularity, strongly contrasting with the humanized quality of "Hermes," exemplifies the Christian ideals of medieval France.

Two religious paintings done in Italy approximately two centuries apart illustrate the manner in which art of the same religion and same country changes.

60. (*Upper*) Giotto's "Deposition from the Cross" is a direct, forceful expression of intense grief, realized through means not unlike those used in the sculpture on the portal of Chartres Cathedral.

61. (*Lower*) Raphael's "Sistine Madonna" has an opulence of form and a mildly sweet physical beauty directly comparable to that found in Praxiteles' "Hermes," as well it might for by the time it was done the classical ideals of humanism had permeated the Christian religion.

The work's success depends on the finished building fulfilling its purpose, on its structural and economical soundness, and on being a flower which did not exist before in the garden of Architecture.

There are many specific excellences of this design worthy of mention— the Temple's concrete, hemispherical dome which dominates the group through its shape and height and produces a serene space for religious ceremony; the folding walls separating the Temple, Foyer, and Assembly which can be opened to provide space for large congregations during high holidays; the well-lighted classrooms placed around courtyards. These details indicate the care given to the solution of a complex problem. But they should not distract our attention from the total design, with its forms ingeniously and rhythmically deployed across difficult terrain, forcefully expressing the purpose of the whole and of each part.

The history of architecture abounds with magnificent examples of churches and temples built to express the religious urges of peoples living in various places, worshiping under varied religions. Chapter 17 introduces other examples which further emphasize the way in which religious architecture grows from its social and geographical environment. We often fall into the easy habit of thinking of one architectural style, usually the Gothic, as being *the* religious architecture, but there is no one religious architecture. The development from Egyptian through Greek and Roman temples to Gothic, Renaissance and modern churches is a fascinating study in the evolution of religious structures.

RELIGIOUS PAINTING AND SCULPTURE

Architecture is only one of many arts in which the religious urge of men has found expression. If it is classified in terms of the human needs that caused it to be created, much of the art carefully guarded in museums is religious. Most of the prehistoric art as well as that of Egypt, Greece, Rome and northern Europe which is studied today sprang from religion, for, until comparatively recent times, the church was the major sponsor of art. A number of examples of religious art, selected because of their variety and contrast, give some idea of the enormous range of this phase of art expression.

The wooden idol (Figure 56) from French Guinea, Africa, is sculpture from a primitive religion, a religion based chiefly on fear—of the sun, of rain, darkness, disaster, and death—and upon gratitude for abundant food and health. Modern psychology holds that a good way to combat fear is to bring it out into the open and face it. Primitive races of men practiced this method of facing fear as a religion by carving grotesque figures which represented their fears and hopes. These carvings became idols, fetishes, or objects of use in religious ceremony. Not a few of them have found their way into our art museums to be admired for their intensity and vigor. Whereas they were once thought to be but the crude carvings of savages, they are now rightfully appreciated as deeply expressive art.

It is an enormous leap in time and spirit, but not in geography, from the African idol to the Sphinx and the Great Pyramid of Khufu at Gizeh, Egypt (Figure 57). Completed almost three thousand years before the birth of Christ, they come very near the beginning of the history of civilized art. The pyramids were built as tombs, and the Great Pyramid, the largest of all, covers about thirteen acres and is seven hundred and sixty feet on a side and four hundred and eighty-two feet high. Except for the three small chambers in the interior and the passages leading to them, it is solid masonry. The Sphinx, also of great size (one hundred and forty feet long and sixty-five feet high), is partly carved from living rock and partly built of stone hauled to the site. A portrait of Khafra, Khufu's son, it stands as one of the world's most monumental sculptures. Both the Pyramid and the Sphinx are calm, majestic, impersonal expressions of one of the slowest-changing religious-social-political systems the world has ever known, and in looking at them one gets the sense of the permanence for which they were built.

"Hermes" (Figure 58), a statue of a Greek pastoral god by the master sculptor Praxiteles, carved over three thousand years later than the Sphinx, is a warm, humanized interpretation of divinity. In contrast to the great size of the Sphinx, "Hermes" is approximately life size, a fact which demonstrates the down-to-earth, human quality of the Greek religion, sharply different from the austere, formalized Egyptian belief. The appealing beauty of this marble has made it a great favorite, and although it may not be the finest example of Greek sculpture, it gives a quick insight into the Greek religion. How different this approach is from that of the Finns who built the churches described above! Can you imagine this statue having been carved in Finland? Certainly not, for it has the warmth of sunny Greece, not the vigor of northern Finland.

In contrast to the physical beauty of "Hermes" which the Greeks admired is the ascetic detachment of the sculptures on the cathedral at Chartres (Figure 59). Compare them with "Hermes." Examples of Medieval Christian art, these figures place such emphasis on spirituality that the shape of the human figure is all but denied. There is little feeling of shoulders, muscles, or hips. Physical beauty, worshiped religiously by the Greeks, found no favor with Medieval Christians. The enormous difference between the two approaches to sculpture developed from differences in religious beliefs. However, it is important that in spite of much obvious differences, they are both examples of religious art.

The "Deposition from the Cross" (Figure 60), a fresco painted about 1305 A.D.—only a few years after the Chartres sculpture—by the great Italian, Giotto, in the Arena Chapel at Padua, shows a return to human interest and emotion. Seldom has there been such mastery of expressive line, such direct and vital gestures intensely portraying passionate grief over the death of Christ. Again we find a warm, human interpretation of religious events, an effort to bring them directly to the emotions of the observer.

The last example of religious art to be discussed in this section is the "Sistine Madonna" (Figure 61) painted by Raphael in the early years of the sixteenth century, approximately two hundred years after Giotto's "Deposition from the Cross." It is interesting to compare and contrast these two landmarks of Italian painting. Both are products of the same religious creed, both belong to the same nation, and, consequently, there is an underlying similarity of expression. Yet there are many differences. In the earlier one, the forms are direct and forceful, show an angular, architectural solidity, and are tightly knit in a vigorous, three-dimensional composition. In the "Sistine Madonna" the forms are much softer, being marked by a gentle, flowing quality quite unlike anything in the earlier work; the composition is somewhat loosely knit, and the appeal is to the more tender and sentimental sides of human nature. These differences, to be sure, arise in part from the differences in the personalities of the two painters, but they also reflect the changes in social and religious thought which took place from the fourteenth to the sixteenth centuries in Italy. These two paintings show again how truly the art products represent their age.

Between such isolated examples were long periods of gradual development, periods of slow transition from one type to another. Changes in art forms are rarely sudden, but occur along with changes in religion, government, and social ideals. Other examples of religious art are Michel-angelo's "Deposition from the Cross" (page 192), Rubens' "Descent from the Cross" (page 212), El Greco's "St. Francis in Ecstasy" (page 234), the silver crosses (page 272), and the temples and churches in Chapter 17.

CHARACTERISTICS OF RELIGIOUS ART

It is time to ask: What are the characteristics of religious art? What binds together the wooden idol of the African Negro, the caressable marble gods and goddesses of the Greeks, the spiritual and detached sculptures of the Middle Ages, the Cathedral at Chartres, the Parthenon at Athens, the churches in your own town. How do the arts of religion differ from the arts of the home and community?

Religion is a realm of life through which man attempts to find meaning for existence, to express his beliefs and ideals, and to relate himself to his fellow-men, his universe, and his God. Because the arts of religion grow from a search for relationships, one of their most significant characteristics is that they belong to a group, seldom to an individual. In fact, one of their prime purposes is to hold the group together in harmony. Thus, the arts of religion are closely akin to the arts of the community, symbolizing as they do the thoughts and feelings of kindred souls. Also like the arts of the community, the arts of religion are idealistic expressions of what humanity strives to be, not merely representations of what it is. Their role is to inspire, to elevate, to lead the observer on to better thoughts and actions. To accomplish these ends, the arts of religion must show, or teach, the observer what these better things are.

However, unlike the typical educational practice of teaching through facts, religious arts teach primarily through the emotions. Seeking to arouse, to stimulate, to inspire, they appeal to man's feeling through the rich, vivid color of stained glass, fresco, or oil paint; through the restless, aspiring arches and buttresses of a Gothic cathedral or through the delicate perfection of a Greek temple; through the stark dynamic forces and tensions of a modern church; through the attenuated, spiritual figures of the Gothic cathedral or the grotesque idols of African Negroes.

In order that this appeal through the emotions shall not be transitory, religious art like religion itself invariably seeks to express feelings and ideals which have the qualities of permanence. No contrast could be

102

sharper than between religious art which holds significance for centuries and posters and advertisements which last for a short time only. All of the great religions—Christianity, Judaism, Mohammedanism, Buddhism— have lasted for centuries because they can arouse in their followers awe and wonder and faith through emotions so deeply rooted that no worldly rulers have final power against them, even though many have attempted to uproot them. Religious art, dealing with ultimate purposes, values, and goals of life, involves not only this life but life in the hereafter. In this way it approaches the infinite, the timeless. And naturally in dealing with such unknowns and unknowables as the afterlife, religious art becomes mystical, inspires great awe and wonder. These qualities mark religious art as something powerful in the lives of men.

If you wish to know more about religious art, any art history book will help. In particular:

Sheldon Cheney: *A World History of Art* (Viking Press, 1937). Presents
historical material in a readable manner.
Hendrik Willem van Loon: *The Arts* (Simon & Schuster, 1937). Places
emphasis on the relation of the arts to all aspects of life.
D. M. Robb and J. J. Garrison: *Art in the Western World* (Harper,
1942). Presents in orderly fashion many of the important facts about
religious architecture, painting and sculpture.

CHAPTER 4 *Art in Industry*

THE breakfast dishes you eat from, the chair you sit on, the rug you walk across, the automobile you ride in—in fact, the majority of objects you use every day are products of industrial art. It is only natural in this civilization that we encounter industrial art often. The illustrations in this chapter and those in Part III give a faint idea of the variety of products available today. Much better is a trip to a local department or dime store, or a glance through one of the larger mail-order catalogues. Never before have so many things been available to so many people.

Today's world is a vast network of cities and towns, and farms and mines, interlaced with a web of split-second communication and swift transportation. Wool is grown in Australia or in our western states; cotton is grown in the South; rayon is produced in Tennessee; mills in Michigan or Massachusetts, New Jersey or England, spin, stamp, dye, and stitch. From Minnesota, Brazil, and Sweden comes the iron ore for the steel in the machines that whir and roar to produce the things we need. Speedy trains and far-driving sea-ships of steel or sky-ships of aluminum bring and take raw materials and finished products. From a hundred corners of our world come the foods on our dinner table; and from our own little corner go the products that we build or process or grow. Our community, tiny or great, is one in a world of communities, each dependent on the rest.

In this world of manufacture and distribution we live our daily lives. We eat and sleep and produce our kind—just as man has done from the beginning of time. But many aspects of our living have changed, and our way of producing art has changed along with them. The shift from individual hand craftsmanship to mass machine production has caused one of the most significant—and upsetting—changes in art history. Before discussing present-day industrial machine art, let us observe the making of hand products in a less complex culture than our own. Self-contained communities are not many in these times. But Mexico and Central

America have such communities. In Guatemala, for instance, there are villages that, until a few years ago, visitors had seldom entered. In these communities the natives, working with primitive looms, potter's wheels and other simple machines, supply the textiles, utensils, and other objects which they need. These are sold or exchanged in the market place (Figure 66). Little is produced that is not consumed in the community.

Communities such as this one, although simple, are highly integrated and the art products are direct and unaffected—as the social order that produced them. A typical example is the weaving (Figure 67) from one of the remote villages in Guatemala. In this little community, as in most places where culture has not been upset by the advent of North American and European ideas and industry, each textile is made for a definite purpose, and no textile is made until it is definitely needed. Where there is communal security there is little necessity to store products for future needs. If a woman needs a new blouse, or a man a new shirt, yarn is dyed, a simple loom is strung and then the cloth for the blouse or shirt is woven. The textile shown in the illustration is a carrying-cloth—for carrying bananas, beans, or babies. Embellished with the symbolic designs of the local village, it has the charm of irregularity, the appeal of the "human touch." The animals and figures are not always in line and some of them are a trifle larger than others. At some points the weaving is tighter than at others. Handmade products invariably have these qualities which are the natural result of their method of manufacture. Wide-eyed tourists from "civilized" countries take great delight in these products which differ so markedly from their own. They exclaim how happy they are to have found something that has escaped the standardization of the machine.

Let us look at the clothing worn by the women of this Guatemalan community shown in the illustration. Despite the lack of machine standardization (which is often cited as one of the blights of this age) all the village women are wearing clothes that are essentially the same: the same materials, the same type of weaving, the same colors and designs. The only differences are those minor ones that resulted from the impossibility of duplicating one hand-made article with another hand-made article. Here, even in this stronghold of the craft tradition, almost untouched by the machine, there is a standardization which cannot be duplicated in a machine civilization, a standardization to which most modern women would object.

Products of craft civilizations are beautiful not because they are individual, but because they conform; not because they vary from every other product, but because they are standardized. The designs in all such products are invariably old. They have been used, with minor variations, for generations. Through the process of use, weak points have been discovered and corrected; satisfactory elements have become established. A craft tradition is a long-time affair, reflecting the simple vigor of an integrated, if primitive, civilization. It is the result of a type of society differing markedly from our own. It produces articles which, much as we might yearn for them, we cannot produce in quantities sufficient for our needs.

The universal use of ornament by primitive peoples is a striking characteristic of their art. Even though their life, made hard by man or nature, demands a disproportionate output of energy merely to keep alive, the craftsman has found ample time and the creative enthusiasm to decorate his wares. Sometimes this decoration grows directly out of the process, as, for example, in textiles exhibiting patterns developed from the weaving process. At other times this decoration may well result from the materials chosen—the color and texture of clay burned to a soft terra-cotta color, the sensuous beauty of silk or wool fibers, the natural grain of wood. These two types of ornament grow directly from the processes or materials. But there are other types of ornament: the animal motives in the Guatemalan textile, for instance, which were consciously and purposefully put there by craftsmen. Such ornament gives stimulation and satisfaction to both primitive and civilized man.

Now, before leaving the subject of industrial art in a highly integrated community to look at the complexities of our own, we might compare a Guatemalan village with an American colonial town—one like Williamsburg, for example. The conditions were not greatly different. Crude means of transportation compelled such communities to be almost self-sufficient. Many families carded and spun wool and later wove it into clothes and coverlets. The blacksmith and metalworker, whose factory, shop, and home were one, occupied an important post in each community. Practically everyone helped in producing the objects of everyday life. The people were craftsmen. They were the industrial artists of their day, producing by hand the products needed by their civilization. Look again at the Williamsburg interiors (Figures 18 and 19) and notice the furniture, candlesticks, textiles and other accessories. We value these early American products because they, like the weaving of Guatemala, express the life of a people.

THE INDUSTRIAL REVOLUTION

The Industrial Revolution got well under way about one hundred and fifty years ago, although the underlying forces had been brewing for some time. It still continues in full force and has profoundly changed our ways of working, living, and, consequently, of thinking. The Industrial Revolution was marked by the advent of power machinery and technological advances. The continued replacement of handwork by machinery has brought on some of the most serious labor problems the world has known. Each new machine throws men out of work, causing discomfort and misery before they can be re-employed in new fields. Craftsmen have fought the machine, looking upon it as a monster which threatens their means of livelihood. One of their most frequent arguments was that it destroyed individuality and beauty in art; that the machine produced only objects which were vulgar and ugly. These protests and arguments we now see as futile, but to the craftsmen they were a part of the fight for existence. They would have nothing to do with machines. They could see in them no new power to make beauty, only disaster and joblessness and ugliness. They were blind to the tremendous advances in speed and skill which were ushering in a new era of mass production, with new possibilities for creating more beautiful and useful things for more people in the rapid machine-manipulation of materials.

The major effects of the Industrial Revolution may be studied through its influence on the products, the workers, and society.

THE EFFECT ON PRODUCTS

The first consideration of the industrialists was to make objects in large quantities and, for this reason, cheaply. Thus a great market would be opened; people who before could not afford many things could now buy in greater quantities. Compared on this count with hand methods of manufacture, new mass production seemed a godsend. A hundred spoons could be made in the same time as one. With labor costs cut, they could be sold for a fraction of their former price. Cheapness, however, was the only virtue of the early stages of the Revolution. The craftsman of the days before machinery had worked long with his tradition and his materials; he had become a competent designer. But by fighting instead of using the machine, he left it without a master. Design went to the dogs. Business men, with no art experience or training, dictated fashions with a comic, clumsy hand. Structure and material were ignored—not intentionally, but because they were not understood. Another factor, the ease with which the machine could reproduce ornament, led to great abuse. In the handcraft products, ornament required time and labor, and was applied thoughtfully. Hours of delicate work were required to paint designs on a dinner plate. Not so with the machine. Any object could be covered with pressed designs in a few seconds. Look at the early stove and package sealer in Figures 72 and 73. And because ornament was so easy, it became an obsession. It was applied to everything, it became the symbol of "art," and, worse, it was used to hide defects in manufacture. Poor carpentry and cheap woods were disguised in profuse carving. Bad joints in metalwork were made less noticeable by being smothered with moldings and gewgaws.

The first phases of the Industrial Revolution had, therefore, distressing effects on art and art products. Development of industry was uncontrolled; cut-throat competition for bigger, faster sales led to a vulgarization and cheapening of design. Fascination with this new power led to a preoccupation with its most immediately apparent virtue—mass production—and all else was sacrificed to roll or stamp out products in abundance.

Gradually conditions changed. Manufacturers, in time, found that, in addition to making products cheaply and in quantity, they needed to raise the quality of their wares. So a period followed, during the early part of our present century, when there was a striking improvement in the quality of manufactured products. Succeeding this was a period during which manufacturers realized that, in addition to inexpensiveness and durability, a product needed to be good-looking. These manufacturers were not apostles of art trying to bring beauty to the masses of humanity. They were hard-headed business men who saw that good-looking products sold better than ugly ones. Art became the partner of business.

Each month brings new products to the market and increasing attention is paid to their appearance as well as to their function. Look first at the mixing bowl, teakettle, radio, and typewriter (Figures 62 to 65), all of which show a *precise* beauty of form growing out of a study of human needs, of the properties of materials, and of the techniques of machine production. Look also at the mass-produced bowl and textile (Figures 69 and 71) which show an *informal* charm usually associated with handcrafts.

In spite of these achievements, it would be a serious mistake to think that we have "arrived." The constant quest for variety and novelty each year drives the manufacturer to seek new designs, and because this quest is often for the sake of novelty alone rather than from real needs, many of the products are ugly. Go through the "novelty" or "gift" section of any store and see how many counters are buried beneath ill-shaped objects. This great number of unshapely products show that tremendous opportunities for improvement still exist. Constantly changing human wants, new machines, new processes, new materials make change inevitable—and we may change for the better or for the worse. You, as consumers, can do much to bring improvements by demanding well-designed products. The manufacturer produces what he can sell, and you are the buyers.

THE EFFECT ON THE WORKERS

The Industrial Revolution increased the division of labor, made men and women specialists in a little part of the process instead of the master or journeyman in the whole. The craftsman no longer designed and fashioned a piece of silverware, but merely superintended the operation of one machine which stamped or pressed the form. Rather than seeing a product "in process" from beginning to end, the workers became cogs, each performing a tiny operation in a vast mechanical system. Often the complexity of the system prevented the individual worker from ever seeing his part in relation to the whole, and because he did not, much of the satisfaction of making things, the joy of his labor was lost. With the introduction of machinery, ordinary work ceased to be creative; it became routine. There is a whole world of difference between designing and producing a coffee-pot in the craft period and in the machine era—between working out the whole idea, and shoving up and down the levers of a machine which stamps out only the spout. Under mass production, a job has a tendency to lose much of its satisfaction to the worker and too often becomes merely a means of making enough money to keep himself alive in order to do more work. Modern machine civilization has, therefore, forced many to hunt elsewhere for satisfaction, has encouraged escapes from reality. New sources of emotional satisfaction have had to be found. This accounts for the popularity of movies showing beautiful women and strong men living in luxury. This accounts, too, for the masses of story magazines, crowded with superheated romance and adventure that pour endlessly from the press into the racks of the four corners' village store and the city pharmacy.

Another and equally serious effect on the workers was brought about by the concentration of industry in large cities. Real estate values in the cities skyrocketed. Factory towns were laid out with no thought for the human lives they were to house. Dwellings crowded shoulder to shoulder, even with vast spaces of land all about. The crowded houses and apartment buildings shut out each from the other the small amount of sun and air that managed to filter through the smoke barrage belching from factory funnels. Muddy streets or dangerous traffic ways were offered to growing children as their only playgrounds. Men read about the open country, but never saw it. The deplorable living quarters of part of our population is one of the yet unpaid bills of the Industrial Revolution. The housing of workers in industrial centers is a pressing contemporary problem, but fortunately a number of private and public groups have given their expert attention to it, and conspicuous progress has been made, as was discussed in the chapter on Art in the Community. The close interrelation of art, industry and city planning becomes evident when we realize how drastically the change from hand to machine production of the art used in everyday life has altered the layout and appearance of our cities and the ways of living of our citizens.

THE EFFECT ON SOCIETY

A social system based on buying and selling is influenced by every shift in industrial trends. The new system of production developed in the Industrial Revolution upset the gradually formulated, century-old labor and craft tradition. Sudden changes caused strife and turmoil and made finding a dominant direction difficult. At such times there is a tendency to fall back on the old ways, on the safe and conservative. This happened in the arts. Frightened by the present and future, people turned to the past for bygone forms. Gothic ornament (but not Gothic structure) was revived for churches and schools, railway stations were fashioned after Roman baths, and post offices and courthouses took their columns and cornices from Greek temples. Present-day revivals of Early American, Colonial, English, and French furniture are part of the same futile attempt to escape our own time. Even our musical programs are composed almost entirely of "classics" culled from the past with only an occasional

110

playing of contemporary work. This is not intended to imply that we should ignore or depreciate historical art which offers endless opportunities for enjoyment and learning. But a vigorous, creative society keeps its energies focused on the present and future at the same time that it gives the past due respect. Fortunately, the past few decades have brought art forms suited to our needs, and one of the purposes of this book is to arouse interest in and understanding of this work.

ARTS AND CRAFTS REVIVAL

During the nineteenth century, there was a strong tendency to split art away from industry. What the machine produced, many said, was always ugly; what the craftsman made by hand was beautiful. Therefore, the argument ran, art and the machine had nothing in common, art and industry were in opposition. In terms of the times, they were in opposition. As a means of livelihood, production by hand methods was being supplemented or, in many instances, being rendered unnecessary by the machine. The economic disaster which millions of people faced colored their reaction toward the machine and toward everything which it produced.

To escape this difficulty, some went further than mere protest and began a movement for the return to craft methods. Thus arose the Arts and Crafts Movement. William Morris, its English founder, was a great social reformer who envisioned an integrated society well housed, working under good conditions and producing worthwhile, beautiful, handmade objects for everyday use. His idea resulted in countless arts and crafts groups which helped turn attention to well-designed products. Today, amateurs profit from handcrafts in terms of personal enjoyment, and professionals make distinguished products, such as the bowl (Figure 68) and the textile (Figure 70), for those who can afford handmade utensils and accessories. These have their place just as do painting and sculpture, for they bring variety and individuality to a machine age. Perhaps even more important, handcrafts promote experimentation, exploration of new materials, and continued first-hand attention to the human element in art, all of which provides the industrial designer with inspiration. Although a craft society as envisioned by the Arts and Crafts Movement cannot be revived, the handcrafts fill a genuine need in today's living.

111

MACHINE-MADE ART AND ITS EFFECTS

Today we recognize the advantages of the machine even though the methods of controlling it are still somewhat obscure. We know that it offers the possibilities of infinite and accurate duplications, great savings in men's time and effort. It has freed the artist so that he may search deeper into human needs instead of occupying his time in beating or hammering out an object which a machine can do with vast, swift superiority.

The Industrial Revolution has given us a wholly new kind of artist: the industrial designer. This is the man or woman who, working with engineers, advertisers, and retailers, designs the trains, airplanes, and automobiles we ride in, the matchboxes and bath towels which we buy. Like the craftsman of old, he understands materials and methods of manufacture. Unlike the old craftsman, he designs but does not execute the finished product. He makes only the plans or a model. The machine will pour it out in as many millions as we will buy. The industrial designer is responsible for the amazing improvement in the appearance of everything from ink bottles and dishpans to airplanes.

Conditions representative of the present phase of the Industrial Revolution may be summed up by again dividing the discussion into three aspects—product, worker, and society.

Mechanical production and technical perfection have given us a new kind of beauty in useful objects—the beauty of precision rather than the charm of handwork. Textiles can be perfectly woven, metals perfectly shaped, glass perfectly blown or molded. Study the photographs of machine-made objects of glass, metal, and wood in the later chapters of this book, and compare them with craft work. Both machine and craft objects have their characteristic beauty; one type can be as beautiful as the other; each has its own special characteristics.

Lowered cost has widened tremendously the market for thousands of needed articles. In response to this increased market, manufacturers have made a great variety of goods available. Never before has a person, even of limited means, been able to select his purchases from such a diversity of designs. Next time you go to a shopping center, count the different designs in glass tumblers offered in the low-price range, and you will probably be amazed to realize that you can choose from so much. While the Mexican glassmaker has been content to produce one type of glass for years, we turn out new designs and colors daily. Some are good, some are poor. One thing is clear: you, the buyer, have an opportunity to select a tumbler to fit your personal needs. You can blame no one but yourself if you fail to make use of this advantage. You no longer have to take only what one maker offers you. You can invariably get good design—if you will look for it.

For the worker, the present phase of the Industrial Revolution has further increased wages and shortened hours. Technological advance continues to throw many men and women out of work and force them into other jobs where they cannot use the skills which they have developed through years of experience. Improved methods of manufacture will always have, as an unfortunate by-product, the displacement of workers with the consequent frustrations and insecurities. In times of prosperity, these insecurities are reduced to a minimum, for displaced workers are readily absorbed. In times of depression, there are grave social repercussions.

Yet in our society these industrial changes have given many others increased leisure and education, and a higher standard of living. Increased leisure has given time to consider beauty, to read about art in books and magazines, to visit art galleries, to form cultivated tastes and opinions on art matters. Increased American education has given great numbers of persons background and training, one aim of which is to increase sensitivity to beauty. The higher standard of living has made it possible for many people to obtain beautiful things. Although the possibilities of more education, leisure and money have not yet been fully realized, the groundwork for richer living has been laid. But now we turn to more specific problems in the arts of industry.

SPECIFIC PROBLEMS

If you want to learn about a person's taste, do not ask him what he thinks about the Italian Renaissance or the Parthenon, because he can too easily quote ideas which he has read but which may mean little or nothing to him. Rather than asking questions, notice his clothes or visit his home. Observe what he *does* about art products when he has a chance. There is the real evidence, objective and undeniable proof of what he believes. Action is perhaps the best index of *thinking*.

FOUR STOVES

The four stoves in Figure 72 show much about the people who designed, manufactured, and bought them. Consider the functions of a cook stove. A stove is primarily a piece of kitchen equipment for cooking food, and it should be designed to perform that function with a minimum of labor and fuel. If it does not do this, it is not a good stove—even though it has proportions as beautiful as a Greek temple! It must also be easy to keep clean. A smooth, simple surface meets this requirement better than one twisted, turned, carved with ornamentation. There should be no unnecessary projections to catch the head, skin or elbow of the unwary housewife who stoops to pick up a pin from the floor or hurries to answer the telephone. There should be toe room underneath to prevent scuffed shoes and a scratched stove. Yet the space for the housewife's toes must not catch dirt or be awkward to clean. Handles and knobs should be easy to see, comfortable and quick to take hold of. The whole stove should look and be sturdy and durable, straightforward and workmanlike. It should appear well balanced, not top-heavy or lopsided; the important parts should be emphasized as dominant features; and all parts should be rhythmically related to each other and the whole design. Finally, it should be so designed that it harmonizes with the rest of the kitchen and relates pleasantly to the refrigerator, cabinets, and sink.

Of the four stoves illustrated, how does the first one meet these requirements? It is probably reasonably efficient as coal stoves go, but does it occupy a minimum of space? What about the dirt-catching space under the stove, the wasted space under the projecting shelves? Metal is a good conductor of heat, and would not these shelves spread, rather than concentrate, the heat? Is it pleasing in appearance? Are the decorations well adapted to the spaces which they ornament—the oven door, for example? We can tell at once that the stove could not possibly be harmonious with the sink, cupboards, table and chairs which are part of the kitchen furniture, unless they, too, were covered with ornament, projecting shelves, and oddly shaped doors. As regards safety (which might well be considered first, not last, since thousands of accidents maim and kill people

62. (*Left*) Mixing bowl by Eva Zeisel is a marked departure from the typical shape. Designed to fit the hand and to make pouring easy, the form takes full advantage of the plasticity of the clay from which it is made. Industrial art of this type demonstrates how *form* (or design) develops out of *functional needs* and the characteristics of *materials*.

63. (*Right*) Aluminum teakettle like the bowl above is functionally designed in terms of use and material. Notice how the spout "flows" out of the body of the kettle as naturally as the water that passes through it, how the handle has been formed to permit easy handling.

64. (*Left*) A straightforward portable radio in a molded plastic case. The legible dial and the functional knobs have been designed as a visually pleasing unit.

65. (*Right*) Portable typewriter designed by Henry Dreyfuss demonstrates how mechanical complexity can be organized into visual and operational simplicity. Only those parts frequently used by the typist are visible; all other mechanism is enclosed. Keys are shaped to fit fingers.

In a handicraft society such as exists in many Guatemalan villages, articles of daily use are limited in variety and represent slowly evolving traditional types. Each village has its characteristic types of weaving and pottery.

66. (*Upper*) In the market place at Atitlan, Guatemala craftsmen display and sell their products.

67 (*Lower*) A Guatemalan textile woven by hand for everyday use. Although such textiles have general similarities, no two are identical. Notice the enlivening variations with which the birds and figures have been treated.

116

Two bowls and two textiles. The vase and textile at the left were made by hand; those on the right were designed for mass production but show clearly the influence of hand crafts. All have rich textures developing from the materials and processes.

68. (*Upper left*) Stoneware bowl in green and brown by Marguerite Wildenhain.

69. (*Upper right*) Free-form bowl designed by Alexander Giampietro for mass production.

70. (*Lower left*) Hand-woven and printed textile made at Cranbrook Academy.

71. (*Lower right*) Machine-woven textile.

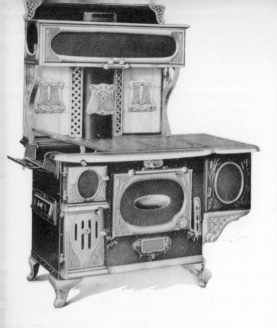

Objects of everyday use have been tremendously improved within the last few decades.

72a, b, c, d. Four stoves showing a progressive simplification of form and adaptation to contemporary needs. Notice the gradual elimination of hard-to-keep-clean distracting ornament and of projecting surfaces which are hazardous in the kitchen, the reduction and final elimination of dirt-catching space beneath the stove, and the treatment of the stove less as an individual object and more as a unit to fit in with other kitchen equipment.

Three designs for package sealers, commonly used in stores to dispense gummed tape, tell the story of industrial design in the last 25 years.

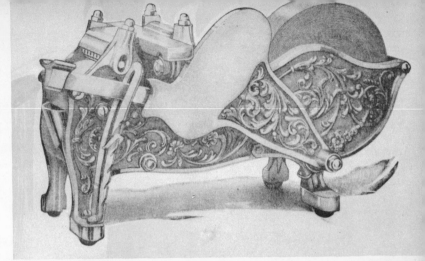

73 (*Upper*) In 1918 the package sealer exposed its mechanism, was embossed with inappropriate ornament as was the early stove.

74. (*Middle*) By 1932 much of the mechanism was concealed in rather crude angular forms poorly adapted to the form of the human hand. Unnecessary projections catch dust, fatigue eyes and hands.

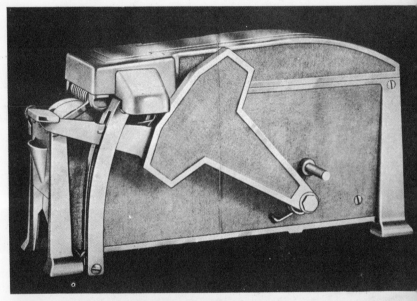

75. (*Lower*) Designed by Egmont Arens in 1941, this package sealer is compact, attractive in appearance, and convenient to use.

Prefabricated mass-production units allow for flexibility and individuality.

76. (*Upper*) Furniture units designed by Charles Eames may be purchased individually, combined in a variety of ways. Based on a standard module as indicated by the grid lines, the pieces fit together harmoniously.

77. (*Lower*) The Ingersoll Utility Unit combines in one prefabricated unit all plumbing and heating equipment needed for a small house. It includes a complete kitchen, laundry, bathroom, and heater compactly arranged to save cost and space. Only the kitchen part of the unit is visible here.

78. The Ford Factory at Dearborn, Michigan, shows the striking new f̲o̲
which have come into being as a result of the needs and techniques of mo̲
industry. Such architecture has a dynamic, aggressive quality which marks
development of contemporary industrial concerns and from this it gains a dram̲
beauty. Basically growing out of their functions, the forms achieve a strong es̲
tic quality.

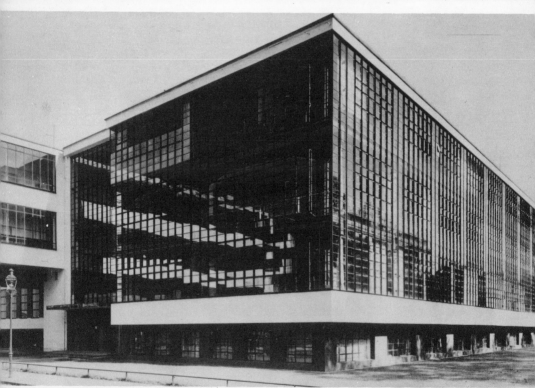

Two contemporary workshops each functional in its environment.

79. (*Upper*) A home factory in Cuernavaca, Mexico, showing the potter working outside his home with a primitive foot-power potters' wheel.

80. (*Lower*) The epoch-making New Bauhaus was designed to house a school to bring art and industry together again as they were in the past.

in their homes) this model gets a flunk! The shelves are perfectly placed for bumping heads, knees and hands, while the legs are fitted to catch toes, brooms and mops.

The second and third stoves represent advancing stages in solving the problem of cooking equipment. They gain in compactness, attractiveness, efficient use of space and safety. But the second stove has panels which, looking as they do like crushed paper, cloth (or is it marble?), certainly do not convey the smoothness of metal or enamel. A further disadvantage is that those panels emphasize parts rather than the whole, making the stove seem to be a number of unrelated units fastened together. This tendency is even more pronounced in the third stove, which looks as though a new unit had been added each year. And do not fail to notice the progressive change in the shape of the legs.

The fourth stove is simple, compact, functional, and would harmonize easily with cupboards, refrigerator and sink. It could be cleaned in half the time required for the other models. Compare the handles on the third and fourth stoves. Why have three different kinds of handles on the one? Observe, too, that every inch of space has been well used in the fourth stove, and that by building the stove down to the floor a difficult cleaning problem has been solved and yet toe room provided. It is good to be able to show such an objective record of progress toward beautiful and functional design in only a few years, and to demonstrate a basis upon which to praise our industrial designers, manufacturers, and customers who have made such rapid development possible. Between the first and fourth stoves are years of cooperative work between artist, engineer, business man, and housewife. Art, science, and business, once declared to be irreconcilable enemies, have quit fighting, and together have developed a product which should bring joy to the user. If such achievement can come out of the industrial system, it merits praise, and those who, with misty eyes, yearn for a return to the simple past should take heed.

But do not get the idea that stove design has stopped. As time goes on there will be others. New developments in heating, in cooking, in kitchen design, all will influence the appearance of our stoves. Just what these changes will be we cannot predict. But changes there will be. The last word in any art form is never uttered.

THREE PACKAGE SEALERS

Figures 73, 74, and 75 show three stages in the design of package sealers. The function of a package sealer is simple: to dispense strips of gummed paper used in wrapping packages. With the exception of two movable parts—the frequently used handle and the infrequently used knob to control the length of the strip—all mechanism can be enclosed. Obviously the handle should be the dominant visual element, and yet when one looks at the first two designs the handle is almost the last thing seen. In the evolution of this object one can see how florid curves and ornament (mistakenly identified with "art") gave way to clumsy angularity (mistakenly identified with the "mechanistic"), and these in turn to simple, basic, unified forms suited to their purpose.

UNIT FURNITURE

Industrial designers are concerned not only with the form of individual pieces but with the manner in which single elements can be used together. Unit furniture which can be fitted together in various combinations is not a new idea but is one which has been intensively explored in the past twenty years. Figure 76 shows furniture designed by Charles Eames as a series of small units each planned for one or more types of storage. Their similarity in size and shapes make possible varied arrangements to fit any type of room or need. Additional pieces can be added as necessary. Their advantage over larger, less flexible chests, sideboards, bookcases, and record cabinets are many: storage pieces can be placed where they will function best; arrangements can easily be changed as family needs change; all space is used with great efficiency: the construction, though light, is very strong; and the pieces can be combined in a compact orderly manner in a variety of rooms.

UTILITY UNIT

The Utility Unit (Figure 77) combines facilities for kitchen, laundry, bathroom, household heating, and other services—all the heating and plumbing needed in a small house—in one integrated core. The efficient grouping of these utilities reduces expensive plumbing lines and saves space. Built on an assembly line, it takes advantage of the speed and precision of mechanized fabrication, eliminates wasteful hand operations. It offers the home builder a well-designed and -engineered, mass-produced solution to one of the major problems of house construction.

The preceding section of this chapter aimed to give some idea of the development of art in industry, to point out how mass-production practices and products differ from those of craft societies, and to illustrate contemporary trends in product design. But for the consumer the most pressing problem is selecting well-designed products from the enormous variety now available. The saleswoman may say, "This is the very latest thing in book-ends. They came straight from New York. Aren't they lovely?" Well, maybe they are and maybe they aren't "lovely." Novelty has no virtue in itself. Fads follow one another as fast as promoters can force them. Distinguishing between objects of lasting interest and those of fleeting appeal requires serious thought and continuous study, but it yields high dividends.

Before you purchase—even better, before you start looking—decide exactly *why* you want the object. Then think about *when, where,* and *how* you will use it. After that it is easier to decide *what* object will be best. While looking through stores, magazines, or catalogues, ask yourself these questions about any object that interests you. How well does it function? How well is the form suited to the function? How pleasing are the form, color, and texture? How suitable are the materials, and how well have they been handled? Make all the comparisons you can on all factors. Study and apply the material on design in Part II and the discussion of materials and process in Part III of this book.

INDUSTRIAL ARCHITECTURE

A change as significant and far-reaching as the Industrial Revolution should, of course, bring a new architecture. And it has. The photograph of an automobile plant (Figure 78) is convincing evidence. In it there is a beauty, very real and very near to all of us, if we regard beauty as primarily dependent on harmonious relationships between functions, forms and materials. Tall cylinders, squat cylinders, rectangular solids and cones are combined in a magnificent composition. Observe the pattern of light and dark, the play of forces, movements, directions with and against one another. And remember that this architecture developed as naturally from the contemporary industrial system as an oak tree from an acorn. It is—and looks—inevitable, an observation which is true of all great art. Great art has no time for falseness, insincerity, self-consciousness. It develops from a social system of which it is a part.

Naturally, a factory such as this is a present step in a long line of evolution. At one time the home was almost universally used as a factory—and it still is in some places. The Mexican craftsman more often than not does his work in one corner of the living room or on his "front porch" as shown in Figure 79. His wife and children generally help him by getting materials ready or by doing minor parts of the work. His whole scheme of living is centralized in the few feet he calls home.

Living and working under one roof in the midst of one's family circle sounds delightfully simple and beautifully integrated to us in the midst of our busy, tangled lives. And when enough space is available and the climate is good and the air pure, the home-factory with its convenience and low overhead costs is not a bad solution. But when living quarters are in crowded tenements which are badly lit and full of foul, lifeless air, and the working hours are long, the problem is different. All in all, the home as a workshop in our world is a dangerous makeshift solution of the problem of industrial architecture.

This was realized most clearly when the introduction of machinery made it impelling to work collectively. Even the simple machinery of the medieval period brought men together in picturesque Guild houses. When the rapid development of power machines around 1800 resulted in many new factories, these were unfortunately designed with little regard for the human beings laboring in them. Working conditions became so bad that "work" took on a new, unpleasant meaning. Often factory doors and windows were tightly locked, and working hours were long, even children working twelve to fourteen hours a day. Somewhat later pathetically futile attempts to "beautify" such factories were made by adding historic ornament—Greek columns, a touch of the Gothic, or a few Romanesque arches—to the outside for the people who looked at them instead of for those who worked in them. An architectural smoke screen was thrown around the factory. But no smoke screen will fool people for long.

To step up production, which depends not only on better machinery but on more efficient workmen as well, engineers began to design clean, functional buildings which were well lighted, well ventilated. Although not always beautiful in appearance, such buildings exhibited the importance of new materials by making full use of their possibilities. Steel construction permitted large rooms without heavy supports or partitions, improved methods of making glass made possible large windows for light and air. The engineer with his interest in function taught the architect a much-needed lesson.

Some architects were ready to learn. The Bauhaus in Dessau, Germany (Figure 80), was designed by the German architect, Walter Gropius, to house "a revolution in art." A combination school and workshop, the original plan was to train young artists to design for a machine age. "Rightness" of design was to be dependent on structure, on the basic shape of the product, not on decoration. Materials were handled and worked until the designers were perfectly familiar with their possibilities and limitations. The educational policy outlined and put into operation at the Bauhaus was one of the most significant recently formulated for the training of artists.

The design of the building was, of course, an outgrowth of the educational ideas. Sometimes called the "Glass Box," one unit of the building has walls made almost entirely of glass. Horizontal bands contrast strikingly with the large glass expanses, but no verticals show on the exterior. Not suited to extreme climates, it is nevertheless one of the most exciting examples of experimental architecture that the world has known. It has its roots deep in our industrial system. But, like all great art, it transcends a period by pointing to a future.

Being at the utilitarian end of the art scale, industrial architecture has special problems of providing for economical operation, of giving workers healthful working conditions. Design and construction are shaped to these ends. Because it is closely related to functional requirements, industrial architecture is likely to express the dominant trend of an age more quickly than other architecture. Few industrialists today will countenance Gothic pinnacles on their factories, although many of them drive modern automobiles to homes built in the medieval manner. Perhaps we should say that there is little or no room for sentimentality in industrial architecture. And, as a result, it stands expressing its age with a magnificent simplicity.

This vitality of design, comparable to the Guatemalan weaver's textiles, arises because human needs have been met directly. No time for affectation leaves much time for straight thinking. Yes, artists do think. And

127

great artists think hard before they arrive at satisfactory solutions. They analyze their problem with skills as precise as those of a great surgeon. What functions must be served by the building, or the chair, the automobile, or the knife? Which considerations are important? What factors are nonessential? They strive for style and avoid fashion. And, if they succeed, their work demonstrates their thought processes. Poor work, of course, demonstrates sloppy thinking too.

Although new, the field of industrial art already has much literature.

Herbert Bayer, Walter Gropius and Ise Gropius: *Bauhaus* (Museum of Modern Art, 1938). A thoroughly illustrated account of the Bauhaus.

Sheldon and Martha Cheney: *Art and the Machine* (Whittlesey House, 1936).

John Cloag: *Industrial Art Explained* (Allen & Unwin, 1946). An English publication of considerable interest.

Norman Bel Geddes: *Horizons* (Little, Brown, 1932). A stimulating discussion of industrial possibilities.

Siegfried Giedion: *Mechanization Takes Command* (Oxford University Press, 1948). A penetrating discussion of the history and theory of mechanization.

Phillip Johnson (ed.): *Machine Art* (Museum of Modern Art, 1934). An excellent survey of forward-looking designs in the middle thirties.

S. Moholy-Nagy: *Vision in Motion* (Theobald, 1947). The best statements of the philosophy and science growing out of the Bauhaus Institute.

Nicholas Pevsner: *Pioneers of the Modern Movement from William Morris to Walter Gropius* (Stokes, 1936). Thorough discussion of the recent history of this phase of art.

Herbert Read: *Art and Industry* (Harcourt, Brace, 1935). An exceedingly penetrating book which is worth anyone's reading.

Herbert Read (ed.): *The Practice of Design* (Lund Humphries, 1946). The special problems and considerations in various fields are discussed in contributions by designers of textiles, pottery, printing, transportation, etc.

Walter Dorwin Teague: *Design This Day* (Harcourt, Brace, 1940). Profusely illustrated book emphasizing industrial design against the social and economic background of the present.

Harold Van Doren: *Industrial Design* (McGraw-Hill, 1940). A book giving a step-by-step account of industrial styling.

CHAPTER 5 *Art in Commerce*

COMMERCE, the lifeline of industry, gives the manufacturer means of getting the finished products across to us, the consumers. Just as industrial art is the art of making things, so is commercial
art concerned with the selling and distribution of things. Advertising,
transportation, communication, buying and selling and financing—these
major fields in our commercial world may be broken into smaller parts.
Advertising: newspaper and magazine advertising, radio and movie advertising, posters—then even further—word-of-mouth, all telling us the appearance of the product, its value to us, and pointing out how or where
to obtain it. Transportation: rail, truck, water, air, and horse and man
power. Communication: telephone, telegraph, mail, radio and direct
speech. Buying and selling: finance, storage, display and appearance of
the product, salesmanship, and the buildings to house these activities.
The art in this world of commerce is fast-moving and busy. It has no time
to slumber in a museum.

We speak of the problems of commercial art as first, to express a
product, idea, or service; and second, to impress the observer forcibly.
Yet we know that expressing an idea in an art object and then getting
someone to notice it is basic to all the arts. The musician composes a
symphony expressing musical ideas, and then hopes for an appreciative
audience; the dramatist writes a play based, perhaps, on a social theme,
and the play is publicly performed; the painter expresses an idea in plastic
forms and colors, and then exhibits the painting. At the root of all art
products is the fundamental idea which is to be expressed for the benefit
and satisfaction of others. In short, art is expression and communication.

But the special problem of commercial art differs from the special problems of the other arts—music, literature, ballet, or those already studied:
the arts of the home, the community, religion, and industry. The aim is
to sell the mass outpouring of high speed machines to as many consumers
as possible. To meet this aim, the idea of the product must be clarified

and uttered in terms so simple and by symbols so readily understandable that even the uninterested passer-by will stop and look. Whereas the arts of the home express comfortable living, the arts of commerce express efficiency. And while the arts of the community—great sculpture, architecture and painting embodying ideals of social unity—are calculated to induce respect and contemplation, the arts of commerce must be so self-evident, so obtrusive, that little study or contemplation is necessary.

Selling and distributing products and services are the functions of commercial art. Stoves, automobiles, furniture, and floor wax—the products of industry—are made to be sold. The problem of selling is integral with that of designing and making a product. The commercial man knows that forms and colors, properly organized, offer direct stimulation to buy his goods.

ADVERTISING

The upper poster in Figure 81 was designed by E. McKnight Kauffer to sell telephone service. It proclaims, "Come on the TELEPHONE." If this poster were in its original size and colors, located somewhere along the path of your daily activities, what would be its effect on you? You would (or so the telephone company hopes) become aware of that important means of communication, the telephone. The word and the picture of TELEPHONE are forceful and direct. You think of what the telephone means, and, to guide your thinking towards two of the best features of telephone service, the artist planned that you think of the handiness of the telephone and of the magical ease with which one can be transported over great distances. Perhaps a further effect of the telephone poster would be your decision to install an extension on the second floor of your home, or to drop in the nearest pay-phone and make a call which had slipped your mind, or—and this is not insignificant—to make you think again what a wonderful thing the telephone is.

The force of this poster was achieved by several means. The design, or arrangement of objects and lettering, is based on a three-sided figure. Notice how, from the word TELEPHONE, the artist has carefully run two lines, one the wire itself, directly to the picture. A simple pattern was achieved by repeating the large triangle of the whole composition in a smaller triangle formed by these two lines and the first three or four letters of the most important word in the poster. The lines and repetition were put there because that was the best way the designer knew of making you think of telephone service. Closer observation discloses other devices to enrich and intensify the design—the relationship of the creases in the hand to the other lines in the composition, the textures on the mouthpiece, and so on. In the representation of the telephone the juxtaposition of simple outline and solid mass is by no means accidental but is carefully planned to produce a dynamic rather than static effect, making it seem that someone is really *handing* you the telephone.

Designing advertisements for magazines or newspapers has much in common with designing posters: a product or service must be made to seem attractive and desirable—even necessary—through the use of illustrations and text. The most obvious difference between the two is that of size. A second difference is that far more time is ordinarily spent in looking at a magazine advertisement than at a poster, and, therefore, the advertisement can project a more lengthy message. The advertisements in this chapter show considerable variety in the products whose merits are proclaimed, the audiences to which each is addressed, the relative amounts of illustrative and textual material, the kinds of illustrations and the styles of type face employed.

Figures 82 and 83 were intended for approximately the same readers, inasmuch as both appeared in the same issue of a current magazine, but the basis of appeal is radically different. Figure 82 has four blocks of text organized around a simple black and white drawing (in the original the ETHYL symbol was printed in yellow). Because the drawing is near the center and because the blocks of text are arranged in a very nearly symmetrical pattern, the effect is simple and restrained. The large amount of white space separates the advertisement from distracting stimuli, and throws into contrast what it has to communicate. Four levels of emphasis are clear: first, "Take a Tip"; second, "Look for these signs of improved gasoline"; third, "The better the gas—the better the car!"; and fourth, the blocks of printed matter on each side of the drawing. Through dominance and subordination, the reader can get at a glance the essence of the message, or he can investigate more thoroughly if he wishes. The design is relatively simple; the effect, thoroughly pleasing.

Figure 83 represents another approach to advertising art, making as it does a valiant attempt to tell a great deal about the manufacturer's product: realistic photographs are combined with humorous drawings; several sizes and styles of type face are used to present facts and to persuade; very little blank space is left for contrast. Advertisements of this kind arouse the reader's curiosity through a direct, personal appeal to his needs and interests, and the design is purposely complicated (so it seems, at least) to prevent the reader from getting the idea quickly. The reader either spends some time and gets the whole story, or he gets practically nothing, for the details are not arranged for rapid perception and comprehension. The basic pattern through which the designer tried to organize these multifarious details is a line starting at the top near the woman's face, directed downward and toward the right by her arms until it meets the iron, then sharply reversed in direction to the cartoon which in turn directs attention to the electric mixer. Such advertisements do not rely for their effect on visual appeal—of which this one has little—but rather on giving the reader facts. A discussion of the total effect of this advertisement could easily become as complicated as the advertisement itself, but it can be summarized briefly: the advertisement is probably good from the manufacturer's point of view in that it attracts attention to and gives information about his products; from the artist's point of view the multiplicity of poorly organized details, the lack of one dominating concept, the unpleasant combination of drawings, photographs and styles of type mark this as mediocre. Were the reading public sensitive to and appreciative of visual design, this advertisement might repel rather than attract attention. Even though it probably sells goods, it has little art value.

The advertisement for Scott radios (Figure 85a) gains effectiveness from a striking photograph contrasted with a geometric pattern of lines. The photograph of the man's head with the spotlight on the ear emphasizes the human factor in sound transmission; the ear phone specifically calls attention to radio mechanism; the vertical and horizontal lines (in addition to being interesting in themselves) suggest the antennae associated with radio and the staff and bar lines used in musical notation; and the noncommittal gray background reminds one of the space through which sound travels. Thus, the advertisement is a subtle presentation of the primary elements associated with the product. The accompanying text, neatly organized in one of the rectangles, is clearly subordinate to the total visual effect.

For some years this company has used the simple device of vertical and horizontal lines until they have become a trademark instantly identifying their advertisements. It is also interesting to note that this use of lines is clearly related to the work of Piet Mondrian, a painter who reawakened an interest in the esthetic potentialities of non-representative, geometric lines and spaces. To a genuinely surprising degree the contributions of experimental painters have directly influenced commercial art by directing attention away from sentimentality and toward an understanding of "the language of vision."

Figure 85b represents a problem more complex than Figures 82 or 84a because a photograph is combined with a line drawing, a problem not always easily solved as may be seen from the above illustration. Furthermore, several styles of type face have been combined in an interesting and effective manner, the combination being effective because the differences have been used to bring different emphasis to various portions of the design—notice how KILKENNY achieves prominence in one place because of its size, in another because of the hand-written quality; how CAVITT-SHAW attracts attention through the strong contrast with POTTERS. The black background, unusual in so large an area, not only acts as an attention-getting device but as a unifying force which brings together the several elements in the composition. The spotting of shamrocks on the map is as varied and interesting as on the plate. The sensitive relation of the plate to the map differs significantly from the uninspired relation of electric iron to coffee maker in Figure 83. Relatively little information is presented by comparison with the other advertisements illustrated, for it relies on subtlety and rich suggestion rather than on an obvious statement of fact. Even the touches of humor distinguish this design and adapt it to the sophisticated audience for which it was intended.

Advertisers have learned through constant observation of the success and failure of their work that certain forms and colors are likely to produce certain effects. Thus, strong contrasts of bright colors, light and dark values, textures, shapes, lines and patterns, help to attract and hold the observer's attention until the idea is sufficiently impressed on him. In the arts of commerce there is far less place for subtlety than in the arts of religion, for example. The communication is clear and straightforward, often to the point of being shocking. Posters must shout their message against the confusion of traffic and jumbled architecture. Magazine and newspaper advertisements must not be overshadowed by the latest news or fiction. The arts of commerce have a stiff struggle for attention—they are not politely placed in properly lighted museums.

Their appeal must be obvious and general, for commercial art is effective only when it sells the product it advertises. Its appeal and claims are addressed to the largest possible audiences, and therefore with a few minor

133

exceptions cannot be esoteric or abstruse. Commercial art is for the immediate present. The manufacturer, unlike the art collector, cannot wait patiently for the public to understand his display.

As a result, current trends and tastes are expressed more quickly in commercial art than in other fields. The advertising man must keep abreast or just ahead of popular preferences, tastes, interests and manners. Since commercial art aims to call forth new wants as an inducement to increased buying, the commercial artist is a keen student of human motives, actions and feelings.

In solving an actual problem, the designer chooses his medium, kind of illustration, style of type and written material on two bases: first, the character of the product, and second, the public which he hopes will be influenced. His first consideration is to find some way of suggesting implicitly as well as explicitly what the product is. When advertising fire or accident insurance, he may use a brutally shocking and upsetting photograph combined with a startling message in bold type. But if he is advertising refined dinnerware or sterling silver, illustration and text will be reserved and tactful. His second consideration is how to arouse the interest and enthusiasm of the public, and even a cursory glance at the variety of advertisements in the periodicals on a typical newsstand will show how this factor influences the design. The pulp magazines differ from their smooth paper cousins as much in their advertising as in their basic content. Further, within the smooth paper magazines differences are conspicuous: compare a periodical planned for the home maker of moderate means with one designed for the wealthy sophisticate; contrast the magazine written for the engineer with that for the artist. Although there are no sure-hit formulas to insure success, there is a highly developed science of advertising art.

In addition, the commercial artist knows that headlines must capture attention, and to this end the words must be direct and appropriate to the product. Although novelty is important, some very familiar catchwords and slogans are long-lived; witness "57 varieties," "Ask the man who owns one," and "Eventually, why not now?" The eyes should be directed from the headline or illustration into the copy which gives the information. In general, the copy cannot be monotonously long, but when this seems desirable, it is divided into columns and paragraphs often subdivided by lines, dots or other devices. In general, the lower part of the advertisement gives the reader such standard detail as the name and address of the company.

All of this and much more the commercial artist knows and uses. Many studies have been made by psychologists on the effectiveness and pleasantness of certain color combinations, on the number of words which the typical observer can perceive under given conditions, on the effect of certain optical relationships or illusions. There is a well-organized body of information at the disposal of a commercial artist. But if for a moment it begins to sound as though he plied his trade according to rule, it should be remembered that imagination and ingenuity, not observance of formula, make art significant. All art depends for its effect to some degree on its power to stimulate jaded senses, to produce vitalizing reactions, and commercial art is far from being an exception.

There is an old familiar saying that "fine feathers make fine birds," and many consumers have been led to believe that fine advertising and fine packaging assure them of superior merchandise. Yet experience proves that such is not always the case. The art quality of the advertising and packaging and the quality of the merchandise are two separate factors. To be sure there is undoubtedly some correlation between the two since many good products are beautifully advertised and packaged. But, on the other hand, a perfectly useless or possibly harmful lotion may come in a beautiful bottle, and a most intriguing poster with sensitively arranged forms and colors may proclaim the poorest ginger ale. The aim of most advertising is to sell a product—whether or not you need it and whether or not it is good. Take pleasing advertisements and packages for what they are, but do not believe that you can always judge the quality of the goods from the design of the container.

PACKAGING

Only a few years ago the country and city grocery store was a confusion of barrels, bins and bags exposing peas, beans, brown sugar and coffee to all who came in. Counters and shelves were lined with boxes and tubs, most of them wide open, holding supplies of soda crackers, colored candies, dried prunes and pickled herring. You asked for a pound of soda crackers: the grocer reached into the cracker box, measured out a pound, and stuffed them in a brown paper bag—but not before handling them several times. You knew little about the quality because you knew nothing

135

of the brand. And your trust in your grocer's scales was all you had to go on to insure your quantity.

Today commercial art recognizes several reasons for selling foods and other products in packages: it is clean, sanitary, efficient; the purchaser has an easy method of identifying the brand he knows and uses; and the appearance of a store can be more attractive. A well-designed package helps sell the product it holds. From toothpaste, stove polish, and harness oil to tomato juice and breakfast foods—all are in new, often attractive packages. Designers must think not only about the looks of the individual package, but also about the appearance that a group of the packages will have, stacked on the shelves of a retail store.

The illustrations on pages 142-43 show some contemporary solutions of the packaging problem. The bottle and box designed for Yardley's perfume is good to look at and to handle and is expressive of its contents. A perfume container should express the daintiness, elegance, and dignity of the product—and of the lady who buys it. More than most commodities, perfume is a luxury and its main appeal must come from the fact that it is above the ordinary necessities of daily existence. The simple, delicately curved bottle with the haughtily poised label and three-tiered cap is a direct play for the attention of the modern woman. The box in which this simple bottle comes is ornamented with gay curves to make a good foil for the bottle. When the manufacturers introduced this product in a fashion magazine, they also took advantage of the literary art. Here is a quotation from the advertisement—suggestive as it is of delicately arched eyebrows and sensitive nostrils:

"Now when new leaves shine under glowing arc-lights—when clear spring moons drench the soft nights with silver, and gaiety rises to a new peak for the year, try the great perfume that is brightening the brighter moments of great ladies on four continents."

Although perfumes, dentrifices, and hair brushes are all sold in drugstores, the differing character of the products suggests different containers. Figure 87 shows co-ordinated packages for one company's line which suggest the character of the products in their simple, refreshing white, dark blue, and light red containers. Packaging a hair brush presents still other problems: the prospective purchaser wants to see the product and yet know that others have not handled it. Figure 88 is an admirable solution. The box reveals yet protects, subordinates everything to the product.

Figure 90 reveals what designers have done to make a product as humble as stove polish more attractive. The contents of the cans are identical.

Which would look better lined on store shelves? Which would you buy? Much attention has also been given to food packaging, and Figure 91 illustrates how breakfast cocoa can be given distinguished treatment. The design emphasizes the shape of the container while adding eye-appeal. Boxes for cleaning tissues have gone through numerous designs before the one shown in Figure 89 was produced. This design indicates where the box is to be opened, identifies its contents from any view, and both attracts attention and expresses its contents in its strong pattern of blue and white.

COMMERCIAL ARCHITECTURE

The needs of commerce find expression not only in advertisements and packages, but in the buildings wherein this busy area of contemporary life carries on its activities. Stores, office buildings, service stations and theaters are all commercial buildings. Commercial architecture means business. It does not fulfill the noble role of community architecture nor the intimate role of home architecture.

The Camera Shop (Figure 95) demonstrates clearly many of the salient characteristics of effective commercial architecture. It is straightforward, efficient, and inviting, and it focuses attention on the merchandise sold within. In fact, the entire store is a display window with only a wall of glass and a low planting bed (for decoration and also to protect the window) separating the store from the sidewalk. Its feeling of openness and continuity with the outdoors is similar to that of the Johnson house discussed in Chapter 1. Setting the window only a few feet back from the street intrigues the passer-by—man loves recesses, nooks, and crannies—and thereby causes him to stop, to take a leisurely look, and probably to step in. The two small display cases at the sides give him sufficient reason to pause while making up his mind and to look more closely at the wares. Nonetheless, his attention will inevitably be attracted back into the store by the lines of fluorescent lights, by the activity around the handsome counters and cases and by the treasures that any photographer knows it must house. Notice how the separation of interior and exterior has been minimized not only by the glass wall but by the continuous wall of corrugated asbestos painted green, by the lines of light, and by the repetition of the shiny metal columns marching into the store. As with

137

all art, the architecture of the commercial world is good in so far as it meets the needs for which it was developed. This shop does that. First, it expresses its purpose; that is, it looks like a store. Moreover, it tells you what kind of store it is through its emblems and general quality. Even were it not for the attractive sign, you would know at once that this store sells something precise and mechanical. Second, it expresses the time in which it was built. We expect—and find—that a shop in Colonial Williamsburg will show the architectural forms expressive of eighteenth-century America, that a shop built today will show the concepts of space and form, the materials and processes of this age. Third, it meets its functions squarely. More than most other types of architecture, that of commerce must be efficient. Commerce has no time for inefficiency, either in its human agencies or in its buildings. This store suggests that you stop: it holds your attention, urges you to come in. Then it is up to the goods and the salesman to make a sale, a friend, or both.

As you walk or ride along the streets of your city, look critically at the commercial buildings. Many of them, perhaps, have been redesigned for better or for worse. Observe the office buildings, the banks, the large department stores. Some, like good industrial or religious architecture, express their functions frankly. The Equitable Savings and Loan Building in Portland and the Philadelphia Savings Fund Society Building (Chapter 17) both exemplify the contemporary trend toward clean-cut efficiency. Today we believe that commerce moves best when it moves most sensibly. That this has not always been thought to be true can be seen from the following example.

The rapidity with which ideals of office design, one type of commercial architecture, have changed in the last few decades can be grasped from a comparison of the Dentist's Waiting Room (Figure 92) and the entrance to an industrial designer's office (Figure 93). The first is a composite drawing but characteristic of the period from 1900 to 1910, providing much to look at and to think about. The furniture design, reminiscent of penmanship exercises, exhibits the belief that complicated forms and shapes are beautiful, an attitude also portrayed by the design of the lighting fixture, the flower vase, the magazine basket, and the Indian-head pillow. The ornaments on the wall add much variety, thereby aiding materially in producing what today we would call a highly confusing room. The deer head and swordfish are typical wall decorations of the period, as are replicas of the painting

138

81. These posters designed by E. McKnight Kauffer are effective because of their simple, dynamic designs and their forceful messages. Posters, and all other commercial art, must put their messages across quickly and vividly. They must attract the attention of the passerby and try to interest him in the advertised product.

TAKE A TIP

Look for these signs of improved gasoline

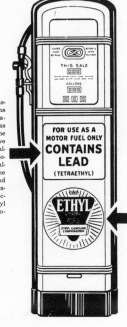

THIS SIGN on a gasoline pump means that lead (tetraethyl), a liquid, has been added to the gasoline to improve its anti-knock quality. "Leaded" gasoline is sold by dealers throughout the United States and Canada. Lead tetraethyl is manufactured by the Ethyl Gasoline Corporation.

THIS SALE

GALLONS

FOR USE AS A
MOTOR FUEL ONLY
CONTAINS
LEAD
(TETRAETHYL)

ETHYL
ETHYL GASOLINE CORPORATION

THE "ETHYL" EMBLEM on a pump or its globe means that the gasoline contains enough lead (tetraethyl) for highest anti-knock, so that your engine's spark can be advanced closest to the point of maximum power and economy, without "knock" or "ping."

The better the gas — the better your car!

This Big Ironing Finished in 2 Hours, 48 Minutes
...WITH New G-E Speed-Iron

Time checked by Good Housekeeping Institute

3 Pillow Cases • 1 Table Runner
7 Napkins • 9 Shirts • 2 Pajamas
2 Dresses • 12 Towels • 2 Aprons
7 Place Mats • 4 Shorts • 3 Sheets
2 Silk Slips • 20 Handkerchiefs

THOUSANDS of women are getting a brand new idea of how *easy* ironing can be! For the G-E Speed-Iron enables them to do the job with minimum of time and effort. That's because it's light in weight—handles easily—distributes heat evenly. Its "dial the fabric" control automatically maintains the correct heat for every fabric—a light signals when desired temperature is reached.

1. 25% Lighter. The lightest weight full-size iron made, weighs only three pounds. Fast heating—uses minimum of current.

2. Less Arm Fatigue. Not pressure but evenly distributed heat by the G-E Calrod Unit does the work.

3. New Hand-Rest Handle. Specially designed plastic handle fits hand perfectly; iron is easier to guide.

AMERICA'S FAVORITE IRON
With The Light That Says "When"

G-E Speed-Iron (The Moderne) $8.95

GE

THE FINEST OF COFFEE EVERYTIME—IT'S AUTOMATIC

To Facilitate Faster, smoother mixing, the new G-E Triple-Whip Mixer is equipped with *three* powerful beaters instead of two ordinary ones! Handy light illuminates inside of bowl. And you have a large selection of speeds!

THREE BEATERS ARE BETTER THAN TWO!

Put Your Coffee problems in the hands of a competent General Electric Coffee Maker! This efficient servant makes perfect coffee! —turns itself off—and *keeps the coffee at proper serving temperature as long as desired!* Only $12.95

Complete with juice extractor $22.75

GENERAL ⓖⓔ ELECTRIC

A contrast between simple and complicated advertisements. Which do you find more effective?

82. (*Left*) A well-spaced, clean-cut advertisement.

83. (*Right*) An advertisement for several products made by the same company. The layout is cluttered and without unity but may, because of these very qualities, hold the attention of persons not sensitive to good design.

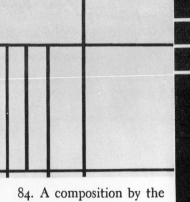

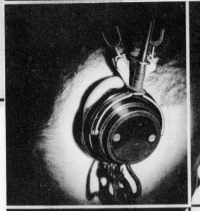

84. A composition by the Dutch painter Piet Mondrian.

Two advertisements in which the forms and total design express as well as describe their products.

85a. (*Opposite*) The arresting photograph of a

Radio amateur? Ship's operator? No. He is the man with the "golden ear." He is one of those with that rare combination of musician's ear and engineer's mind who listen to every finished Scott radio-phonograph first. They do the final testing and adjusting, to make sure that the Scott's technical and tonal perfection has come true. For you? Yes, tin ear or golden ear, for you if you're restless for the finest and fortunate enough to be able to afford it. ... Write for the name of your Scott dealer. Scott Radio Laboratories, Inc., 4430 Ravenswood Avenue, Chicago 40, Illinois.

man with a microphone to his ear is made even more interesting through contrast with the vertical and horizontal lines. This basically simple pattern was derived from the experiments of Mondrian.

85b. An advertisement for dinnerware decorated with shamrock leaves. The white-on-black map of Ireland both contrasts and harmonizes pleasantly with the photograph of the plate: both map and plate have undulating outlines and show shamrock leaves, although the treatment is sufficiently varied to maintain interest. Compare the sly humor in the treatment of "Blarney" with the broad humor in Figure 83.

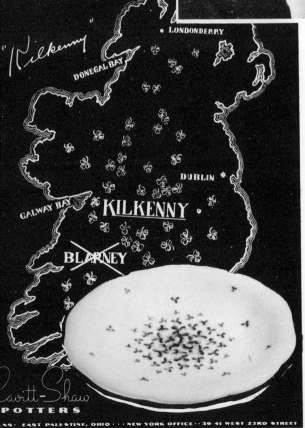

141

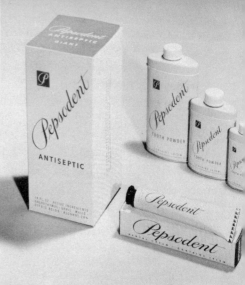

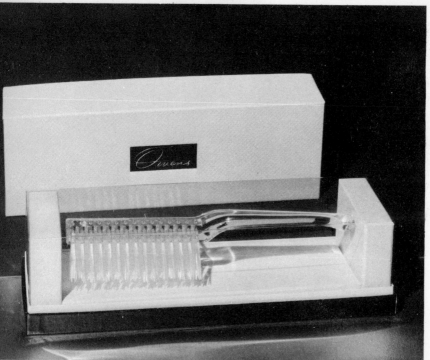

Three examples of packaging which are good to look at, good to handle, and which express their products.

86. (*Upper left*) A perfume bottle and container suitable for a luxury product.

87. (*Upper right*) Packages marked by a refreshing, clean-cut character.

88. (*Lower*) A package which displays yet protects a handsomely designed brush.

89. (*Upper*) A package design related to the manner in which the package is used and identifiable from any view.

90. (*Lower left*) Old and new designs for cans of stove polish showing notable improvement in legibility.

91. (*Lower right*) A container of more than average subtlety of design.

The design of offices shows one of the most rapid changes in contemporary art.

92. (*Upper*) Perkin Harnley's water color of a waiting room of a dentist's office typical of the period 1900 to 1910 has a variety of dust-catching forms which the majority of persons today would find wearisome.

93. (*Lower*) The office of McStay-Jackson in Chicago illustrates the current trend toward simple, comfortable, efficient forms. The design has a strong basic unity which encompasses the varied forms, has textures, and colors, and a pleasant, inviting quality.

144

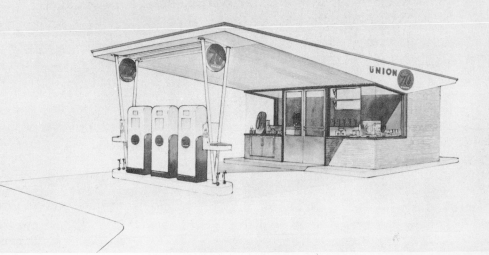

Two structures designed for effective sales and service.

94. (*Upper*) The service station designed by Kem Weber is a remarkably straightforward example of commercial architecture. Notice the manner in which the entire structure has been unified by the shape of the roof and the attention-getting repetition of diagonal lines.

95. (*Lower*) The Camera Shop in Berkeley, California. The integration of indoor and outdoor space is reminiscent of the Philip Johnson house and characteristic of all phases of contemporary architecture.

Two office buildings designed by Frank Lloyd Wright are outstanding examples in the development of contemporary architecture. The Larkin Company Administration Building, built in Buffalo in 1904, shows a notable unity of interior and exterior.

96. (*Upper*) The massive geometric forms of the exterior of the Larkin Building still offer striking contrast to the nondescript characterless exteriors of the office buildings typical of most cities.

97. (*Lower*) The interior of the Larkin Building is dominated by a spacious court illuminated by a skylight.

146

98. (*Upper*) The exterior of the Johnson Building, built between 1936 and 1939, shows interlocking curved walls of brick with bands of glass tubing emphasizing the basic forms and lighting the interior.

99. (*Lower*) The interior of the Johnson Building gives an unusual feeling of light and space. Notice the slender, tapering, structurally efficient columns.

The North Shore Shopping Center designed in 1947 for a site near Boston, Massachusetts, is an architecturally co-ordinated group of stores.

100. (*Upper*) Surrounding an open mall, the shops are connected by arcades.

101. (*Lower*) The shops designed as a consistent unit show integration of indoor and outdoor space.

of Sir Galahad and the Colosseum the symbols of culture. Almost every surface in the room is broken by ornament or pattern of some sort.

Figure 93, showing the entrance to an industrial design office, illustrates the contemporary trend toward plain colors and surfaces, simple forms clearly defined. Most noticeable is the architectural, or structural, character of this office. Each part seems to belong to the whole. The simple but attention-getting sign above the door, the stout frames of the entrance door and flanking windows, the grillwork ceiling which diffuses fluorescent light, and the built-in furniture all contribute to an impression of frank sturdiness. Interest is achieved through these strong basic forms; through the natural grain of wood in the walls, counters, parquet floors, and grilles; and through the shaggy texture of the rug. Because of its simplicity, the office provides an excellent background for displaying the work of this firm and a relaxing place in which to sit. This is indeed a far cry from the dentist's office furnished some forty years before.

In spirit, the Union Service Station (Figure 94) is closely akin to the Camera Shop. Not so many years ago it was common practice to make filling stations look like something they assuredly were not—Normandy cottages, Old English Inns, Colonial shops, and even Dutch windmills. Today that approach is seldom followed because designers agree that service-station design is chiefly a matter of using common sense and sensitivity in producing a unit that is efficient in operation and attractive in appearance. If you were driving around looking for a service station, you would have no trouble in spotting the one illustrated. Its bulk looms sharply and cleanly, displaying clearly the name of the company. It is important that this be prominent—most people are particular about the brand of gasoline they buy.

One of a series established by a design-conscious company, this station is planned for open highways or rural areas. It is as clean-cut in appearance as it is efficient in structure. The inverted-truss roof rises welcomingly from the enclosed section to rest on slender supports in line with the gasoline pumps. The roof and canopy can be prefabricated of steel, while the walls of the enclosed section may be of stone, brick, wood, or metal. The large window areas make the interior light and pleasant and tempt the traveler in need of refreshment for himself or accessories for his car to look within.

A study of two office buildings will conclude the discussion of commercial art; both are among the most brilliant examples of architecture of our century. Frank Lloyd Wright, pioneer in commercial as well as in religious and domestic architecture, designed the Larkin Building which was erected in 1904-1905 (Figure 96). Striking evidence of the architect's genius, the building looks as modern today as it did when newly built, and it looks far more modern and better suited to its purposes than most office buildings designed since. Strikingly and forcefully simple, the exterior at once commands attention by its dominant masses of brick, denoting our industrial age. Why so few windows? The building is in a section of Buffalo which does not offer attractive outlooks, and the air in this section is dust- and smoke-laden. Therefore, much of the light is brought in from the top through skylights visible in the interior view. Notice the straightforward but attractive iron fence, the unusual entrance gate. The severe, restrained ornamentation emphasizes the simplicity and solidity of the primary masses, and is in keeping with the austere quality of the building. The interior (Figure 97) is organically related to the exterior— the same qualities, the same forms, even the same materials give the whole building a compelling unity. The ingenious manner in which filing equipment and desks have been made part of the architecture is further evidence of the architect's ability to conceive his problem, the designing of an efficient office building, as a unified whole, not as a series of unrelated parts.

Again Frank Lloyd Wright triumphed in his design for the offices of S. C. Johnson and Son, Racine, Wisconsin, which were completed in 1939. Study the photographs of this office building (Figures 98, 99) and read the observations made by the editors of *Life*.*

FRANK LLOYD WRIGHT OFFICE BUILDING SHOWS SHAPE OF THINGS TO COME

The new administration building of S. C. Johnson & Son (wax polish) was designed by the master modern architect, Frank Lloyd Wright. It is genuine American architecture, owing nothing to foreign inspiration, different from anything ever built in the world before. Spectacular as the showiest Hollywood set, it represents simply the result of creative genius applied to the problem of designing the most efficient and comfortable, as well as beautiful, place in which Johnson Wax executives and clerks could do their work.

---

* The following quotations are reprinted by special permission from *Life* magazine

"This building," says Architect Wright, "was designed to be as inspiring a place to work in as any cathedral to worship in." Wrote the financial editor of the Milwaukee *Journal* on viewing it last week: "It is like a woman swimming naked in a stream. Cool, gliding, musical in movement and in manner. The inside of an office building like a woman swimming naked in a stream? Yes, that's right."

The building is proof against earthquake, fire and sound. The walls are of warm red-brown brick, lined with thick cork and concrete. Bricks were specially baked in 200 shapes to fit the building design. At the left is a "carport" which opens on main entrance of building. At the right is the main workroom. On the roof are penthouse offices for executives. . . . Two "nostrils" . . . suck air into conditioning equipment. Heat radiates evenly from steam pipes laid space-savingly under the concrete floor slab. Heat apparatus is controlled to synchronize with the movement of the sun.

The main workroom, which occupies most of the building, seats 200 clerks. On mezzanine are offices for special workers. Architect Wright's most revolutionary space-saving innovation is the "golf-tee" supporting pillar which is only 9 inches in diameter at the floor. . . . The pillars mushroom into a diameter of 18½ feet at the glass-tubed roof. . . . Frank Lloyd Wright, to prove to a skeptical Wisconsin Industrial Commission that his novel "golf-tee" pillars were really strong enough to support the building, put on a convincing demonstration. Propping up a pillar at the building site, he had sand and cast iron piled on until the weight reached 60 tons, a weight much greater than could be supported by the same amount of material in a conventionally designed pillar. Next day the pillar was found unflawed. . . . Note the round desks, which have cutout space for typewriter and comptometer, "swinging-tills" instead of drawers.

The dynamic, vigorous curves of the exterior, the clear, clean, free sweep of space of the interior, combine to make this truly significant architecture. Wright's two buildings, designed for similar purposes but built thirty-six years apart, show many similarities and some differences. This is to be expected, since each building is a product of its own age. These two buildings, excellent and forceful in their meeting of human needs, give high hope for the future of art in America.

The Problem of Human Needs

The shop-lined main street of Williamsburg served as an adequate eighteenth-century commercial center when most shoppers came short distances on foot and the congestion and hazards of automobile traffic were non-existent. The shopping center at Greenbelt with stores grouped around an open plaza convenient to parking space has been mentioned as a twentieth-century solution. The proposed designs for the North Shore Center (Figures 100 and 101) for suburban Boston show a commercial center geared to the convenience of the automobile shopper. Strategically located near the convergence of three highways, it has 3000 parking spaces, handsome buildings designed to attract customers, covered walks connecting all buildings for shoppers' protection from inclement weather, and a feeling of unhurried spaciousness given by the open mall. The department store is at one end, the recreational facilities at the other. The restaurant, near the theater, has an outdoor dining terrace bordering a pool which in winter will become a skating rink. The character of the center will be protected through a belt of land zoned for public and residential use.

Commercial centers of this type represent a great advance over the unplanned, uncontrolled, hetereogeneous collection of buildings lining traffic thoroughfares—the typical shopping center of today. They are in line with the trend toward decentralization, toward planning land and buildings for maximum human benefit. They show due regard for the shoppers' needs: adequate transportation facilities; shops grouped efficiently; protection from rain, snow, and excessive sun; buildings designed harmoniously, and pleasantly grouped around an open green. This one further demonstrates the type of cooperation needed in this sort of venture. Owned by the Conant Real Estate Trust, the project was planned by the National Retail Recentralization, Inc., as general consultants; Kenneth C. Welch as economic surveyor; Frederick J. Adams as site planner; Ketchum, Gina and Sharp in association with Anderson and Beckwith as architects; and Arthur and Sidney Shurcliff, in association with Thomas Church, as landscape architects. Art of the community requires the services of many experts.

The following books treat in detail various aspects of commercial art:

Art Directors Annual of Advertising Art (Watson-Guptill).
Faber Birren: Selling with Color (McGraw-Hill, 1945).
Joseph Binder: Color in Advertising (Studio, 1934).

Richard Chenault: *Advertising Layout* (Heck-Cattell, 1946).

Austin Cooper: *Making a Poster* (Studio, 1938).

Alexander Dorner: *The Way Beyond Art* (Wittenborn, 1947).

Egbert Jacobson (ed.): *Modern Art in Advertising* (Theobald, 1946).

Henry Russell Hitchcock and Phillip Johnson: *The International Style: Architecture since 1922* (Norton, 1932).

Morris Ketchum, Jr.: *Shops and Stores* (Reinhold, 1948).

Frederick Kiesler: *Contemporary Art Applied to the Store and Its Display* (Brentano, 1930).

Ben Nash: *Developing Marketable Products and Their Packaging* (Mc Graw-Hill, 1946).

Matlack Price: *Advertising Design* (McGraw-Hill, 1947).

Paul Rand: *Thoughts on Design* (Wittenborn, 1946).

PART II

The Problem of Organization

Introduction

A COMMERCIAL poster and a religious painting, a Gothic cathedral and a prefabricated filling station, a Greek vase and a ten-cent store flower pot, although designed to meet different human needs, are related because all are organizations of the plastic elements: form, line, space, color, and texture; all embody principles of design. Having investigated, in the first section of the book, the life sources from which art emerges, we now focus attention on the second major problem in art, the problem of organization, the ways in which these human expressions become orderly; in other words, the design and composition found in all art products.

The study of design has at times led to serious errors. Too often design has been elevated to a position of undue prominence, being considered the essence of art rather than means to an end. This minimizes the importance of function and expression as well as the vital role played by materials in the forming of an art object. To be sure, organization is essential to good art, but the organization should grow out of the *purpose* of the art object and the *materials* from which it is made. Overconcern with design and organization has frequently led to the formulation of rigid arbitrary rules which restrict creativity and block fresh, direct appreciation. The study of design should be an expanding rather than a contracting experience.

Principles, however, have great value in that they pull together varied experiences which might otherwise remain chaotic, and in that they serve as guides for future activity. In thinking about design principles two considerations are of major importance. First, the principles should be based on the widest possible variety of experiences in order that they be truly comprehensive and generally applicable. This demands continuing study of three aspects of our world: *human reactions* to varied organizations of form, line, texture, color, and space; *natural design* as found in a tree or leaf, a rock or mountain, the movement of waves on a lake or

157

smoke from a chimney; and *contemporary and historical art* from all parts of the world. Such broad continuing study protects us from evolving narrow principles and making trite applications and allows us to experience with open eyes the new interpretations constantly discovered by creative workers. For example, the principle of rhythm has often been narrowly interpreted as being only graceful, flowing movement. Such limited understanding of rhythm betrays the fact that it was based only on selected types of experiences and would very likely prevent one from enjoying those paintings in which rhythm is angular and staccato. Similar examples could be cited from many inflexible statements on the principles of color harmony.

The second consideration to bear in mind is that the organization of each art product should grow out of the specific conditions from which the problem arises. These conditions include, first, human needs, and second, the resources (both human and natural) for meeting those needs. For example, in the chapter on Art in the Home we discussed the functional and esthetic problems both of the individual and of the community, and saw how within the limits imposed by geography and by technology, those problems were solved. We saw how the diversity of available house-building materials—ice, straw, wood, brick, metal, glass, and so on—created a diversity in the type, or organization, of human dwellings. As we study other forms of art, we shall be more and more aware that the organization of significant works of art arises out of needs and resources. It does not come from thin air.

Finally, the organization of an art product should in itself afford the observer a stimulating experience. If—and there are quite a few "ifs"—the artist is sensitive to form and color, if he is imaginative, if he analyzes his problem thoroughly, if he chooses his materials well and handles them skillfully, the chances are that his design will be marked by spirit, vitality, and intensity. It will give the spectator a new and enlarging experience. It may be that colors are combined in a refreshing way or that a new vision of space and form are revealed. If, on the other hand, rules are slavishly followed, the result will probably be uninteresting, and neither the observer nor the artist will have grown from the experience.

This second section of the book deals with principles or organization in art. Two aims of organization are stated and discussed: FORM FOLLOWS FUNCTION, and VARIETY IN UNITY. The plastic elements—*form, line, space, texture,* and *color*—are the means which the architect, painter, sculptor, commercial and industrial designer, in fact all artists, use for the expression of their ideas and concepts. The principles of design—*balance, con-tinuity*, and *emphasis*—are ways of using the elements to achieve the aims of form following function and variety in unity.

Throughout the history of art the principles of organization stated in this section of the book appear to have operated consistently. Thus, the desire to have form follow function, to secure variety in unity, and to produce a measure of balance, dominance and subordination, and rhythm mark the work of artists in primitive and sophisticated, Oriental and Occidental, democratic and autocratic societies. Although the exact means by which these ends are attained differ remarkably, the basic goals are similar. As you study the principles, try to relate them to what you have learned about the functional and expressive qualities of art objects, and to the aspects of your daily life in which art occurs.

CHAPTER 6 *Two Aims of Organization*

T HE superb form in a soaring gull is one of nature's most thrilling sights. Its body and wings, magnificently poised and wrought, are like a piece of fine sculpture. We call it beautiful, write songs and poems to praise it, because the natural beauty that arises from forms suited to their purposes stimulates man esthetically. Nature abounds in other forms clearly expressing their purposes or function. The bodies of fishes, the roots, stems, and leaves of plants, our own eyes and hands, are examples. In fact, if these forms were not adapted to their functions and environment, they would long ago have perished—like the dinosaur or the giant ferns and vegetation now a part of the Pennsylvania coal deposits.

FIRST AIM: FORM FOLLOWS FUNCTION

In art there are also forms clearly designed to meet their functions: forks and spoons with which to pick up and convey food to the mouth; chairs which are shaped to fit easily and support comfortably the human body; cooking utensils, such as percolators, double boilers, or muffin tins shaped for special cooking needs. There are objects planned primarily for esthetic satisfaction: paintings, sculpture, etchings, and many others. But in every case, FORM FOLLOWS FUNCTION. If it is the function of a painting to arouse feelings of excitement, tenseness and perhaps anger, then every square inch of that canvas, every vivid brush stroke of the artist, is governed by this function: each color, shape, texture, or line strives to fulfill this end.

No familiar object has had a more exciting evolution in the search for forms clearly adapted to and expressive of their function than has the automobile (Figure 102). Only a few years ago we had automobiles designed like carriages—minus the horse. The emphasis on "up-and-down" lines made them look like boxes set on wheels. As the motor was improved, greater speed became possible and the shape of the car was changed. Engineer-designers began developing automobiles to lessen air resistance, provide greater safety and comfort, and give better expression to their function. The automobile salesman has not overlooked the sales appeal of the new forms. These forms, suggested at first primarily by functional needs, were refined to increase their beauty. Although progress has been made in the last fifty years, many of the changes are superficial, some of them actually decreasing the efficiency of performance. Certainly today's automobile is but one stage in an evolutionary process which will be intriguing to watch during the coming years. The shape of the car of the future will differ from that of today, but, based on our present knowledge and technology, might look similar to that shown in Figure 103.

The architect faces, and has always faced, a problem similar to that of the automobile designer because he, too, is dealing with functional forms. When Louis Sullivan was a young architect working in Chicago in the 1880s, the problem of skyscraper design had just arisen. Commercial buildings were shooting up to new and great heights because cities were growing, land was becoming scarce, steel construction had been developed, and elevators were being perfected. And yet—the architects failed to turn their eyes from the past, continued to load these magnificent steel frames with ornaments developed for and copied from Greek temples, Roman baths, and Gothic cathedrals. Turn to page 450 and contrast the clean, sharp forms of the Philadelphia Saving Fund Society Building with the meaningless Gothic arches and pinnacles and Turkish mosque, all lifted many stories from Chicago's busy Michigan Avenue. Here is an admirable contrast of form which does, and form which does not, follow function.

Sullivan saw the absurdity of coating a steel frame with gargoyles, columns, cornices, buttresses, and pinnacles (see his Wainwright Building on page 450). It was he who emphasized the slogan FORM FOLLOWS FUNCTION. This principle, axiomatic from the beginning of architecture, led to such well-known forms as the Greek column and the Gothic arch. No principle is more important; none has been more influential in turning the attention of contemporaries to a due regard for functional form. Today it is widely accepted, even though not always understood or followed.

If the term "function" is to be interpreted narrowly as referring only to utility, then it would seem that artists work in a way which is dual-purposed: they seek not only to make a product useful and expressive of its use (functional) but also to make it beautiful (artistic). But are these two aspects of the artist's work separate? If function is defined as "the natural and proper action of anything" the concept includes considerations of both use and beauty. Generally speaking, functional forms in nature are beautiful—the soaring body of a sea-gull, the microscopic shape of a paramecium, the foliage pattern of a redwood tree. In articles designed by man beautiful forms frequently develop naturally. But at times the functional form may not be pleasing in appearance and it becomes necessary to change, alter, or refine the design in the interests of greater beauty. At other times two forms may be equally efficient but with noticeable differences in esthetic merit. Then a choice must be made, and this choice is determined largely by the designer's sensitivity to beauty. Thus truly functional art forms are determined by utilitarian and esthetic considerations so closely interwoven that it is difficult to distinguish one from the other.

Nearly all of the art illustrated in this book has form which follows the function. Notable exceptions, however, are the early automobiles shown above, the early kitchen stoves, and the iron bench (Figure 160). But you see many others every day: radios disguised as everything from chests of drawers to rows of books; Colonial secretaries from which spring folding beds; electric lights imitating candles—in fact, all of those objects which conceal, rather than reveal, their true nature and function. It would be illuminating to make a list of all violations of this principle which you see in one day.

SECOND AIM: VARIETY IN UNITY

Compare the recently built Courthouse in Brooklyn, New York (Figure 104), with the façade of the Farnese Palace, Rome, Italy (Figure 105), designed by Sangallo and Michelangelo about four hundred years ago. Which building looks like a series of separate units piled together? Which looks like *one* building developed from one idea? Which is richer in variety? Both buildings are basically simple cubes, both have three horizontal divisions, both expose a masonry surface. But at about this point similarities cease.

The Farnese Palace is definitely horizontal in feeling: it is noticeably longer than it is high, the horizontality of the three rows of windows has been accentuated by the string courses, and the structure is capped by a magnificent cornice. The Brooklyn Courthouse, a little higher than it is long, shows no such definiteness. The lowest unit is neither horizontal nor vertical, the middle is somewhat vertical, and the top is mildly horizontal. One feels no driving force integrating the three, no real conviction about its basic form, and consequently one gets no dominant single impression of the whole.

Certainly the varied window shapes and sizes, the different character of the surfacing materials, give the Courthouse variety of considerable range —but this variety seems added on to, not growing out of, a basic idea. The Farnese Palace encompasses more variety within a restricted range. Look, for example, at the detail around the windows. On all three tiers it is fundamentally the same, yet each shows enlivening differences. The rectangular windows in the ground floor are topped by a horizontal projecting and modified cornice; those on the second are rectangular but with alternating pointed and arched pediments; while the top floor windows are rounded, fitting nicely into broken pediments. Thus, straight, pointed, rounded, and broken shapes are progressively integrated into a rhythmic pattern. Similar analyses could be made of other details. Try one for yourself. The Farnese Palace has a richer variety within a greater unity than does the Brooklyn Courthouse. VARIETY IN UNITY is fundamental to art.

Unity, or the state of one-ness, invariably results from the strength and clarity of a single and motivating idea. It is for this quality that the art of children and primitive people is often praised. Both are able to rule out things that do not belong more easily than minds confused and disorganized by too many unassimilated experiences. If you ask a child to draw a picture of a slippery day, he busies himself at once with what to him is most characteristic of a slippery day: people falling down on icy streets. He is willing to use his forms and colors in any way he sees fit to put that idea across clearly and directly (see Figure 106).

Significant mature artists, like children, penetrate superficialities and eliminate irrelevancies to drive straight to their goal. David Alfaro Siqueiros' "The Sob" (Figure 107) focuses full attention on the content he wishes to portray. The tense weariness of convulsive grief is expressed in every fiber of the strong arms and clenched fists pressing against the face to restrain sobs. The overpowering unity is strengthened by the asymmetry of the two arms and the individualization of the hands and fingers. These two pictures demonstrate a high degree of one-ness, or unity.

It is the purpose of unity to focus interest on the art object so that the object fills the whole field of attention. If you are to enjoy it thoroughly, the art object must stand out separately from other objects within the field of vision. This is why it is often tiring to visit an exhibition of paintings in which each clamors to be looked at, and you respond by glancing in every direction, trying to see three or four at one time. Next time you set out for an exhibition of paintings, make up your mind to look at only a few in the whole collection. Your enjoyment of the exhibition may be greater than if you walked in and made your eyes drunk with a hundred or so different pictures. You will notice that if the unity of an art object is forceful enough (this assumes a certain amount of sensitivity on your part), your attention is riveted, and you feel compelled to "stay with" the object.

Unity, besides focusing attention, has two other effects. First, the art object becomes easier to "take in." Second, it becomes easier to remember, because it provides a central idea. Rather than looking at and trying to remember many things, you are concerned with only one. Based on common sense, this effect of unity makes for economy of effort and leads to genuine satisfaction.

Study again the four stoves and the three package sealers in Chapter 4 and the automobiles in this chapter. Notice how distracting or irrelevant forms present in the early examples have been discarded while the important ones have been strengthened. There are probably changes which you could make in your own living quarters to make them more pleasantly unified. What are they?

Unity grows out of many conditions, is dependent on many factors. Some ways of controlling and directing the observer's attention to give a greater sense of unity are:

1. *Limiting the Amount Included in the Object.* Do not let the diversification growing out of an idea get out of control. An individual can attend to a limited number of things or ideas at one time. He cannot look at a dozen unrelated colors, a dozen isolated forms at the same time, and no art object should impose such a strain upon him. Thus, a well-planned display window in a department store will have greater unity than the usual junk- or pawn-shop window. We can stand before the latter with great interest, but we are held not by the unity, but by the chaos; our

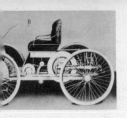  

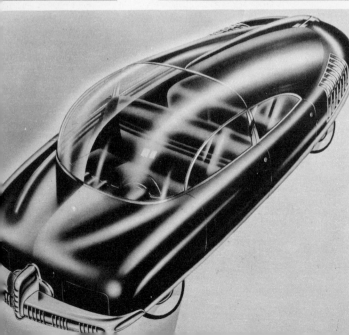

Automobile design in the past fifty years shows a progressive understanding of FORM FOLLOWS FUNCTION.

102. (*Upper*) Early designs show little concern with human comfort, expose their mechanical complexity. Designs from 1896 to 1946.

103. (*Lower*) The problem is still not completely solved. Will this be the car of the future?

165

Two buildings having similar architectural detail yet varying greatly in esthetic quality.

104. (*Upper*) The Court House in Brooklyn, New York, shows an excessive variety of window treatment which detracts from its unity.

105. (*Lower*) The façade of the Farnese Palace in Rome, Italy, has a richness of variety which contributes to a powerful unity.

In all expressive art, whether done by children or mature artists, each part contributes directly to the whole.

106. (*Upper*) A child's drawing, titled "It is slippery," expresses emphatically what happens on a slippery day.

107. (*Lower*) "The Sob" by David Alfaro Siqueiros is a powerfully direct portrayal of human sorrow.

108. "Assia," a bronze by the French sculptor Despiau, shows strong simplified forms. Compare the apparently complex foliage shapes with the clearly organized forms in the statue.

response is not esthetic, it is chiefly one of amazement or curiosity or acquisitiveness.

2. *Observing the Principles of Design.* The principles of design have developed as aids to keeping and holding interest in art objects, and naturally they lead to unity. A house, a picture, a person out of balance makes us feel uncomfortable. Noise without rhythm or speech without emphasis leaves us with little or no feeling of esthetic satisfaction.

3. *Selecting Details, Materials, etc., in Harmony with the Basic Idea.* For example, if a house is of contemporary design, greater unity will be developed if the furniture and gardens are also contemporary. Each part of a total composition should strengthen the original concept, and this demands constant attention to the desired result in selecting everything used.

4. *Surrounding the Art Object by Suitable Enclosures, Such as Frames, Walls, Fences, etc.* These devices aim to separate the object from its surroundings in order that attention will be focused on it. Compare the effect of a framed with an unframed picture, a furniture arrangement in the middle of a large showroom with the same arrangement in a home room enclosed by four walls.

Variety, the other partner in this pair, arises from any type of opposition or contrast, is developed from diversity of materials, differences in forms, in colors, in textures, or in space arrangements. Variety, in fact, is produced by means exactly opposite to those leading to unity, and the manner in which it is developed is of great importance.

Variety should develop out of unity, not be added to it. The expansion and development of an original idea produce a healthy differentiation. Nature provides a stunning example of potential diversification in unity: the acorn. It is a complete thing in itself but one which is capable of development. If it is planted, it sprouts and starts to grow. Out of it develop roots, stalk, leaves, bark—parts of conspicuous variety. Instead of a simple-appearing little acorn there is a large tree, performing many different functions, possessed of many different parts. Yet all these parts (variety) are of a piece. They all belong to and have developed out of the acorn, just as in the musical form of "theme and variations" all developments, varied as they may be in tempo, rhythm, modality, or tonality, arise from the central theme.

The same kind of development from an original idea is apparent in our daily activities. A boy decides, for instance, to learn to ski. First, he sets about getting a pair of skis, the most important element in the situation outside of himself and the snow. When he finds that he likes skiing and plans to do a lot of it, he purchases a pair of ski pants, then a ski jacket, and hat, mittens, and scarf. He improves in his ability to ski. He studies types of snow, he buys different kinds of wax, he practices types of turns —stem turns, Christiana turns, jump turns. Thus a complex pattern of behavior develops out of a simple interest in skiing—a complex pattern, yet wholly unified by a central idea. Art, too, can be as organic as nature or our behavior pattern when it stems from a central idea.

In summary, variety, or lack of sameness, is often spoken of as the spice of life. It is also the spice of art. For relieving monotony and thus holding attention, variety is quite as valuable and necessary as unity. The two complement and supplement each other. In a well-planned design the two interact with and balance each other, steering a mid-course between monotony and chaos. Variety gives vitality by way of contrast. For example, a small area of bright color vitalizes large dominant areas of somber color in a painting; it emphasizes and even highlights the somberness which the artist sought. Naturally, however, if variety is carried too far, unity is lost. Then the whole is lost in the parts: a building becomes a collection of doors, windows, decorations; a room becomes a random collection of furniture; a painting becomes an assembly of objects. In great art, attention is kept on the whole; the parts take their appointed places. There is no competition; everything cooperates. To achieve variety in unity is an aim of all art. When present it leads to profound human satisfaction and enjoyment. Second only to FORM FOLLOWS FUNCTION, VARIETY IN UNITY is an ideal held by artists from the dawn of history to the present day.

FORM FOLLOWS FUNCTION and VARIETY IN UNITY are two considerations basic to the understanding and the making of beautiful things. When an artist, whether in the home, the community, the church, commerce, industry or other sphere of human endeavor, works to create beauty he bears in mind these two aims of organization, and using the elements of form, line, space, texture, and color, he organizes his materials to achieve his purposes.

CHAPTER 7

The Plastic Elements

THE poet or the novelist uses words—nouns, verbs, adjectives, pronouns—when he expresses his *verbal* ideas. The composer of songs, symphonies, and swing uses tones of different time lengths, in different combinations, in different relationships—when he expresses his *musical* ideas. The artist, whether painter, architect, sculptor, or engineer, uses similar elements—form, line, color, texture, and space—when he expresses his plastic ideas. These five elements at the disposal of the artist who seeks to express a fundamental idea or fulfill a human need are present in every art object. These—and the two basic principles, FORM FOLLOWS FUNCTION and VARIETY IN UNITY, which govern their use and combination—are in the artist's mind when he plans to build a house, make a water-jug, or dress for a game of golf.

Much as chemical elements—hydrogen, oxygen, nitrogen, or iron—make up chemical compounds, these plastic elements are basic in the plastic arts. The human arm, for instance, may be thought of as cylindrical in *form*, light red-orange in *color*, soft and smooth in *texture*, and, finally, as occupying a certain *spatial* position in relation to the rest of the body of which it is a part. The painter or sculptor in representing a human arm pays attention to each of these elements, not as separate, discrete aspects but as organically related components of visual appearances. He may concentrate on one or more at a time, but he sees each one in its context.

Each shape has a particular type of existence, a character of its own, which the artist uses in infinite variation to express his plastic ideas. A pyramid, for example, can be defined as a conelike, triangular figure with a plane polygonal base. When fairly low and broad, it rests on its base as one of the most stable forms in art or nature. Look again at the Pyramid of Khufu on page 95 and think of mountain ranges. These suggest permanence and durability. When tall and thin but still resting on its base, as in church steeples or the Washington Monument, a pyramid leads the eye and spirit upward in an aspiring manner. If, however, a pyramid is inverted so that it stands on its apex, an opposite effect results. Then it becomes one of the least stable forms, suggesting topheaviness, uncertainty, imminent change. These variations on a theme only introduce us to the range of possibilities inherent in the basic shape. A pyramid can be large or small in size; three-sided or many-sided in structure; erect, horizontal, or tilting in position; rough or smooth in texture; light or dark in value, red or blue in hue, and bright or dull in intensity. Further, it can be solid as the Egyptian pyramids or open as a radio tower, and it can be made of paper, straw, wood, stone, concrete, metal, or glass. In addition to existing as solids, pyramidal forms can be represented on two-dimensional surfaces in drawings, paintings, and prints. However it may be treated, the pyramid retains its characteristic of progressing in one direction toward a point. What wondrous possibilities the artist has in a shape as basically simple as a pyramid!

A sphere, by way of contrast, is a body bounded by one surface, all points of which are equidistant from the center. It has one continuous surface—no top, sides, bottom or angles. In position, it appears to be highly unstable for it can roll easily in any direction. In durability and permanence, however, it exceeds even the pyramid: there are no corners or angles to break off or wear away. Like the pyramid, the sphere can be any size, any color and texture, but it cannot vary in basic shape. The sphere always appears to be self-contained, with all of its forces in sustained equilibrium. There are, of course, many other solids with rounded contours, as a look at natural objects will reveal: pears, watermelons, potatoes; eggs or amoebas; or the parts of the human body—eyes, ears, or heart. In fashioning the plastic elements into art, the artist exploits the essential character of each to express his ideas. He is free to select, to transform, to imagine. Look through the illustrations in this book and list all of the ways in which pyramidal and spherical forms have been used. Better yet, look around your school, home, and community and see how many examples you can find. Then try to figure out why these forms were used, what they express.

Each form, line, color, texture, and space is experienced not in isolation but in relation to its surroundings, and the surroundings do much to alter its effect. Imagine the Pyramid of Khufu transported from its setting on the expansive sand of the Egyptian desert to a valley in the Rocky Mountains. It would still, of course, be large, pyramidal, and impressive, but by comparison with the towering pyramidal peaks, it would seem smaller and less significant than in its own environment. Or try to imagine the community of Williamsburg set down on a New Mexican desert. In the soft light of Virginia, the formal buildings of Williamsburg nestle charmingly in their green surroundings; in the glaring sunlight of New Mexico, the colors would seem weak, the ornamentation over-refined and precious.

The importance of relationships is further exemplified by the phenomena of optical illusions. Figure 109 shows that shapes of identical size do

109. Optical illusions forcefully demonstrate the importance of relationships. *Left,* the two circles are exactly the same size; *middle,* the two segments of the line are equal in length; *right,* the vertical lines are parallel.

not appear the same in different surroundings and that parallel lines do not always appear to be parallel. We have all had opportunity to know how dissimilar the same thing appears under different conditions. Thus, the successful business man appears to be of great importance when seen in his well-furbished office with his organization at his finger tips; when seen in swimming trunks on the beach, he may seem less significant than a college athlete. The movie heroine without benefit of sets, make-up, and lights may not have her glamor. We might well raise the question: Is the same object always the same? The answer is no. Things are greatly modified by their context, and this is true of every form, line, color, texture, and space the artist employs. All artists take advantage of, or counteract, optical illusions to suit their purposes. On pages 468-69 are listed several devices used by the Greeks to overcome optical illusions in architecture.

The Problem of Organization

One further important characteristic of the plastic elements deserves mention. Like magnets and like people, the plastic elements generate a field of force extending beyond their boundaries. We all know that the force of a magnet extends beyond its physical limits, and we know how a great actor or musician can project the force of his artistry to audiences of thousands of persons. The plastic elements have this same power. The symbolizing star forms in Van Gogh's "Starry Night" (page 397) extend their centripetal vigor to all parts of the canvas. In "Steamer 'Odin,' II" (page 233), Feininger actually indicates these projecting forces by lines and forms pressing beyond their outlines. Moreover, this projected force goes beyond the confines of the painting to the observer, who is psychologically stimulated and energized. In organizing any art object, the significant artist does not regard forms and colors as inert spots but as energies as lively as those in an atom—and as important to control. As with the atom, the forces in the plastic elements have to be released before they can serve the artist. Releasing and directing the energy in a form or color so that it carries to the observer are as important in art as releasing and directing physical forces are in science.

FORM *

In this section we will look at form without too much regard for its fellow ingredients, although we know that such isolation of a plastic element is quite arbitrary. It is just as difficult as trying to listen for all the sixteenth-notes, or for just the French-horn part, in a good piece of music: if the music is good, you hear musical ideas, not a great mass of mechan-

---

* Warning! *Form* has two meanings! In the larger sense, it is the total problem of the second section of this book, that is, the total organization of all the parts so that the fundamental idea or human need is clearly expressed. In the smaller sense, as used in Plastic Elements, it means mass or shape—as of an arm or Despiau's statue. When used in this restricted sense, it leaves out not only the other plastic elements, but the principles governing their use and combination, materials and processes, and the relation of all the parts of an art subject to the big, underlying thought—the human need. The authors deliberated long before deciding to use the word *form* in this second, smaller meaning within that section of this book which deals with form in the larger sense. But no other words would quite fulfill the descriptive power of the word *form*. Both *mass* and *shape*, upon a moment's reflection, will fall short of what this first plastic element really means. Later discussion will help clarify the distinction between the two meanings of *form*. It is important that this distinction be well understood.

174

ical parts. It is as difficult as trying to detect the kinds of spices in a barbecue sauce or a fruit cake.

"Assia" (Figure 108), a bronze statue by the French sculptor Despiau, illustrates clearly and simply this first and most important of the plastic elements—form. Form describes the structure or shape of an object and seems the most inclusive and unchanging truth about objects. Nature and art show how really few are the primary forms to which all others are related. Buildings, bookcases and other furniture are usually composed of cubes or other rectangular solids; oranges, apples, electric light globes and domes on state capitols are shaped as spheres or parts of them; evergreen trees, volcanoes, panicles of flowers, radio loudspeakers and cream separators are basically cones; tree trunks, human arms and legs, grain elevators, pencils and smokestacks are cylinders. How many of these simple forms are used in Despiau's "Assia"?

Despiau's bronze statue grew from a clay model. At first this clay was a meaningless mass of unrelated shapes with as little plastic significance as bread dough. The sculptor transformed his shapeless clay into art. As subject matter he used a female figure, but it is not a literal copy of nature. His aim was not merely to reproduce what he saw in his model but to create a statue which would communicate to the observer a fundamental idea of dignity, restrained power, and serenity. He eliminated irrelevant details so that basic structure would be intensified. Head and neck, shoulders and arms, breasts, torso, and legs have been strengthened through emphasizing their relation to such primary forms as spheres, cylinders, and cones. All parts are rhythmically related through strong poised curves; each part develops from those adjacent through subtle transitions. By such means the statue is invested with dignity and serenity.

Form in sculpture can be realized in many other ways, as shown in the "Eagle" and "The Boxers" in Chapter 9 or the illustrations in Chapter 16. When form has been so treated, it gains an importance that goes well beyond merely recalling the object from which it was adapted. Form gains a significance of its own, a meaning beyond that of the model who posed for the sculptor. Clive Bell has aptly described this result as "significant form."

Let us take another example. A painter is painting a portrait of a young man. The subject wears a coat and both his arms are bent. Wrinkles appear in the sleeves, and each time that he extends and flexes his arms the wrinkles occur a little differently. As the light in the room changes the shadows change. The sleeves which encase his arms may look quite different at five o'clock than at one. Actually his arm is the same—through all these changes of covering and light its general form is unchanged. The variations which have appeared on the surface are all trivial, accidental. The fact that on one cloudy day it was dark at five o'clock and it was impossible to see the arms of the model clearly, while the next day was sunny and all details were sharp, is certainly accidental so far as the true, fundamental, or significant form of the arms is concerned. The painter interested in portraying basic, fundamental form would pay little attention to the shifting, fleeting changes of light because his interest leads him to the forms underneath. It is the difference between appearances and realities. On page 234 you will find a strong contrast between a painting with well-realized form and one that has merely pictured light as it fell on the objects. Study these two illustrations carefully.

In painting, as in all of the other arts, form can be handled in a great variety of ways. George Bellows in "Dempsey and Firpo" (page 231) and Grant Wood in "American Gothic" (page 398) treat form in a more or less literal manner: light, shade, and shadows are used to convey an illusion of three-dimensionality. The forms in "Dempsey and Firpo" are full of force and energy, those in "American Gothic" staid and stable, as befits the different ideas expressed in the two paintings. Both, however, are compact and self-contained. Stuart Davis in "Summer Landscape" (page 230) uses simplified, flat forms, poised in space to express the stillness of a warm day. The forms are even more self-contained than are those of Bellows or Wood, and they have been reduced to flat planes. Roundness or squareness is indicated by direction of line, contrast in color. Only the lilt of the tree, the free rhythmic forms of the other foliage and the sky, suggest a gentle movement. In striking contrast are the vehemently dynamic forms in Van Gogh's "Starry Night" (page 397), the surging movement in El Greco's "St. Francis in Ecstasy" (page 234). Sculptors, too, transform natural shapes to suit their need. In the nineteenth-century "Eagle" (page 230) the outspread wings, the strong neck and body, the cruel head and talons have been given a quivering tension not only by their basic structure but by the pulsating representation of feathers and claws. Archipenko in "The Boxers" (page 231) has forsaken textures to give vividness to the energy which he felt to be the essence of a boxing match. Different as they are in the handling of form, "The Boxers" and the "Eagle" are equally compelling.

Form, therefore, is structure. It is not surface. It refers to the skeleton and muscles of the body rather than to the skin, to the trunk and branches

176

of a tree rather than to the bark, to the whole organization of a building rather than to the decoration. It can also refer to the forces and tensions that make the object what it is. Form is more than outline or external surface.

All the visual arts are concerned with form. Sculpture, architecture, and the industrial arts deal with actual, three-dimensional form. Of these, sculpture is the only one which deals with exterior form alone. You do not get inside a statue, but you quite definitely get inside a building, and you at least put your hands in vases or chests of drawers. Seen and used from both inside and outside, architecture and the industrial arts—the hollow arts, in one sense—add many new complexities to the problems of the designers of form.

Good architecture and good industrial art allow their outward forms to be governed by what goes on inside them. As was discussed in Part I, a house is a place to live in; it is the home of the family. The inside, therefore, is the most important part and should be carefully designed to meet the needs of the family. If the exterior forms of the house clearly express the interior forms, the house is well on the way towards becoming a good piece of art. If a factory expresses on the outside that its inside is for efficient manufacture, it is in that respect a good factory. Thus we find that throughout the use of forms there is a guiding principle which says that the inner content or purpose or function governs the outer appearance. In other words: form follows function.

Ornamentation in architecture, industrial art, or any other art is the elaboration or enrichment of basic structural forms. We have already run into the problem of ornament several times and have found that it arises from a deep sense of beauty which compels such artists as the Guatemalan native to apply figures and embellishments to such simple utilitarian household objects as carrying-cloths and cooking vessels. The application of ornament calls for a highly developed sensitivity for the relation of forms to each other. Ornament should not just be stuck on something, like shutters on a contemporary house, or Renaissance brackets on a present-day electric street light. The ornament should be related to the object which it graces, should help that object fulfill its purpose, like the cross on the Finnish church (Chapter 3), or the restrained use of decoration in the parlor in the Raleigh Tavern in Williamsburg (Chapter 1), or the decorations and bands that make the dishes (Figure 111) suitable for a formal dinner.

In the Royal Copenhagen plates (Figure 111) notice that the floral decorations and bands are integrally related to the size of the plates and that the flowers have been simplified into a conventional design which fits the shape of the plates and adds to their elegant appearance. In the center of the plates is a floral motif which provides a focal spot of interest and further adds to the circular shape of the plates themselves.

Because of the universality of ornament, it is worthwhile drawing some generalizations regarding its use. (1) *Size.* Ornament should bear a strict relation to the size of the basic form of which it is part. For example, a textile printed with large patterns may well be used in curtaining the windows of a sizable room but would not be suitable for a woman's dress. (2) *Shape.* Ornament should be related to the basic shape of the object and intensify it through repetition or contrast. In the American highboy (Figure 113) the carving emphasizes the roundness or the rectangularity of the different parts, strengthening the character of their basic shape. (3) *Material.* Ornament should grow out of the nature of the material. Outstretching or protruding forms, for instance, suggest themselves in materials having considerable tensile strength such as wood or metal, but are less appropriate in glass or clay. (4) *Association.* The associations aroused by ornament should be in harmony with the object's function—it would be unpleasant to eat from plates decorated with rattlesnakes or night-crawlers, and it is not too pleasant to step on rugs or sit on chairs covered with realistic flowers. (5) *Quality.* Finally, ornament itself should be significant and expressive—lively, vigorous, refined, peaceful, or whatever the function, form, and material indicate. It should not be a sterile, unimaginative pattern which merely clutters the surface but should contribute its own spark of life.

Check these generalizations with the silverware shown in the photograph of the Royal Copenhagen porcelain. Here the ornament is so thoughtfully related both in shape and in size that it almost appears as if there is no ornament at all. Many industrial products have not been designed as thoughtfully as these pieces. It is easy to find plates that writhe under their load of flowers, woodland scenes, and street views. Silverware with awkward handles and clumsy ornament is common. Kitchen stoves laden with roses and arabesques were once common sights.

It is the form, therefore, of an object which gives it the dominant characteristics by which it is recognizable. Compare the simple, cylindrical shape of the ordinary earthworm with the relatively complex structure of a mud turtle or with the highly complex form of man. Or compare the Early American cupboard, dating from 1660-1680, with the American

178

highboy which is dated some sixty years later. These two sideboards (Figures 112 and 113) clearly indicate that they are storage cupboards of some kind, but they tell the careful observer considerably more. One is heavy, thick and solid, and expresses much of the spirit of the first period of Colonial America. It recalls the puritanical philosophy and manner of living of the early Americans and is in perfect harmony with the simple, severe clothing they wore. The other piece is as delicate and refined as the first one was vigorous. Notice the delicate finials, the slender curved legs, the elaborate fan-shaped decorations. These decorations and forms are of the eighteenth century, a period of powdered wigs, hoop skirts and gracious aristocracy.

Contemporary furniture tells equally much about those who buy and use it. What about the forms of the furniture in your own home? Are they strong and sturdy, delicate and graceful, or clumsy and awkward? Do you feel easy about letting them speak for you? Much of our thinking and believing is expressed in the things we say and do, the objects we make and buy, and the furniture, dishes, pictures, and houses with which we live.

LINE

In one respect the graphic arts of drawing and painting are exceptions to the above discussion of form. In making a painting or a pencil drawing we cannot work directly with form, as can a sculptor. Instead, we work with symbols and conventions that indicate form. The simplest of these is line. Look at the drawing of three youths by Pablo Picasso (Figure 114). There is no shading or modeling, yet without any of these devices Picasso has succeeded in defining human forms in a most convincing manner. Notice the three-dimensional quality in the head and hand at the extreme left. Notice how the differences between hair and textiles have been indicated. Form, texture, and space have all been represented by using line only. A wealth of suggestion and indication have been portrayed with an economy of effort. (In case you think that effective line drawings are as easy to do as they appear to be, try one.)

Contrast Picasso's drawing with the one of the Mexican mother and child by the Mexican artist, Diego Rivera (Figure 115). Notice in particular the hands and faces in the two drawings. Do you get different

179

reactions from them? Why? One is delicate and reposed, the other is strong, moving, almost brutal. Forget the subject matter: turn the pictures upside down. The difference still exists because it lies in the quality of the line of the two artists.

Creative artists are always seeking new ways to express their observations, and few have been more inventive than Paul Klee and Alexander Calder. Look at Figure 116 to see the geometric interplay of line in Klee's "Family Promenade (Tempo II)." Ruled lines enclose angular planes which depict four persons and two dogs taking a walk. By avoiding the obvious ways of drawing, Klee takes us into the realm of fantasy and

ACTION   BONDAGE   HUMOR

110. Abstractions representing Action, Bondage, and Humor show the expressive possibilities of line.

whimsy. He reveals a new aspect of familiar objects and activities. The next time you see persons and dogs walking, remember this drawing. You will probably find that it looks more like the subject matter than you would have guessed.

In "The Hostess" (Figure 117) Alexander Calder treats line three dimensionally. With rare perception, he has grasped—and caricatured—a typical gesture of a hostess greeting her guests. Such actions, especially if exaggerated, have their humorous side, and that is what Calder wishes to convey. Art, like drama and literature, can be humorous but not often is it expressed as subtly with line alone as in these two examples.

For proof that mere lines and shapes can be expressive, look at those labeled Action, Bondage, and Humor in Figure 110. Even if they were not labeled and you were asked to guess their meaning, the chances are that you would come close to the words used in the caption. Try these drawings on your friends. Tell them the three titles and ask them to indicate which title applies to which drawing. Action may be described in many ways: quick movement, speed, motion, excitement, etc. Bondage might be constriction, enclosure, repression, depression, etc. For humor we might say wit, merriment, whimsicality, facetiousness, and so forth.

The list of adjectives that could be used to describe the expressive power of line (form, space, color, and texture as well) would include most of those listed in Roget's *Thesaurus*. Here are a few: long or short; thick or thin; pointed or obtuse; straight, curved, or zigzag; vertical, horizontal, or diagonal; ascending or descending; advancing or receding; expanding or contracting; fast or slow; staccato or legato; vigorous or serene; majestic or playful. These are only sets of extremes between which there are infinite gradations. And these qualities never occur in isolation. A line may be long, thick, straight, and vertical; or it can be short, thick, straight, and vertical. The two will not give the same effect. A statistician could spend several lifetimes computing the potential permutations. You can spend a lifetime experimenting with or merely appreciating the suggestive eloquence of the plastic elements.

Why is it, however, that an artist with a few simple lines on a flat piece of paper, or with sticks and stones organized in space as architecture, can project to us the essentials of human experience? Perhaps we will never know the answer, but here is a thought: When we are tired and lie down to sleep, we assume a horizontal position—invariably the things that mean repose to us are horizontal objects such as large, calm bodies of water or flat, gently rolling hills and meadows. When we are up and about, we move in vertical positions, and when vertical lines are seen in pictures with horizontal lines, the vertical ones look more awake and strong. When we run or are otherwise unusually active, our bodies assume a diagonal position, head thrust forward, balance somewhat precarious, elbows and knees forming angles like those in the sketch called Action. It seems, then, that forms have a definite, distinct basis in human experience, that an artist may make a building, a statue, a painting, or a piece of furniture look restful, or alive and imposing, or excited and moving.

Line, however, is not always used to express deep human emotion and experience in this manner. Often it is used merely for a conventional representation of objects—the line drawings of a building prepared by an architect, or the drawings of a bridge made by an engineer; the lines drawn on maps to represent rivers, roads, or contours; or the lines drawn on paper to represent words. Such use of line is primarily utilitarian, a convenient way of communicating our ideas to another person. To be sure, there are strong possibilities for beauty in the lines of a well-printed page, a well-drawn construction detail but their major purpose is utilitarian. Whichever the emphasis—expression of human emotion or communication of factual materials—line is an important plastic element at the disposal of the artist.

SPACE

When Mozart was asked what he thought was the most beautiful music, he replied: "No music." He meant, of course, the moments of pause and rest, of total silence, which occur in every piece of music. In some of Mozart's own scores are moments of "no music" a hundredfold more eloquent than the music which surrounds them. Likewise we are familiar with the dramatic pauses used by actors on the stage or screen, speakers on the platform, to emphasize a mood or a point. Often no words effect far more than a thousand could. We think of the saying: Silence is golden.

More and more widely understood and sensitively used is the corresponding element in the plastic and graphic arts: space. We judge a room by the space that is enclosed as much as by the forms and colors and textures used to enclose it. The manner in which the space areas of a building have been designed—called spatial organization—is one of the major factors on which a building is evaluated, criticized, and enjoyed. This is quite just because the space in architecture is the portion which we use. The walls have meaning and function only as they enclose space effectively. Contemporary architecture is being thought of more and more as the organization of space, less as solid mass.

In the photographs of the contemporary living rooms designed by Mies van der Rohe and Greta Grosman (Figures 121 and 123), notice the free, open, extending, unrestricted space. They are, however, quite different. The room by Mies is simple, defined as it is by relatively few, smooth-textured planes at right angles to one another. That by Grosman is more complex, being based on organic forms rather than on rectangles and showing a rich interplay of solids and voids. Yet in neither room is there any feeling of tight enclosure, peephole windows, or cramped movement. Since the dawn of history man has sought space sufficiently enclosed to protect him, and yet open enough to allow him to live comfortably within it. Natural caves were a readymade solution for primitive man; then came the cavernous temples and tombs such as the Egyptians built. Later the Greek, Roman, and Gothic builders succeeded in making building lighter, space more flexible. And in modern times came steel and glass to permit a new freedom in the handling of space. Architectural history shows a constant trend toward greater use of space—space flexible and free.

If we could suddenly step into Anne Hathaway's cottage (Chapter 1) and from there into the Tugendhat home (Figure 121), we would realize at once the contrast between historic and modern architecture. On the basis of these two examples we could list such specific contrasts as small versus large windows, rough versus smooth textures, pointed versus flat roofs, picturesqueness versus precision. But these differences are only external manifestations of a fundamentally new approach to the problem of enclosing livable space. To the Elizabethan or the American Colonist, architecture was strong, solid shelter against the dangers and discomforts of the out-of-doors, and it was highly important that the architecture by its very appearance assure the occupants that they were warm, protected, and safe. Together with the materials and type of construction, this led to an architecture in which space became a matter of tight enclosure, a series of boxlike rooms with peephole windows and doors. It is no exaggeration to say that the greatest single difference between the architecture of the past and that of the present lies in the handling of space, the third plastic element.

Gardens, too, are primarily compositions in space, with trees, shrubs, walls, and buildings acting as dividing and accenting elements, with the ground as a floor and the sky as a roof. When functionally planned, they extend the house into the outdoors, carry living space beyond the building walls, so that people may enjoy nature planned and controlled to meet their needs.

Beyond architecture and gardens, however, stand cities, our most extensive and important organizations of space. In them, houses, stores, public buildings, factories, streets, parks, and boulevards are all units of a great space planned for the manifold activities of the civilized human being. The whole discussion of the Arts of the Community (Chapter 2), especially the section on the planning of Greenbelt, Maryland, was a consideration of how space could best be adapted to community life. Even larger projects such as the Tennessee Valley Authority carry the practice and theory of space organization into startling proportions. Think of how your own community, your country, or your state *could* have been planned to take best advantage of its resources.

The Problem of Organization

We turn from such gigantic examples to the arts of painting and drawing, etching and photography, which deal with symbolic rather than actual space. They use two dimensions instead of three. Therefore, a major problem in these arts is to represent adequately both *form* and *space*. Look *again* at the Picasso drawing (Figure 114) and see how this problem has been handled. It is quite evident that one boy is standing behind the two others, that the arm and hand at the extreme left are in front of the leg. We feel certain that there is space between the different forms. Picasso accomplished this by carefully directing his lines to suggest boundaries for both form and space. The Rivera drawing (Figure 115) is considerably flatter, i.e., it has less space. This is not because Rivera is less capable than Picasso, but because his subject did not demand the same open treatment. The element of space in each of these drawings is as different from that in the other as the subject matter and the line quality. In Chapter 15, the problem of spatial organization in painting is treated in some detail, but in order to get a head start look again at two paintings in Chapter 9. In Bellow's "Dempsey and Firpo" (page 231) space is represented by the devices of literal perspective: parallel lines converging toward vanishing points and objects diminishing in size and value contrast as they recede. In Davis' "Summer Landscape" (page 230) there is no fixed point of view, no systematically converging lines. And yet both give a substantial feeling of space. In Picasso's "Three Musicians" (Figure 118) form and space are expressed by flat planes some of which are brought forward by their size, shape, and color while others recede. As with line and form, space in painting can be handled in many ways.

There are two phrases that arise from a discussion of space. One is *spatial organization*, by which is meant the design of forms, textures, and colors in three dimensions (actual or symbolic). The other is *space division* which refers to the two-dimensional or surface quality of such things as textiles and printing. There is a world of difference between these two phrases, and the concepts which they describe. An architect, for instance, who is interested primarily in space division spends his time decorating the façade of his building—he plays with arrangements of openings and the ornaments on a surface. But if he is interested in spatial organization, as he should be, he is concerned with the relationships of solids and voids throughout the *whole* building. He regards openings and ornamentation as expressions of the space-plan of the building, not as mere decorations on a surface.

If this discussion of space seems brief, it is because the organization

111. Plates and silverware on which ornament is nicely related to basic shapes.

112. (*Left*) American cupboard, 1660-1680, showing robust, vigorous forms.

113. (*Right*) American highboy, 1725-1750, with delicate, graceful forms.

114. A drawing by Pablo Picasso in which solid forms and empty space are convincingly represented through line alone. Sensitive line expresses the character of the dancers.

Rivera

115. In this brush-and-ink drawing Diego Rivera has used heavy lines to depict a Mexican peasant and child. Contrast the line quality with that in Picasso's drawing; in both, line has been used to *express* as well as to *represent* the subjects.

187

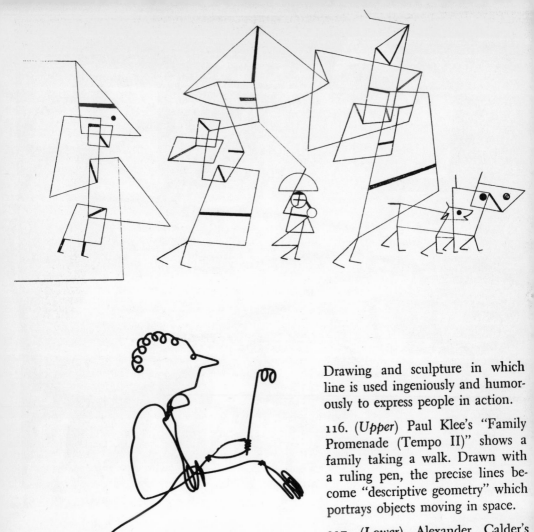

Drawing and sculpture in which line is used ingeniously and humorously to express people in action.

116. (*Upper*) Paul Klee's "Family Promenade (Tempo II)" shows a family taking a walk. Drawn with a ruling pen, the precise lines become "descriptive geometry" which portrays objects moving in space.

117. (*Lower*) Alexander Calder's wire sculpture called "The Hostess" might be described as a line drawing in three dimensions, for in it line actually carves and defines space.

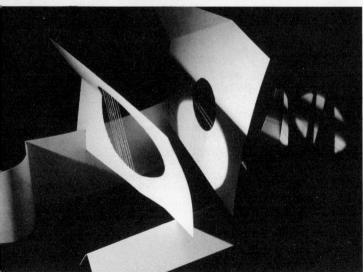

118. (*Upper*)
Pablo Picasso's
"Three Musi-
cians" reduces
three-dimensional
form to two-
dimensional
planes. Notice
how some planes,
such as the book
of music and in-
struments, stand
in front of the
planes depicting
the figures, there-
by creating a
sense of space.

9. (*Lower*) An experimental "Light Modulator" constructed of paper and string
study the relation of light to space. Explorations such as this have influenced
hitecture and industrial design as well as painting and advertising.

189

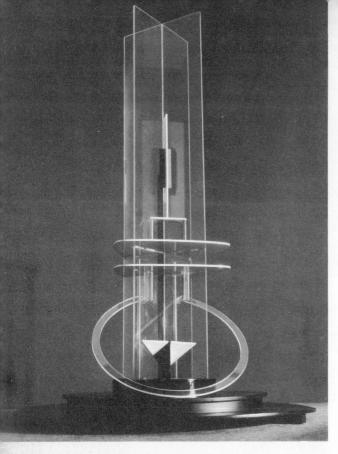

A construction and living room in which space has been organized in precise geometrical manner.

120. (*Upper*) A Column, or Space Construction, by Naum Gabo explores the spatial geometry of transparent materials. Compare with "All the Elements" on the opposite page.

121. (*Lower*) The space in the living room of the Tugendhat house designed by Mies van der Rohe is given rectangular definition by enclosing planes of solid and transparent materials.

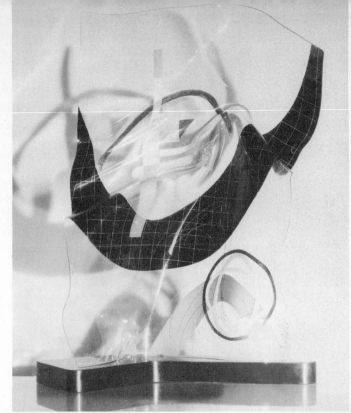

Space can also be modulated with free forms reminiscent of natural shapes.

122. (*Upper*) Moholy-Nagy's "space-modulator" is called "All the Elements." Molded Plexiglas has been painted, scratched, and drawn on to produce a lively pattern of transparency and opaqueness which varies in changing light and casts complex shadows.

123. (*Lower*) Greta Grosman's living room attains an organic quality from the predominance of nongeometric forms in contrast to the rectangularity of the living room opposite.

124. Michelangelo's "Deposition from the Cross" portrays four figures in a coherent organization of form, line, and space.

of space has already been dealt with extensively in Part I and will be considered again in Part IV. Space, far from being merely "what is left," stands with form as one of the two major plastic elements. Our understanding of the importance of space in art has been enormously expanded by recent advances in science: rapid transportation on land, sea, and through air; communication by wire and through air; aerial photography; and astronomical explorations of the vast, complex, interplanetary space. Artists have kept pace with scientists and have pushed forward their concepts of spatial organization. Mobility and fluidity, as well as stability and rigidity, have been the subject of experimentation. Alexander Calder (Figure 139) has incorporated actual movement into abstract design through the use of free-swinging shapes. Touched by the hand or a gentle breeze, his discs suspended from wires cut through their surrounding space to describe fascinating rhythmic patterns.

Sculptors, such as Gabo (Figure 120), have made geometric constructions of transparent and opaque materials which increase our sensitivity to what happens between solids. Designers, such as Moholy-Nagy and Charles Eames, have made their contributions. In "All the Elements" (Figure 122), Moholy-Nagy has molded Plexiglas by hand, then painted and scratched designs on it. Seen in changing lights with its varying reflections and shadows, it well deserves to be called a "Space Modulator," for it adjusts, regulates, and tempers the space in which it exists. While working out the designs for his furniture (page 269), Charles Eames produced the boldly molded plywood shape (page 233) which vigorously carves its enveloping space into new dimensions.

But not all of these experiments have been done in art intended solely for esthetic satisfaction. Eames' molded plywood form is directly related to his chairs, and Greta Grosman's room in Figure 123 shows forms in the extending, non-rectangular davenport, the irregularly shaped table, and the free form of the lowered ceiling that exemplify revitalized concepts of space.

What are these concepts? First, increased emphasis is placed on the continuing character of space. Architecture tends to merge inside with outside space; cities extend into the countryside with no moats or walls to mark their limits. Less emphasis is put on enclosure and boundaries, more on expansiveness and extension. Second, space is treated as being integral with form, line, color, and texture. In the House of Ideas and the Johnson house in Chapter 1 we saw how space was modulated by and integrated with form, texture, and color, and in Moholy-Nagy's "All the Elements" how difficult (and unnecessary) it is to separate space from form, texture from color.

Third, the multi-dimensionality of space has been more fully recognized. Although strictly speaking there are still only three spatial dimensions, in Moholy-Nagy's and Eames' abstractions and in Grosman's room we are conscious not only of verticals and horizontals but of the infinite variety of diagonal and curvilinear directions and relationships.

Do not think for a moment that these concepts were invented in the twentieth century. The builders of Gothic cathedrals, the painters and sculptors of the Renaissance, and the artists of the Orient were well aware of effective spatial organization. But modern artists have continued the progress shown in history and have added their contribution.

CHAPTER 8   *The Plastic Elements:*
Continued

W E have seen how form, line, and space play their parts in giving quality or character to art objects. And when we discussed houses, oil paintings, textiles, furniture, and other objects for their form, line, or spatial qualities, you must have noticed now and then that another element tried to assert itself. You will realize this immediately if you close your eyes and run your fingers over this page, then over some article of clothing you are wearing, and then over the arm of the chair you are sitting in. Do the same with sandpaper, fur, and glass. Your fingers will report differences—smoothness, roughness, silkiness. This is *texture,* the surface quality of an object. Differences in texture can be as striking as roundness and squareness (which are differences in form) or red and green (differences in color), and are of great importance in giving character to an object.

TEXTURE

Of the five plastic elements, texture deals most directly with the sense of touch. The surface of an object produces tactile sensations when we touch it: these are called *tactile values.* Tactile value is best appreciated when object is actually felt with the hands. This was brought sharply to the attention of the managers of a store which retails women's wearing apparel. In a newly altered department, coats and dresses were kept in sight but out of reach behind glass doors. The customers objected. They wanted to *feel* the clothes, and soon the management found it necessary to alter this department again so that their customers could *feel* what they were looking at. Because we touch clothes many times

195

every day, we have become highly conscious of their tactile values. When we buy a suit or dress, one of our first impulses is to feel the material, because the hand, as much as the eye, aids in making the selection.

Sensitivity to texture is equally important in determining the materials used in architecture and furniture. Turn to Chapter 1 and notice the natural textures of thatch, wood, plaster, stone, and hedge in Anne Hathaway's cottage; notice the equally interesting but more delicate textures in the Williamsburg interiors. In these examples, variety and sensuous beauty were attained by allowing each material to reveal its own character—the grain of wood, the brusque shagginess of thatch, the fibrous quality of textiles, the smoothness of glass and metal.

The contemporary architect and designer have at their disposal a great variety of textures. Efficient transportation permits them to use woods, metals, and stones from far countries; modern science has given them a treasure of new materials such as structural glass, stainless steel, ribbed plywood, and countless synthetics. Were it not for this renewed interest in texture we would still be repeating the all-too-common type of interior that has no surface richness or variety: everything is smooth and painted, everything is slick—and passes unnoticed. The surfaces do not even look smooth—just monotonous. In contrast to these, the House of Ideas in Chapter 1 and the Hanna House (Figure 145) use a variety of woods, textiles, brick, and glass so that your finger tips tingle as you look at the photographs. Look through the illustrations in this book to see the variety of textures used by architects and designers.

Painters, too, have reawakened to the richness and vitality given by textures. Academic painting of the nineteenth and twentieth centuries placed high premium on porcelain-like smoothness. The smoother the surface and forms, the more the painting was admired. But Cézanne, Van Gogh, Picasso, Marin and others—the innovators of the nineteenth and twentieth centuries—rediscovered the values of textures. Look again at the purposefully used textures in Siqueiros' "The Sob" (Figure 107), at Klee's "Beride" (Figure 127), which is almost a study in texture, and then at the two advertisements (Figures 128 and 130). In "Resistance" the rough textures of rugged countryside and architecture pervade the whole painting; in "Diversification" the basic smoothness is emphasized by subtle indications of the surface qualities of fruits and vegetables, tennis racket and mandolin, tire and spark plug. You will also notice that historical and contemporary sculptors use texture, as shown in Michelangelo's "Deposition from the Cross" (Figure 124), Despiau's "Assia"

196

(page 168), and the illustrations in Chapter 16. When next you look at original painting or sculpture, study their textures carefully.

How should textures be used? What are the determining principles? Mind well that here, as in all other aspects of art, there are no dogmatic rules or laws. It is rather a matter of relationships, of appropriateness to function and to material.

First, the texture of an object should be in character with its form and color, strengthening both of these elements. The form and color and texture of an object all do the same thing—they express its reason for being. Therefore, they are related in purpose, and, in that way, reinforce each other. We may, for instance, compare the textures in two art objects of widely different purpose and time: Anne Hathaway's cottage and a modern automobile. In the hand-crafted cottage the forms are irregular, informal, picturesque, expressing not only the materials from which they are built and the manner in which they were processed but a great deal about the period and the persons of that period. The colors are the colors of natural materials. We expect to find—and do find—natural, rough, irregular textures. In contrast, the modern, mass-produced automobile is designed for persons who speed over highways. Its forms show not only the purposes for which the automobile was designed, but the scientific precision with which it is built. The modern automobile is smooth and sleek; the colors are uniform, show no variations. The smoothness of the automobile and the roughness of the Hathaway cottage are textures which, like the forms and colors, have grown out of the basic character of the two things.

Second, textures used in combination should show definite relation one to another. They may be harmonious, that is, have something in common, or they may be deliberately selected for contrast. Just as color and form are related to texture, different textures in the same object should be related. In an individual's clothing, for example, many colors, forms, and textures are present. Yet, all of them, when well-organized, contribute to the total desired effect. The desired effect naturally grows out of the intended function. Thus, a girl clad in rough tweeds and shoes with crepe-rubber soles gives the appearance of going on a hike or a picnic. A sleek silk sash at her waist or a filmy bit of lace about her collar would seem out of place because sleek silk and filmy lace have little in common with tweeds. To be sure, contrasting textures may be used for variety and emphasis, but these contrasts must be carefully planned. Thus in the above example a silk neckscarf might well be used for comfort and be related to the texture of the girl's face. But the larger areas, the more important textures, should be harmonious, leading to a unified effect.

Another complicated problem in textures, already referred to, is that of the home interior. Many interesting problems of relationship, harmony, agreement, and variety beset the person who seeks to make the furnishings of a room the direct, functional, and beautiful solutions to everyday living that they should be. Here, again, it is of first importance to have a basic idea, and to select textures in harmony with this idea. Thus your room may be predominantly (but not entirely) smooth and silky to give a feminine effect; rough and woolly to give a masculine effect; or you may desire the more neutral effect of textures, neither rough nor smooth, but intermediate. You will avoid using oiled-silk curtains against sandy-rough plaster, or bristly wool curtains against sleek tiles (unless, of course, you have in mind a very striking contrast). You will avoid these combinations because the two materials in each spring from different basic ideas. You would do better, in the interests of harmony, to hang oiled-silk against tile, rough wool against sandy plaster. As you look at the photographs of interiors throughout this book you will find many which show harmony through repetition, contrast through opposition.

COLOR

In one of Dickens' books there is a conversation between two stable boys in which one of them tries to get the other one to visualize a world without color—grass that was not green, a sky that was not blue. The other boy is not bright enough to handle such an idea and wonders vaguely about his companion's sanity. It is difficult to imagine a colorless world; we cannot blame the second boy for refusing to enter the discussion with his friend. We would probably agree with him that the whole notion was not worth discussing; nature without color is unthinkable—except for the color-blind.

Not many years ago, however, living rooms and dining rooms were frequently almost without color. They were painted or papered in cream and taupe, taupe and cream. Woodwork and furniture were brown, walls were tan, curtains cream, and the floors taupe. The effect was dreary. The people living in them seemed to have a fear of color. They used it as little as possible and in combinations that were foolproof, even if monotonous. In the industrial arts color was either used carelessly or avoided. The story is told that some years ago a well-known automobile manufacturer said, "You may paint my automobiles any color you wish as long as they are black!"

Recently, the attitude toward color has changed as more about its power has been learned. The automobiles made by the company of the manufacturer quoted above are now available in a range of colors. Women's clothes have always been sold almost as much on the basis of their color as on their cut or materials. And today men's clothes, which have known periods of drabness, are available in carefully studied colors. In furnishing homes, the importance of color is continuously brought to attention by magazines featuring illustrated articles on effective color. Commerce and industry have learned the power of color: girls in a factory complained of cold when the temperature was at 72 degrees, but the complaints ceased when the blue-green walls were painted coral; men lifting black metal boxes complained of strained backs, but when the same boxes were painted pale green, said that the "new, lightweight" boxes made a real difference; a chain of New York restaurants speeded its turnover of customers and increased its receipts 50 percent by changing its color scheme from a quiet gray-green to a stimulating red and yellow. Other reports are equally amazing: flies tend to avoid blue, and night insects keep away from an orange light bulb; barnacles, a pest of the shipping industry, avoid hulls of ships painted white or light green, seek those that are dark. Clearly, color is a powerful force.

THE NATURE OF COLOR

Physicists tell us that white (or apparently colorless) light, such as that from the sun at noon, contains all the colors of the spectrum: violet, indigo, blue, green, yellow, orange, and red. These are so balanced and blended in daylight that the effect is white. When this light strikes an object, certain of the colors are absorbed, others reflected. A lemon, for instance, absorbs all color rays except the yellows which, reflected to our eyes, give the lemon its color. Leaves reflect only green rays, and, therefore, we say that leaves are green. A red apple reflects only the red rays. Thus the color of an object is determined by the rays which are reflected to our eyes, and those which are absorbed by the objects. In transparent objects the light passes through rather than being reflected from the surface, but in passing through certain rays are filtered out.

199

The Problem of Organization

This, however, only begins to describe color. If you have ever tried to describe a color to a friend, you know the difficulties you had. You might have seen a carpet which appealed to you, and you began, "The carpet was red." But that was not enough: was it scarlet or maroon? Was it dark or light? Was it a bright, clear red, or was it a dull, gray red? If the rug you saw was a dull, dark red, you probably found that you had to use at least *three* terms, something like those mentioned, to describe the color with even reasonable accuracy.

Color has *three dimensions* or *attributes*. They are *hue, value,* and *intensity.* These three dimensions we will look at separately in order to understand better how all three of them combine to produce the world of color that we know. Our study will be concerned only with color obtained through pigments.

Hue, the First Dimension

Hue is the name of a color. Blue, red, green, yellow, purple, and orange are color names or hues. We see immediately that hue, alone, says very little about color; it does not say anything about its lightness or darkness (value) or its brightness or dullness (intensity). But about hue alone there is a considerable amount of information good to know and much easier to grasp if the other two dimensions of color are momentarily held off.

Look at the hues labeled (1) on the color wheel (Figure 125). They are red, yellow, blue—the *primary hues.* Since they cannot be obtained by mixing other pigments, they are "originals" or "primaries." If they are combined in the proper amounts, these primaries will produce nearly every other known hue. They are basic; from them comes the infinite variety of color we see in art products.

The hues labeled (2) on the color wheel stand between the primaries and are formed by mixing equal parts of two primaries. These are the *secondary hues*—green comes from equal parts of blue and yellow; purple from red and blue; orange from red and yellow.

The hues labeled (3) are produced by mixing a primary with a secondary hue. These hues are known as the *tertiary* hues and complete our twelve-hued color wheel.

The color wheel demonstrates one point: hues are changed by adding or combining neighboring hues. Red, for instance, became red-violet when it was combined with violet. If more violet were added, the hue would be changed again. Actually, then, the twelve hues on the color wheel are only a beginning. There can be an infinite number of hues.

Hues also have an effect ranging from warmth to coolness. Red, red-orange, orange, yellow-orange, and yellow are warm hues, associated as they are with the sun, fire and other sources of heat. Conspicuous, cheerful, and stimulating are these warm hues; they stand out prominently, have an effect of coming towards you and for this reason are called *advancing* as well as *warm* hues. A red flower is conspicuous from a distance, a red bathing suit stands out above others on a beach. In contrast to these warm hues are the *cool* ones: green, blue-green, blue, blue-violet and violet. They are inconspicuous, restful, and sometimes depressing. Instead of advancing, they *recede* and are known as *receding* hues. They call less attention to themselves as, for example, blue blossoms in a flower patch. They also suggest distance, since faraway objects—mountains, trees, and so on—generally appear more bluish than those near by. There are also some borderline hues, like yellow-green and red-violet. They have neither outstanding warmth nor retreating coolness and seem to possess instead an odd combination of these two qualities. They appear to stand midway between "red hot" and "blue with cold."

Painters make good use of this characteristic of hue. If a painter wishes a landscape to be cheerful and stimulating, he uses reds and yellows, the warm colors. If he wants the opposite effect, cool hues will dominate his canvas. In neither case, however, will his painting be uniformly warm or cold. Foreground objects will be in warm, advancing colors; background objects in cool, receding colors. This is one means of establishing a feeling of distance in a painting. But there are exceptions to this general observation; look for them the next time you visit an exhibition of paintings.

Besides warmth and coolness, hues have another characteristic which arises from the effect different colors have upon each other when they are placed side by side. Some combinations of hues are especially harmonious when used together, such as blue, blue-green, and green. There appears to be no conflict or clash, but rather a restful sensation. On the other hand, if blue is placed beside orange, there is an immediate feeling of conflict or opposition or excitement. Hues, then, when placed side by side, may produce effects ranging from harmony to contrast. Furthermore, from looking at the color wheel, we see that hues adjacent to each other are the more harmonious, and those opposite from each other are the more contrasting. Those hues which are adjacent to each other on the color wheel (for example, red, red-violet, violet) are spoken of as neighboring, related, or *analogous* hues. From hues arranged this way we get color harmonies. Hues that lie opposite each other on the color wheel (for example, red and green) are called *complementary* hues, and complementary hues are the ones that give us contrast.

If any two complementary colors are mixed in proper amounts in the pigment pot, they will produce gray or complete neutrality. If they are not mixed, but are placed next to each other in their pure states, they intensify each other. Red, next to green, appears redder than when alone, and the green appears greener than when seen in isolation. Blue and orange, yellow and violet—these complementary hues affect each other similarly. This phenomenon, known as simultaneous contrast, is of the greatest importance in combining colors. Thus, if a person is sun-tanned, but wishes to look even more bronzed, he will wear blue or blue-green to contrast with the color of his skin because the skin is a red-orange (higher in value and lower in intensity than the red-orange on the color wheel). What would a red-cheeked person wear who wished to appear less florid? A sallow person who wished to appear to have more color?

Although many historic painters were familiar with these phenomena, the first group of painters to make extensive use of the effects resulting from a careful juxtaposition of hues was the school known as the Impressionist. These artists found, for example, that a green lawn in a painting appeared to be a more brilliant and vibrant green if painted by laying streaks of yellow next to streaks of blue—in other words, if the secondary hue (green) were broken * into its two primary components, blue and yellow. The pigments applied to the canvas in this way gave the effect of being combined when observed from a short distance. By working in this way, this school of painters were able to reproduce certain effects of light with uncanny accuracy and vitality.

Value, the Second Dimension

Value describes the lightness or darkness of a color. It has been mentioned before that every hue possesses a certain degree of lightness or darkness. The value scale (Figure 125) shows seven value steps of green, orange and violet which are labeled *high light, light, low light, middle, high dark, dark,* and *low dark.* Adding white to the top and black to the bottom gives nine regular steps. This classification is somewhat arbitrary:

---

* From the fact that the Impressionists broke their colors down into the primary hues comes the expression "broken color."

actually there may be an almost infinite number of degrees of lightness and darkness.

The hues in the color wheel also differ in value. Yellow is very light, violet is very dark, and the other hues range between these extremes. The values in which the hues are shown in the color wheel are known as normal values; that is, the values most characteristic of each hue. They correspond to the seven steps in the value scale. Thus, starting at the top of the color wheel, and going down either side we get:

Value Step	*Hue*	*Hue*
White		
High light	Yellow	Yellow
Light	Yellow-green	Yellow-orange
Low light	Green	Orange
Middle	Green-blue	Orange-red
High dark	Blue	Red
Dark	Blue-violet	Red-violet
Low dark	Violet	Violet
Black		

A moment's reflection will show that we ordinarily think of hues in somewhat this way: yellow, for instance, usually comes to mind as a light, bright yellow—the color of a lemon or a dandelion. Violet usually is thought of as a dark color—the color of a violet or grapes or plums. To be sure, there are dark yellows and light violets, but these are not characteristic values. In this connection there is an opportunity to clear up a common misuse of color terminology. The words *tint* and *shade* are often incorrectly used. Tints are values above the normal, shades are values below normal. Thus, pink is a tint of red, maroon is a shade of the same hue; sky-blue is a tint, navy-blue is a shade.

How is the value of a hue changed? When we *raise* the value of a hue, we add more light to it; we make it capable of reflecting more light. If we wish to *lower* the value of a hue, we reduce the light which it can reflect. With pigments this is most readily done by adding white or black, although the process of raising or lowering the value of pigments is apt to be accompanied by unavoidable changes in hue and intensity.

And now that definitions are completed, we can see what different values can do.

First, what effect does value have on the apparent size of an object? Usually, but not always, the higher the value the larger the object appears to be. Many are the ways in which this observation can be carried into daily living. Darker clothes help make the overweight person look smaller; lighter clothes help the underweight person seem heavier. Painting the walls of a room in high values makes the room seem larger and more spacious; painting a house dark makes it appear smaller. *But* the value contrast between an object and its background is also important because great contrast makes the object conspicuous. Thus, a davenport or chair covered in dark material will probably look larger against a white background than would one upholstered in lighter material. In general, high values increase apparent size—but not always.

Second, what is the relation between values and apparent distance? When you look out over a view that includes distant trees as well as those near by, you will observe a difference in the appearance of the trees. The faraway ones, of course, seem smaller—but what about the values? Besides appearing smaller, the distant trees will be lighter in value and will show less contrast. It will be almost impossible to distinguish between one tree and another because there is so little contrast in values. The nearby trees, on the other hand, will show a great variety of values. Lighter and less contrasting values make objects appear far away.

In art, these observations on value changes effected by distance are in common use. It is the constant problem of the landscape painter to make his flat canvas convey the impression of space. From observing natural effects, he paints foreground trees in striking value contrasts and generally darker than those in the background. Already we have mentioned that he employs warm colors for the foreground and emphasizes them with cooler colors in the distance. Thus he uses both value and hue to create a feeling of space on his canvas. If he paints an abstract composition, he follows the same principles, for, in abstractions as in naturalistic work, some planes recede, others advance. These observations are used by other artists as well. Architects and interior architects also increase or decrease apparent sizes by using value wisely. A ceiling that is too high, for instance—what can be done to make it look lower?

Third, how do value contrasts affect the outlines of objects? Compare Figures 128 and 130. In which of them do you see the individual objects most quickly and clearly? You will see at once that strong value contrasts emphasize silhouettes, thereby calling attention to the objects; closely related values tend to minimize shapes and outlines. In "Resistance" the figure and goat in the right foreground and the buildings in the left background are scarcely noticeable whereas in "Diversification" the bottles and shoe seen against the chair or the fruit and vegetables against the cabinet are easily perceived. In "Resistance" everything builds into and reinforces the central figure to portray the unity of all forces in a struggle; nothing stands alone. In "Diversification" the diversity of packaged products is expressed by black and white separation of the many objects.

Painters make conspicuous use of this phenomenon. Notice in Rubens' "Descent from the Cross" (Figure 132) how those heads in strong value contrast to their backgrounds stand out much more clearly than do the others. Or compare the living room and the hat store shown in Figures 129 and 131. In the living room, the value range is small and one object blends with the other. In the hat store, the light value of the case and table make them very conspicuous when seen against the dark floor. These two rooms represent equally good—but different—ways of handling value contrasts.

Fourth, what happens when two different values are seen so that one is the background? If the darker value is in the background, the value seen against it will appear lighter. The reverse of this is likewise true. It is not an uncommon experience for drapery clerks to have people bring back draperies with the remark that there had been a substitution, that the draperies delivered were not the ones selected in the store. If you find that a dark-blue chintz displayed against a wood-paneled wall is much to your liking, remember what will happen to it if you hang it against cream-colored walls at home. It will look gloomy, much darker than it did in the store. It is well to remember that values in themselves are of much less importance than values in relation to their surroundings.

Intensity, the Third Dimension

Intensity, the third dimension of color, refers to brightness or dullness (purity, saturation, or pigment strength) of a color. Notice that when we say a color is bright we do not necessarily mean that it is light. Intensity describes the grayness or degree of neutrality of a hue, and is independent of value. Thus, pink is a light red, but it may be dull or bright in intensity. In other words, pink is a high value of red, but it may be of any intensity ranging from a bright pink to a dull pink. In the case of the red carpet, *intensity* tells how bright or pure the red is, and *value* tells how light or dark it is.

The scale of intensities (Figure 125) shows two degrees between full intensity and neutral for six hues. The intensity of a hue is lowered by mixing it with its complementary; that is, yellow with violet, blue with orange, and red with green. Notice that midway between each of the pairs of complementary hues, both in the color wheel and in the intensity scale, is gray or complete neutrality.

Intensity differences may be described as *full intensity, two-thirds intensity, two-thirds neutral,* and *neutral.* There can, of course, be many more intensity steps than those indicated and named above, but these have been found convenient to remember and use.

Now is the time to complicate the problem. *We can vary the intensity of any value of a hue.* It is possible to take a low-value red (maroon) and vary the intensity to produce intense maroons and dull maroons— but we find that the brightest maroon we can make is less intense than normal red. Similarly, lavender is never as intense as violet. From this we learn that the full intensity of a hue occurs when that hue is at its normal value (as in the color wheel, Figure 125) and, further, that raising or lowering that value of a hue *from normal* automatically lowers its intensity.

The final observation regarding intensity is again the question of relationships. You will notice in the colors around you that the apparent intensity of a color depends to a large extent on the surroundings in which it is used. You can easily conduct a series of simple experiments which will illustrate this far better than words can. Hold a piece of bright green paper or cloth in front of (1) dull red, (2) white, (3) black, (4) bright blue, (5) bright yellow. Does the background alter the brightness of the green? Against which background does it seem most intense? With intensity as with value, relationships are more important than the thing itself. Colors can be made to seem more or less intense, depending on their surroundings.

ON USING COLOR

Color plays such an important role in our lives that it is logical to suggest that the use of it be governed by the way it affects us. We assume that a baby's discrimination of distance and form is not sharp because he reaches for every brightly colored thing that comes within the range of his vision. As he grows older, he gains a better understanding of distance and form until, finally, he is able to distinguish subtle variations in form and even small units of distance. Color, as light reflected from objects, has played a major role in enabling him to understand spatial relations. Definiteness of planes, sharpness of edges, value contrast and color intensity were some of the clues by which he learned to distinguish cubes from spheres, near objects from distant ones. A cube, for example, he saw as three planes, each different in hue and value, related at right angles, and with sharp edges. A cone or sphere was marked by subtle gradations, showed no sharp edges. Distant objects were less definite, had smaller contrasts of hue, value, and intensity.

Color has also a strong effect on our moods. Church architects consciously plan not only the shape of the building but the color as well, in order to put the observer in a religious mood. Were the same architects to design a tea-room or a service station, they would use colors in different relationships from those in a church.

Since color does have this influence on us, psychologists and artists have spent much time investigating it. Some of their findings are these:

1. *Stimulation:* red, yellow, and orange are the most exciting and stimulating hues; green is fairly neutral; some blues and violets affect us as grave, somber, or depressing.

2. *Attention Value:* red, black, green, and orange attract most attention when seen against white. The advertiser who wishes to attract your attention to his poster will use red because he has found that color to be the most efficient color for this purpose. Check—you will find that red is the color most frequently used in advertisements. But it is also true that in some instances advertisers want you to read their message from a distance, and for this purpose black on yellow is superior to any other combination. Many state highway departments have found that motorists find it easier to read road signs with black letters painted on a yellow ground. Architects make similar use of colors in creating focal points in rooms; painters also, in attracting your eye to the important parts of their pictures. An unusual situation, however, attracts more attention than a commonplace one: a red coat on a man would attract more attention than a red coat on a woman. Strong hue contrasts, especially of complementary colors, also arrest the observer's attention.

3. *Color Preferences:* red and blue are the most popular colors, yellow and orange the least. Fairly pure colors (when seen alone) are preferred to those of low intensity. On the whole, women prefer lighter colors,

men prefer darker. So far the results of the tests are fairly consistent, but when the preference for combinations of color is studied, there is almost no agreement. While it is true that from time to time fads bring certain color combinations into prominence, such preferences seldom endure long.

By pulling these observations together, expanding them and adding to them, we can outline a few generalizations about the intelligent use of color. No principle is always good; do not expect these to be infallible. They are suggestions, not rules.

1. A Color Scheme Should Have a Basic Plan or Idea

Art is generally more pleasing when it develops from a basic plan or idea. Color and color schemes are no exception. When working with color, decide what general effect you want and what special conditions you are trying to satisfy. Do you want the result to be stimulating or restful, bright or dull, loud or quiet, cool or warm, harmonious or contrasting, striking or unobtrusive? Colors producing these effects have been worked out into more or less formalized color schemes because it has been found that they follow certain general patterns and that these patterns are capable of wide usage. In the following pages where these types are discussed, the examples given for each one will use colors that occur on the twelve-color wheel (Figure 125). But do not forget all our discussions on hue, value, and intensity—that these three dimensions of color may be subjected to innumerable variations. Blue and orange, for instance, at normal value and full intensity would create an effect harsh and even garish. But think for a moment how these two colors may be altered, how they appear in different situations, as a dark brown suit with a blue tie, natural oak furniture against a royal blue wall, brown oak leaves against a blue sky or storm clouds, a blue bathing suit on a sun-tanned body. Some of the more typical, basic color schemes are discussed in the following paragraphs.

Color schemes of related or harmonious colors tend to give a quiet, restful effect if strong value contrasts and strong intensities are avoided. Schemes of this type are composed of variations of one hue or of several hues which lie close together on the color wheel. The simplest of these is the *monochromatic*, in which all colors are of one hue. Monochromatic color schemes may be made entirely of blues (light blue, medium blue, navy blue), or of greens (light green, dark green, gray-green), or of oranges (tan, orange, brown), or of any one hue. The word

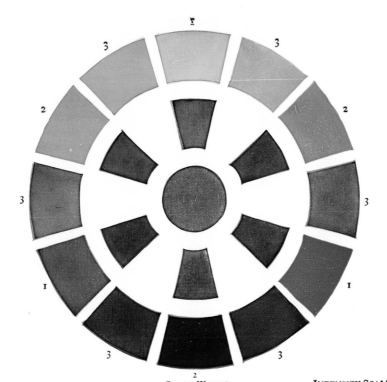

VALUE SCALE COLOR WHEEL INTENSITY SCALE

High light — Full intensity

Light — Two-thirds intensity

Low light — Two-thirds neutral

Middle — Neutral

High dark — Two-thirds neutral

Dark — Two-thirds intensity

Low dark — Full intensity

The color wheel shows a sequence of hues in the following order, beginning with yellow at the top and proceeding clockwise: yellow, yellow-green, green, blue-green, blue, blue-violet, violet, red-violet, red, orange-red, orange, yellow-orange.

The value scale shows seven values each for the three hues: green, orange, and violet. Those containing white disks are at full intensity.

The intensity scale shows two different degrees between full intensity and neutral for six hues. The intensity is lowered by mixing the hue with its complementary, the hue on the opposite side of the color wheel. The dimensions are approximate only. (From *The Art of Enjoying Art* by A. Philip MacMahon as adapted from *Commercial Art* by C. E. Wallace; by permission of McGraw-Hill.)

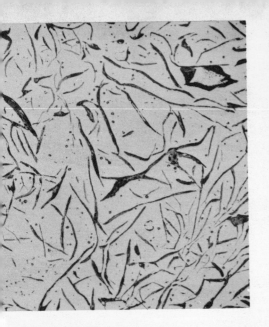

126. (*Upper*) Microphotography reveals the structure of selenite (*left*) and cast iron (*right*) and shows varied textural patterns.

127. (*Lower*) Paul Klee's "Beride (Town by the Water)" weaves water, boats, docks, buildings, and a person into a pattern of textures.

RESISTANCE! U. S. supplies to Yugoslav patriots—in paper packages.

CONTAINER CORPORATION OF AMERICA

An advertisement and a living room in which closely related values tend to merge varied forms.

128 (*Upper*) In Tibor Gergely's "Resistance" people, buildings, and landscape become closely related by means of limited value contrasts and liberal use of textures.

129. (*Lower*) In the living room designed by Michael Goodman, objects are drawn together by means similar to those used in the poster above.

An advertisement and store with sharply defined forms resulting from strong value contrasts.

130. (*Upper*) A. M. Cassandre's "Diversification" deliberately brings each of the many objects into prominence by skillful use of black against white.

131. (*Lower*) In the hat store designed by Edwin H. Cordes objects are clearly separated by value contrasts.

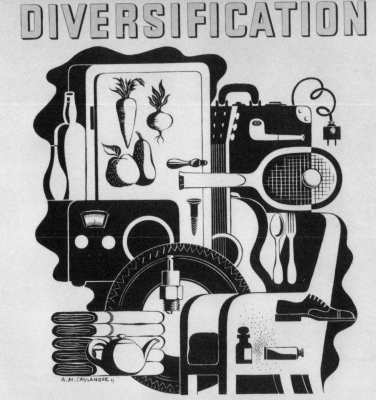

DIVERSIFICATION

A paperboard package for every product

CONTAINER CORPORATION OF AMERICA

A.M. CASSANDRE 17

132. Peter Paul Rubens' "Descent from the Cross" magnificently integrates all
the plastic elements in a profoundly expressive painting.

monochromatic, then, simply means "one hue." In this scheme it is necessary to vary the values and intensities. Naturally, if a monochromatic scheme is unified to a high degree, it may even become dull and monotonous if this unity is not handled carefully.

Analogous schemes are composed of hues and their variations occurring next to each other on the color wheel; for example: blue-green, blue, and blue-violet; or yellow, yellow-orange, and orange. The colors in an analogous scheme must have some basic hue in common. In the first example given it was blue; in the second, yellow. Analogous schemes offer more chance for variety in clothing ensembles, interior decoration and window displays. In general, related color schemes (monochromatic or analogous) are restful and harmonious, and are used for those art objects which we spend considerable time with, such as our rooms or our clothes.

Color schemes of contrasting colors are at once more stimulating and, perhaps because of this, harder to handle. Opposing rather than related hues are used. In this group of contrasting schemes, the simplest is the *complementary*. Here the basic hues are any pair occurring opposite each other on the color wheel: red and green, red-orange and blue-green, violet and yellow.

A modification of this is the *split-complementary* which is composed of any one hue and the two hues located on each side of its complement. An example of a split-complementary scheme is yellow with red-violet and blue-violet. Violet, the complement of yellow, was split into blue-violet and red-violet. Thus the contrast is less shocking than in the simple, complementary scheme.

Another color scheme is known as the *double-complementary*. Here we use two adjacent hues with their respective complements. Observe the color wheel again as we select a typical double-complementary scheme: red-orange and orange with blue-green and blue.

The final type of contrasting scheme is the *triad*. This is a brilliant color scheme made from any three hues that are located equidistant from each other. Red, yellow, and blue or yellow-orange, blue-green, and red-violet are typical examples of triad color schemes.

By way of summary we find that there are two general groups of color schemes: those made of related colors and those made of contrasting colors. In the first group there are these types: monochromatic and analogous. In the second group there are: complementary, split-complementary, double-complementary, and triad. Look about you for examples of these types. What type of scheme are you wearing today? What type was used to decorate your room? What type of scheme do you prefer in your clothing and surroundings?

2. *Color Should Be Related to the Forms on Which It Is Used*

Imagine for a moment that you are an interior decorator and that your client wishes to have two rooms decorated. One is a bedroom for a young girl which is to be furnished with graceful, slender furniture; the other is a man's den which is to be furnished with solid, masculine-appearing pieces. Would you use heavy, rich colors on the delicate furniture or the massive pieces? The heaviness and solidity of the furniture in the den suggest rich, dark colors, do they not? In this same way the industrial designer plans for the colors of his products; so, too, does the painter for his paintings. Each tries to emphasize the fundamental character of the art object by selecting colors which have the same general feeling as the forms. The color grows out of and is dependent on the basic form.

In great art such relationships of form and color occur naturally, inevitably—the artist is probably not aware of them as such, although he has undoubtedly spent many hours achieving mastery over his materials and techniques. The artist's chief aim is to communicate something to you. He selects both forms and colors to build and express his message. If he is designing a typewriter, he wants it to look efficient. He wants the chair that he designs to appear to be comfortable. Naturally, then, form and color must be similar in character because the two must play together, must aid each other.

3. *Large Areas Are Generally Low in Intensity—Small Areas Bright*

This is the Law of Areas, a safe guide to color usage, and one which is followed quite generally. The large elements in a room—the walls, floor, furniture—are usually duller than the small accents—vases, lamps, pictures. Buildings often have small areas of bright decoration against large walls of low intensity colors. A dress may be gray or blue with a few touches of bright color. The Law of Areas always produces conservative effects which at worst may be dull, at best dignified. But what about an evening dress which is a bright scarlet or a brilliant blue? Or a painting or a room done entirely in vivid hues in large areas? Paintings, rooms, evening dresses and other art objects which disregard the Law of Areas are striking and stimulating, and the reasons for disregarding the principle are, therefore, justifiable. Exceptions, it seems, can be quite as important as the rule.

4. Simultaneous Contrast May Alter the Appearance of Any Color

If you turn back and read about simultaneous contrast, it will not be necessary to develop this point more than to call attention to the fact that hues, values, and intensities affect each other. This can be a fascinating study in itself.

5. Other Guides

Equality of hue, value, or intensity—since it gives no emphasis or contrast—is usually not as pleasant as variety. Just as some parts of music should be louder, some softer, so some portions of art objects should be brighter, duller, darker, lighter. Notice that if you vary hue, value or intensity, interest and attention are more easily aroused.

Light-yellow, orange, and red (and their variations) are the most unifying colors. They appear to draw together any objects seen against them. Blues and greens—the cool hues—tend to separate objects for which they form the background. This suggestion has many applications, but one common one occurs in furniture arrangement. If you wish the pieces of furniture in your living room to seem closely related, give them a warm background. If you wish each piece to stand out more or less prominently, give the furniture a cool background.

Color applied in equal-sized areas is just as unsatisfactory as equality of hue, value, or intensity. A painting in which the areas of color are equal will not hold your attention long. It is difficult to find a painting in which this occurs, although there are many examples of living rooms in which no color predominates, in which all seems monotonously the same.

The discussion of color has included many principles and ideas. Before going on to the summary it would be well to review these. The best way is to apply them to things in your everyday life: your clothes, your home, your town. Ask yourself many questions. To what type of color scheme does your own room belong? How could it be improved? Does it have too many colors—or too few? Does it look cluttered and confused—or monotonous? What color or colors would you use on the walls if you could repaint them?

Do the clothes that you have on today follow any basic color scheme? How would you describe it? Could you have made a better selection from the clothes you now own? Which colors are most suitable for you? Why?

Is the town in which you live cheerful and colorful, or is it drab and depressing? Would you like to see more color used in architecture? Have you noticed the subtle colors of natural materials—the differences among various woods, stones, and fibers? Have you observed the differences in color among the so-called white metals—nickel, chromium, aluminum, stainless steel? If you have not, start looking at once. Becoming sensitive to color variations in nature and art is a stimulating pastime. Enjoy it!

THE FIVE PLASTIC ELEMENTS: CONCLUSION

The plastic elements described above are important to the degree to which they affect human beings in the normal activities of life. Following are excerpts from a letter written by a woman after living in her modern, functionally designed house—a house in which form, line, color, texture, and space were carefully considered to achieve the two aims of organization: FORM FOLLOWS FUNCTION and VARIETY IN UNITY. In her letter she tells how these elements governed not only her way of living, but the ways of her children and husband—the whole family:

> Yesterday and today have been two very hot days, but our new house is very cool both to bodily and emotional feel. We are so excited these days—after years of living in old, inefficient houses—finding out that ours is acting as the architect said it would. It is now over 90 degrees outside, but the indoor thermometer registers 76 degrees, and we haven't even begun using our cooling system yet—such is modern insulation.
>
> Still more I would be interested in studying the psychological effect of color and space on people. I know that the effect of these on the insane has been worked on, but I mean color and space on normal people like us. It seems that in this house we just can't be tense and tied in knots. The minute we enter it our worries and burdens seem to drop at the door and leave us free. The rowdy youngsters are less boisterous and quarrel-

some, and yet by no means unnaturally so. Our friends all wonder what has happened to my husband. Instead of being somewhat morose and silent—as he usually has been, poor man, with all the responsibilities of his office hounding him at home too—he has become very chatty and genial. That boredom which showed up when he was with dull people seems to have left him.

The hours are never long enough we spend in this house. It has had a very disastrous effect on me. I don't want to do a thing when I close the door behind me and find myself inside but, like Ferdinand the Bull, just sit and look and listen and smell and feel. If I didn't have League work to do and deadlines to meet I would lead just such a pleasant animal life as his. This is what a real house does to us all.

A HAT STORE

We look now at the way in which the five plastic elements have been organized in an attractive store designed to sell men's hats (Figure 131). From the viewpoint of function, notice first that the merchandise is well displayed, permitting the customer to get up to and handle the hats if he wishes. The stock is displayed on open shelves and in this way the hats themselves become one of the chief decorative features of the store. The whole interior is businesslike and masculine; it gives an impression of orderliness and decision that should help a man in that difficult task of choosing a hat.

Form and Line

The basic form of the store is given by the enclosing walls, ceiling, and floor. This determines to a large degree the final appearance. The irregularity of the walls furnishes a note of informality which has been carried out in the entire scheme. The recessed shelves, indirectly lighted, are simple rectangles with metal shelves accentuating the horizontal lines which dominate the entire scheme. The display cases and tables have rounded corners because they permit easy traffic through the store and because the rounded forms offer a needed variation from what might have been an excessive rectangularity. The furniture is mainly of two types. A settee, built into one corner of the room, becomes part of the architectural background quite as much as do the display shelves. The

217

metal chairs, on the other hand, contrast in every way with the background, and, consequently, stand out as decorative accents. The repetition of round shapes in the hats and lighting fixtures performs a similar function of decorative accent. This type of treatment, where a few rounded shapes are used in contrast with many squared ones, is an excellent example of variety in unity.

Color

The four walls are paneled in pine, finished not in the conventional manner but with a bluish-gray cast. With the royal blue carpet, this gives the store a generally cool color scheme and, consequently, a soothing, restful appearance. Color contrasts have been provided in the terra-cotta red hat cases which were installed as a part of the wall treatment. The furniture is upholstered in chartreuse, yellow, orange, and maroon; the large maple tables are painted chartreuse; and the interiors of the tie cases are yellow. Thus, a *triad* color scheme has been used against a neutral background. Additional contrast is provided by the silvery aluminum chair frames and hat racks and the mural painting of old New York. Notice, too, that the value pattern is good: the dark floor gives a feeling of solidity, the light walls of openness. The hats and neckwear are contrasted well with the background. The aim of the designers of this shop was to use color so that the discriminating might purchase their hats in this shop; and they succeeded admirably.

Texture

Perhaps the most noticeable textures are those of the natural woods in the walls and furniture. The plate glass used throughout the store creates, of course, a familiar contemporary smooth surface. The softness of the carpet contrasts with the hard plastered ceiling, the smooth metal chair frames and shelves. The merchandise itself furnishes still more rich textures from fabrics of many kinds. In the painting above the mirror there is an accenting texture directing attention to one of the chief focal points in the shop—a place where a customer may sit and rest.

These textures are calculated to display the merchandise and to sell it. It is the purpose of everything in the shop to throw the merchandise into relief, to call the customer's attention to it. By using background textures that are smooth and hard, the goods for sale, since they are soft and rich in tactile qualities, are in striking contrast—this is a far better way to show merchandise than to have the background texture the same as the goods. This is good business, good psychology, good art.

Space

Have you ever gone into stores, especially china and glass stores, where too much merchandise displayed on too many small tables gave you the feeling that you were in constant danger of knocking something over? But this hat store offers striking contrast to that type of planning, for here the open space invites you to roam around, to go from one display to another. The horizontal lines in the shelves and fixtures have been carefully calculated to lead your eye around so that you become fully conscious of spaciousness and of hats. The plain dark carpet, contrasting with the lighter walls and furniture, adds to this feeling of roominess. The vertical lines in the paneling above the cases, in the doors and mirrors, emphasize the vertical space (or height) of the room. The irregular walls, dividing the store into several interesting units, offer a measuring stick with which to estimate the space far more easily than if the walls were straight and without variety. The plan shows that this irregularity in the walls came about also as a means of providing storage space, shipping rooms, and service rooms. Another means of helping you get your bearings and estimating spaces is in the placing of accents, such as the small round display table, the square table and chair, and the neckwear case. All in all, space has been wisely utilized in this store; like its fellow elements, form, line, color, and texture, it plays its part in making this a successful hat store.

RUBENS' "DESCENT FROM THE CROSS"

In concluding this discussion let us turn from contemporary examples to a great work of the past (Figure 132) which magnificently integrates the plastic elements. Created between 1611 and 1614 by Peter Paul Rubens, the greatest of the seventeenth-century Flemish painters, "Descent from the Cross" orchestrates form, texture, color, and space symphonically. The eight figures are organized around the central body of Christ in a dynamic complex of curves with a predominant downward movement expressive of tragedy. Form is depicted in a genuinely plastic manner, sharp and well defined at times, merging into the enveloping space at others. The varied textures of rough and glistening textiles, wood and metal, ground and sky, flesh and hair, not only strengthen the representation of form but add visual enrichment through their unified variety. Using the full range of color possibilities, Rubens ran the gamut of light to dark values, pure to neutral intensities, warm to cool hues to produce a rich, vibrant chromatic effect.

The spatial organization merits special attention because this painting shows deep understanding of pictorial composition. It is not merely a two-dimensional design, nor is it merely a record of what the eye sees or the camera reproduces. Based on interweaving diagonals, attention is carried obliquely from top to bottom, side to side, near to far. The dominant spatial movement is between the two figures at the top of the cross through the white cloth and body of Christ to the three Marys in the left foreground. This is balanced and strengthened by subordinate movements between far objects at the left and near objects at the right, especially the movement from the two figures on the ladder through the head of Christ to the head of the bearded man. A sense of scale and of deep space is given if one looks from the bowl in the lower right corner (the object nearest the spectator) diagonally to the small tree in the distance at the left (the object farthest from the spectator). Paintings such as this show the esthetic possibilities of the plastic elements.

What has been done in this section might well be done for any art object. Try it with the Johnson house or the Carpenter garden in Chapter 1, Refregier's mural in Chapter 2, or the Leversbach Church in Chapter 3. Then look about you—your room, your college library, your most recent purchase, the advertising across the way. How have the plastic elements been used in each of these?

Of the books on this subject we suggest:

Faber Birren: *The Story of Color* (Crimson Press, 1941) concerns color in relation to the history of man.

J. C. Chase: *An Artist Talks About Color* (Wiley, 1930) for a first-hand report of what an artist thinks.

H. and V. Goldstein: *Art in Everyday Life* (Macmillan, 1940) for the chapter on color.

Hilaire Hiler: *Color Harmony and Pigments* (Favor, Ruhl, 1942) explains one artist's system in detail.

Gyorgy Kepes: *The Language of Vision* (Theobald, 1944) is a stimulating account of visual elements and their psychological effect.

M. Luckiesh: *Color and Colors* (Chapman, 1939) tells more of the nature of color and its use.

M. Luckiesh: *The Language of Color* (Dodd, Mead, 1930) is an interesting, non-technical discussion of the effects of color

L. Moholy-Nagy: *Vision in Motion* (Theobald, 1947) is an extremely significant discussion of the plastic elements in relation to various fields of art.

Ralph Pearson: *Experiencing Pictures* (Brewer, Warren & Putnam, 1932) gives an excellent discussion of the plastic elements in relation to various fields of art.

CHAPTER 9

Principles of Design

W E found that when an artist sets out to create an art product in response to human need, the design he seeks is determined by two basic aims: FORM FOLLOWS FUNCTION and VARIETY IN UNITY. To carry out these aims, we found that the artist has at his disposal five plastic elements: *Form, Line, Space, Texture,* and *Color.* But is there anything to guide the artist in organizing these elements. Are there any general principles which will help him to relate forms, colors, and textures to one another in developing a design which has functional form and unified variety.

It would be strange indeed if, after man had been practicing art for untold centuries, there were no such principles. They exist and they are basic to all art. However, one must not assume that they are formulas of success, or that they are easy to apply. The principles of design are not hard-and-fast, narrow rules, which set boundaries on what the artist can do, but are rather norms established by many generations of men.

Perhaps it would be well for us to approach a study of these principles through observation, by making a somewhat detailed comparative analysis of two house exteriors. One of these houses has been selected because it is attractive; the other, because it is unattractive. It will be our task, through observing the way in which each of them has been designed, to see precisely why one of them is more pleasant than is the other.

TWO HOUSES

Look at Figures 133 and 134. In Chapter 1, we observed that a house should be functional and meet individual needs, be related to its site and its community, be worth the money invested, and be satisfying in appearance. In this comparison we shall assume that these two houses have equally functional plans, are equally well related to their communities, and cost the same amount of money. In other words, we shall compare them on the basis of appearance alone. Holding the above considerations equal, we are struck by the fact that one house is more pleasing than the other. One house looks orderly, unified, inviting, the other ungainly and haphazard. These are total impressions of the houses as *wholes* as we first come upon them, or view them from sufficient distance to see each at a glance. But total impressions, important as they are, do not suffice. Why is one gracious, the other awkward? In many ways the houses are much alike: both are constructed of wood, have sloping roofs and small porches, and have approximately the same number of similarly proportioned openings. The difference lies in the ways the units have been organized.

If we look at the general shapes of the two houses, we find that both of them have similar masses: a large major section to which is added a smaller one. In the first house, the main mass is symmetrical: one half is the mirror image of the other. This symmetry produces an effect of sureness, stability, and repose. The small wing at the right, adding weight to its end of the house, in reality destroys the formal equilibrium established in the main section. This kind of organization, however, has become so sanctioned by tradition that it is accepted without question. Possibly we do not object to it because it relieves the monotony that might result from the too rigid symmetry of dormers, windows, and ornamentation, and gives the house a pleasantly casual air.

The second house certainly pretends to no formal arrangement of its elements. The door is distinctly off-center. It might be argued that the door was set to the left as a counterweight to the small porch on the right, but logical as this sounds, one look at the house tells us that this is no satisfactory explanation. The point of the gable coming in the exact center of the mass sets up a central axis so insistent that it demands respect. Whoever designed the house ignored the dominant centrality and tried to make another center of the doorway. As an afterthought he weakly echoed the stronger axis by placing one insignificant attic window under its apex. Half close your eyes and look at it. You will notice the effect of too much dark on the left side—and that the attic window and gable peak fight with the doorway for the center of balance.

Perhaps the word *balance*, indeed, is one we ought to remember.

223

The Problem of Organization

We can analyze the relationships among the elements in these houses in another way. The first house shows two horizontal parts, each interesting in itself and each related to the other. The door and windows of the dominant main floor achieve horizontal continuity through their uniform heights, repeated shapes, and almost, but not quite, identical spacing. The subordinate roof and dormers energize this pattern through a contrasting, yet related, pattern of repetition. Thus each part has its own measured movement, but there is also a strict vertical relation between the dominant and subordinate parts. Notice the easily perceived and satisfying axial relation of the center dormer to the door, which binds them together vertically. The end dormers, placed midway above the lower openings, accent the strong beat of the first floor openings. Furthermore, if you will cover all but the left end of the house, a triangular relation among the three windows becomes evident, and this triangularity echoes not only the roofs of the dormers but the roof of the whole house.

Even a glance reveals the repetition of horizontals in the roof, clapboards, cornice, and window mullions; and the repetition of verticals in the windows, shutters, chimney, and porch. In order that this recurrence of straight horizontals and verticals does not become too insistent, curves in the porch opening, cornice detail, and window lights in the door add variety. The crisp, lively curves reflect and complement each other, furnish a beat of their own—a counter-beat, subdued and subordinate, which enriches the basic rectangularity. Further study reveals that the doors and windows have approximately the same proportions as the main mass of the house, only turned the other way. The shutters also are similar in proportion to the front wall of the house from ground to cornice. Much of the sense of "belongingness" of the different parts of the house can be accounted for by such relations. The parts are so strongly bound together that we feel a continuing idea pervading the building.

Both openings and materials progress in size from bottom to top. Not only are the windows on the second floor smaller; the shingles are finer in scale than the clapboards below. The larger, stronger, coarser forms are at the bottom and give the house an organic quality—as if it had developed naturally, much as a plant which has large leaves at the base, smaller ones at the top. Such refinements help make a house look strong and stable.

The second house suffers from a notable lack of continuity, especially in the fenestration. The window placement shows no continuity horizontally or vertically, top, bottom, or sides. Although there are only seven openings on the front, there are five different sizes and proportions (as compared with eight openings of three sizes in the first). It is true that all are related through their rectangularity, but their unpatterned placement and varying sizes does not allow this shape similarity to count for much. There is no discernible relation among the proportions of the windows, doors, shutters, and whole house such as there is in the first house. Aside from the inevitable repetition of horizontal and vertical lines, the house stands as a discontinuous assemblage of shapes. It has, in other words, little rhythm or continuity.

Perhaps *rhythm* and *continuity* are two other words worth remembering.

Now for a moment let us consider the houses in another way. While we are still looking at their general shapes, we are bound to notice that one of them gives the effect of being horizontal, lying steadily, as it were, on the ground; while the other seems to have no dominant direction. Is this something important? If we look closer at the first, we find that all the major forces in it are horizontal: the walls of the two masses, the roof, the visual unit of door and windows. This horizontality, of course, is challenged by many verticals: the door, the individual windows, the shutters, the dormers, and the chimney. These units, however, less strong than the horizontals, serve as a contrast to the dominant lines, and give the composition a rightness, a controlled accent that is neither under- nor over-done. The other house looks boxy. Neither verticals nor horizontals dominate, nor have they been used with any perceivable sensitivity to the manner in which they might have related one to another. They neutralize, rather than intensify, each other. We may say in general, then, that shapes which have a definite direction and movement are usually more pleasing. But before we try to draw a principle out of this fact, let us observe some of the individual features of each building.

In both houses the doorways have been accentuated by architectural details. This is as it should be because the doorway, through which we enter and leave a house, deserves attention. In one, the doorway is made to stand out by its size, color, and small panes of glass. Even though it is set apart, one feels its kinship to the other openings on the first floor. In the other, the portico certainly stresses the doorway, but it becomes obtrusive rather than important. The portico is too heavy and crude for the door and, for that matter, for the rest of the house. It leaves the door

225

cringing, cowering, and insignificant—the rest of the house looking weak and fragile. Its relation to the windows is obscure.

The windows of the two houses are also worth study. It will be readily agreed that the windows of a house should express the interior, and in most houses the first floor rooms are of greater importance than are those on the second floor because we spend most of our waking hours in the living, dining, and cooking areas. The windows in the first house form two clearly distinguishable units: those on the first floor tell us through their size and contrasting shutters that they are the major ones, while those in the dormers are clearly secondary. The windows in the second eloquently enough tell us that the third floor is unimportant. But that is not telling us much. How about the first and second floors? Here we find nothing but confusion. There is no stress, no emphasis on what is important.

And perhaps *emphasis* is also an important word to keep in mind.

In our discussion of the two houses, we have inevitably touched on the way that various plastic elements may be used to produce different effects, and we have seen that *balance, continuity,* and *emphasis* are important elements in determining whether these effects are pleasing or displeasing. But what about the aims of organization as regards these houses? Does the maintenance of balance, continuity, and emphasis help the artist achieve these aims? Let us look at the houses briefly once again.

Most of us will agree that a house should look homelike, that it should not only function well but should express its *function* through its *form.* Although there is no single form that expresses "home" to everyone, most persons would agree that one looks more like a home than does the other. Why is this true? In large part because the low horizontal mass of the first house rests securely on the ground and thereby gives a feeling of repose and belongingness. Such horizontality is restful and makes a house appear comfortable and inviting. Then, too, one has a sense of order which contrasts strongly with the haphazard awkwardness of the other. Such factors as these contribute toward making the first house a structure expressing pleasant living.

There is little question about which of the two houses is more unified. The door and four windows on the first floor of the first house are similar in character and shape and are aligned across the top. Thus, these five elements form a major visual unit. But notice that each set of two windows becomes a secondary unit because the spaces between them are less than the spaces between the door and the windows. Variety has thus come in to give interest and vitality to what might have been a monotonous repetition of similar shapes. Such variety in spacing quickens and enlivens a design. The three dormer windows add further variety through their position and shape, yet they are clearly related to the total design. In contrast to the basic rectangularity, curves appear in three places. Even the curves vary one from another. Thus, unity is achieved through a major consistency of shape and placement, but monotony is avoided through obvious and subtle variations.

Whereas all of the parts in one house are of a piece and fit together nicely, those in the other have no consistent relation. The house appears to have been built without a well-prepared design, as though it had been assembled by adding one thing to another. Parts are repeated and parts are varied, yet the result is both chaotic and monotonous. It emerges with no basic unity—and with no interesting variety.

We have used these two houses to introduce the discussion of design because they are relatively simple in organization and because they represent the type of design you can see in the residential sections of your own community. The fact that one is superior to the other can be analyzed and explained in simple terms. This should not lead you to think, however, that all design in art is as rudimentary as are these houses. Basically perhaps it is, for even the most complex and intense designs of Michelangelo, El Greco, or Frank Lloyd Wright can be reduced to simple outlines. But in developing these outlines into full-fledged plastic organizations, such artists exhibit enormous range of imaginative yet ordered relationships, surprising yet consistent nuances, dynamic yet controlled contrasts, so that their work is as powerful—and as subtle—as life itself. Forms intensely express their function, unity pervades each variation. They handle their ideas and materials with such consummate mastery that in the presence of their great works one shares the exhilaration and satisfaction of magnificent creativity.

WHY DO WE HAVE "DESIGN"?

Design serves us in several ways.

First, design aids the artist in communicating his idea to the observer. Thus if a designer wishes to create an exciting, dramatic building for a new movie theater, he will organize the parts of the building to produce that effect. In contrast, if he wishes to give an effect of restfulness, ease, and quiet, such as is desirable in a library, he will use a different type of organization. Therefore, when we see an art object, whether a salt cellar or an office building, we ought to view it in terms of the ideas the artist was trying to convey.

In *The Innocents Abroad*, Mark Twain tells how he roared to the captain of the ship taking him back to America that the coffee served at his table was disgraceful. The captain smelled and tasted the brew. Then, smiling benignantly, he said: "It *is* inferior—for *coffee*—but it's pretty fair *tea!*"

We, too, must avoid using "tea" criteria on products intended to have "coffee" characteristics.

The *first* step in communicating the idea is to engage the observer's attention, to focus it on the art object. This is no small task in a world full of lively stimuli hitting our sense organs from all sides. Sometimes the artist has to make his design shout above the clamor of conflicting forces in order to gain our attention. To do this he may resort to strong color contrasts, dynamic diagonal lines or forms, or pictures of unusual objects.

The design, however, must do more than merely attract your attention— it should hold your interest until you get the idea. The design of a roadside advertisement must be such that you get the idea or message while driving along at thirty to fifty miles an hour. You would hardly expect the design of an El Greco painting (Figure 143) to do this. A roadside advertisement is a temporary thing, and must be simple. An El Greco painting tells of more profound matters, and by its complexity requires more time for understanding. Its design will be carefully calculated to hold your attention until you understand the message it bears. It takes a much simpler art message to sell a cigarette than to illumine a deep religious feeling.

Remember well that the fundamental idea which inspired any design is more important than the design itself. The design is merely a means to an end. Sometimes unworthy goals are attained through superb design, as when a well-disciplined army ravages a country. Here the design is excellent, the goal is vicious. Similarly in commerce, the most beautiful advertisement may aim to sell a harmful product. But, fortunately, there are many art objects in which design and idea are both deserving of praise.

228

Two houses of Colonial derivation markedly different in quality of design.

133. (*Upper*) This house has pleasantly proportioned masses, well-organized doors and windows.

134. (*Lower*) In contrast to the above, this house is visually displeasing.

A wood carving and painting which gives an effect of quiet and repose.

135. (*Upper*) "Eagle," carved in wood by an unknown nineteenth-century American, is symmetrically balanced and looks as though it were poised ready for flight.

136. (*Lower*) "Summer Landscape" by Stuart Davis brilliantly portrays the quiet restlessness of a summer day. Notice the balance of light and dark, of varied textures, shapes and sizes. The rhythmic pattern is inventive and playful.

Sculpture and painting with violent action portrayed through active balance of thrust against thrust, tension against tension which express the dynamic movement of a prize fight.

137. (*Upper*) Archipenko's "The Boxers," a terracotta sculpture, shows natural forms simplified and abstracted to emphasize movement and force.

138. (*Lower*) Bellows' "Dempsey and Firpo" vividly reports a knockout blow. The diagonal composition is asymmetrically balanced and the rhythmic pattern is vigorous. The three major figures are emphasized by their size, position, and value contrast with the background.

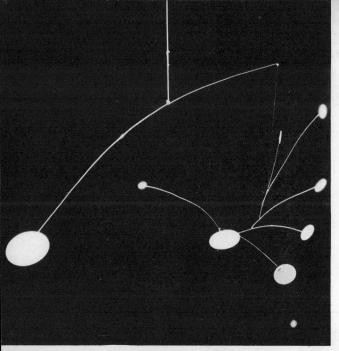

Calder's "Mobile" made of aluminum and steel wire provides convincing evidence of the relation between movement and the principles of design.

139. (*Upper*) At rest, the "mobile" is a subtle example of informal balance, rhythmic shapes and directions, satisfying emphasis and subordination.

140. (*Lower*) In motion, the balance and rhythm become even more evident.

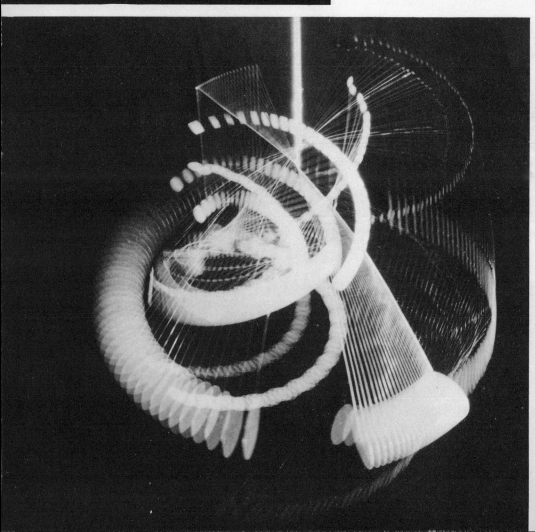

Sculpture and painting with strong pattern of movement achieved in different ways.

141 (*Upper*) Eames' plywood abstraction has unfolding, curvilinear forms reminiscent of the organic nature of wood.

142. (*Lower*) Feininger's "Steamer 'Odin,' II" achieves its continuity through expanding geometric forms.

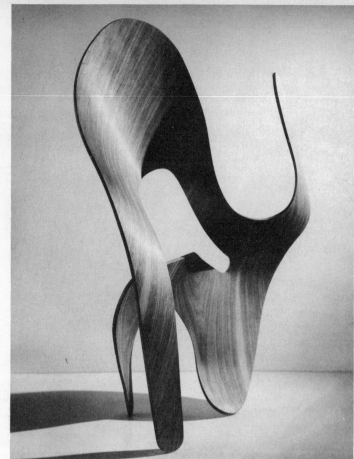

Two paintings markedly different in rhythmic organization.

143. El Greco's "St. Francis in Ecstasy" shows forms pervaded by an intense, all-pervading continuity.

144. Sargent's "The Fountain" shows the forms of man and nature as loosely organized as in a casual snapshot. Although marked by technical brilliance, the painting is little more than a pictorial comment.

Two rooms markedly different in quality of design.

45. (*Upper*) Living room in Hanna House designed by Frank Lloyd Wright. The forces are dynamically balanced, the movements are measured, and the parts are emphasized in proportion to their importance.

46. (*Lower*) Living room in Shoreland Hotel in which the furnishings are indecisively balanced, discontinuous, and all demand attention.

Two illustrations which show the need for visual dominance and subordination in our surroundings.

147. "If you want my advice, I'd get plain curtains. There's so much going on in your rug." Helen Hokinson's cartoon forcefully makes its point.

148. The Royal Courts of Justice in London, England, show a conglomeration of poorly related elements and details which lacks effective dominance and subordination.

Second, design aims to organize the appearance of objects so that they are more readily comprehensible and useful. Nature, in many of her aspects, is chaotic and unorganized from the standpoint of human use. In order to make nature serve our purposes we reorganize her resources: we plant and remove trees to gain better streets and parks in our towns and cities; we reorganize the human form to transform it into sculpture; and we shift and alter the objects in a landscape in order to produce a well-composed painting. In architecture, we plan and order windows, doors, etc., to produce a pleasant, easy-to-look-at pattern; in a room we choose and select furniture with a basic, guiding idea in mind.

Third, design aims to put the observer in harmony with the purpose of the object. As an example, the art discussed in the chapter on Religion was created to place its observers in a religious attitude. This art was spiritual, aspiring, uplifting, eternal. In contrast, the art illustrated in the chapters on Industry and Commerce was businesslike, expressing efficiency, order, regularity. Designers control and direct our actions through the careful choice of forms, colors and directions. It was natural, for instance, that the designers in the Middle Ages should stress vertical directions in their church sculpture and architecture, because the religion of the period emphasized heaven and hell and spires were to point, like long fingers, to heaven itself. And it is natural that present-day designers stress horizontal lines in our airports and railway stations because in them the emphasis is on getting from one place on the earth's surface to another.

Fourth, design often aims to give the observer experiences which are new and expanding, which take him away from the humdrum repetition of eating, sleeping, and working. A magnificent combination of colors, whether in a sunset or an abstract painting, is an event at once stimulating and satisfying. The design of a piece of civic sculpture may at once lift an ordinary citizen from his everyday existence, impress him with the nobility and worth of his community, and help make him a better member of the state.

THE THREE PRINCIPLES OF DESIGN

For centuries men have been struggling with the problems of design, experimenting with colors, forms, and textures. It was gradually found that there were certain principles exemplified not only in works of art but in the products of nature as well. These principles were generalizations based on observations of many examples—observations, furthermore, that are equally applicable to new examples. As these principles of design were discovered and formulated, some used them in studios and classrooms as a short cut to teaching art—a person had only to learn the rules and apply them in order to be an art authority. These principles of design became a formal body of laws which in time began to smell musty, in spite of the fact that nearly every writer on art stated them in a new order. As a revolt against this excess, others approached art with no principles other than those growing out of a particular situation. The first group erred in starting with rules rather than with situations, erred in formulating rigid laws. The second group made the mistake of having no guiding principles as such and thus failed to see how the arts of various periods and in various fields were related.

Between these two extremes there is a middle ground, one perhaps more sensible, more workable, nearer the truth. We believe that there are basic design principles representing centuries of observation as to what constitutes pleasantness and unpleasantness in art and in nature. These are not stiff, rigid, unbending laws, but are principles capable of infinite variation to suit different materials, different purposes, different periods. They are flexible principles which can serve as guides and as checks in the creation and enjoyment of art objects.

BALANCE, THE FIRST DESIGN PRINCIPLE

Losing your balance on an icy sidewalk is no fun. Neither is unbalanced design, for balance is probably the major principle in design as well as in life. In discussing the two houses above we noticed that balance plays an important role in our reactions to art. A sense of stability, permanence, equilibrium, is sought by everyone this side of an asylum.

The classical illustration of balance is the pair of scales in the hands of blind justice. The weights on one side almost exactly equal those on the other (one scale is depressed slightly as a symbol of mercy). These are inactive weights pulled by the force of gravity. But balance is more energetically shown in such sports as skiing. The skier must balance himself in ever changing manner or suffer a spill. When he speeds down a slope, he must continuously shift his weight to maintain equilibrium. When his weight is equally balanced on both feet, he goes in a straight line. If he wants to change direction, he must alter his balance. Thus, balance is not always static but can be intimately related to moving forces and tensions as is illustrated in the photographs of Calder's "Mobile" (Figures 139 and 140).

There are three main types of balance: *formal* or *symmetrical, informal* or *asymmetrical,* and *radial.* Although they seldom occur in isolation, discussing each type separately will give clearer understanding of their characteristics and effects.

Formal, Symmetrical, or Passive Balance

Formal balance is that type of equilibrium in which one half of the object is the mirror image of the other. It occurs in many aspects of nature such as flowers or leaves (when viewed from above) or the human body standing at attention (when viewed from front or back). Because of man's bilateral symmetry many of the objects he uses—clothes, chairs, tables, and desks—are symmetrically balanced. Formal balance is also a determining factor in classical architecture of which the Governor's Palace in Williamsburg (Chapter 2), the Farnese Palace (Chapter 6), or the Parthenon (Chapter 17) are examples. It is not often found in painting or sculpture although the poised "Eagle" (Figure 135) shows a high degree of symmetry as do the placid "Summer Landscape" (Figure 136) and the controlled "Sob" (Chapter 6). As these examples show, formal balance usually gives a sense of stateliness, dignity, and formality. The effect is static rather than dynamic, poised rather than moving, passive rather than active. At best symmetrical balance seems permanent and reposed, at worst merely inert.

When should formal balance be used? The above paragraph provides the basis for the answer: namely, whenever we wish to produce a reposed, formal effect. Often, however, it is used merely because it is easy to achieve. Hanging a picture, or placing a door or fireplace, in the center of a wall automatically puts the wall in a state of balance; but the centered picture may not give the most pleasing visual effect and the centered door or fireplace may not be most satisfying from the functional point of view. Thus, formal balance, useful as it is, should be employed only when it leads to the desired effect.

Informal or Active Balance

An object in which the weights or attractions on each side are equal— but not identical—illustrates informal, or asymmetrical, balance. The side

239

view of the human figure shows this type of active balance. The principle of the lever, as used in physics, further illustrates the idea of informal balance: a man could hold his own against a freight car if the proper leverage were supplied him. In formal balance a man must be balanced by another man his own size.

Naturally, the effects of informal balance are quite different from those of formal balance. It stirs the observer more quickly and more vigorously. It arouses an immediate reaction, a curiosity to see what makes the object well balanced. Because it is less obvious than formal balance, it tends to attract attention and to set the observer thinking. Informal balance suggests movement, spontaneity, or sometimes casualness. Focal points are not dead stops placed in the center, but are pauses in a dynamic design.

Many art problems suggest informal balance. Notice the advertisements in any magazine or those in Chapter 5. Very few are symmetrically balanced because advertisers know that informal balance attracts and holds attention. Observe, too, that paintings and sculpture which express violent action, such as Bellows' "Dempsey and Firpo" (Figure 138) or Archipenko's "The Boxers" (Figure 137), or deep feeling, such as Rubens' "Descent from the Cross," are balanced asymmetrically. Or study houses planned functionally, such as those in Chapter 1, and you are likely to find that rooms, windows, and doors are not formally balanced. Look at well-planned furniture arrangements in living rooms, bedrooms, kitchens, and bathrooms. Notice that the parts are seldom repeated and balanced exactly. Informal balance is generally found in objects that demand attention, express action or deep feeling, and in arrangements of objects planned for efficiency. The increasing use of informal design in contemporary products of all kinds is also a reflection of the movement toward greater casualness and informality in manners.

Radial Balance

This is relatively an unimportant and infrequent type of balance, characterized by the fact that all parts radiate from a center, like the spokes in a wheel or the petals on a daisy. This movement from a central point makes that point a strongly focused spot, a bull's-eye to attract and hold attention. Radial balance is really a type of highly formalized balance, involving many repetitions, but with a strong circular sense of movement. Examples may be found in decorated dinner plates, round hooked rugs, the circular halls in some public buildings, and the rose windows in Gothic cathedrals.

CONTINUITY, THE SECOND DESIGN PRINCIPLE

It is satisfying to watch the graceful, regular, and flowing movements of a good dancer, and to notice how they relate rhythmically to the music. Such a dancer is much more pleasant to observe than one whose movements are without pattern—uneven, uncertain, and rambling like a beginner learning to dance. A continuing, recurring and developing pattern makes rhythmic movements. The many different kinds of dance steps —the graceful waltz, the jerky one-step, the unpredictable fox-trot, the languorous tango, the ecstatic rumba—gain their popularity because they are rhythmic patterns of bodily movement. This rhythmic flow which goes by many names is basically continuity, and although it may find its most obvious expression in the dance, it pervades all fields of art.

A comparison of two paintings, "St. Francis in Ecstasy" by El Greco (Figure 143) and "The Fountain" by Sargent (Figure 144), shows how different painters handle the rhythms in a composition of figures and landscape. The first point of difference is the subject matter: one is a simple garden scene showing a lady taking a painting lesson; the other is a scene of religious ecstasy. In "St. Francis" there is a pulsating, vigorous movement pervading every inch of the canvas—inflaming the sky, the figure, and the foreground with intense vitality. All parts of the picture build into one exciting, organized pattern of movement. In the painting of "The Fountain" there is no strong moving pattern. The two figures are arranged casually before a naturalistic background hanging like a curtain at the back of the painting. The lady is perched on a stone pier as she paints. Water gushes from a spot between the man's head and the easel. It shoots out of the top of the picture, and then falls back into it. The picture is a brilliant impression of a garden scene—nothing less, nothing more.

Between these two paintings is a vast difference in organized movement, continuity, rhythm, recurrence, or repetition. As fundamental in nature as in art, continuity is found in the beat of the heart, the ebb and flow of the tide, the change of seasons. These, undisturbed, create a graceful continuity. Interference may bring awkwardness, discomfort, or even death. Undoubtedly much of our satisfaction from rhythm in art—be it dancing, music, poetry, or painting—comes from its similarity to the organic rhythms of breathing and walking, and from the bigger rhythms of nature's phenomena.

241

The Problem of Organization

Specifically, continuity is necessary in art for a number of reasons. *First,* it attracts and holds our attention by giving the object vitality, life, or intensity. Half close your eyes and look again at the two paintings: forget the subject matter and look only at the dark-and-light pattern. Which holds your attention longer?

Second, continuity aids in establishing order and regularity by making things easier to look at, easier to grasp, and easier to understand. Compare the Courts of Justice (Figure 148) with the Governor's Palace in Williamsburg, or the two houses at the beginning of this chaper. The value of orderly, continuous relationships is obvious from these comparisons. It is interesting to notice in each example what and how many forms are repeated, how different forms are related to each other.

Third, the rhythmic pattern of an art object is a potent force in expressing reactions or moods, as already observed in the paintings by El Greco and Sargent. Another example of contrast may be found in the telephone advertisement and the perfume container. One suggests strong, dynamic, fast-moving rhythms; the other, delicate, subtle, leisurely patterns. A good advertisement tells through its rhythmic pattern something of the nature of the product it proclaims. Rhythm may be used in equally expressive ways in all other art products.

Fourth, continuity, in the form of repetition, leads to harmony. When we say that the furniture in a room is harmonious, we mean that certain forms, colors, and textures have been repeated and emphasized. In a contemporary living room, harmony is often achieved by repeating simple forms, natural textures, and colors. In historic rooms, as those in Williamsburg, harmony was created by repeating delicate moldings, ornaments, and floral patterns.

Continuity in an art object is introduced by one or both of two devices: repetition and progression. Repetition, the simpler device, is used extensively in advertising, where it pays well. A form, a color, or a texture is used again and again until a pattern is established. This may act as a structure or groundwork for other developments in the design. Repetition must be carefully handled, lest its constant reiteration become irritating or senseless. The small child who keeps yammering, "Mamma, I wanna cookie, I wanna cookie, I wanna cookie," may get the craved-for delicacy, but he runs the risk of so irritating mamma that she may give him something else instead. In contrast, the ceaseless ticking of a clock becomes, eventually, a part of the background, unnoticed, meaningless.

Progression is a more dynamic device than repetition. It is the transition or sequence produced by increasing or decreasing one quality. In music, a progression of loudness, or crescendo, means *more*, MORE, and MORE loudness. It builds up attention. A color progression may go from gray, through dull greens, to bright green (Figure 125); a size progression may go from very small to large, or large to small, as in the branches of a tree; a shape progression may be one like that of waves which mount higher and higher and then break in a mighty roar upon a rocky reef. At times, repetition and progression are interchangeable. A row of columns across the front of a building illustrates repetition because they are repeated at regular intervals. But if this colonnade is seen from a raking (oblique) position, the result is a progression because the farthest column will look smallest, and, from it, each column in orderly progression will apparently increase in size as it nears the onlooker.

Notice in El Greco's "St. Francis in Ecstasy" (Figure 143) the progressive change in size, shape, and direction of the V-shaped forms in the left sleeve which pull your attention down toward the hand and over toward the skull. Notice how the elongated, pointed shapes are found in every part of the painting but that no two are identical. Always there is change, a progressive development from one form or shape to another. In Feininger's "Steamer 'Odin,' II" (Figure 142) geometric forms emerge from one another, in Eames' abstraction (Figure 141) curving forms unfold and grow.

EMPHASIS, THE THIRD DESIGN PRINCIPLE

Perplexed by many patterns, the lady in the cartoon (Figure 147) is facing a major crisis such as occurs in the lives of many homemakers—the selection of draperies. Her friend wisely suggests that she buy a plain textile because "there's so much going on" in her rug! This is a good phrase to remember. Imagine a painting in which all the colors were equally bright, or all the areas of equal size. Worse, imagine both in the same painting! The effect would be one of hysterical confusion—or deadly monotony. Imagine a living room in which all surfaces—of the rugs, chairs, draperies, walls—were patterned, say, with flowers. Everything would clamor for attention. There would be no rest spaces, no dominant areas.

Best defined as giving the proper importance to the parts and to the whole, the principle of emphasis is basic to all life's activities. It is the process of separating the essential from the less important.

Three reasons for emphasis are:

1. *To relieve monotony.* To furnish variety by holding and releasing attention. A blank concrete wall, like a blank sheet of paper, does not hold your interest. But if the wall is accented with windows or decorations of sensible shape and size which are separated by panels less arresting, the effect is different. Your attention will now be held by the decorations and you will pay little notice to the spaces between.

2. *To simplify the appearance of objects* by calling attention to the important parts. The confusing, unpleasant effect produced by a painting or a living room in which all the parts are of equal importance has already been mentioned.

3. *To give an impression of unity* by emphasizing those parts most expressive of the basic idea in the art object. Turn to page 450 for a photograph of the Chicago Tribune Tower. Here the architect was intent upon giving an impression of verticality, and consequently he subordinated all the horizontal lines. He made the windows and panels appear as continuous, dark, vertical stripes. You do not notice the horizontals in the building. In contrast, another architect strikingly emphasized horizontals in the Philadelphia Savings Fund Society Building (page 450). Each building has developed a striking total effect by the judicious consideration of dominance and subordination. Compared with the typical criss-cross building in which neither horizontals nor verticals are dominant, the Philadelphia Savings Fund Society Building achieves architectural distinction.

The question may be asked: How many dominant elements should be used in an art product? It is impossible to give a general, final answer because each art problem has its own particular needs to meet. A mural painting, for instance, may well have a goodly number of dominant points of interest because it usually covers one or more walls. But a magazine cover, only a few inches square, can rarely afford more than one. Many other considerations come up. Color, for instance: it is necessary to heed carefully the attention values of colors. A small spot of red will attract much attention outdoors because nearly everything else is green. In a firehouse, where red predominates, a patch of green would stand out more strongly than red. Furthermore, bright colors are more dominant than dull colors: notice which flowers first attract your attention when you look at a garden or in a florist's window.

Size also has an effect on emphasis. A davenport will demand more attention than a near-by chair; a horse more than a cat. Large objects not only fill more of our field of vision, but experience has taught us that they are to be reckoned with. Thus, other things being equal, the large object attracts attention, creates emphasis.

Unusual shapes will also aid in creating emphasis. The commonplace is avoided by advertisers, who rack their brains finding phrases and illustrations unusual enough to attract attention to their product or message. It is a deep-rooted human trait to pay attention to that which is different. The artist knows this human characteristic well and designs his buildings, paintings, furniture or stoves accordingly. Look again at "St. Francis in Ecstasy" (Figure 143). Notice how the angular distortion of face and background calls attention to the head of the figure. Notice how the elongation of the hands, silhouetted against the dark background, makes them dominant notes.

Finally, emphasis is achieved by grouping important elements. Building entrances usually have decorated doorways, windows, and possibly colonnades or towers. In well-planned living rooms, large furniture, paintings, and lamps are used together to compose a major group. In paintings, the principal elements—figures, buildings, or trees—are usually organized in one dominant group so that a powerful emphasis is achieved.

CONCLUSION

In concluding the discussion of design principles, let us look at a living room from the Shoreland Hotel (Figure 146) and the living room of the Hanna House (Figure 145). There is little inherently wrong with the furnishings of the Shoreland room if you concentrate on one piece at a time, but that is almost impossible because each item—draperies, davenport, chairs, and corner cupboard—clamor for attention. It is as though you ate a piece of poorly stirred cake, and instead of tasting cake, you tasted eggs, flour, butter, and vanilla separately. The Hanna living room, in contrast, gives an impression of *living room* not *furniture*.

Let us consider how these two rooms demonstrate the principles of design. First, *Balance*. Although the Shoreland room seems balanced, the arrangement is so casual and purposeless that it all but defies analysis. Quite different is the active stability of the Hanna living room in which the massive brick wall is counterbalanced by the large windows. Second, *Continuity*. In the Shoreland room the chair and table legs, the upholstery and drapery materials show many repeated curves, but there is little or no progression throughout the room. One part does not lead smoothly to the next. In the Hanna living room, a dynamic continuity, based on hexagonal shapes, interrelates all parts. The lines of the brickwork, mullions of the windows, strips on the ceiling intensify the measured movement of basic forms.

The most striking difference between the two rooms is in *emphasis*. In one you look at everything, in the other, a few centers hold your attention. In the Hanna house the wall of brick and the wall of glass dominate all else, and the furniture, especially the built-in seat at the left and the table at the rear, becomes a subordinate part of the architecture.

When you look at art objects during the next few days or weeks, concentrate your attention on their organization or design. In order to sharpen your observations and judgments, ask yourself questions similar to these:

1. *Does the art object, whatever it may be, give you the impression of one basic idea?*

   Example: A building should give the impression of an organized mass expressing its purpose; it should not look like a collection of doors, windows, chimneys, and what-nots.

2. *Is there enough variety to hold your attention?*

   Example: A building or painting should have enough variety of form, line, color, texture, and space organization to hold your attention. The length of time during which an art object holds your attention should be in proportion to its importance. Thus, a painting is more important than an advertisement, a church more important than a gasoline filling station, and hence we expect more variety or interest in the painting or church.

3. *Does the general composition seem well-suited to the purpose?*

   Example: Horizontal rather than vertical masses suggest contemporary family living (with the possible exception of apartment buildings), whereas we still, rightly or wrongly, think of religious buildings as being predominantly vertical. Remember, too, the comparison cited above of an advertisement for a telephone and for perfume.

4. *Is the object easy to look at?* (Have the forces, movements, or directions been well-controlled, or do they look haphazard, disorganized?)

   a. *Are the various weights and forces in a state of balance?*

      Example: A living room should not have the furniture all placed against one wall; a painting should not have all interest crowded into one side (unless this is deliberately planned to produce a certain effect). In brief, the art object should give a feeling of being balanced, of being in a state of equilibrium.

b. *Are the parts emphasized in proportion to their importance?*

Example: The furniture in a living room is more important than the background, and should not be subdued by beflowered carpets and beflowered wallpapers. Similarly, the important words in an advertisement or package should be dominant; the less important, subordinate.

c. *Does the whole design have continuity?* (Are the parts rhythmically related?)

Example: In a landscape painting the trees should be related to the ground forms and the sky. Suggested movements ought to carry the attention from one part of the picture to another easily. The same holds true in architecture.

Worthwhile readings on design principles are not numerous.

A. W. Dow: *Composition* (Doubleday, Doran, 1928) for a long time the standard book on the subject and still worth reading.

H. and V. Goldstein: *Art in Everyday Life* (Macmillan, 1940) for their chapters on design principles.

Winold Reiss and Albert Schweizer: *You Can Design* (Whittlesey House, 1939) for its interesting layouts and approach to design.

Adolfe Best-Maugard: *A Method for Creative Design* (Knapp, 1935) an abstract, amusing and somewhat superficial approach to design.

Gyorgy Kepes: *Language of Vision* (Theobald, 1944) for a good recent statement of the problems.

PART III

The Problem of Materials and Processes

Introduction

MAN takes raw materials from nature and creates art products. Sometimes he treats them sympathetically with a true understanding of their possibilities and limitations. Sometimes he ignores or fails to appreciate the qualities of his materials, forces them into inappropriate shapes, uses them so that they do not reveal their natural beauty.

The relation of materials to other aspects of art is important, no matter what the product. Let us take Rockefeller Center, illustrated in Chapter 17, as an example. Long before steam shovels bit out clay and stone for the vast foundations, men planned for the thousand different needs such buildings must serve, studied these needs in detail and in relation to the total design. Even such small items as doorknobs, light switches, and hand railings were considered along with the more fundamental problems of steel construction and the general appearance of the buildings. In solving each of these problems, the matter of materials was important because if buildings are to contribute to the welfare of those who work or find other pleasures in them, the steel and wood, stone and concrete, metal and glass of which they are built must be used efficiently and attractively.

Even a chair, although much simpler than a whole building, is complex both from the standpoint of design and materials. A primary problem is the choice of material: it may be made of wood, steel, cane, or plastics. If it is to be made of steel, the question of how best to treat the surface arises. One possibility is plating it with another metal, such as chromium. The selection of suitable upholstery is another problem. Should it be smooth and slick, repeating the metal texture, or should it be rough and shaggy for contrast? Another item of the greatest importance is the consideration of the room in which the chair is to be used. A chair well suited to a modest home may be quite out of place in a movie director's office, and the converse is equally true. The method of manufacture will in

251

its turn affect all of these other factors. Machine fabrication produces different results from those achieved by hand tooling.

As aids in solving these manifold problems, designers have isolated certain conditions which affect and determine the use of materials. The first of these is function. In the two preceding parts of the book dealing with human needs and organization we saw how function determines to a large extent the form of art objects, but function also affects the choice of materials. Obviously, the damask used in upholstering a davenport is not suitable for use on a kitchen chair because such a textile, even apart from economic considerations, would not withstand the hard wear given kitchen furniture. Expression is another controlling factor—the expression of elegance implied in damask is out of place in a kitchen where utility and efficiency are more in order. The type of design, shape or form desired is a third controlling factor. In fact, design and materials are so inter-related that it is almost impossible to consider them separately. Each material has inherent possibilities and limitations which determine to a large extent what can and cannot be done with it. Glass cannot be made as thin and extended as metal and remain strong; stone leads to shapes and textures quite different from those of concrete. Not only the material itself, but the way of working it, affects the design. Thus, clay may be shaped by hand, or cast in molds; wood may be carved and worked by hand, or machined into large sheets of plywood.

This leads to another point: in materials and processes lie the most obvious differences between the plastic and graphic arts and the musical, dramatic, dance and literary arts. The plastic-graphic arts use stone, metal, paints, brushes and plastics to build visual objects; music employs various instruments to produce tones; literature employs words. Although in the problems of human needs and organization all the arts find much in common, the materials and processes differentiate the arts fairly sharply one from another.

We are now ready to consider the third major aspect of art creation and appreciation: the problem of materials and processes. Part III will include discussions of the materials, their characteristics, possibilities and limitations as well as some of the processes whereby they are transformed and made suitable for human use and enjoyment. The chapters include wood, metal and plastics, ceramics and glass, textiles, the graphic processes and photography.

CHAPTER 10

The Three Virtuosi: Wood, Metal, and Plastics

$$W$$OOD and metal are two of nature's most abundant and useful resources. In no small way is the progress of man measured by his increasing ability to shape these materials to meet his needs. To these two natural materials, man has added a third type: plastics. Made from such humble ingredients as milk and soy beans, plastics emerge in all the colors of the rainbow, in rich textures, and in shapes varying from a simple button to a radio cabinet. These three materials lend themselves to almost any treatment, and can be fashioned into a tremendous variety of objects. Because of this almost unlimited range of possibilities, we call them "The Three Virtuosi." The use of wood and metal in architecture and sculpture will be discussed in Part IV. Our concern here will be chiefly with furniture and household implements which show intelligent, sympathetic handling of these materials.

WOOD

Observe the uses to which wood has been put in the contemporary dining room (Figure 149). The table tops and utility chest are made of East India laurel—beautiful in color, texture, and grain. When correctly finished, it is ideal in hardness for furniture. The designer, Gilbert Rohde, could have specified other materials; the table top could have been made of a slab of glass, a plastic, or metal. But none of these materials has the organic quality of wood. They all have a colder, more formal appearance. For this reason many people prefer to use wood in their homes and elsewhere when they want to establish a feeling of warmth and intimacy.

Naturally, it is the grain in wood that gives it the appearance of having a history of growth, an organic nature. Paint or enamel a board well, and to all appearances and touch you cannot tell it from any of a number of similarly painted plastics or metals. Therefore, if wood is to display its most important characteristic qualities, it is used so that its grain will show. The grains in the various woods differ widely; compare the grain of a breadboard or noodle-board (which is probably either birch or pine) with the grain of the East India laurel in the Gilbert Rohde dining room pieces. Turn to page 432 and look at the grain in "Venus in Red Cherry."

The grain is dependent primarily on the kind of wood: spruce, maple, oak, walnut, birch, rosewood, pine, fruitwood, ebony, teakwood, myrtle, cedar, and many others. Second, grain is affected by the way the wood is processed (Figure 151): whether it is sawed across the grain (end grain), plain-sawed or quarter-sawed; the way it is sanded and smoothed and prepared for its protective and preserving coatings of oil, wax, or stain. Finally, grain is much affected by the way in which it is finished: oils, stains, and varnishes have varying effects on different woods.

The color of wood differs, too, according to its kind and manner of treatment. The several oaks are naturally in the yellow range; rosewood, cherry, and mahogany are red; walnut is brown. Through the use of stains the natural color of wood can be altered to almost any color, sometimes with excellent, sometimes with unpleasant results. As an illustration, oak stained to look like mahogany is a travesty on both woods, but oak may be stained, bleached, waxed, and finished in varied ways to produce unusual and satisfying results. The Gilbert Rohde furniture shows two treatments of wood, first, that which brings out the natural color and grain of the East India laurel, and, second, that which, through bleaching, produces what is called blond wood, as the inside of the open shelf of the chest. This particular use of bleached wood adds interest to the piece of furniture; in color it is well related to the upholstery material of the chairs and, in this way, serves in unifying the room. Wood is easily bleached; nature does much of it herself, as you no doubt have noticed when strolling along a beach, picking up pieces of bone-white driftwood. Cabinet makers bleach wood with acids. If you want to bleach wood yourself, you will find it easy to do with common laundry soap, which, applied over a long enough period of time, will turn any wood almost white. If you want to hasten the process, any of the several bleaching compounds used in the home laundry, or those prepared specifically for bleaching wood, will do it faster.

Without proper treatment, wood rots and crumbles rather quickly. Furthermore, the surface of wood is usually too soft and absorbent to be stain resistant and readily cleaned. These are disadvantages, but if the wood surface is well protected, they can readily be controlled. Oils of various kinds tend to preserve wood, and if used alone, darken it slightly but still reveal the natural color and grain. Varnish, shellac and clear lacquer perform similar functions, but give a gloss surface far easier to keep clean. Wax and wood-fillers harden and protect the surface without noticeably changing its appearance. Opaque paints contain oils which penetrate as well as pigments which form a durable surface. Some woods, such as cypress, pine, or spruce, even without protection will last indefinitely. Used in outdoor construction and becoming more weatherbeaten through the years, these woods become a rich gray in color that blends beautifully with any rural landscape.

The density of wood is an important factor governing its use. Some wood is light and fibrous, like balsam fir, and cannot be used for furniture nor for such construction work as will require much strain or hard wear. Ironwood, at the other extreme, is so hard, tough, and heavy that it is difficult to handle, as any camper who has tried to chop it will tell you. But its hardness and toughness make products which are sturdy and durable. Between these extremes are hundreds of woods, all adaptable to many uses. Furniture is made from those which can stand usage and wear, houses are built from those which are easily handled by carpenters, and yet are strong enough to make a sturdy building. White pine fills the whittler's heart with creative joy, but oak will whip up his temper and dull his knife.

The grain of wood, mentioned before chiefly as a surface feature, is as important as density with which, when the working qualities of wood are considered, it goes hand in hand. White pine, the aforementioned whittler's joy, cuts and carves almost as easily against the grain as with it—which explains why countries which abound in this wood (northern United States and northern Europe) have indulged in so much woodcarving and sawing in their native arts. The wood invites the carver's knife and allows him to turn out the most fantastic forms his mind can conjure. Fir, however, objects even to grainwise cutting. Woodcarvers dislike it and wrecking firms offer little money for the privilege of salvaging a building made from fir. All woods, therefore, must be studied for their working qualities so that the right wood is selected for its specific purpose.

The Problem of Materials and Processes

The ease with which it can be worked, the number of uses it fulfills, and its natural, intimate beauty make wood a popular source-material just as much as does the fact that it is plentiful. The three bowls illustrated (Figure 152) show to advantage many of the desirable characteristics of wood. Even in the picture we get the "feel" of the bowls, the smooth, warm surfaces that are so pleasurable to the touch. They demonstrate the ease with which wood can be worked, the range of colors, from very light to almost black, which it can take without effort, and perhaps as important as any, the grain, never the same yet always arranged in organic patterns.

Wood has been used structurally, as in building and furniture; decoratively, as in woodcarving and turning, veneer work and paneling. It has also been put to decoratively structural uses, as in the turned legs for furniture, the carved timbers of a ceiling. In all these uses, wood has shown itself to be a true virtuoso; it scarcely has known abuse because its nature is so flexible. In the days when metals were expensive and difficult to handle and before our present era of plastics, wood served even more uses than it does today. In architectural construction, metals, concrete, and fabricated materials have been found to be better suited for some purposes and have in many instances, particularly in large buildings, almost entirely replaced wood. In domestic building, however, wood is still by far the most commonly used material. In a sense, wood has been liberated from tasks better performed by other materials, yet it still remains one of our most important and versatile materials, and, while being supplanted in some areas, its range of usefulness is being increased in others as the following section shows.

Wood, ordinarily, is limited in the sizes in which it is available. Always present, too, is its tendency to split and warp. Plywood, made of several layers of wood tightly joined, overcomes these limitations, yet preserves the advantages of wood. In making plywood, large logs are rotated against knives which cut from the surface of the logs continuous sheets of wood about the thickness of heavy cardboard. Several such sheets are stacked so that the direction of the grain alternates from one piece to the next, and by the use of glue (or resin, if it is to be used out of doors), terrific pressure, and fairly high heat, are formed into large sheets of a light yet exceedingly tough and durable material. The terms 3-ply or 5-ply refer to the number of thin sheets of wood in the finished plywood.

Plywood, long used for packing boxes and rough temporary construction, is fast winning a respected place for itself as a dignified building material. It is being used increasingly both on the exterior of houses as a finish material, and in the interiors for floors, walls, and ceilings. It is obtainable with the top visible layer in unusual and expensive wood, such as mahogany, walnut, harewood, which, although quite as decorative, is far less costly than solid pieces of wood. Not all plywood is well used, however. Fir plywood, frequently used on the interiors of cheaply constructed buildings, is often treated with dark stain to emphasize a grain which is already overvigorous.

Figure 150 introduces us to newly discovered possibilities of plywood and new technological processes which rank high in importance in man's long effort to make wood behave as he wants it to. Designer Charles Eames found through experimentation in his own apartment that he could mold plywood as he wished. When his apartment oven exploded, he carried on in a bakery, later in a well-equipped laboratory. During the war he turned his attention to the design of efficient molded plywood splints and stretchers which, like the furniture he had developed, take advantage of the flexibility and strength of laminated wood.

Eames' furniture is remarkable for many reasons. The organic shapes echo those of the human body; the clear articulation of parts, especially in the chairs, is equaled only by the Windsor chair and a few other examples in the history of furniture design; the designs show unusual vitality and sensitivity in their sculptural character. Then there are more prosaic but significant factors. The furniture is light in weight, uses wood economically, and many pieces, notably the tables, are demountable. The processes of manufacture show a degree of standardization and simplification highly desirable in industrial production and include three significant developments.

In the first of these processes, the wood is rapidly and precisely molded under heat and pressure. In the second—the "Cycleweld" process of shock welding—a sheet of synthetic resin is placed between the parts to be joined, and a special electronic instrument transmits sufficient heat in a few seconds to the resin to produce a bond stronger than the wood itself without injury to the wood. In the third process, the wood is impregnated with resin, thus becoming completely weatherproof and hardened against scratches and dents. So thorough is this impregnation that the furniture may be left outdoors indefinitely and washed down with the hose when necessary. The wood can also be impregnated with brilliant dyes which reveal the grain while bringing new color possibilities. Few if any examples of contemporary industrial design show as complete mastery of the varied problems of human need, design, and processes and materials as does Eames' furniture.

Akin to plywood, although much older, is veneer, which is made by gluing a thin sheet of wood over wood of inferior quality. Most furniture has a veneered surface, as you can discover by opening a bureau drawer and examining the edge of the drawer panel. Veneering makes possible high quality surfaces on inexpensive furniture, but it is by no means a mark of cheap furniture; in fact veneered furniture has many advantages over that made from solid wood, and includes much that is expensive. Flexwood, another recent development, is a product in which paper-thin sheets of wood are fastened to a flexible backing, such as a sturdy paper, and used in interiors like wallpaper on either flat or curved surfaces. The effect approximates that of a wood-paneled room, but the absence of discernible joints gives it in most cases a thin applied appearance.

Skis and snowshoes are bent into shape by being treated with live steam. So, too, were the Eames chairs. This is not a new process, but it has been used widely in the past few years in the manufacture of furniture and referred to under the name of bentwood. Furniture of this nature has an elastic appearance that is closely akin to the effect of metal. Bending wood into harmonious shapes is another instance of capitalizing on one of its inherent potentialities.

In the above discussion of wood only those uses were mentioned in which its essential appearance was not altered. But wood can be ground into a pulp, chemically and physically treated, and made into a miraculous variety of materials: rayon, paper, insulating materials, medicine, and wall board. Some of these products then pass on to realms with which we are not concerned. The others, like rayon and new building materials, are discussed on other pages.

METAL

The George Washington Bridge in New York City (Figure 153), ably photographed by Margaret Bourke-White, is a masterpiece in metal. The graceful span between towers is 3500 feet (two-thirds of a mile), and the rugged towers are 600 feet high. No material but metal could have made possible this magnificent modern structure, and the most striking characteristic of metal is thus demonstrated: its great tensile strength. But metal, like wood, is a virtuoso among today's source materials, and bridge construction is only one of the multitudinous uses man has found for it.

Although there are many different kinds of metals and combinations of metals (alloys), most of them have several "metal" characteristics in common. They are all strong and durable; they have a luster when polished that is always attractive and in some cases highly coveted; and they can be shaped, molded, or cut into extraordinarily fine detail. Even though metals will corrode and tarnish, in lasting qualities they surpass most other materials. Because metals come from inorganic sources and are subjected to many refining processes, they have in most instances a cold, formal, impersonal quality. Metals invariably look cool, and in cold weather actually feel icy to the touch. Unlike wood, they have little feeling of warmth, softness, or intimacy. Whereas woods seem soft and workable, metals seem hard and unyielding.

It should not be concluded from the above that all metal textures are unpleasant. Far from it. Few things are more delightful than the gleam of well-polished pots and pans in a kitchen, more exciting than the metal sleekness of an airplane, more to be treasured than the richly glowing highlights in metal pins, or rings, or necklaces. Contrast the bright, sharp, efficient surface on the kitchen spoons and beaters in Figure 155 with the soft, diffused, inviting texture of the Georg Jensen silverware and necklaces in Figures 154 and 157. Metal, indeed, is as versatile as wood.

Perhaps because structural metal came to us by way of the factory, there is some prejudice against the use of metal in furniture, as the chairs shown in Figure 149. In appearance they are radically different from wooden chairs because the designer used his material in such a way as would make best use of its great strength and modern methods of fabricating metal. The seats, cantilevered from the front supports, are perfectly strong and give the chair a most satisfying elasticity. Notice, too, that the metal tube, which comprises the structure of the chair, is continuous, because metal tubing can be fabricated in indefinite lengths. Reducing the number of joints to a minimum (one in this case) is sound engineering because of the difficulty of making joints and their potential weakness. Metal furniture is light in weight and easily moved about.

259

It is simply cared for and not subject to many of the frailties of wooden furniture: loose joints, warping, splitting. Used chiefly in offices and waiting rooms, metal furniture is finding increased acceptance in homes as well.

One of the most striking characteristics of metals is the ease with which they can be fabricated into all manner of products. Under pressure metals can be forced to assume almost any shape. The illustrations of the making of a spoon (Figure 156) and the making of a pitcher (Figure 158) show clearly the processes involved in the production of these two products, the one by machine, the other by hand. In making the spoon, dies for its front and back are carefully made, and once they are completed an indefinite number of spoons can be stamped in a heavy press. The pitcher, however, is made by hand without the aid of a mold, and considerable skill is needed to raise a symmetrical container from a flat sheet of metal. Figure 159 shows another handmade product, a superbly designed covered bowl. Notice the broad, flat, highly reflecting surfaces in contrast to the sharp, full-formed detail. The ornament has been not only sensitively designed, but skillfully placed to enrich and attract attention to the important parts of the composition. This is an excellent illustration of the principles discussed in Part II.

Metal is such an agreeable material in the hands of a skilled metal-worker or a machine that almost anything can be done with it, and consequently it is subject to many misuses. The iron settee (Figure 160) is a misuse of metal because here the intention was to mislead (if possible) the observer into thinking this was a rustic wood bench. One touch would be sufficient to disillusion even the most obtuse. Metal is always a fabricated material and the forms it has been forced to take in this bench are unnatural both to metal and to machine fabrication.

The forms in the kerosene lamp holder on the left in Figure 161 are obviously machine fabricated but they tend to obscure the function of the holder—to hold the lamp. In the redesign on the right the metal appears more frankly as metal, and the support more frankly as a support, rather than as a bit of foliage in metal. The frank, functional use of metal in this redesigned lamp shows how forms, which follow their intended function and develop naturally from the possibilities and limitations of the materials from which they are made, almost inevitably give pleasing designs. Although they may not necessarily be distinguished, they are at least pleasant.

The Three Virtuosi: Wood, Metal, and Plastics

Metals, as commonly used, are either metallic elements extracted from various ores, or alloys composed of two or more metallic elements. There are many of them, and as they differ in cost, availability, density, malleability, color and other qualities, they vary in use. Following are a few of the metals in common use today.

Copper was one of the first metals to be discovered and used by man. It is a rich, glowing orange in color, but when exposed to weather, it assumes a characteristic and attractive green surface, or patina. Being fairly inexpensive, easily worked, and attractive, it is commonly used for coins, water pipes, electric conduits, cooking utensils and decorative ornaments. Occasionally, it is used for roofs.

Bronze is an alloy of copper and tin. It is hard and durable, and like copper takes an interesting green color when weathered (patina again). United States Standard Bronze is composed of 90 percent copper, 7 percent tin, and 3 percent zinc. This is not an official formula, nor is it the only one. In some Greek bronzes the copper content is as low as 62 percent, while in some recently discovered Inca bronzes the copper content is as high as 94 percent. The United States Standard is, however, the most commonly used formula at present in this country. Bronze is widely used for casting statuary and medals, and for plumbing fixtures, ornamental metal fences and gates, and church bells.

Brass, in many ways, is a cheaper substitute for bronze, being compounded of zinc and copper instead of tin and copper. It is much used for plumbing fixtures, electrical fixtures, and as a base for such objects as coffee pots and watches, which are plated with gold, platinum, nickel, or chromium. Brass was very popular several decades ago, just as chromium and stainless steel are now; automobiles used much of it, and brass chandeliers and beds were common.

Britannia Metal is one of the many alloys in popular use, made from tin, antimony, and copper. Easily worked, polished and maintained, it is used as a substitute for pewter. (Pewter, an alloy of 4 parts of tin to one of lead, is seldom seen any more on the commercial market, most of the objects sold as pewter being in reality britannia metal, which in appearance and durability is superior to pewter.)

Gold. The natural beauty of gold has made it one of the most treasured of human possessions, despite the fact that it is too soft for most purposes. It is usually combined with other metals and made into jewelry or coins. It is made white by platinum, green by silver, red by copper, and brittle as glass by lead. The most malleable of metals, a single gram can be drawn into a wire two miles long, and an ounce can cover 1200 square feet; a fourteen-inch cube of it weighs a ton. It can be hammered into sheets 1/280,000 inch thick and in the form of gold leaf is often used to cover statues, domes, ceilings and, as lettering on wood, metal, or glass. It is also easily plated on cheaper metal bases, and even the least expensive jewelry is sometimes plated with gold, microscopically thin.

Iron. This metal and its end-product, steel, are the great metals of our age. Steel is comparatively new; iron has been used for centuries. Their great strength, abundance, and low cost make them very widely used construction materials today.

Aluminum is one of the most abundant of the metallic elements, being a constituent of clay. Until a few years ago, it was prohibitively expensive until simple ways of refining it were developed. It is now widely used and low in cost. Being both light and strong, it is used extensively in construction of objects where these characteristics are needed, as in airplanes, furniture, trains. It is an excellent *conductor* of heat, and therefore used in the manufacture of cooking vessels. It is also an efficient *reflector* of radiant heat (as from the sun), and is used to solve many difficult problems in insulation. It is softer than steel and takes on a finish which is both pleasant to see and feel (see the brushed aluminum handles on the chest in Figure 149).

Chromium and *nickel* are similar in color to aluminum or stainless steel and take a high polish. They withstand exposure and abuse better than iron, steel, copper, or brass, because they are harder. Chromium has largely replaced nickel; it is more serviceable, takes a much higher polish, and will not tarnish. Good for kitchenware, chromium has also been used in place of silver for ashtrays, silverware in general. Both chromium and nickel are colder in appearance, when compared with silver, because they are bluer in color.

Silver is a precious metal, like gold, and also like gold, it is malleable and takes a high polish. It tarnishes easily, and silver corporations have a standing offer of many thousand dollars for anyone who can produce nontarnishing silver. The rich quality of this material cannot be successfully imitated in other metals; it will remain long as a favorite for the manufacture of articles of personal use. The Georg Jensen pieces (Figures 157 and 159) show well the rich, plastic qualities of this metal.

This list is not complete, of course. It leaves out many pure metals and also the bewildering array of alloys: there are literally hundreds, most of them designed for very special purposes like permaloy, which is used in transatlantic cables. In recent years there has been a great increase in the use of alloys which banish the worries of rust and stain. These alloys are usually iron combined with chromium, sometimes with nickel, silicon, or aluminum.

It is almost as difficult to imagine our world without metal as to imagine it without color. From airplanes to safety pins, from suspension bridges to wrist watches, metal products surround us on every side. Steel construction has given a new character to our architecture while other uses of metal have made possible our systems of heating, lighting and plumbing. But in addition to such utilitarian concerns, the beauty of various metals is as widely appreciated today as ever. Metal is truly a basic material in modern living.

PLASTICS

Plastics are a triumph of the chemist. He has taken ordinary materials such as cotton, resin, soy beans, formaldehyde, salt and silica and through the magic of chemistry has created crystal-clear substances that look like glass but will not break; tough, brilliantly colored strips that may be woven into chair seats and backs; flexible, transparent material that can be made into serviceable belts and suspenders; surfaces that cannot be scratched or marred, and that resist acids. Plastics are a young giant in the industrial world, a fledgling just beginning to feel its strength whose possibilities have as yet only been hinted at. The study and production of plastics are young—only since about 1930 has their manufacture been carried forward on a big scale. Yet, so rapidly has this development taken place, that it is now almost impossible to look around without seeing a plastic of some kind. A portable radio case may be made entirely of plastic; if not entirely, at least the tube sockets and the dials will be. The kitchen contains plastics in knife handles, parts of electrical kitchen appliances, perhaps the clock case. Elsewhere plastics may be used for such things as flower vases, dishes, table and counter tops, camera and automobile and dashboard fixtures.

Figures 162 and 164 show one of the newest and most versatile of the plastics—Lucite—or chemically speaking, methyl methacrylate, one of the acrylic resin plastics. It can be made crystal clear, translucent or opaque, delicately tinted or brilliantly colored. Readily cast or molded into any desired form (like metal), it can also be sawed, cut, machined, or tooled (like wood). Figure 164 shows some of the products, in this case automobile parts, that are commonly made from Lucite. It readily lends itself to carving, and thus provides the sculptor with a new medium. In addition to being endowed with this amazing host of potentialities, Lucite created a sensation when it was discovered that it can conduct rays of light in other than straight lines. Thus, light introduced at the end of a long strip of Lucite emerges at the other end with practically undiminished intensity no matter whether the strip is straight, coiled, or twisted. Interestingly, too, the light that emerges is a cold light. The only practical use that has been made so far of these last two mentioned properties is the preparation of doctor's and dentist's instruments where a light source without heat has long been hoped for. However, the decorative and architectural possibilities are enormous.

The manufacture of plastics varies. With some types the product is molded in forms under great pressure, and the shapes which the material can take are limited only by the molds that can be made. Other plastic products are cast by methods similar to those used with clay or metal, rolled, pressed into sheets, or formed by extrusion. Probably no other group of products known to man can be shaped and formed in so many ways, a fact which explains why they are called *plastics*. The ease with which they may be handled in a variety of ways, together with the abundance of the materials from which they are made, are perhaps their greatest virtues, but they have many other assets. Their wearing qualities are considerable: they are light, yet exceedingly tough; they are pleasant to touch but do not scratch or mar easily; they can be made in almost any color, and since the coloration is part of the plastic, there is no likelihood of the color wearing off or fading, as often happens with wood finished with paint. Plastics do not corrode, rot, or disintegrate except under unusual circumstances. Objects made from plastics do not readily reveal their origin. Like metals, plastics are ordinarily lacking in textural interest, and the finished product in no way resembles the natural materials from which it was made. Thus, a plastic made from milk may look very much like one made from carbolic acid. Because of this and because of their novelty, there is a tendency, as with every new discovery, to try to make plastics imitate older and more familiar materials. It is not uncommon to find plastic table tops in imitation of marble, and other plastics in imitation of wood; convincing as these imitations sometimes are, a frank acceptance of the inherent possibilities of plastics leads to results far more significant. Plastics have qualities of their own which extend the range of effects possible in many art forms. Therein lies their distinctive contribution.

Plastics fall into about fifteen groups depending on the materials from which they are made. Six of the more important groups will be discussed briefly.

The *cellulose nitrate* plastic group, of which the best known representative is Celluloid, was the most common of all plastics up to ten years ago. Despite the fact that it is highly inflammable and in some forms affected by sunlight, plastics in this group were widely used for fountain pens, piano keys, toys, tool handles, and spectacle frames.

The *phenol-formaldehyde resin* group, typified by Bakelite, is used for such varied products as automobile and airplane parts, camera cases, electrical insulation, and telephone equipment. Although it was discovered in 1872 that carbolic acid and formaldehyde when mixed produced resin, the commercial possibilities of the discovery were not realized for some years. Molded by thermo-setting (in hardened steel molds under pressure and heat), this group of plastics shows unusual resistance to water, chemicals, and heat. By a process of lamination, layers of this plastic are frequently used as a covering for cheaper materials, as on table tops, wall coverings, counters, and paneling on cabinets. Formica, Textolite, and Insurok are among the better known examples.

The *formaldehyde-hardened casein* plastics go back to the discovery that milk mixed with formaldehyde produces a substance which early in the century in France and Germany was known as "Galalith," or milkstone. However, since plastics made of milk did not withstand well the extreme climatic changes in this country, they have been superseded by more durable types. Although important at one time, they are little used in this country today except in the manufacture of buttons. Other proteins such as soy beans and corn are being used with greater frequency here, and show great promise of development.

The *cellulose acetate* plastics find a place in the knobs, handles, instrument panels, and steering wheels of nearly every make of automobile, and since about 1921 have been used extensively as a safety photographic film supplanting the dangerously inflammable celluloid.* Generally molded by heat, this plastic is obtainable in sheets, rods, tubes, and powder form. Because of its unlimited color range and because it may be molded speedily and economically, the cellulose acetate group has met with wide approval. The transparent forms are seen in screwdriver and saw handles, pen and pencil barrels, combs, costume jewelry, and lighting accessories. One type called *Tenite* has found an interesting use in strips woven into simple patterns for the seats and backs of chairs.

The *vinyl resin* group, known for a century, has been promoted in the business world for only a decade. Because of their toughness, resistance to moisture and chemicals, some of these plastics are used for floor tilings, phonograph records, and coatings for concretes and metals; other forms because of their transparency are used as binders in safety glass, substitutes for window glass, and strangely enough, for women's shoes.

The *acrylic resin* group has already been referred to in discussing Lucite. The plastics in this group may be completely colorless or highly colored. Their elasticity and stability under light and weather have made them useful in manufacturing safety goggles while their optical properties adapt them to lenses of various kinds. Other forms are used for protective coatings or impregnating leathers and textiles. In addition to Lucite, this group includes Plexiglas and Crystalite.

CONCLUSION

Wood, metal and plastics share in common the fact that they may be processed in a multitude of ways, and formed into an endless number of objects for human use. In enjoying and judging products made from these materials the criteria and principles of Part II and the concepts of Part I of this book are of first concern, but this should not cause us to overlook the materials from which an object is made. It is true, for instance, that a waste-basket can be made from wood, metal, a plastic, or a combination of these materials. In any of these it will function well.

---

* Celluloid is still used, however, for commercial motion-picture film. This is why elaborate fire-prevention methods are necessary in regular motion-picture theaters. Cellulose acetate, or "safety" film, as used in all amateur work including 8 mm. and 16 mm. home movies, shrinks rapidly in storage to an extent that makes it unacceptable for use in regular commercial theaters.

And yet, we hasten to say that any of these materials may be abused and result in products in which the design, abstractly considered, may be good, but not suited to the material from which it is made.

This brings up basic considerations of the use of materials. Is it true that metal must look like metal—no matter how pliable it may be? That iron should not be made to look like wood, that the plastics should not be forced to imitate marble, no matter how closely they are able to approach it in appearance?

The answers to these questions take us in the direction of philosophy and morals. Do you value sincerity and frankness? Do you want honesty in art? Or are you going to be content with imitation and pretense? These are weighty questions, and your answers to them will govern many of your reactions to art objects.

Naturally, your first activities should be to look at and to feel wood, metal, and plastics in all their various forms. Your own home, your school, your office, your automobile, your furniture and hardware stores, your mail order catalogues are alive with these materials. Study them. Question whether they are used well or poorly.

Some suggested readings are:

Herbert Bayer, Walter Gropius and Ise Gropius: *Bauhaus* (Museum of Modern Art, 1938). An excellent account of the Bauhaus approach to the use of materials.

Marta and Sheldon Cheney: *Art and the Machine* (McGraw-Hill, 1939). A thoroughly readable account of machine-made art.

Gordon Logie: *Furniture from Machines* (Allen & Unwin, 1947). A survey of the technology of industrially produced furniture.

Laszlo Moholy-Nagy: *Vision in Motion* (Theobald, 1947). Chiefly for the excellent illustrations of experimentation in wood, metal, and plastics.

Herbert Read: *Art and Industry* (Harcourt, Brace, 1935). Probably the best exposition on the role of materials in the production of useful, beautiful objects.

The Encyclopaedia Britannica: Articles on Wood and Metal.

For more technical reading on the handling of materials:

William J. Becker: *Woodworking Made Easy* (Bruce).

J. B. Butler: *Problems in Metal Work* (Manual Arts Press).

Raymond Cherry: *General Plastics* (McKnight and McKnight).

A. Cirino and A. F. Rose: *Jewelry Making and Design* (D. Van Nostrand Co.).

The Problem of Materials and Processes

John Cloag: *Plastics and Industrial Design* (Allen & Unwin, 1945).

J. H. DuBois: *Plastics* (American Technical Society, 1942).

V. C. Fryklund and A. J. LaBerge: *General Shop Woodworking* (Mc-Knight and McKnight, 1940).

Ira S. Griffith and George B. Cox: *Essentials of Woodworking* (Manual Arts Press, 1947).

Arthur Koehler: *The Identification of Furniture Woods*. Circular No. 66 (U. S. Department of Agriculture).

Dale E. Mansberger and C. W. Pepper: *Plastics: Problems and Processes* (International Textbook Co., 1938).

The potentialities of wood and metal are explored by contemporary designers.

149. (*Upper*) Furniture by Gilbert Rohde has slender continuous metal tube supports, large flat surfaces of wood.

150. (*Lower*) Charles Eames uses wood plastically, taking full advantage of its strength, workability, and beauty in sculptural forms.

Different methods of working wood lead to varied results.

151. (*Upper*) Oak sawed in three ways—end grain, plain-sawed, and quarter sawed reveals three kinds of pattern.

152. (*Lower*) Bowls of sturdy, simple design illustrate the solidity of wood

153. The George Washington Bridge in New York City takes full advantage of the tremendous tensile strength of metal. Contrast the slender metal supports with the massive stone columns of the Temple of Ammon in Chapter 17.

We use metal in almost every daily activity. Sometimes it is used primarily for embellishment as in jewelry, at other times primarily for utility as in kitchen utensils, but most often its utilitarian and esthetic qualities are combined as in silverware for the table, watch cases, or lighting fixtures.

154. Handwrought crosses in silver show the decorative possibilities of metal, but the slender chains use the tensile strength of metal just as does the George Washington Bridge.

155. Kitchen spoons of functional design of metal and wood can have forms suited to each material. The wood handles stay cool and are pleasant to hold, the metal stems and bowls are strong and easy to clean.

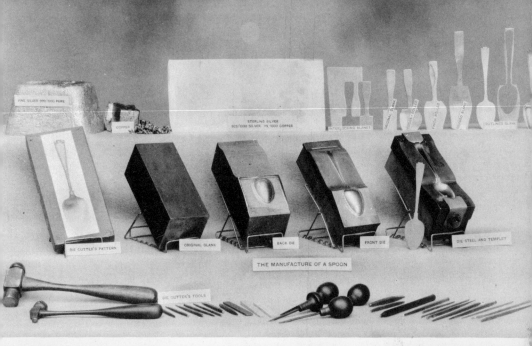

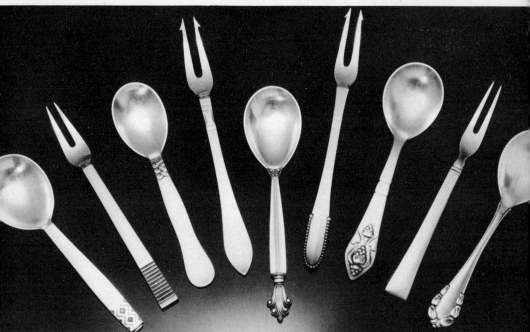

Transforming metallic ore into forks and spoons is a complex process based on the malleability and ductility of metal.

56. (*Upper*) In making silver spoons by hand, flat sheets of silver are cut and then shaped in a mold.

57. (*Lower*) Spoons and forks of distinctive design. Notice that the ornament logically concentrated near end of handle and at junction of bowl.

PIECE FLAT STERLING SILVER
1 ST. STAGE OF PROCESS

Finished Pitcher

2 ND. STAGE OF PROCESS

3 RD. STAGE OF PROCESS   4 TH. STAGE OF PROCESS   5 TH. STAGE OF PROCESS   6 TH. STAGE OF PROCESS

SILVERSMITH'S HAMMERS   METHOD EMPLOYED IN MAKING A PITCHER   HANDLE SPOUT & BASE   TOOLS USED IN CHASING

Handworking a flat piece of metal into hollow ware is comparable to making a vase from a lump of clay *except* that metal is not plastic as clay and must be heated and hammered.

158. A pitcher is literally "raised" from a disc of silver.

159. A silver bowl of unusually beautiful design. The subtle contours and concentration of rich ornament against plain surfaces emphasize the beauty inherent in silver.

274

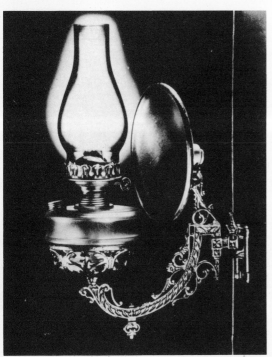

Metal can be used badly and frequently is.

160. (*Upper*) The rustic bench of metal designed to imitate wood is a travesty on both materials. Imitations of one material with another are seldom if ever successful. The bench also looks remarkably uncomfortable. Compare with Figures 149 and 150.

161. (*Lower*) Old and new designs for kerosene lamps.

Plastics are invading the field of industrial design and bring with them a host of advantages and disadvantages not found in natural materials.

162. (*Left*) Lucite salad bowl and oblong tray with different surface finishes. Smooth Lucite is used for handles of serving fork and spoon.

163. (*Right*) Nylon plastic makes a translucent tumbler which resists breakage and damage from heat.

164. Lucite is used for many automobile parts.

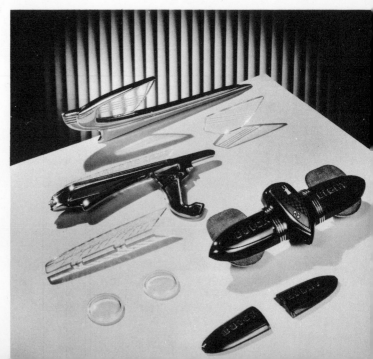

CHAPTER 11

Ceramics and Glass

CERAMICS

THE field of ceramics includes such widely varied products as porcelain, drain pipe, butter crocks, crucibles, tableware, flower vases, figurines, fireplace tiles, terra cotta, rough stoneware water coolers, and false teeth. Behind this array of products is a history notable for its length, widespread activity, and comparative simplicity. This section will be confined, however, largely to a discussion of pottery, tableware, and ceramic sculpture as these are the objects that fall within the scope of this book. Many of the general processes described are applicable to all ceramic products.

When or where arose the art of fashioning vessels from clay and hardening them by heat, no one knows. But somewhere a primitive race of men must have learned that the clay with which they lined their wicker baskets could be made more waterproof, harder, and insoluble if it were heated to a high temperature. This way of making pots, this plastering of clay inside a wicker frame which burned off in the firing, was used centuries ago by primitive races. Other ways of making suitable ceramic ware developed, and slowly, as the centuries passed, practices became more and more refined. Somewhere it was discovered that different clays turning different colors in the firing could be used for colorful decoration. Elsewhere it was learned that quartz pebbles develop a shiny surface if heated in wood ashes—and from this happy accident may have developed the process of glazing.

Most of the fundamental processes in ceramics were known to the Egyptians before the decline of their empire. Even more surprising, we have not surpassed in many respects the ceramics produced long ago by the Persians, the Egyptians, the Chinese (Figure 165), and other peoples. The art has long ago reached the stage where genuine steps ahead must be few and far between. We do have to our credit the discovery of new clays, and the development of new glazes, faster and more accurate methods of mass production, and controlled firing. We have applied power to turn old machines, made accurate thermometers and thermostatic controls for kilns, and improvements in the chemistry of ceramics to meet the many new demands of modern living, such as insulators for high-voltage electricity, or crucibles for the chemist's experiments. But the fundamental methods are still much the same, and in some parts of the world pottery is made today just as it was in ages past.

Today, almost everyone may own good ceramics. Whereas in 1750 only the rich could afford a set of dinnerware, today the advantages of machine production have so lowered the cost that good dinnerware is available in even the low-priced stores. We will turn first to the basic materials, and then to the processes by which our dinnerware, pottery casseroles, insulators, and vases are made.

THE BASIC MATERIALS

Simple as the basic material, clay, may seem, it is found in many different textures, degrees of hardness and plasticity. Some of it is coarse, and is suited only to heavy, crude types of ceramics; some of it cannot stand the necessary high temperatures without melting. On the other hand, the clays used for refined porcelains and insulators are wonderfully fine in texture and can withstand very high temperatures. Also, as mentioned above, clays differ in the colors they take after firing. Some turn red, others tan, others brown. Some remain gray or white. Notice, the next time a piece of ceramic ware breaks in your home, the color of the clay under the glaze.

All clays have three ingredients: a plastic element or "clay substance"; a non-plastic element made up of sand, flint, bone, or aluminum—this is the element that makes the mixture keep its shape in the drying and firing processes; a flux or solvent, such as potash, lime, or lead. It is the proportions of these three parts that determine, first, whether or not the clay can be worked and shaped, and, second, whether it can survive the drying and firing without undue deformation.

Clay, after it has been fired, changes physically into an entirely different substance. Whereas previously it was plastic and porous, the heat of the fire changes its color, texture, and physical nature into a material which disintegrates far more slowly than textile fibers, wood, or metal.

278

Pottery, because of its small size and physical constitution, survives for centuries with only slight changes, and gives us some of our most useful and reliable records of the way in which earlier peoples lived.

The variation that is possible in glazes is unlimited, although there are few basic materials. Glazes are made from clays, minerals, and mineral oxides. Different minerals cause different colored glazes, but the complication only starts there. Different amounts of a mineral may result in quite different colors, or again, a glaze fired at one temperature may be quite different in color than when it is fired at a higher temperature—and this does not exhaust the possibilities for complication. For example, oxides of copper, iron, and cobalt, under normal kiln conditions, produce green-blue, brown or yellow, or blue, respectively. However, if the intake of oxygen into the kiln is limited, these mineral oxides will produce red and purple, olive green to grass green, and black, respectively. The statement still stands that basically ceramics is comparatively simple, but in its details it becomes staggeringly complicated.

THE PROCESSES

There are three major steps in the manufacture of ceramic ware: (1) shaping the object, (2) drying and firing and (3) glazing.

Shaping by Hand. One of the earliest methods of making pottery was that which we call today the "pinch or scoop" method. The vessel, whatever it may be, is simply pinched and modeled from a ball of clay. The result, naturally, is crude—as anyone who has made mud-pies will know. The first refinement in the art of potting was the coil method. Here the potter starts with a disc of clay to which he attaches ropelike strands of clay which he has previously rolled out. These strands he builds up in layers of coils, smoothing and pinching them together as he works, until the general shape is complete. Then, when his coiled pot is nearly dry, he may still further smooth and polish it with a smooth pebble if he so desires. This method is employed even today by Indians and other primitive people.

The tombs of Egypt, Babylon, and Assyria have yielded evidence that, as early as 4000 B.C., the machine known as the potter's wheel was in use. The simplest form was a heavy flat disc of stone or metal which could be rotated by hand. Later an improvement was added in the form of a heavy wheel below the one on which the potter manipulated the clay, which could be kicked around by either the potter or an assistant

(Figure 79). A further improvement in the wheel was the "kick-wheel" in which the lower balance wheel was set in motion by a lever which was operated by the foot of the potter like the treadle of grandfather's grindstone. In this type, the potter was better able to regulate the speed of the wheel. Power machinery came along later, and, although it did not change the principle of the wheel, it did greatly lessen the physical exertion required of the potter.

The shaping of clay on a potter's wheel is called *throwing* (Figure 166). The clay is carefully prepared, mixed and kneaded so that it is of uniform consistency, entirely free of air bubbles, moist enough to be workable, yet not so moist as to lose its shape. A ball of this prepared clay is thrown on the center of the wheel which is then set in motion. The first task of the potter is to *center* the mass of clay by pressing on the sides and top of the revolving ball. Then, when he has a squat, symmetrical, truncated cone of soft clay (Figure 166a), he begins to open it by pressing heavily with both thumbs into the center of the revolving mass while steadying the thumbs by pressing on the outside with the palms. When the potter's thumbs have forced a hole in the center of the cylinder, he begins to press with one hand on the inside and with the other hand on the outside. This forces the clay to rise in a cylinder between the hands (Figure 166b). From this point on, the potter shapes his pot by pressure on the inside or outside (Figure 166c), according to the direction he wishes the curve of his pot to take. Infinite variety is possible—the skill, taste, and imagination of the potter are the important limiting factors.

The cookie jar in Figure 167 is a consummate example of the potter's art. The full, flowing contours show clearly the shaping of a plastic material on a moving wheel. The handles, too, partake of the same plastic quality. Few ceramic products can surpass this one in form or in sensitive handling of a pliant material.

Shaping in a Mold. Very little of the ceramic ware sold today is made by hand because, although it gives us some of our finest pieces, the expense of such hand production puts it beyond the reach of the average buyer. In commercial production, it is customary to design the piece carefully on paper, and then to turn a plaster model on the wheel. From this, plaster molds are made. Some of the handsome ware in Figure 172 was produced in molds.

Hollow ware—vases, coffeepots, pitchers—are generally cast in molds. A one-piece mold of a simple shape in which the top is the largest dimension can be made by simply pouring plaster of Paris over the original shape—leaving one end open, of course. If the shape is more complicated and has undercuts or extrusions, it is necessary to build a mold of two or more co-ordinated and interlocking pieces. Then, when the plaster has hardened sufficiently to retain its shape, the original clay model is removed, and the mold carefully dried.

The illustration (Figure 170) shows a potter in the process of casting a piece of pottery. Notice that the mold is in three pieces, one for the bottom, two for the sides, and that these three pieces are being held securely together. Into this mold is being poured a mixture of clay and water called *slip* which looks like thick cream. The plaster of Paris mold, being very dry, readily absorbs water from the slip that comes in contact with it. Thus, there is built up on the inside of the mold a layer of clay which varies in thickness according to the length of time the slip is left in the mold. When the casting of clay formed by the absorption of water into the mold is thick enough, the remaining slip is poured out. Then the piece is allowed to dry until it has shrunk away from the mold sufficiently to permit safe and easy removal. After this the mold must be dried thoroughly before it is used again. In the meantime, the cast piece of pottery is smoothed; seam marks from the mold and other faults are removed. This must be done before it dries too thoroughly. Also at this time, any handles or knobs that were not cast with the main part are fastened on. Notice in the picture the pieces that have been removed from molds, and the other molds about the work shop.

Shaping with a Jigger. Jiggering is a process of making duplications of an original piece by means of the potter's wheel (Figure 171). Cups, saucers, plates, most bowls and many platters are usually jiggered. A plaster disc, having the profile of either the inside or outside of the object to be jiggered, is fastened on the wheel. As this plaster disc revolves, a tool, bearing the profile of the other side of the object and firmly set in a stationary arm, is brought to bear upon the pancake of clay that has been pressed down over the plaster disc. Thus the front and back are made in one operation much faster and with greater standardization than is possible for the potter working without such a machine. Plates are usually made with the upper surface formed by the plaster disc and the lower surface fashioned by the tool. Cups and bowls are made in the reverse fashion. Jiggered pieces are finished and dried like cast ones.

The Problem of Materials and Processes

Drying and Firing. The drying of a clay object, whether made by hand or machine, should be a slow process. It must be done evenly, else the clay will warp or crack. Products that vary in thickness must be particularly evenly dried because they will quickly crack open if dried too fast. Therefore it is a definite, practical advantage to keep ceramic shapes comparatively simple and of uniform thickness. During the drying process, a clay product will sometimes shrink as much as 10 percent. In the firing process, it may shrink another 8 or 10 percent. The potter who makes objects for a specific purpose must remember to take this shrinkage into account, or he will find that his product does not measure up to the specified requirements.

Drying and firing should not be confused. Dried clay products are not serviceable as containers. They break easily, and contact with a liquid will dissolve the clay. Real firing in a specially built oven or kiln actually changes the composition of the material. This change is called *maturing.* The terms that indicate whether or not a pot has been subjected to great or little heat are *high fire* and *low fire.* Most red or brown earthenware, such as that used in flower pots, matures between 1733 and 2030 degrees Fahrenheit, and is called low fire ware. Gray and buff stoneware, such as most of our tableware, can be matured at 1841 degrees, but usually is carried to 2174 degrees or higher. True porcelain (we often call it china) is translucent and white when mature, and must be fired between 2237 and 2534 degrees, or at high fire.

Ware before being fired is called *green ware.* The first firing is known as *biscuit fire,* and hardens, but does not vitrify, the ware. Most ware is fired twice, first for the biscuit fire, the second time for the glaze. At a certain temperature, varying for different clays, the ware becomes vitreous, that is, it is no longer porous. Low fire ware, such as flower pots, is porous, but can be made waterproof by suitable glazes.

Glazing. Glazing is perhaps the most fascinating process in ceramics, offering as it does almost infinite opportunities for developing colorful coatings for clay products. Glazes serve three major purposes: to make the ware non-porous; to provide color; and to give a surface pleasant to touch. Similar to glass, not only in name, but in chemical composition, glazes belong to the chemical compounds known as silicates because silica is their characteristic ingredient. Typical glaze formulas, expressed in chemical terms, show three divisions. First, the base—such as lead or lime—which classifies the glaze as a lead glaze or a lime glaze. Second, the alumina and boron oxide which regulate the flow of the glaze in the kiln. Third, silica which determines the "fit" of the glaze to the body.

Unless the glaze and the body have the same coefficient of expansion, one may shrink faster than the other while cooling after the great heat of the glaze firing. The result will be either (1) crazing or crackling, where the glaze develops many fine lines or cracks, as in your old dinner plates, particularly those which have been put in a too hot oven, or (2) shivering, where the glaze flakes off the body itself. In the first case the glaze shrinks more than the body; in the second the reverse is true. Sometimes crackling is planned, and the added surface texture in some wares contributes to its attractiveness, as in Figure 169.

DECORATION

Much ceramic ware needs no decoration because the shape and glaze are completely adequate to meet all esthetic requirements (Figures 167 and 172), but on certain products, some type of decoration may be desirable. As in the other arts, decoration on ceramics is best when it is integrally related to the basic shape of the ware. Since most ceramic products are circular or spherical, it follows that most decoration employs curves and circular forms. There may be opposition to the circular, of course; otherwise ceramic decoration would be tame and insipid. But downright contradiction or violation of the circular feeling is not often successful. Look again at the Sung vase and notice how beautifully the floral design fits the shape of the vase, or look at the examples of plates (Figure 168). Plates made with a lip and well suggest that these two basic divisions be respected in the design: it is implied by the form of the plate that the design of the well (the flat inner surface) shall not trespass upon the space allotted to the lip (or rim), and likewise, the border shall not wander over into the center of the plate. This does not mean that they cannot be related to each other, for the closer the relation between the ornament on lip and well, the better.

The types of decoration are legion, but may be classified from the point of view of process, as decoration applied (1) before biscuit-firing; (2) before glaze-firing; and (3) after glaze-firing.

Decoration before Biscuit-firing. While a piece of hand-thrown pottery is still in a plastic state, even while it is still on the wheel, it can be decorated with concentric raised or lowered rings, thumbprint borders, and sketches or swirls in the body of the pot. This type of decoration is usually coarse, and, therefore, is especially suited to large plates, bowls, and jars. If pottery is allowed to become partially dry, bits of clay can be pressed on to make raised borders and similar decorative devices. Mass production pottery may have the design pressed into the mold on which it is formed, as the plate in Figure 168b.

At the stage in the drying process known as *leather hard* (when the ware is hard enough to be handled safely, but not so dry that the clay powders or chips when cut away) several kinds of decorating can be done. First among these are the incised decorations. Concentric lines can be incised with a sharp tool while the pot is revolving on a wheel, or other designs and motives may be cut into the leather-hard clay. A second type is excised decoration, produced when the background is cut away to leave the design in relief (Figure 169). A third type is that in which the decoration actually pierces the clay, the holes being all or partially filled by the subsequently applied glaze.

Ceramics can also be decorated by using slip in various ways. One process, called by the Italian name of *sgraffito*, is produced by covering the whole piece with slip different in color from the clay of the body. Making the design involves scraping off the outer slip to show the color of the body in certain areas. A variation on the slip theme is the application of contrasting clays with brushes, a method which leads to free, vigorous designs, as in some Pennsylvania Dutch and Mexican pottery. Also one may inlay large surfaces of cutback body with a contrasting color.

Underglaze Decoration. Biscuit ware may also be decorated in a variety of ways. Suitable pigments mixed with water, glycerine, and oil can be painted on with a brush; underglaze crayons giving effects much like pencil drawings can be used; or designs may be stamped with a sponge or rubber stamp. It is at this time, too, that decalcomania prints are applied. Decalcomanias are lithographic prints on thin paper that transfer from the paper to the pottery with comparative ease. These are similar to the decalcomanias, generally of floral design, available at hardware stores for applying to furniture, and they are likewise similar to those which children transfer to their arms. Most dinnerware with colored designs is decorated by the decalcomania transfer process, as in Figure 168c. Covered with a transparent glaze, the transfer remains quite secure between the body and glaze.

One of the commonest types of underglaze decoration in handmade pottery is underglaze painting as in Figure 177. In work of this sort the design is painted with a brush on the biscuit ware much as one would paint a design on paper or canvas. The mineral oxides used in the painting change color when fired so that the decorator must know his material well to plan his results. This method may produce soft rich effects as in the illustration where the result, with the subtle gradations and clear, almost transparent colors, is much like water color. The glaze, usually clear, which covers the painting, serves further to unify the decoration.

Overglaze Decoration. Overglaze decoration is the term used to designate all forms of decoration applied after the ware has been glaze fired. The china painting so popular in our mothers' and grandmothers' day was of this type. Overglaze decorations generally are painted on with a brush and then fired to a temperature much below that which originally bonded the glaze to the body. Tints and lines and gilt may be applied in overglaze decoration; in fact, all gilding is done after the glaze-firing. Overglaze decoration is easy to do, but may wear off with long use. Decalcomania and other transfer prints may also be applied after the glaze fire, but, like overglaze decoration in general, they do not withstand the ravages of time and frequent washing.

CERAMIC SCULPTURE

Ceramic sculpture has been a consistently popular medium of art expression for centuries. Peoples as varied as the ancient Greeks and Egyptians, the Chinese and Mexicans, have all produced statues of human and animal forms in clay to use as symbols and decorations. The Mexican painted pigs are typical examples. Recently there has been a renewed interest in ceramic sculpture on the part of contemporary American sculptors and ceramists (Figure 178) with the result that much excellent work is available for use in home decorations. Because a piece mold can be prepared from the original sculpture, a great many replicas can be made and marketed at relatively low costs, making ceramic sculpture one of the few forms which the typical person can afford to have. Notice the way in which it has been used in the rooms pictured in Figures 1, 7 and 10 in Chapter 1.

GLASS

Glass is both handsome and useful. Along with steel, it has been one of the leading materials used in the development of new ways of building.

The Problem of Materials and Processes

From office buildings and factories to barns and family dwellings, the change brought about by the use of modern glass has been almost phenomenal. In spite of its long history, glass more than other natural material seems to belong to the twentieth century. Never before have its magnificent possibilities been used to such advantage.

Glass itself is no new product; it was known to the Egyptians who developed it as a stepchild to ceramics. It was used by the Romans. The craftsmen of the Middle Ages wrought the vibrant stained glass windows of Gothic cathedrals. But for many years glass was a great luxury; windows were few and far between. In the eighteenth century window panes were taxed as a luxury, and country squires disguised their casements with pigeon houses. It is within comparatively recent times, however, that the repertory of glass has been expanded. Glass has now descended from the luxury class to that of a necessity. Scientists have pondered and experimented, and from their laboratories have come glass blocks as strong as common brick and better insulators than their clay counterparts, huge sheets of clear plate glass, tremendous reflecting lenses for astronomical uses, such as the one at Mount Wilson Observatory in California, safety glass for vehicles of transportation, glass which can be made into diving boards, glass that can be seen through in only one direction, and even wearing apparel of glass—shoes, hats, sweaters, and dresses.

In the previous chapters we have seen examples of the new technical—and esthetic—potentialities of glass, especially as used in architecture: the liberating indoor-outdoor relationships made possible by the glass walls in the Johnson House (pages 10 and 11) and the Bauhaus (page 122); the sales value of the glass wall in the Camera Shop (page 145); and the efficient illumination secured through glass in the walls and ceilings of the Johnson Wax Company Office Building (page 147).

These, together with the examples which follow, illustrate the possibilities of this, as yet, most useful transparent material. Glass, however, has drawbacks which limit its use. Foremost is its notorious brittleness and fragility, a difficulty that is being partially overcome through lamination, as in shatterproof windshields, and through improved formulae and processes of manufacture. Still, however, with the exception of small amounts of flexible glass experimentally produced, glass has little of the tensile strength of wood or metal. Another, and less important, disadvantage is its inability to withstand sudden changes in temperature. To a large extent, this limitation has been overcome in the type of glass widely used in cooking ware. In spite of these limitations, glass still remains one of our most useful and spectacular materials. It can be thick or thin; formed into almost any shape; transparent, translucent, opaque; crystallized or filled with bubbles or a host of other textures; without color or with almost any color from a delicate tint to a deep gemlike richness; blown, molded, cast, pressed, rolled, or spun into threads; cut, engraved, etched, or sandblasted. And as though this were not enough, it is made from common materials, is inexpensive to manufacture, and is remarkably resistant to deterioration.

THE MATERIAL

Glass is a product of sand, a silicate material, as were the ceramic glazes discussed above. It is made by the melting and fusing at very high temperatures of sand and some alkali, such as sodium or potassium. These two substances are basic, but many others may be added to give special qualities. To produce crystal, the finest glass made, lead to the amount of 25 to 50 percent by weight is added. Color is produced by adding various chemicals; red comes from gold and copper oxide; blue from copper or cobalt oxides; and yellow from cadmium and uraniums. Other effects, such as opacity, bubbles, or crystallization, result from chemicals or the way in which the glass is treated.

BLOWING AND MOLDING GLASS

In making blown glass, a hollow metal rod is dipped into molten glass, withdrawn at the right moment with the desired amount of glass clinging like heavy molasses to one end. It is rolled on a polished slab, then blown into a bubble (Figure 176). Working with the simple tools used for centuries—the workman's bench, the flow-iron, the shears, the rough calipers, and wooden paddles—the craftsman expertly develops the final form. As the final product is being shaped it is subjected to rolling, twisting, and shaping with the simple tools while the glass is hot and malleable. Because the glass can be worked only at high temperatures, the process is frequently interrupted to reheat the object in small ovens or "glory-holes." Added forms, such as stems, feet, handles, or blown ornaments are successively "dropped on." The finished products must be cooled slowly, for if subjected to sudden temperature changes they will shatter. Few craft processes are more fascinating to watch than that of a skilled glassblower.

And few art objects are more serenely beautiful than a simple, unadorned piece such as is shown in Figure 174.

Most glass products today are made entirely by machinery, being either blown or pressed into cast iron or wood molds. This ware may often be detected by the careful observer because of the seam lines of the mold. In your home, you will find several examples: perhaps in the kitchen you will discover that some of the glassware there has this telltale seam mark. Look at the milk bottles or glass cooking utensils.

To produce cast glass, as the fish in Figure 179, molten glass is poured into a mold, and the resultant product is solid, not hollow as in cast pottery. Such products are usually thick, and consequently exploit to the fullest the play of light and the liquid, sparkling quality of glass. Notice in the fish how the modeling is brought out, not so much by the light falling on it, as by the light coming through it.

ORNAMENTING GLASS

Two schools of thought are current in modern glass designing. One maintains that glass should be utterly simple (look at Figure 174 again), that the fluid, reflective, elusive quality of perfectly designed clear crystal is most satisfactory. The other school holds that decoration enhances the clarity and brilliance, that the quality of the material is heightened through contrast, and that greater richness of form and meaning results. As with most other issues of this type, both schools have their points, and there is a place for both plain and decorated glass. Cutting, engraving, and etching, discussed below, are the ornamenting techniques most widely used today—the too prevalent smothering of glassware with enameled flowers, fruits, and vegetables does not merit discussion.

Cut Glass. Glass has long been cut to provide surface decoration, add fire to the crystal, or, more often, to conceal imperfections. The cutting is done by a steel wheel fed with coarse abrasives to remove the bulk of the glass, then the piece is successively polished on stone and felt wheels until the surfaces regain their original brilliance. When the design, material, and workmanship are good, the reflected and refracted light gives a dazzling effect. With the development of flaw-free glass and the trend away from elaborate decoration, the cut glass that graced our grand-mothers' sideboards with its saw-tooth edges and heavy ornamentation has fallen from favor. That this technique still holds possibilities, however, is shown in Figure 173, a heavy cut crystal vase aptly called "Whirl-pool" and showing a lively and varied pattern of light.

Engraved Glass. The technique of engraving glass has enjoyed wide popularity among contemporary glass designers and has led to many handsome pieces, one of which is shown in Figure 175. Although this is not a new technique it has enjoyed a heartening renascence chiefly in the Scandinavian countries and in the United States. Engraving is usually done on the finest crystal (glass with a high lead content), and the resulting product is more than likely to be expensive because designing and engraving are done by master artists and craftsmen. Vases such as this one are fashioned entirely by hand as described above. After the shapes have been formed the master engravers work on them at small bench lathes, into which scores of interchangeable copper wheels can be fitted. The glass is pressed upward against the revolving wheel which is fed with a fine abrasive of linseed oil and emery dust. Working with only visual reference to the designer's drawing, the engraver must use great judgment as well as technical facility in interpreting the design on the glass. The result is a shallow intaglio which, by optical illusion, seems to be in low relief. Although the engraving is seldom deep, the effect can vary from delicate to heavy modeling. Good copper wheel engraving is easily recognized by its sharp, full forms, and sensitive modeling. It is easy to distinguish from etched glass (described below) or from ornamentation produced by sandblasting through a mask, for neither of these gives the sharp clarity of line or the full modeling of form that come from engraving. The design on the vase in Figure 175 is notable for the way in which the sinuous lines relate to, without monotonously repeating, the form of the vase. This is ornament genuinely related to its form.

Etched Glass. Etching is a common method of decoration on inexpensive glass, and one which can be easily done in the art room. First all the areas of the object not to be etched are covered with a *resist* that is like a coating of wax. Then the glass is exposed to hydrofluoric acid which eats the unprotected areas to a texture which we commonly refer to as frosted. This type of decoration is often used on table glassware—tumblers, goblets, and so forth.

ARCHITECTURAL GLASS

The window panes in your house were made by one of two processes. Ordinary window glass is made by *drawing,* a machine process by which glass cylinders usually about forty feet long and three feet in diameter are blown, cut in sections, placed on a stone surface, heated, and smoothed with a block of wood. Plate glass is made by *rolling*; that is, molten glass is poured on an iron casting table, and distributed and smoothed to a thickness of about one-half inch by massive iron rollers. Superior in quality, plate glass must be ground and polished, and is considerably more expensive than the typical window glass. These processes had their beginning in the seventeenth century, but it has been only in recent years that glass in large clear sheets has been produced this way. In the time of Shakespeare, window panes were small because they were not made by the rolling process. Usually the Elizabethans blew bubbles of glass and then flattened them out into circular, or bull's-eye, panes, seldom larger than six inches in diameter. These had to be fastened into leaded frames, and the total result, at the best, was a highly unsatisfactory window as far as visibility was concerned. The transmitted light, however, was interestingly varied, and the windows were handsome to look at— but not through! If the Elizabethan wanted to look at his garden or at a passer-by, he simply had to open the window. Today we make sheets of glass over fifty feet long. This glass is clear, almost free from flaws, and makes magnificent windows in our contemporary buildings.

Although the most important, clear window glass is not the only kind of architectural glass. Factories have long made use of many kinds of "industrial glass"—translucent glass, glass reinforced with mesh, and the like. The recent introduction and ready acceptance of glass building blocks has extended the architectural possibilities of glass enormously. The Johnson Wax Company Office Building illustrates how bands of glass tubes can be used to provide soft, even light. Finally, architectural glass includes the magnificent stained glass windows generally found in Gothic churches (Chapter 17).

GLASS TEXTILES

During the last few years, glass manufacturers have given us a new product, and a startling one—glass textiles. These textiles are woven of fine glass fibers, and possess many distinct advantages. They are fireproof and sunproof, and will not shrink or mildew. Since glass is non-absorbent, they will not stain, and any spot which gets on them can be easily removed. Glass textiles are admirably suited for lamp-shades and draperies, and will undoubtedly develop other possibilities. The fibers have no elasticity, as do those of wool or cotton, so that glass textiles in their present state are not suited for clothing. They also have a lustrous finish which limits their use. But these are new products, and it is unwise to try to predict the future of glass textiles.

CONCLUSION

Ceramic art has been practiced since the dawn of civilization, and today is universally practiced throughout the world by methods which differ only in efficiency from those of the early potters. Glass, somewhat slower to develop, has recently come into its own as one of the materials deeply expressive of this age. Ceramics and glass have much in common. Both are made from inexpensive materials, clay and sand, found in all parts of the world. Both of these materials are made plastic so that they may be shaped—clay by the addition of water, and sand by subjecting it to great heat. Intense heat permanently alters both clay and sand so that neither ever returns to its original state. Other common qualities are that products of clay and glass are limited in size and more or less fragile. And the list of similarities does not stop here, for both were very expensive at one time, but have now been made inexpensive through improved machine fabrication. Finally, both show great variety in color and texture, and are pleasing to look at and to feel. Even though glass and ceramics are used for hundreds of objects which affect our daily living, recent research indicates that we have only begun to explore their possibilities.

The following publications on ceramics and glass are worth reading.

The Encyclopaedia Britannica: Articles on Ceramics and Glass for good factual summaries.
D. M. Billington: *Art of the Potter* (Oxford Press, 1937).
C. F. Binns: *The Potter's Craft* (Van Nostrand, 1932) for one of the best discussions of pottery and pottery making.
W. Buckley: *Art of Glass* (Oxford Press, 1939) for a good discussion of glassware.
Warren E. Cox: *Book of Pottery* (Crown, 1944).
J. W. Dougherty: *Pottery Made Easy* (Bruce Publishing Co., 1939).
Julia Duncan and Victor D'Amico: *How to Make Pottery and Ceramic Sculpture* (Museum of Modern Art, 1947).

The Problem of Materials and Processes

G. M. Forsyth: *Twentieth Century Ceramics* (Studio Press, 1936) for contemporary trends.

G. S. McKearin: *American Glass* (Crown, 1941).

W. A. de Sager: *Making Pottery* (Studio Press, 1934) for clear presentation of the process of making pottery.

Helen E. Stiles: *Pottery in the United States* (Dutton, 1941).

Sidney Waugh: *The Art of Making Glass* (Dodd, Mead, 1937). Notable for its excellent photographs of the process.

165. Chinese vase, Sung Dynasty (about 1108 A.D.). A wheel-thrown vase of exquisite shape. The vigorous decoration emphasizes the roundness of the form.

Throwing ceramics on a potter's wheel is an age-old art still widely practiced.

166. (*Upper*) Four stages in forming a vase: centering the mass of clay; beginning to form the vase; shaping the neck and lip; and finishing the vase.

167. (*Lower*) A stoneware cookie jar by Arthur Baggs clearly shows its origin on the potter's wheel in its strong round forms which need no ornamentation. The handles retain the plastic quality of wet clay.

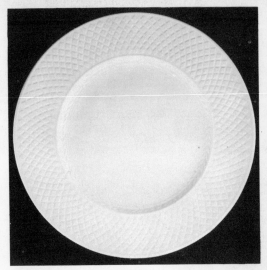

Decoration on ceramics may or may not be deemed necessary.

168. (*Upper*) Four Spode plates with various types of enrichment all emphasizing the basic shape of the plate.

169. (*Right*) Earthenware bowl by Dorothea Warren O'Hara with excised decoration. Note crackle lines which add interest to the glaze.

Mass-produced ceramics are made in molds or with jiggers and jolleys.

170. In casting pottery, liquid clay is poured into absorbent molds. The vases in the background have been made by this method.

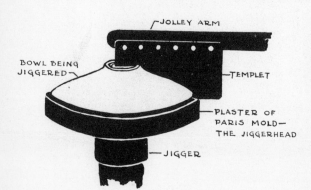

JOLLEY ARM

BOWL BEING
JIGGERED

TEMPLET

PLASTER OF
PARIS MOLD—
THE JIGGERHEAD

JIGGER

171. Diagram of jigger and jolley. The Jiggerhead forms the inside of the bowl or plate, the templet on the jolley arm forms the outside.

172. Straightforward, beautiful ceramic shapes made by casting and jiggering.

Glass may be cut to increase its prismatic effect or left without decoration.

173. (*Upper*) A contemporary cut glass vase which brilliantly exploits the rich sparkling quality of the material.

174. (*Lower*) A bowl of heavy glass. Compare the pattern of light in this bowl with that in the vase above.

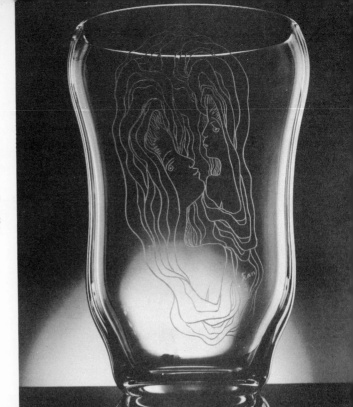

175. (*Upper*) Engraved glass vase designed by Jean Cocteau in which the design is nicely related to the sensuous shape.

176. (*Lower*) The art of glass blowing survives as the method of making the highest quality of glass objects.

177. (*Upper left*) Plate by Henry Varnum Poor with free handling of underglaze painting.

178. (*Upper right*) "The Creature God Forgot," ceramic sculpture by Victor Schreckengost.

179. (*Lower*) Fish of molded glass. Transmitted light gives a liquid, moving quality.

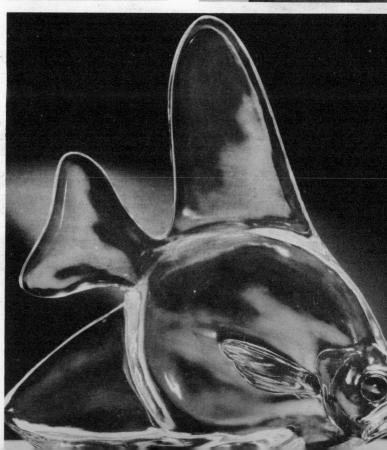

CHAPTER 12 *Textiles*

O UR range of contacts with textiles is broad, for we not only use them to upholster furniture, to cover floors, and to hang at windows, but we wear them for protection and adornment. The selection of suitable textiles for any of the many functions in which they serve us brings to light a number of facts concerning fibers and methods of fabrication. A typical problem in textile selection is a good introduction.

Suppose you set out to buy a man's summer suit. Your interest will be centered on the texture, weight, porosity, and wrinkling qualities of the textile as well as on style. Following are some of the materials the salesman may show you.

Seersucker is a well-known cotton summer fabric characterized by its familiar light, grayish-blue stripe and crepe weave. In recent years there have been variations of seersucker. New patterns have been substituted for the traditional blue and white stripe, while the crinkle is kept. Being highly porous, it sets up little resistance against the summer breezes. A suit made of seersucker weighs only about one and a half pounds, but since most cottons do not hold their shape, a seersucker suit will, all too soon, look wrinkled and baggy.

Linen is highly absorbent (that is why it is favored for dish towels), and the smoothness of its fibers, aiding circulation of air, helps keep one cool. But linen comes from a vegetable source (flax), and does not have the springy quality found in animal fibers, such as wool. Linen suits spend most of the summer in the laundry, and the expense and annoyance of keeping one up through a season have turned many away from them.

Rayon and other synthetic fibers are becoming increasingly popular. While not yet in as great demand as other suitings, they have certain advantages. These fibers have the admirable quality of being wrinkle resistant—at least the wrinkles tend to fall out overnight from a properly hung garment—but most rayons cannot be easily laundered and many of them still spot and stain easily.

Tropical worsted is wool finely spun into a fabric from which suits weighing about ten ounces less than the average wool suit can be made. It is popular because it is cool, has the appearance of an all-year-round suit, and yet has the desirable qualities of crease-resistance and porosity.

Worsted gabardine is a perennial favorite because it is probably the dressiest of summer suitings. But where it gains in appearance, it loses in coolness. It is a tightly woven wool material, heavy, as summer materials go, and some gabardines become unpleasantly shiny.

Worsted and mohair is a mixture usually woven into a herringbone pattern and, although heavier than tropical worsted, it does have the necessary hardness (from the mohair) to keep its shape better.

Palm beach cloth is a mixture of angora, mohair and cotton—animal and vegetable fibers. The angora and mohair help make the material wrinkle free, and, for this reason—since the material is light and extremely porous—it is used all over the world for both men's and women's summer clothes.

It is plain to see that, even in the limited range of summer suitings, there is a variety to choose from, and that one of the factors which largely determines the kind of textile the loom will yield is the raw source material. Although the above illustration did not introduce all of the raw materials, it gave an example of each of the major types: vegetable fibers, such as cotton and linen; animal fibers, such as wool and mohair; and manufactured fibers, such as rayon. The raw material must be a fiber of some kind, the possibilities and limitations of which we now turn to.

THE RAW MATERIALS OF TEXTILES

THE VEGETABLE FIBERS

Cotton, probably our most common fiber, in its natural state is usually white but may be brownish. The short fibers grow as twisted hairs covering the seeds of plants raised in many parts of the world. About 60 percent of the cotton crop comes from the southern United States, the remainder from such widely separated places as Egypt, India and Brazil. The fibers are separated from the seeds by the well-known *cotton gin,* invented by Eli Whitney; carded and drawn further to clean as well

302

as to make them parallel; spun into threads; and finally woven into a host of products. Cotton is widely used because it is inexpensive and has fairly good wearing qualities for clothes, sheets, towels, draperies and curtains as well as for bagging, packaging, belting, and even highway construction.

Linen comes from the fiber growing around the woody pith of the flax plant which has been in cultivation for at least 7000 years. One stem may yield as many as 25,000 fibers, each averaging $\frac{1}{1000}$ of an inch in diameter and as long as three and one-half feet. The fibers are separated, made parallel and spun into thread. Flax fiber is capable of being worked to a high polish without losing any of its other qualities of tensile strength and absorbency. Fibers like these can be spun into extremely fine threads which, in turn, may be woven into products (like handkerchiefs) of delicate sheerness but with more absorbing quality than silk. Beautiful tablecloths and napkins, sheets and pillow cases come from weaving such thread and have strength, smooth, even texture, and that much-prized feeling of freshness. Linen, however, wrinkles easily and this restricts its use in some ways. Flax fibers may also be spun into heavier threads, and woven into textiles with interesting, rough textures well suited to summer sport clothes, draperies and tablecloths. Rugs having unusual wearing and decorative qualities are also being produced from flax fibers.

Jute and hemp, growing in tropical and semi-tropical countries, produce a fiber not unlike that of flax but much rougher and coarser. They are used chiefly in the making of rope and coarse rugs and mats.

THE ANIMAL FIBERS

Wool is not hair, but rather an undercoat which later develops into hair; it is much finer than hair. The sheep, and not all sheep at that, is one of the few animals that bear a fleece of wool and no hair. The wool fiber varies in thickness from that of a spider's web to that comparable to coarse hair, and this accounts for the variety of wools: Merino, Shetland, Cashmere, and many others. The fibers are combed out and twisted into threads much as the cotton fibers are. Good wool can be given a variety of textures which can be used to advantage. Wool can be woven into textiles as smooth as are some gabardines or as rough and shaggy as are tweeds and homespuns. A rich carpet in velvet weave and plain color, made from wool, has a luster and an air of luxury and solidity that is impossible to duplicate in any other fiber. And, because wool is a

303

tough fiber, it may also be made into closely woven, heavy fabrics such as tapestries. The subdued luster of wool fibers gives these textiles a warm, living tone which makes them pleasant to touch.

Horsehair is thick enough and long enough in its original state to use without further processing. Its hard, shiny quality results in extremely stiff, grating products. *Camel's hair* is wool; it is the winter undercoating which camels shed in spring and makes wonderful winter-coat material. Actual camel's hair is sometimes used as is horsehair for textiles and, of course, is widely used for paint brushes. Other animals which produce hair used in textiles are the goat, alpaca, llama, and rabbit.

The story of the manufacture of *silk fibers* by a lowly worm from the mulberry leaf is such a favorite that it need not be told here. Silk fibers are strong and very long in contrast to most fibers which are short. Silk fibers are also very fine, and can be spun into threads of great slenderness, and subsequently woven into the thinnest of textiles; or more fibers can be spun together to produce threads and cloths of heavier weights. Because it is extremely tough and has natural luster, silk has long been a favorite for woven or knitted sheer, clinging textiles. Stockings of gauzy texture and transparency may be fabricated from this material; shimmering satins and soft chiffons are likewise natural products of silk. And yet, if the process of finishing and refining is not entirely completed, products appear which are quite contrary to the popular notion of silk. They may show the typical silk luster but with more roughness as in shantungs or pongees, or they may be coarse and somewhat rough. Known as raw silk, these materials are more like wool in appearance than we usually think it possible for silk to be, and they make excellent drapery substitutes for the ubiquitous cretonnes and monk's cloths.

MANUFACTURED FIBERS

By processing such materials as wood pulp or cotton, chemists have produced artificial fibers, referred to by such trade names as Rayon, Bemberg and Celanese. The process, although very complex in actuality, may be described simply. Cellulose products (wood, cotton, etc.) are transformed into a liquid state called viscose by being treated with different chemicals. This viscose is then forced through tiny nozzles, each with many holes, into an acid bath. Contact with the acid solidifies the viscose, and a thread results. This thread may be composed of as many fibers as there are holes in the nozzle, and may be of infinite length if desired. It is spun as it is wound on the bobbins. The whole process by which wood is transformed into synthetic threads is accomplished in one long, but continuous, manufacturing operation.

Originally the ugly duckling of the textile industry, these synthetic fibers have undergone remarkable development until now they are very widely used. At first all textiles made from these fibers resembled silk more closely than other fibers because of their shiny surface, and even now the great majority of them are closer to silk than to cotton or wool in appearance. However, these fibers seem to take easily to developments of all sorts and we may expect today to find synthetic materials which look almost like wool. The chief difference between the natural and the more recent synthetic fibers from the viewpoint of the consumer seems to be that the synthetic textiles must be handled with greater care. The regular processes of washing, cleaning and pressing with hot irons affect synthetic fibers in various ways, a fact which is attested by the carefully worded cleaning instructions which accompany these products.

There are other manufactured materials which are used in textiles. Cellophane (another cellulose product) is often cut into strips and woven. As mentioned above, glass may be transformed into suitable threads. Occasionally, gold and silver are used for weaving rich brocades and tapestries, although such gold and silver thread is not accurately called a manufactured fiber.

MAKING TEXTILES

It is plain to see that the raw material is important in determining the use and appearance of a textile. So, too, is the processing of the raw material—the preparation of it and actual making of the textile. Four classifications cover the territory of fabrication: weaving, knitting, felting and lace-making.

Of these four, weaving is the most widely practiced. Knitting is second, with felting and lace-making trailing along as distinctly less important. The manufacture of textiles has changed little in fundamental processes since they were first developed. The Guatemalan in Figure 182 is weaving in the same way as her ancestors did for centuries. But great advances in

machinery during the past one hundred years have made the textile industry a gigantic one: factories now produce textiles in quantities the
very thought of which would have staggered the imaginations of those
who patiently toiled for days for a few yards of goods. Manufacturers
continue always to combine new materials, to refine the old ones, to
produce an endless variety of products. They battle to introduce new
colors, new designs, new textures, with the result that the products from
the power looms of today surpass anything man ever dreamed of—in
quantity, at least. But the processes remain fundamentally the same.

WEAVING

Weaving is the process of interlacing threads at right angles—as simple
as that. It can be done on a piece of cardboard cut into a crude loom, on
the primitive contraption of the Guatemalan, or on the magnificently
complex power looms of a great mill. No matter what the loom, there
are three fundamental movements in all weaving: (1) separating the warp
threads into two or more series, thus forming an opening for the passage
of the filling (warp); (2) "picking" the filling through this opening, by
hand on a hand loom, by power on a machine loom; (3) beating back
the filling thread just run through to form a tight interlacing. These
movements are well illustrated in Figure 183.

The variety of weaves seems enormous when you look through the textile displays of a large store (or mail-order catalogue), but they may be
classified as follows:

Plain weaves including the following three general types:

Tabby in which the warp and weft threads are interlaced in simple
alternations, as in muslin, dress linen, burlap, and canvas.

Rib in which a rib is formed by having a thicker warp than weft (or the
reverse), as in rep, poplin, piqué.

Basket in which two or more warps are crossed by two or more filling or
weft threads, as in monk's cloth.

Twill weaves which have a diagonal rib across the material as in serge
and herringbone, produced by having the filling thread go over one and
under two or more threads, instead of under one and over the next.

Figure weaves in which simple or complex patterns are woven in the
plain background, such as damasks, brocades, tapestry. Machine weaving

306

of this type is done on a Jacquard loom, a highly complex mechanism in which the weave is controlled by small cards through which holes have been punched. These look like player piano records, and the principle is much the same.

Satin weaves in which a series of warp threads remain on the surface with a cross thread at intervals. This tends to eliminate the textures typical in most weaving, and produces a characteristic sleekness.

Pile weaves which give us our velvets, corduroys, mohair, terry cloth, bath towels and rugs are produced by allowing the weft threads to remain in loops above the surface. Sometimes these are cut (as in velvet), sometimes left as loops (bath towels).

The apparent complexity of weaving will frighten you much less if you will look carefully at different textiles with a magnifying glass. The differences in weaves will then become more readily apparent, and you will have little difficulty in classifying—and understanding—them.

KNITTING

Knitting is the interlocking of loops of yarn or thread by means of needles, and it may be done slowly by you or grandmother in the parlor or with lightning rapidity on knitting machines. A striking—and often annoying—characteristic of knit goods is that they may become unraveled if a thread breaks. Knitting, of course, gives us our socks and stockings, sweaters, underwear, and jerseys.

FELTING

Felting is nothing more than matting or pounding together fibers to form heavy cloths. Felt hats and certain types of floor coverings are produced in this way. There is no regular textural pattern in felts, although the fibers, especially if they are large or rough, give varying surface qualities.

LACE-MAKING

Lace-making in which threads are interlocked in various more or less open patterns does not enjoy the popularity that it did when lace collars and lace curtains were tokens of a certain degree of wealth. More than other fields of textile design, lace-making has suffered from a lack of new designs suited to contemporary needs.

Each of these processes gives a product of distinctive characteristics, fitting it to perform certain functions well. Each of them results in distinctive textures and patterns which range all the way from the coarse, rugged roughness of burlap to the soft suppleness of fine wool jersey, from brash tweeds to smooth satins, from crisp cellophane to rich tapestries. We may be thankful for this variety, but it is a danger as well as an opportunity. To choose with care the textile used for any purpose is possible today, but choosing with care demands understanding. What do we look for? Suitable fibers, suitable processes and appropriate, pleasing designs.

PRINTING ON TEXTILES

Many textiles used today are enriched through patterns printed on the woven fabric (Figures 181, 188, 189, 190, 191, 194, 195). They are now so common that it is startling to realize that their widespread production is relatively recent in western civilization. No one knows when or where printed textiles originated, but it is believed that they were first produced in India and Egypt. Although India prints were highly valued by the Romans, textiles were not printed in Europe until the latter half of the seventeenth century. Once introduced, the process was rapidly developed and within a hundred years many factories had been established.

There are three basic ways of printing designs on textiles: *block-printing*, *intaglio printing*, and *stencil printing*. These processes are almost identical with those used in printing on paper, and because the latter are discussed in some detail in the following chapter they will be only briefly mentioned here.

Block-printing is done from blocks, usually of wood, into which a design has been cut. The coloring agent is applied to the block, the block is pressed onto the textile, and the raised portion of the block prints the pattern. Each color in the pattern requires a separate block, and when done by hand, each is printed individually. Usually a hand process, block-printing is suited to patterns in which the design is rela-

Textiles gain interest from the fibers used, the method of weaving, and applied decoration such as printed patterns.

180. (*Upper*) Experimental textiles woven with plastic threads by Barbara Beardsley show variety of texture and pattern.

181. (*Lower*) Two printed textiles by Frank Hinder. "Ngaboni" (which signifies "Look— behold") was developed from a study of aboriginal Australian art forms. "Doodle-Dot" shows imaginative forms developed from a skilled designer's "doodling."

(Opposite page) Contemporary weavers have explored the possibilities of old and new materials to produce varied effects.

184. (Upper left) Translucent gauze of silk and wool mohair handwoven by Menlo Textiles.

185. (Upper right) Hand weave by Dorothy Liebes made with cotton warp, flat plastic strips, and metal braid.

186. (Lower left) Cotton fabric with bands of loop texture handwoven by Menlo Textiles.

187. (Lower right) Hand weave by Dorothy Liebes of wool, cotton chenille, raw silk, three types of metal strips and silk cord.

Printed patterns range from naturalistic to abstract forms.

188. (Upper left) Print called "Geraniums" shows geranium plants in naturalistic colors.

189. (Upper right) Adrian Feint's "Foliage" was suggested by the falling leaves of autumn.

190. (Lower left) Angelo Testa's "Cat-Tails" is a linear design in brown, blue-green, and gray.

191. (Lower right) Angelo Testa's "Line in Action" is an abstract pattern of black lines on bands of yellow and white.

182. (Upper) A primitive Guatemalan hand loom on which textiles such as shown in Figure 67 are woven.

183. (Lower) Four-harness hand loom which permits more complex weaves than the Guatemalan loom. Notice the four treadles which separate the warp threads in four ways, and the shuttle on which the filling or weft is carried back and forth.

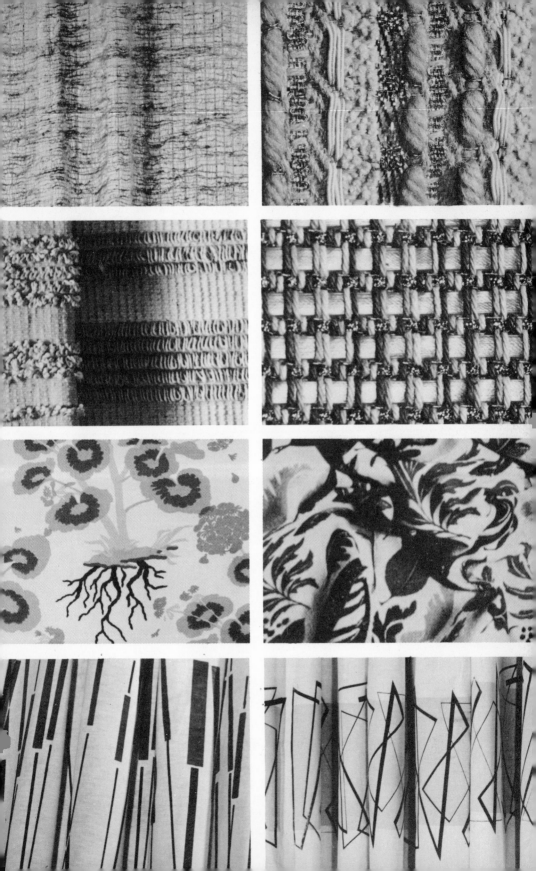

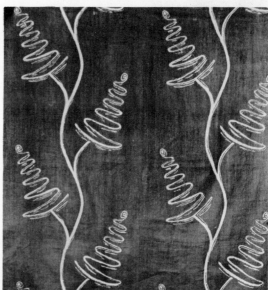

Many textiles are designed to be seen in folds.

192. (*Upper left*) Eighteenth-century woven damask from Williamsburg.

193. (*Upper right*) Modern damask used in Williamsburg shows nice relation of textile pattern to architectural ornament.

194. (*Lower left*) Contemporary print of conventionalized foliage.

195. (*Lower right*) Compare this treatment of patterns with that in Figs. 188-192.

tively simple, the repeated motives are of fairly small size, and the number of colors is limited.

Intaglio printing is a machine process done from engraved copper cylinders on a rotary press and is basically similar to rotogravure printing on paper. Although each cylinder prints but one color, as many as sixteen colors can be printed in one run through the press. The process imposes few limitations on the designer: the pattern can be simple or complex, repeated motives as large as the circumference of the cylinder, colors as few or many as the designer wishes. Because of its flexibility, speed, and precision, intaglio printing is widely used.

Stencil printing is usually done with a stencil of stout paper or wood. The design to be printed is cut out of the stencil; color, applied with a stencil brush, reaches those parts of the textile exposed through the cut-out stencil. Primarily a hand process, stencil printing has been intensively developed in Japan but is not widely used elsewhere. Silk-screen printing is a variation of the stencil process and is increasingly being used in the production of distinctive textiles.

TEXTILE DESIGN

Textile design is the organization of the form, line, texture, color, and space of woven fibers to achieve the aims of FORM FOLLOWS FUNCTION and VARIETY IN UNITY. The character of the design develops from three sources: the qualities of the fibers; the processes by which they are woven; and the decoration (if any) applied after weaving.

The qualities of the fibers deserve first consideration because it is the fibers with which the designer begins. We have seen that different fibers have special possibilities and limitations: jute is naturally coarse and stiff, silk is fine and soft. Mohair crinkles and twists when subjected to heat to give the irregularities noticeable in Figure 184. The manner in which the fiber is processed also affects the final result. Flax, for example, can be spun into fine threads suitable for weaving sheer handkerchiefs, or it can be made into coarse yarns adapted to the manufacture of rough, long-wearing rugs. Silk can be refined so that it attains a high luster or it can be used as raw silk to give softness and smoothness without being shiny. In Figures 184 to 187 we see differences resulting from the use of silk and wool mohair; cotton, plastic strips, and metal braid; cotton used alone; and cotton chenille, raw silk, metal strips, and silk cord. Thus, the character of the fibers and the manner in which they are processed is the primary source of textile design.

The second consideration is the way in which the fibers are interlaced to form a textile. We have seen how different weaves give different results (look again at Figure 180). When the pattern arises from the structure of the material, it is often referred to as structural design of which there are many standard types: muslin, rep, monk's cloth, satin, and terry cloth. There are also many less familiar ones, such as those shown in Figures 186 and 187 or in the master weavings of the pre-Columbian Peruvians. Structural design permits great variation in the general character of the textile and the uses for which it is suitable. Another way of enriching textiles during the weaving process is shown in the Guatemalan fabric illustrated in Chapter 4 or the damasks shown in Figures 192 and 193. In these, yarns of different colors, weights, or fibers are introduced to produce shapes of various sorts. Such woven patterns show great variety: conventionalized animals and human figures in the Guatemalan textile; formalized foliage in the Williamsburg damasks; geometrical shapes and abstract symbols in Early American coverlets and Navajo rugs.

The third consideration includes the several ways of ornamenting textiles after they have been woven: embroidery, appliqué, and printing. Embroidery and appliqué, usually done by hand, produce raised designs either through needlework or sewing other materials onto the fabric. Although both give rich patterns and textures, they are infrequently used today. Printed textiles, however, are so abundantly available that they deserve thought. The designer of printed textiles has almost complete freedom to do what he wants, and this freedom is both valuable and dangerous—valuable because it encourages experimentation and creativity, dangerous because there are few controls inherent in the process. The designer can take a natural object such as a geranium plant (Figure 188) and paint the leaves, flowers, stems, and roots in natural colors. He can then spot this statically on the textile, loosely filling in the voids with falling petals. Or he can remove his design a step or two from the literal appearance of nature, as did the designer of "Autumn Foliage" (Figure 189). This print shows leaves organized into a strongly rhythmic design which is far from a literal copy. The designer can treat his subject matter even more abstractly, as did Angelo Testa in Figures 190 and 191. In "Cat-Tails" the basic shape of the plant has been expressed in simple

314

forms to give a pattern nicely suited to the flatness of textiles and pleasing when seen either stretched flat or hung in folds. In "Line in Action" there are no recognizable objects because in this print the designer wished to express directly and abstractly a feeling of action and movement. Whether one wishes accurate representations of flowers and leaves, conventionalized treatments of natural objects, or purely abstract pattern is largely a matter of taste. It is worth noting, however, that in the history of textiles few which copy nature literally hold interest for more than a short time.

In appraising textile design it is well to remember that textiles are *two-dimensional, continuous* surfaces. Strictly speaking, of course, all have a third dimension, and contemporary weavers as well as those in the past have created textured surfaces pleasing to look at and touch. Nevertheless, in comparison with objects of clay or metal, textiles are essentially flat and any design destroying this planeness is questionable. Not a few printed designs, especially those with bunches of flowers almost bulging off the cloth or scenic designs diving into space, fall into this category. To be sure space can be indicated to increase interest, as in "Cat-Tails" where the large forms stand somewhat in front of the smaller or in "Line in Action" in which some lines advance and others recede. But a textile is flat and the designer should bear this in mind.

With minor exceptions, textiles are not only flat but are continuous. They come by the yard or bolt and are usually seen in sizable areas. If one aims to strengthen and emphasize the nature of his materials, he will not want to destroy this basic continuousness. He will want to direct attention easily and pleasantly over the surface, to relate each part to those adjacent rhythmically. Only on rare occasions will he want a series of disparate spots attracting attention to themselves and thereby distracting attention from the whole. Isolated motives of the sort that tempt you to count them one by one can be particularly trying.

As with other types of art, in appreciating textiles we think about the way in which they will be used and concern ourselves with their functional qualities. And equally important, we look for textiles which have spirit, imagination, creativity. They should be useful—but not dull.

The tremendous variety of textiles available today makes the problem of selection easy and difficult at the same time—easy because if you look long enough you can invariably find what you want, difficult because the variety is confusing. To become more conscious of the textiles which you see, try making a list of those seen in one day. Feel them carefully to notice their tactile qualities because—mark this well—most textiles are designed to be felt. Try also applying the criteria listed above. Then, if you wish to learn more, read:

Z. Bendvre and G. Pfeiffer: *American Fabrics* (Macmillan, 1946).

Kate Van Cleve: *Hand Loom Weaving for Amateurs* (Beacon Press, 1935) is good for beginners in the art of weaving.

H. Coats: *Weaving for Amateurs* (Studio Press, 1941).

Anthony Hunt: *Textile Design* (Studio Press, 1937) combines theory and practice.

F. Kean: *Art Weaving* (Heath, 1937) considers weaving as an art.

Ethel Mairet: *Handweaving Today, Traditions and Changes* (Faber & Faber, 1941).

Herbert Read: *Art in Industry* (Harcourt, Brace, 1935) for the best brief discussion of textile design.

M. Trilling and F. Williams: *Art in Home and Clothing* (Lippincott, 1936). A good practical handbook.

Isabel Wingate: *Textile Fabrics and Their Selection* (Prentice-Hall, 1935) is a consideration of textiles from the consumers' viewpoint.

The Encyclopaedia Britannica's excellent article on Weaving.

CHAPTER 13 *Printing and the Graphic Processes*

PRINTING

THE book which you are reading is an example of the art of printing. The type used is called Electra; the black and white illustrations were reproduced by the Polytone process of lithography; and the color chart was reproduced by four-color process printing.

So accustomed have we become to the printed page—the newspaper, the magazine and the book—that we easily forget that machine printing on paper came relatively late in man's history of accomplishments. The art of printing as we think of it today had been known in Europe for only fifty years when Columbus discovered America. Before man abandoned the old, laborious process of copying by hand the books storing the world's knowledge, the Egyptian and Greek temples, already centuries old, were beginning to crumble. With the exception of some graphic processes described in this chapter, printing is one of the youngest of the plastic-graphic arts.

However, the principles and processes on which printing is based had long been known. In India designs from woodblocks had been impressed on textiles for centuries, and as early as 900 A.D. the Chinese were familiar with block printing on paper. There is evidence that the Chinese used movable type of clay and tin in the eleventh century, and that a Korean book was printed from cast type in 1409. However, it was not until the middle of the fifteenth century in Europe that Johannes Gutenberg began making movable type of individual letters. We stress the point of *individual letters* because pictorial woodblocks, made by a process similar to that illustrated in Figure 198, were widely used. Furthermore, a few words had often been carved on these pictorial block prints and

317

printed with them. Thus the line of development is from (1) pictorial woodblocks to (2) woodblocks with a few words on them (like home-made Christmas cards) to (3) individual letters.

At first this type was set by hand, and printed in crude *platen* or job presses—presses in which two flat surfaces are forced together to make the printing. The capacity of such early presses was about 300 pages a day. Think of the time it would take to print a best-selling novel or a Sunday newspaper on such presses! By 1814 power-driven cylinder presses were giving 1000 pages an hour, and today our giant rotary presses have many times that capacity. The *cylinder* press differs from the platen press in that the paper is fed on a cylinder but the type is carried on a flat surface. In the next development, the *rotary* press, both type and paper are on cylinders, making possible much greater speed and efficiency.

As the speed of printing increased, attention was turned to the process of setting the type, and in 1885 the linotype was patented. The improved form of the linotype in use today is a very complex machine. A skilled operator works at a keyboard similar to a typewriter. As he presses each key, a matrix or mold of the letter is released and carried to an assembler. When molds for a full line of words have been assembled, a cast or slug is made. Then the molds are returned automatically to their proper places. Printing is done from the cast.

As you thumb through magazines looking at the different classes of types used, you will undoubtedly think that there are hundreds of different ones. There are. However, almost all relate to three major classifications:

black letter   roman   *italic*

The black letter is the earliest, having been introduced by Gutenberg in imitation of the hand-copied books of his day. The roman or Italian was developed in the fifteenth century after the classic roman lettering carved on monuments. The italic is of more recent origin. These have given rise to many variations.

There are two other distinctions worth noting. The weight (lightness or heaviness of value) of a type face refers to the width of lines in the letters. There are four standard classifications:

lightface
standard
boldface
extrabold

Type also varies in width:

extended
standard
condensed
extra-condensed

Thus the printer has to make three major decisions: which classification of type to use, which weight and which width. After selecting the exact type, the typographer needs give his attention to the kind of paper on which the type will be printed, the kind and quantity of illustrations or decorations, and the margins which will surround his printing. Apply these criteria to the printing in Figure 196, and to the printing you see in newspapers, magazines and books:

1. Legibility comes first. Printing is a means of communicating ideas, and if it fails to function efficiently, that is, if it is not legible, it has little to recommend it.

2. The style of printing should be in harmony with the content of the printed matter. In more familiar words, the form should be determined by the basic idea. Although this cannot be achieved in all printing, it may be in well-designed books and advertisements.

3. The printed text should be pleasingly related to illustrative materials used with it whether they be photographs, drawings or paintings.

4. The aims of organization—FORM FOLLOWS FUNCTION and VARIETY IN UNITY—as well as the principles of *balance, continuity* and *emphasis* apply with full force to the art of printing.

Printing is the means through which we do a great deal of our learning. There are few who do not read at least a little every day. Here, then, is an art of daily life, an art which affects us profoundly. Look critically at the printing with which you come in contact. Is it pleasing? Legible? How could it be improved?

Printing of words is only one branch of this art, the other being the printing of pictures, to which we now turn.

THE GRAPHIC PROCESSES

About noon, in Brooklyn, the President's wife christens a ship. A photographer records the event, and later that day, across the continent in San Francisco, pictures of the christening are printed in the evening newspaper. Photographs are wired across the country with the speed of electricity, and reproduced by the thousands in a few minutes. Strikingly different is the example of an artist who labors long and patiently to produce a small number of drypoints or etchings. Yet both are examples of the graphic arts serving real but different contemporary needs. The *graphic processes* are those printing processes by which pictures or designs are reproduced, generally in quantities. Because of the relative cheapness of the product these processes afford most persons a means of establishing contact with good art. Some of the graphic processes, such as drypoint and etching, are hand processes, essentially methods of *creating* art.* Others, such as photoengraving, are mechanical methods of *reproducing* art.

Another method of dividing the graphic processes is in terms of the type of printing surface from which the print is actually made. In all printing the basic problem is to treat a surface so that part of it will print, part of it will not. Three different types of printing surface have been developed, and, consequently, three methods of printing. They are relief printing, intaglio printing, and planographic or surface printing. The rubber stamp is a good example of *relief* printing—printing in which the inked surface is raised. *Intaglio* printing is the direct opposite —the printing area is lowered. *Surface* printing is done from a flat plate —the inked portion is neither raised nor lowered. Each process as it is discussed in the following section will be designated according to the classification into which it falls.

THE HAND PROCESSES

The Woodcut and Linoleum Cut (A *Relief Process*). The woodcut and linoleum cut are the simplest of the *relief* printing processes. Almost everyone has seen examples of them. You may have received one as a Christmas card from one of your more industrious or artistic friends, or you may have seen them used as book illustrations, or you may have done one yourself. The materials are wood of even grain—beech, apple, pear, or sycamore—or battleship linoleum; a cutting tool which may be a pocket knife or a set of especially designed knives or gouges; printing

---

* Expression and communication are quite as important in these arts as in painting and sculpture, and much of what is said in Chapters 15 and 16 applies equally well to the creative graphic processes.

AN EXHIBITION OF

Woodcuts & Wood Engravings

BY

Hans Alexander Mueller

FROM

book published by Pynson Printers

December 15, 1939

NOW ON DISPLAY

SEVENTH FLOOR · TIMES ANNEX · 229 W 43

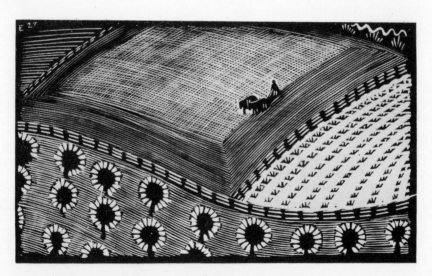

196. (*Upper*) An example of well-designed printing.

197. (*Lower*) Wharton Esherick's woodcut illustration for Walt Whitman's I WATCHED THE PLOWMAN PLOWING shows tectural effects secured with different woodcut tools. The design is in white lines and areas silhouetted against the black background.

321

Woodcuts can be in black and white or in color, can show much detail or place emphasis on simple forms.

198. A detail of Albrecht Dürer's "The Knight and Man-at-Arms" shows a woodcut in which the design is in black lines against a white background. Compare with Figure 197.

199. "The Lantern Maker" by Yoshida is a Japanese wood block printed in color. All forms have been simplified and conventionalized.

oo. (*Upper*) Rembrandt's "Christ Healing the Sick," an etching.

o1. (*Lower*) Georges Braque. "Job." A drypoint in the cubist manner. "Job" was a popular brand of cigarette.

202. (*Upper*) Honoré Daumier's "The Too Hot Bath" is a lithograph which shows the rich blacks and textured grays possible in this medium.

203. (*Lower*) Silk screen printing used on a cover of an exhibition catalogue. Silk screen permits broad simplified handling of pictorial forms and lettering, as in the above example, and is also suitable for more detailed work.

ink; and suitable paper. The designs are frequently worked out on paper, and transferred to the wood or linoleum before the cutting begins. Then the chips begin to fly. Not all woodcuts, however, are done by amateurs. The range of effects obtainable from woodcuts makes them highly prized, and artists from Albrecht Dürer to the contemporary Howard Cook, Lynd Ward and Raoul Dufy have put this medium to good expression.

There are two types of woodcuts: the black line and the white line. The black line (Figure 198) may closely resemble an ink drawing, and, in fact, it came into being as a method of reproducing such drawings. It is characterized by the fact that the black lines are left standing, the background areas being cut away. The white line (Figure 197) is the opposite: here the line is cut away, and the background left standing. A moment's reflection will reveal that the second method is probably a better use of the medium because in it the cutting tool works on the positive part of the design. In no way is it an imitation of a drawing. Closely related to woodcuts are wood-engravings, once widely used for reproducing pictures. They are done on the end grain of wood with special tools, and generally show much more detail than do woodcuts.

Printing from such blocks need not be confined to paper, but can also be done on fabrics. India prints are good examples of block prints in color on textiles. The process is exactly the same as on paper except that the design is repeated countless times to produce an all-over pattern. More than one color is generally used which merely means that separate blocks for each color are cut and printed one at a time.

The Japanese Color Print (A *Relief Process*). This popular Oriental art, examples of which exist in almost every Japanese and not a few American homes, is a type of woodblock printing. The process is exactly the same as that described above: the design is prepared, and transferred to blocks of wood which are cut and printed, each color demanding a separate block.

Japanese prints are almost universally admired today for their subtlety of design and color. Their strong, basic organization, simplicity and unity, have influenced the work of many modern painters. "The Lantern Maker" (Figure 199) by Yoshida is a characteristic example: a commonplace scene lifted to importance by imaginative vision and competent technique. Notice the striking, asymmetrical balance of dark and light; the textures in lanterns, robe and screen; the circular movements in the foreground, the vertical movement in the background; and the judicious use of carefully placed contrasts—the dark paint in the dishes, the brushes, the inscription on the lanterns.

Etching (An Intaglio Process). The term *etching* comes from a German word which means "to eat." In making an etching the artist works on a plate of copper or zinc. He coats this with a thin, even layer of *ground*—a waxy material which will resist acid and yet be easily penetrated by a needle. Generally, so that he may better see what he is drawing, he blackens the plate with candle smoke. Then, with blunt needles of different sizes and shapes, he scratches lines through the waxy ground so that the metal is uncovered. All these preliminary steps, of course, must be made with the next process, that of the actual etching, in mind.

The etching (eating in) occurs when the plate is immersed in an acid, generally perchloride of iron, known as the *mordant*. Wherever the etcher's needles have exposed the plate or, in other words, wherever the wax has been scratched away, the acid attacks. A plate can be given a single immersion in which case all lines will be of equal darkness. If a variety of lines is desired, a *stop out* is applied to those lines which the etcher thinks are deep enough, and the plate immersed again in the acid. This stop out, which is either shellac or asphaltum varnish, protects the bitten lines from further action by the acid. This procedure of stopping out lines that have been bitten to the desired depth can be repeated many times resulting in a variety of widths and darknesses in the final etching. When all the lines in the plate are bitten to what appears to be the proper depth, the plate is wiped clear of the ground and stop out, and is ready for printing. If lines are weak in places, they may be deepened through the use of a graver which both deepens and broadens the etched lines, practically all etchings being touched up in this way.

Now comes the inking. The ink, specially prepared for printing etchings, is either rolled or stamped into the incised lines of the plate, which has been warmed to increase the ink's fluidity. When all the lines have thus been thoroughly charged with ink, the surface of the plate can be dragged with a soft cheesecloth which spreads the ink slightly from the confines of the incised lines. This is known as *retroussage*, and is done in order to remove from the print the coldness and hardness of a line which is wiped clean.

The final step, the printing, is done on a heavy press. The bed of the press is of cast metal which moves forwards and backwards between two metal rollers below and above. The plate is centered on the press bed and placed face up, and the paper (which has been dampened) is laid on top of it. Blankets of extra fine felt are placed over the paper, and the whole is run through the press under firm pressure. The damp paper is forced through this pressure into the incisions in the plate. The ink held in these incisions is, therefore, transferred to the paper.

The finished etching has many characteristics which make the identification of the process comparatively simple. The lines on the print are raised—run your fingers over an etching and you will notice this. The plate also leaves several marks on the paper: you will see the impression left by the edges of the plate (the plate mark), and in addition the whole area of the paper which has been in contact with the plate will be slightly darker than the borders because of a film of surplus ink. Closer examination of an etching will show how the ends of the lines are square cut, a result of the eating of the acid. This characteristic differentiates the etching from its brother and sister graphic arts, the drypoint and the engraving, in which the lines are more or less pointed at the ends.

The etching, "Christ Healing the Sick" (Figure 200) by Rembrandt, stands today, as it did three centuries ago, as one of the truly great works of art in any medium. The subject matter and the intense sympathetic treatment make it a noble expression of religious ideals. The dramatic diagonal organization of darks and lights gives great force to the group of figures with Christ in the center. But we are here more particularly concerned with the manner in which the medium of etching has been used to produce these results. Careful examination will show that line is the plastic element used to gain the effects. At the extreme left the lines stand clear and distinct, defining form and space by merely enclosing areas. As we move into the center of the picture, the lines are woven into a pattern of textures and values so that we are less conscious of the individual line. Finally, at the extreme right, the lines are hardly noticeable in the rich grays and blacks. But line is the major element on which the composition is built, and is a major factor in giving it a flexible, lucid, almost transparent, quality.

Only a limited number of prints can be made from an etching plate, and each print is numbered consecutively. Editions vary in number from about fifty to several hundred. Subjection to the repeated process of printing flattens the plate, and tends to make each succeeding print somewhat less rich. Etched plates are sometimes coated electrolytically with steel, thus making possible an almost unlimited number of prints.

327

These prints are in no way inferior to those made from the untreated copper or zinc plate.

Drypoint (An Intaglio Process). It is so difficult to distinguish an etching from a drypoint that only the practiced eye, acquainted with all the details of the two processes, can be reasonably sure. (See Figure 201.)

The difference in the process lies in the way in which the lines are put in the plate. Acid is not used in making a drypoint. Instead, the worker draws directly upon a plate of copper with a point of sharpened steel or a diamond or ruby point. Greater freedom of drawing is permitted with the diamond or ruby point. The tool in scratching the lines on the plate throws up a tiny ridge of metal, just as a plow throws up a ridge of earth as it proceeds down the field. This ridge, called the *burr*, causes a softness in the lines of the first prints to be made. This softness of line, distinguishable in Figure 201, is a highly prized and distinguishing characteristic of drypoints.

The inking and printing of drypoints are essentially the same as for etchings, except that care must be taken not to destroy the burr. Editions in drypoints seldom run more than fifty prints (because the burr is worn off in the printing), of which the first twenty-five are invariably the richest. Drypoint plates are also sometimes coated with steel, which permits the pulling of many more prints.

Engraving on Metal (An Intaglio Process). Several examples of printed matter produced from engraved metal plates are in common use: postage stamps, paper money, and engraved calling cards. At one time, copper engravings were widely used for pictorial subjects, an example of which is the drawing of Brasenose College (page 55).

Engravings are made on plates of copper, steel, or zinc. (They are also made on wood, but these belong to the relief processes.) Strong tools, called burins, which are triangular in shape and gouge out V-shaped channels, are used in cutting the design directly into the plate. The deeper a line is engraved, the wider it becomes, and the heavier it prints. Some engravings, as the one of Brasenose College, are done by hand. Machines may also be used in the actual engraving process, giving a precise, methodical and hard appearance to the finished print, quite apparent in either stamps or paper money. Close study of an engraving —notice a dollar bill—will show an interesting variety of treatments, such as parallel lines of varied widths, dots, dashes, cross-hatching and others. These are much more apparent when seen through a magnifying glass.

328

An engraving is inked and printed in much the same way as described above for the other intaglio processes.

An engraving is a more methodical and stiff piece of work than either the drypoint or etching, the latter being free and sketchy. But, for the purposes of stamps, cards, money, bonds and certificates, engraving is a fitting and satisfactory process. In the past, engraving was more extensively used for such things as book and even magazine illustrations, but it has been almost completely superseded by the photoengraving processes mentioned below.

Lithography (A *Planographic Process*). Study the reproduction of the lithograph, "The Too Hot Bath" by Daumier (Figure 202), and you will see that lithography is a medium which permits great variety of effect. By this process it is possible to obtain lines or areas which are mealy and soft, silvery and rich, black and oily, or sharp and crisp.

The steps in the actual process are as follows. (1) The drawing is done on a slab of stone * of a special sort found in Bavaria, with a greasy crayon composed of wax, shellac, tallow, soap, and lampblack. (2) Flooding the stone with nitric acid changes the surface *not* covered by crayon to one which repels grease or oil, and changes the surface covered with crayon to a substance insoluble in water. (3) When ready for printing, the stone is moistened with water which soaks into the untreated areas. (4) Printing ink, rolled over the surface, adheres only to those portions which are not wet (that is, the portions on which the crayon has been applied). (5) Paper is then applied, pressure exerted, and a print is produced. Thus part of the surface of the printing plate is greasy and holds the greasy ink, part is wet and repels it, and although the surface is neither raised nor lowered noticeably, a print with white, black and all values of gray is made.

Commercial lithography follows the same basic principles outlined above but makes more extensive use of machine methods. It frequently was, and is, employed for color printing, separate plates being made for each color. Although at one time colored illustrations in books were widely reproduced in this way, the process is now used chiefly for such things as large bills and posters.

Silk Screen Process. This is one of the newest of the graphic processes, having been used in this country only since the beginning of the century.

---

* Lithographs are frequently done on zinc or aluminum plates instead of on stone, or the original drawing may be done on paper and transferred either to stone or metal.

The Problem of Materials and Processes

It is basically a *stencil* process especially well suited to flat or textured areas such as are commonly found in commercial posters, signs, and pamphlet covers (Figure 203). Many artists, however, are using this process for the production of silk screen prints, or serigraphs, and have attained remarkable results. The process is also being used for making reproductions of paintings. Silk screen printing is popular, too, because the materials are inexpensive, the process basically simple. The name derives from the silk bolting cloth or special stencil silk stretched on a wooden frame with sides several inches high. The silk is then treated so that the mesh in some areas is left open to allow paint to pass through, but is closed or impervious in others. Each color used requires a separate stencil.

Stencils are frequently made with nu-film or pro-film, as it is commercially named, which is a specially prepared, transparent, amber-colored sheet laminated with several layers. The steps in the process are as follows: (1) The outlines for the first color to be printed are cut out, but *only through the top layer of the stencil.* (2) The film is then securely fastened face down to the silk screen. (3) The backing film, which was not cut through, is carefully removed. This leaves part of the silk covered with the top layer of the film, the portion to be printed uncovered. The stencil is now ready to print the first color. The process is repeated for each color used. The screen may be cleaned, the film removed, and the silk used again. There are also several other methods of preparing the stencil, involving the use of such materials as tusche (a black liquid with wax particles used in lithography), glue and shellac, and imitation shellac.

In making the print, the stock on which the printing is to be done is placed below the screen. A specially prepared oil paint—thick but light— is poured along the edges of the silk within the printing frame. The paint is drawn across the screen with a squeegee and forced through the uncovered portions. The stock is removed and the next piece is printed.

As mentioned above, the silk screen process is becoming increasingly widely used for posters and other commercial work for runs of anything up to several thousand. For greater quantities, other mechanical processes are usually employed. The two distinctive advantages of silk screen are: first, its initial cost is much less than for most printing processes; second, it can be used on substances on which a metal plate will not print, such as wood or glass. In fact, it is being widely used for printing labels on milk bottles, designs on tumblers, and the like. It has also been widely used for printing textiles when only a relatively small quantity of each pattern is wanted. More recently, a number of artists have begun to make silk screen prints of the subject matters commonly associated with colored woodblocks and paintings, and are producing very distinguished results. Thus, the process is midway between the hand and the mechanical types.

THE MECHANICAL PROCESSES

Almost all of the pictures reproduced in books, magazines and newspapers are done by one of the *photo-mechanical processes*. These processes permit reproductions to be printed in almost unlimited quantities. As the name implies, light plays an important part in these highly mechanized processes. In all of them the design or picture, known as the *copy*, is photographed onto a photo-sensitive plate which is acted on by chemicals to prepare it for printing. Of the important types, *line cut*, *three-color*, *half-tone* and *four-color* are relief, but *commercial lithography* (mentioned above) is planographic, and *photogravure* belongs to the intaglio group.

The Line Cut (*A Relief Process*). The most distinctive feature of the line cut is that it prints but one value, usually, although not necessarily, black (see Figure 82, page 140). This renders it suitable for reproducing pen and ink drawings, woodcuts, or wood-engravings because all of these show only black and white.

The making of a line cut, though highly mechanized and complex in action, is basically simple. (1) The copy is photographed onto a photo-sensitized glass plate, thus giving a negative. (2) A similarly sensitized zinc plate is exposed to this negative, and the original design becomes an acid-resisting photographic print on the metal plate. (3) The metal plate is put into a bath of nitric acid which eats away those areas not intended to print. This leaves the design standing in relief. (4) The plate is locked in a press, properly inked, and the copies begin to roll out.

In order to give an effect of textures or stippling in a line cut, the *Ben-Day Process* is frequently used in such work as newspaper advertisements and comic strips. In this process various textures, prepared in advance, are photographed onto certain areas of the plate before the acid bath. These may be readily distinguished from half-tones because in the Ben-Day Process these textures never show variation or actual shading: they print as flat, textured areas.

The Three-Color Process (*A Relief Process*). Frequently, it is desirable to print a drawing, advertisement or something similar in more than one color, and the simplest process of color printing is the three-color. The principles and methods are identical with those in making line cuts, except that a separate plate is made for each color. Like the line cut, three-color printing never shows shaded variations; each color is printed flat. The name is somewhat misleading because as many colors as necessary may be used, but it serves to distinguish it from the four-color process.

The Half-Tone Process (*A Relief Process*). Almost all newspaper and magazine reproductions of photographs, drawings or paintings which show variations in value, but have only one hue, are printed by the half-tone process. In general the process is similar to the line cut with one important difference: the copy is photographed through a screen composed of two pieces of glass with parallel lines ruled on them, the lines on one piece of glass running at right angles to those on the other. A picture photographed through this screen emerges as a series of dots which are transferred photographically onto a metal plate coated with sensitized gelatin. After being treated to an acid bath similar to that of the line cut, the printing plate is composed of a series of dots. The dots in areas of high value are small, in dark areas they are large, their size depending on the amount of light which strikes the plate in the process of photographing the copy. The screens are described by the number of lines to the inch: a 60-screen, common in newspaper work, has 60 lines to the inch (3600 dots per square inch); a 400-screen, used in fine printing on coated paper, has 400 lines to the inch (160,000 dots per square inch). Although you can see the dots in newspaper work with the naked eye, you will need a magnifying glass to see them in finer printing.

The Four-Color Process (*A Relief Process*). This is an extension of the half-tone process into the field of color. The original picture, which is in color, is photographed through color filters and half-tone screens to produce yellow, red, blue and black (4 colors) half-tone printing plates. To accomplish this "color separation" half-tone negatives for yellow, red and blue are made. The copy is first photographed through a blue filter which permits only the yellow rays to pass, and thus gives a record of all the yellow in the original; second through a green filter to obtain reds; and third through a red-orange filter to obtain the blues. The fourth plate is made with practically all hues eliminated, recording only the major values. The printer now has four plates, one of which is used to print only yellow dots, another red, another blue, and the last black. Through different-sized dots and their combinations practically any color can be duplicated.

This method of printing is widely used. The color plates in many books and magazines are done by the four-color process, and you can perhaps distinguish the dots with the naked eye. Study some four-color plates through a magnifying glass, and notice the structure of the dots. As in half-tone the entire range of values can be reproduced and, in addition, color. Although four-color reproductions are often excellent, they frequently lack the depth and richness obtainable in collotype or rotogravure.

Photogravure and Rotogravure (Intaglio Processes). The rotogravure sections of newspapers, printed characteristically in brown or green, are well known to everyone. Rotogravure is a more familiar process than its parent photogravure. The processes in both are essentially the same except that rotogravure, as the name implies, is printed from a rotary press. The gravure processes give prints that have a rich, velvety quality not possessed by any of the other photo-mechanical processes, with the exception of the collotype.

The copy to be reproduced is photographed onto a sensitized carbon tissue covered with gelatin. The carbon tissue is then exposed to light through a ruled screen (as in half-tones) which has from 150 to 175 lines to an inch, or about 25,000 squares per square inch. The copy is thus reduced to a multitude of microscopically small dots. Next, these dots are transferred to the copper plate or roller, which is then etched in a bath of ferric chloride. This leaves the surface of the copper composed of innumerable little squares eaten away to different depths by the action of the acid.

In the printing, these little squares are filled with ink which is transferred to the paper. Those squares which are shallow hold little ink and, therefore, print light; those squares which are deep hold much ink and, therefore, print the dark portions of the picture. In half-tones (a relief process) it will be remembered that the round dots all printed the same value, but varied in size. In photogravure the squares are the same size, but vary in value.

The preparation of plates in rotogravure printing is the same as for photogravure, except that in rotogravure the plates are cylindrical. Two cylinders are used for printing, one being the etched cylinder, the other being the impression cylinder which forces the paper against the ink-laden, engraved cylinder. Since rotogravure printing is done at very high speed, and the papers must be folded immediately, the printed paper is passed over a heated drum which dries the ink.

Photogravure and rotogravure also lend themselves to fine color printing. When this is done, color separations are made as in the other photo-mechanical processes, and a plate is made for each color.

333

The Problem of Materials and Processes

Collotype (*A Planographic Process*). Most of the large and more expensive reproductions of paintings and drawings available today, and occasionally the plates in books, are made by the collotype process. With this method of printing remarkably faithful reproductions of paintings in color can be made. They are characterized by a richness, depth and subtlety of color that makes them readily distinguishable from most four-color reproductions. When observed closely with a magnifying glass, a collotype will seem to have a somewhat mealy texture quite different from the regular dots and squares of the half-tone or photogravure.

The process of making collotypes begins with photographing through color filters (as in the four-color process) the original painting or design. Each color-separation is photographed onto a photo-sensitive gelatin plate, which is then treated so that inks will adhere to those areas in which that color is to appear in the final print. These plates are inked and printed in a manner more or less similar to four-color plates. Great care is taken with collotype, however, to get the final print close to the original copy and a good collotype may be given as many as eight or nine printings, each with a color different in some way from the others.

From the point of view of materials, collotype printing is one of the least expensive of color processes. That prints are fairly expensive to purchase is due to the fact that only a limited number can be made from each gelatin plate (a metal plate such as used in four-color work can print a great many more copies), and that greater care is taken to secure accurate reproduction. In spite of this, collotypes are becoming available at increasingly lower prices, and have done much toward bringing faithful reproductions of paintings to a wide public.

CONCLUSION

The printing of words and pictures is one of the most important means of communication among men. Three basic processes of printing have been developed: relief printing, intaglio printing and planographic printing. Each has advantages and limitations, and all are in use today. In their search for methods to create and reproduce their work, artists have developed many graphic processes of which only a few have been mentioned. Aquatint, mezzotint, soft-ground etching, stipple and crayon engraving, and wood engraving are among those which, although they have

334

made a contribution, are not now widely practiced. Because fine prints may be reproduced fairly readily, they offer nearly everyone an opportunity to bring original pictures into homes, offices and school rooms.

Scientists, working along with artists, have brought to a high point of technical perfection a number of means of reproducing photographs, paintings, drawings—in fact, all kinds of pictorial representations. These have made possible the widespread use of illustrations in books and periodicals, and have encouraged the publication of several magazines which depend on pictures, rather than on text, to put across their stories. It is no exaggeration to say that the perfection of photo-mechanical methods of reproducing pictorial materials has done much to turn attention to and increase appreciation of the visual aspects of our environment.

For reading you many enjoy:

John Taylor Arms: *Handbook of Prints and Print Makers* (Macmillan, 1934). A good book written by a worker in the field, which means that you get first-hand information.
Thomas Craven: A *Treasury of American Prints* (Simon and Schuster, 1939).
Harold Curwen: *Processes of Graphic Reproduction in Printing* (Oxford University Press, 1934). An excellent account of both hand and mechanical print processes.
Leon Friend and Joseph Hefter: *Graphic Design* (McGraw-Hill, 1936). A beautifully illustrated account of commercial printing.
Aline Kistler: *Understanding Prints* (Associated American Artists, 1936). Tells how prints are made and how to judge them.
D. C. McMurtie: *The Book: The Story of Printing and Bookmaking* (Covici-Friede, 1937).
John C. Tarr: *Printing Today* (Oxford, 1946).
D. B. Updike: *Printing Types: Their History, Forms and Use* (Harvard University Press, 1937).
Carl Zigrosser: *Six Centuries of Fine Prints* (Covici-Friede, 1937). A good historical survey of prints.
The Encyclopaedia Britannica, under the name of each process, contains excellent, rather technical discussions.

If you are interested in trying your hand at lettering or print-making, read:

Grant Arnold: *Creative Lithography* (Harper, 1941).
Claire Leighton: *Wood Engraving and Woodcuts* (Studio Press, 1945).
Clifford Pyle: *Etching Principles and Methods* (Harper, 1941).

335

The Problem of Materials and Processes

Harry Shokler: *Artist's Manual for Silk Screen Print Making* (American Artists Group, 1946).

Harry Sternberg: *Silk Screen Color Printing* (McGraw-Hill, 1942).

Sallie B. Tannahill: *P's and Q's: A Book of Letter Arrangement* (Doubleday, 1939).

Levon West: *Making an Etching* (Studio Press, 1932).

ARLY in 1948 the publishers of *Photography*, a quarterly designed to appeal to advanced amateur and professional photographers, announced that they were changing the name of the magazine to *Photo Arts*. The editor commented on the change:

> The word *Art* in our photographic century has been a flaming one around which historic battles have been fought. Although the fighting is over the controversy lingers on in abated bitterness, but bitterness none-the-less. There are photographers —usually very fine ones—who will have no truck with the word, as well as those—very often bad ones—who refer proudly to their prints as Art with, note, a pompous capital A.*

Those discriminating photographers who dislike to be called artists obviously do not want to be classified with people they think are an impractical, unworldly lot of longhairs. We would heartily agree with them, if all artists were longhairs. But as we watch artists at work, listen to their explanations, we discover that those who do significant work are usually not impractical dreamers. They are serious workers who deplore sensational methods and quackery.

Many years of exacting scientific research gave us photography. It is safe to say that no other medium employs so many highly trained mechanical, chemical, and optical engineers. Photography is complicated. For this reason the mechanical problems involved in making a print often place most of the emphasis on craftsmanship. But photography is also a way of communicating ideas, just as is painting, etching, engraving, or any other art. When the materials and processes of photography are handled by someone who has something to say, photography can be a genuinely expressive art.

---

* Quoted by permission from *Photo Arts*, Spring, 1948. Bruce Downes, editor.

THE CAMERA AND THE FILM

Suppose that you have acquired a simple box camera, some film, developing supplies, and the necessary materials and equipment for making prints.

THE FILM

There are many kinds of film available to the amateur photographer: those that are so sensitive to light that even on dull, cloudy days good results are obtained; films that permit tremendous enlargements to be made from the negatives; films that are extrasensitive to the colors below red (infra-red) and can be used where other films are useless. The spool is a double coil, the first one of light-proof paper one end of which you see; the inner coil, which you cannot see, is the film itself. This is a strip of material as wide as the spool and long enough to supply the number of negatives stated on the package. The *base* material of film is any of several transparent substances. In amateur films, it is usually cellulose acetate. On the base is the *emulsion*, a thin layer of gelatin in which are suspended silver halide crystals. These crystals are the real photographic (light sensitive) medium; they form the actual image on the negative. It is because they are so sensitive to light that they must be guarded against accidental exposure. When the film is locked in the camera and the shutter is tripped for the exposure, the halide crystals will record the scene. Note, however, that if you were now to remove the film from the camera and look at it, it would be quite blank. Although the crystals have been activated by light, they still do not change in appearance. Here we have one of the great mysteries in photography. The image is there, although unseen; it is called a *latent image*. Later, when the film is in the developing bath, a remarkable change takes place in the emulsion. The silver halide crystals that were activated by light are changed to metallic silver. The image you see in a negative or on a print is pure silver!

Spooled film is seldom used in the larger professional cameras. For these cameras film is supplied in pack and sheet form so that each sheet can, if desired, be processed separately. Movie film is a continuous strip, hundreds of feet long, with sprocket holes on the sides to accommodate it to movie cameras and certain small still cameras. Finally, for negatives on a rigid base, the emulsion is coated on glass. Here, obviously, the word *film* cannot apply: these are called *plates*.

THE LENS

When you open the camera to thread the film into it, observe what makes up the box. There is a lens at one end supplied with a shutter that can be tripped, and a trackage system which, after the box is closed, unwinds the film and places a section of it directly opposite the lens.

The most important part of a camera is the *lens*. It is the eye. A lens may be optically simple, as in the box camera, or highly complex. To a degree, increased complexity in a lens increases its picture-making qualities; also, unfortunately, its cost. The manufacture of a good lens is a costly process because it is largely one of elimination and compensating for defects and aberrations so that the final product approaches that most remarkable of lenses, the human eye. Study enlargements of negatives made in different cameras. This is a good test of a lens. Do not, however, confuse faulty camera operation and poor darkroom work with lens quality. These are more often the cause of inferior pictures than is a bad lens.

Lenses are also available for special work. There are lenses, such as those used by wild-life photographers, which have a telescopic effect and permit the photographer to station his camera at an extraordinary distance from his subject. There are lenses which "see" an extremely wide angle—even wider than the eye. Such lenses are useful when the photographer attempts to obtain a picture indoors where space is so limited that he cannot back away from his subject. If, however, the lens produces either a wide-angle or a telephoto effect, the lens will distort the perspective. A normal lens does not distort perspective unless the user blunders too close to his subject. A picture taken with a wide-angle lens is characterized by an over-emphasized foreground. The opposite effect, an over-emphasized background, is the result of a telephoto lens. Forceful and dramatic effects can be obtained by these lenses.

THE IRIS

The photographic usefulness of a lens is greatly increased if the amount of light which it gathers can be controlled. A window shade allows us to vary the amount of light that enters a room by means of a simple device which, in effect, lessens the area of the window. Built into the photographic lens is an iris-like diaphragm. By means of it, the effective area of a lens can be changed at will, the only limit being the diameter of the lens. Because an iris type of control is too costly to use in low-priced cameras, a much simpler and also much less flexible type of control is provided. A camera thus equipped usually provides no more than two choices: one almost the full diameter of the lens and one scarcely larger than a pin-hole. When the photographer learns more and more about light, he becomes increasingly skillful in choosing the proper setting of the iris. The amount of light which gets to the halide crystals in the emulsion determines the correct exposure. The various positions of the iris are known as F-stops. For a thorough explanation of this photographic problem, one should consult either of the first two books in the list at the end of this chapter.

THE SHUTTER

But the lens must also be provided with a means of keeping it closed so that no light will reach the film until the moment of exposure, the crucial moment when, for only a fraction of a second, light is allowed to enter the camera. The box camera shutter has one speed, about $\frac{1}{30}$ of a second, but the more complex cameras have shutters which provide a wide choice of speeds, from 1 second to $\frac{1}{1000}$ of a second. Thus the photographer has two means of controlling the light that enters his camera: first, the *iris*, which is built into the lens and allows him to increase or lessen the area of the lens; second, the *shutter*, which allows him to control the duration of the exposure.

For ordinary work, the commonly used shutter speeds are those of $\frac{1}{25}$, $\frac{1}{50}$, and $\frac{1}{100}$ of a second. In certain industrial work and sometimes for striking speed studies, as of a pirouetting figure skater, speeds are needed that are beyond existing mechanical shutters. It is then necessary to provide a sudden burst of intense light, timed to flash at the incredible speed of 1/100,000 of a second. Figure 208 is an example of the possibilities of speed photography. Sports photography also demands fast shutter speeds. You perhaps have observed pictures of the rapidly moving runners at a track event taken at such slow shutter speeds that the figures were blurred. In order to "stop" the action of a fast runner it is necessary to use a shutter speed of at least $\frac{1}{1000}$ of a second.

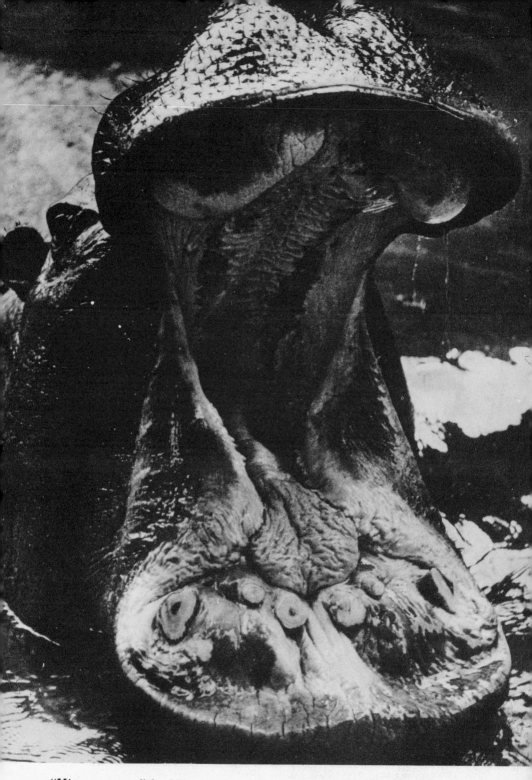

204. "Hippopotamus" by Ylla demonstrates photography's speed in documenting bizarre facts.

205. "Pennsylvania Station." A remarkably brilliant photograph with strong contrast of dark and light in the center and subtle variations of gray at the edges.

206. Arthur Siegel. "Lyric Singer." A photograph in which two separate negatives are printed on one positive.

207. Arthur Siegel. Photogram. Such prints as this are achieved by placing object directly on sensitized paper. There is no negative. Note the similarity to many abstract paintings.

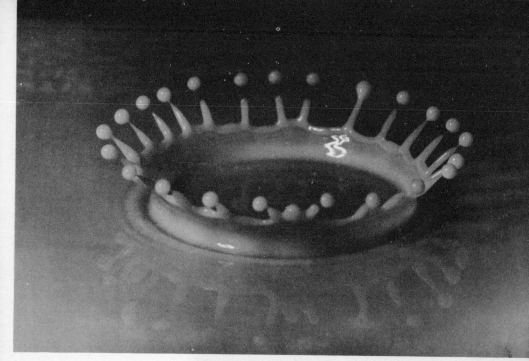

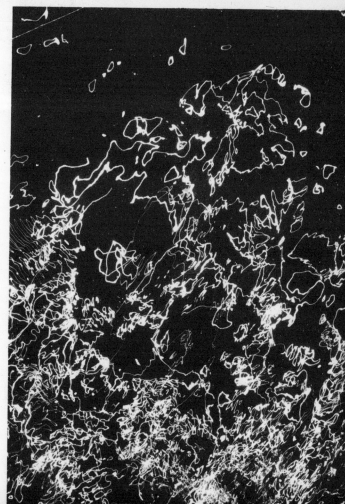

208. (*Upper*) "Splash of Milk Drop," a photograph taken at 1/100,000 of a second by Edgerton, Germeshausen and Grier, revealing a new world of reality.

209. (*Lower*) Harry Callahan. "Moving Highlights on Water," a time exposure. This is no photograph of "an instant of reality," but of an occurrence over a period of time.

The type of film and filter used make great difference in the final result; three photographs of the same landscape.

210. (*Upper left*) Taken on film not sensitive to color differences.

211. (*Upper right*) Taken on panchromatic film through a yellow filter.

212. (*Lower*) Taken on infra-red plate with infra-red film, the value pattern and relations are completely changed.

The composition of a photograph is frequently improved by *cropping* to eliminate irrelevant or distracting detail and to emphasize what is important.

213. (*Upper*) A photograph with some portions of interest but with poor composition.

214. (*Lower*) The same photograph after cropping.

215. "Sailboats" is a brilliant study of action registered in strong contrast of light and dark.

Of the other accessories and attachments to the camera, we need make no detailed accounting here. Whatever the accessories—view-finders, exposure counters, delayed action releases, parallax correctors, automatic film transports, focusing aids—remember that they do not make the picture, only the man behind the camera does that. One camera accessory, the *light meter*, however, must be mentioned here because it helps us to understand that light is the medium of photography. *Photo-graphy* means *light-writing*. Because the light reflected from an object, not the object itself, makes the photograph, it is clear that some means of measuring the light present on a scene would be a valuable aid in making a picture. Light meters, usually called exposure meters, use photo-electric cells which accurately measure the quantity of light.

MAKING A PHOTOGRAPH

Some critics insist that photography is not an art since to take a picture one need only point the camera at a subject and trip the shutter. The camera, they say, does all the work. But it does not; some things the camera does not do: it does not choose the subject, it does not decide how much of the subject to include in the frame, it does not gauge and compensate for lighting conditions. These are done by the photographer. By the simple act of choosing his subject the photographer becomes an artist. When he shows a desire to record, if only as a humble keepsake, a small child's moment of pleasure in a new toy or a friend's graduation gown, he does what any artist ever does. He seeks to communicate an idea.

When he explores his subject in order to find what first aroused his desire to record it, he moves toward being a better artist. No subject, however pretty or attractive, is art. Whatever is good or bad in art is not in the subject, it is in what the artist does with the subject. When a photograph is bad, the fault lies in the photographer, not in the subject. When a photographer misunderstands his subject or fails to see it clearly, when he is careless in his camera techniques or in his darkroom skills, he is not an artist. Just trip the shutter? No!

In photography, as in the other arts, the artist controls his medium. The painter selects and prepares his canvas, supplies himself with a variety of brushes, is discriminating about the quality of his pigments and oils. The photographer, too, desires that whenever possible his equipment be capable of the job it has to do. In order to make clear the processes of photography, a hypothetical photograph will be followed from its inception in the mind of the photographer, through the taking of the picture, developing and enlarging it, to the final print. The photograph, for reasons of simplicity, will be taken by a simple box camera. It should be noted, however, that a box camera is inadequate except for the most casual kind of recording. Although it is a camera complete in essentials, it throws too many mechanical hurdles in the way of a wide range of expression.

We, however, go on to take a picture with our box camera. It will keep our problem simple as well as demonstrate how the photographer, like all artists, continually strives to express and communicate an idea.

THE IDEA

One good way to think of any picture is in terms of what it does to the person who looks at it. A picture made in this way, and the process of making it, from beginning to end, will be stimulating. Ansel Adams, the famous California photographer, teaches his students that the final print is *felt* (not *seen* with mechanical accuracy) in such a way that the procedure of making the print may be thought of as backward, from the final finished print to the first steps preliminary to tripping the shutter.

Our hypothetical picture is to be sent, instead of a letter, to a friend, inviting him to visit and enjoy the hospitality of a new house. The first step is to choose the subject. The doorway of the new house seems to express the thought behind the taking of the photograph: it is broad, welcoming, and friendly. The door is wide open, the brick path continues into the house to become the floor of the entrance hall, the low-massed shrubs around the doorway give way to colorful potted plants in the entrance. The roof of the carport (open-air garage) extends over the doorway, drawing the eye to the focal point of the house.

TAKING THE PHOTOGRAPH

An experimental glance into the view finder of the camera tells us that we are too close. The doorway looks cramped for space. Gradually, as the camera is moved backwards the various elements of the composition shift around until the door assumes the dominant position the architect had intended it to hold. The shutter is clicked; then, other angles are explored and snapped until eight exposures have been made.

DEVELOPING THE PHOTOGRAPH

In the darkroom—and this room is really dark, not a glimmer of light enters it—are three trays with liquids. In the first one is the *developer*, a solution in water of several chemicals that will turn the light-struck silver halide crystals into metallic silver. There are many kinds of developers: The X-ray photographer uses a developer, for instance, which will yield negatives of great contrast. The landscape photographer may search, instead, for a developer that gives a long scale of grays from almost black to almost white.

In the second tray is cool *water*, about 70° F., which temperature, incidentally, will be found in all three trays.

The third tray is filled with the fixing agent, commonly called *hypo*. This bath stops the action of any developer that may be lingering in the emulsion and fixes the image by rendering neutral all those silver halide crystals that were not affected by light and which, therefore, were not changed into metallic silver by the developer. Photographers sometimes add other ingredients to this bath. It is common to find a hardening agent in the hypo which will render the surface of the gelatin coating on the film quite tough and resistant to scratches caused by ordinary handling. This toughening of the gelatin—actually, it is tanned, like leather—is not so thorough that the dry negatives may be handled the way many people do.

The film strip is unwound, a clip put at each end, and then pre-soaked in the tray of plain water. Pre-soaking takes the curl out of the film and makes it much easier to handle. Ordinarily, when the film becomes so flaccid that it has no further tendency to curl, it is time to begin the actual developing.

The length of film is moved through the developer for five minutes or so (the actual time is usually stated on the label of the packaged developer), then returned to the same water in which it was pre-soaked. It is rinsed up and down for a minute, and drained so that it will not carry excessive water—and of course there are small quantities of developer in it—to the hypo tray.

To fix the image that has now been developed it is necessary to remove those halides that were not changed into metallic silver. A few

351

seconds in the hypo bath will suffice, but it is well to stay on the safe side, not turn on a light for at least three minutes. Light can no longer affect the emulsion. The halide crystals have either been changed into metallic silver and are a part of the negative image or they have been rendered harmless by the hypo and are a part of that solution. The strip of film in the hypo tray is now a series of eight negatives.

After about ten minutes in the hypo solution the film is ready for washing. This process removes the hypo from the swollen gelatin. The film is transferred to a tray into which flows a gentle stream of cool water and left for about fifteen minutes. A piece of soft, clean chamois, soaked in cold water and wrung dry, is used to sponge gently the excess water off both sides of the film. The film is hung up to dry with the hope that no dust floating in the air nearby attaches itself to the emulsion. When dry, it is cut into the eight negatives.

Only a good negative yields a fine print. Of all the steps toward the final print, few are more important than the making of the negative. Here in a microscopically thin layer of gelatin are imprisoned millions of grains of silver. Although they look black because they are rough, unpolished, and do not reflect light, they are the finest of silver. Studied under a microscope, these silver grains would seem to be scattered formlessly in the clear gelatin, but out from under the powerful glass and viewed from even a close angle, they gather and cluster to make an image, in reversed values, of the original scene. Thus, the negative is a record of the light reflected from the scene, gathered by the lens, and directed to the emulsion of the film where it leaves its mark in reversed values by the clustering of silver grains within the gelatin.

MAKING THE PRINT

In order to make a print of the best negative of the doorway, the scene is re-photographed on to a paper-based emulsion by transmitting light through the negative. The processing of the exposed paper follows basically the same procedure as with film: development, fixation, drying.

Contact Prints. The simplest way to make prints is by the *contact* method. A piece of photographic paper is placed in firm and even contact with a negative, as in a *printing frame,* a device that looks and operates very much like a small picture frame. In fact, a picture frame may be used as a substitute. You then have a sandwich; glass, negative, photographic paper, and any kind of firm backing. If the glass side of this sandwich is held a foot away from a lighted 40-watt lamp bulb and the rest of the room kept dark, the paper will become exposed by the light that shines through the negative. The length of the exposure (the time the lamp is on) is dependent on many factors such as the brightness of the light, the distance between the printing frame and the lamp, the density of the negative image, the sensitivity of the paper, and several others. The further processing of the print—developing, fixing, washing, and drying—is exactly the same as the following processing of enlargements.

Contact prints are an exact duplicate in size of the original negative. When films are sent to commercial finishing plants for processing, contact prints are ordinarily returned to the customer unless he orders enlargements.

Enlargements. Enlargements offer many more possibilities than do contact prints. Some beginning photographers make satisfactory enlargers from their cameras, and a brief description of the way in which this is done will help us understand the technique of enlarging. The outer casing of the camera is removed so that only an open box with the lens at the bottom is left. The negative is placed at the open end so that it is opposite the lens in the same position that is ordinarily occupied by part of the long strip of film. The negative is secured at its edges with photographic scotch tape which is black and opaque. Next, to provide a shielded, directed light source, a round hole is cut in the bottom of a two-pound coffee can in such a way that the socket end of an electrical extension cord can be forced into the hole. A 75-watt bulb is screwed into the socket, and the open end squeezed to slide over the back of the camera about an inch. The can and camera are held together with black scotch tape.

After the room lights are turned out and the extension cord plugged in, the whole contrivance is held in such a way that it can be raised or lowered over a piece of white paper until the image is as sharp as possible. The enlarger is then in focus. A box camera gives only one size of enlargement. If the distance between lens and negative can be altered, as is possible with cameras equipped with bellows, enlargements of various sizes can be made. The enlargements a box-camera enlarger makes will be too large. Later we will learn why.

Enlarging paper (frequently called *projection* paper) is coated with a light sensitive emulsion of the same basic material, but different type, as film. The blank sheet of paper, on which the preliminary focusing was done, is replaced with a piece of photographic paper.

353

The Problem of Materials and Processes

The enlarger lamp is turned on for one minute.

Think of all that happens during this minute: a stream of light passes through the negative, unimpeded through the transparent areas and hindered in the darker, denser areas. These rays are gathered by the lens and directed to the paper surface where they focus once again. *The darker areas of the negative supply the paper surface with less light and the lighter, thinner areas of the negative supply the paper surface with correspondingly more light.* The values are being reversed. The latent image now building up in the emulsion of the paper, if we could see it, is the beginning of a *positive* of the original doorway scene.

Processing the print is very similar to processing the negative. The paper is submerged in the developer solution for a full minute. The paper is drained for a few seconds, plunged into cool water where it gets a good soaking, drained again, and finally submerged in the hypo solution for ten minutes.

The first exposure is almost sure to be either too long (too much light) or too short (not enough light). If the print is too dark, the next exposure period is decreased by, say, one-half. If too light, the exposure may be doubled. This trial and error method is continued until as good a print as the original negative and the equipment will allow is obtained.

Then, after the print has *fixed out* for ten minutes, it is washed under the cold water faucet for about a half hour. When the prints are washed, the excess water is removed from their surfaces with a clean sponge or cloth, and they are laid on a towel for an hour or so, until they are almost dry and begin to curl. They are then pressed in a large book or letter press so that they will dry fairly flat.

EVALUATING THE PRINT

"The Doorway" is still not completed. It needs to be trimmed and mounted to bring out its best features. There is the possibility of using only a part of the print, as described below, to improve the composition. The ethics of this procedure are argued by photographers, with one group maintaining that a shot, once recorded on a negative, should not be altered. Another group contends that the selective processes of the photographer, begun when he first takes a picture, may be continued to the completion of the print—the creator having the right to make use of any or all of a negative or print as suits his purpose. It is undoubtedly true that the better the photographer, the less use is made of any tricks or devices to improve his prints.

An aid for exploring picture possibilities of a print is easy to make. Two L-shaped masks are cut from stiff white paper, the legs of each about 2 inches wide and about 10 or 12 inches long. When these masks are placed over a print so that there is a border all the way round, it is easy to give the picture any shape one pleases, and the continuity and emphasis of the picture can be changed remarkably. This is called *cropping*. In Figure 213 a random record shot is thereby lifted into a class of high pictorial value by cropping as in Figure 214. According to many people Figure 215 is over-cropped. They say that in the original print, of which Figure 215 is a cropped version, the sailboats are back far enough so that the pennant on the first one is also visible, giving the composition more freedom. When a picture is cropped so much that the principal subject is brought too far forward, an effect is produced which seems to choke the composition. The effect, when overdone, is unpleasant. If done carefully, the effect may be dramatic. *Choke shots*, as they are commonly known, have been popular in recent photographic exhibits.

Now for a critical analysis of our hypothetical print, "The Doorway." The image may lack definition; it looks blurred. Several factors contribute to this defect. First, the quality of the original camera lens and the quality of the enlarging lens. Because lens quality is important in image definition and clarity, an inferior lens which sells for a few dollars is incapable of yielding the results obtained from a good lens. Enlargements beyond 5 x 7 inches made from ordinary box camera negatives are not pleasant because of the almost complete breakdown in image quality.

The second cause of the possible lack of sharpness and snap in "The Doorway" arises from a quite different source. Here we mention *grain*, the bugaboo (and needlessly so) of many photographers. Recall that a strip of film is coated with an emulsion containing silver halide crystals that turn into clusters of metallic silver when developed. These clusters are of such microscopic size that the human eye, unaided, cannot detect them. When an enlargement is made, it is impossible to escape the enlarging of these clusters because they *are* the image. Naturally, when bigger and bigger enlargements are made, the more noticeable these clusters become until finally the eye recognizes them as such. This effect is called *graininess*. Some films are inherently more grainy than others. In general, *faster* films are grainier than *slower* films. Graininess may also be caused by improper developing techniques. But the chief cause is enlargement, and the only cure is to get a larger camera. The larger the camera, the larger the negative and, consequently, the smaller degree of enlargement is necessary to make a picture of given size. But remember that it is the grain (silver clusters) that makes the photographic image. The person who finds grain objectionable may be like the person who rebels when he sees the brush strokes of an oil painting.

Another quality in "The Doorway" may be the lifeless appearance of the image. It does not have the brilliance of "Pennsylvania Station" (Figure 205) and of "Sailboats" (Figure 215). The gray values in "The Doorway" are few. The picture is flat. Observe the values in Figure 212 and notice how they jump from one step to another. The picture is "contrasty." Perhaps this quality in Figure 212 goes beyond what "The Doorway" required. It does indicate, however, that the photographer, when he knows his materials, can control the contrast in his pictures. Many causes may have contributed to the flat quality of "The Doorway." Most important is *subject contrast*. A subject that has too much contrast, a landscape scene that includes areas intensely illuminated by the sun and areas deep in shadow, for instance, must be carefully studied by the photographer so that in his print of that scene both the highlight and the shadow areas are in pleasant relationship. A dull subject, such as a street scene on a dark and cloudy day, must be so handled that the final print is not even flatter than the original scene. The photographer controls the contrast of his pictures by several means: increased or decreased shutter speeds, different types of film, variation of the methods of film development, different types of photographic paper, and variation of the enlarging techniques.

In the print of "The Doorway" the small patch of sky may be a meaningless dead white. Figures 210 to 212 explain why. Different emulsions are sensitive to colors in different ways. One very quickly learns that although negatives show only steps in gray, these steps are in response to color. In Figure 210 the picture is ruined by the action of too much blue and ultra-violet light. If we could examine the sky area in the negative of this picture we would find that it is very much overexposed. When this negative is in an enlarger, such a small amount of light from the enlarger lamp penetrates the dense sky area that the emulsion of the printing paper receives little or no light. In Figure 211 values throughout the entire picture are altered by means of the yellow filter. Blue light, which is a part of the green light of the foliage and grass, is held back, rendering those objects lighter and, in this case, better. The ultra-violet light in

356

the pond's reflections is also brought under better control. The sky is rendered as gray and the clouds show up against the gray. Notice, in passing, that when the photographer made Figure 211, he improved the composition by only a slight shift of his camera position. The lawn has now a more dynamic quality and this, in turn, adds more vitality to the trees in the background.

Further technical analysis of "The Doorway" must give way to a more important kind of observation. We leave this technical department knowing that we have not completed the list of mechanical problems in a print: simple blunders such as camera shake, careless handling of the film, developer stains; these problems and many others even more complicated we leave to the ambitious experimenter who will find them himself, all too soon.

How much better would "The Doorway" be if the picture had been taken with a better camera, with more suitable film, with a yellow filter, if the negative had been processed and the enlargement made with more adequate equipment and knowledge? Mechanically, the picture would be vastly improved. It would be, perhaps, nearly technically perfect. But what of the original intention when it was decided to photograph the doorway of a new house? Does the picture show hospitality, invitation to enter? The picture may fail in its original intention, however perfect it may be mechanically.

Our problem is to find how "The Doorway" could have succeeded. We must go back to the original thought behind the making of the picture. We must learn how, in photography as in all the arts, to make our final evaluations in terms of the artist, not the materials. This is the problem of the critic of photographic prints and this is your problem when you see photographs.

When we hear Horowitz play the Tchaikovsky "Piano Concerto," our enjoyment and evaluation of his artistry supersede our knowledge of the laws of harmony, the rules of composition, and the array of devices at the disposal of the composer who writes music for the piano and the orchestra. We think above the mere mechanical details of piano playing, the machinery of the instrument, the tensile strength of the cast iron frame, the chemical content of the steel in the strings, or the quality of wood in the sounding board. We hear more than a series of tones played in rapid succession. We hear music.

The judges who select the best photographs in a show take it for

357

granted that the photographers all had good cameras, that they knew how to use them, and that they employed the best of materials which were so skillfully handled in the darkroom that there is no question of their knowledge of materials and processes. A good judge of photographic prints evaluates the pictures before him on the same basis as the judge of a showing of oil paintings or water colors or sculpture. What is that basis? For an answer we turn to the opening pages of this book and paraphrase our former words: Human needs are not only for practical things. Frequent, certainly, are the desires for experiences other than eating, working, sleeping, or traveling. It is no feeble urge that compels us to seek ways to express and to communicate our thoughts and ideas, feelings and aspirations through paintings, drawings, etchings, photographs, ceramics, sculpture, textiles, and a host of other products.

We look at our hypothetical photograph and it may say nothing. It communicates nothing more than the dull fact that a doorway is there. Or perhaps it really gives a feeling of friendliness, welcome, and hospitality because the angle was well chosen to express those ideas, the composition is good, and the processes and materials have been handled adequately. Whatever the quality of the final result, going through the process step by step has indicated the many problems that the photographer must solve. Technical skill and good materials are important, but they alone cannot produce art. Human sensitivity and creativity are needed for that.

SOME AVENUES OF EXPERIMENTATION

So accustomed are we to photographs in newspapers, magazines, and vacation albums, that we forget the possibilities for experimentation. But new areas for exploration have been opened by photographers who are searching out the possibilities of their medium quite as much as are the experimental painters and sculptors. Several examples of this type of work are illustrated in Figures 206, 207, and 209.

Figure 207 is a photogram by Arthur Siegel made by placing objects directly on light-sensitive paper and exposing it to light. It is, therefore, not a photograph in the usual sense because there is no negative and the result is an original which cannot be duplicated in the conventional way. Photograms invariably show considerable interest in form and texture and bring to attention new facets of the character of various objects and

358

materials. "Lyric Singer" (Figure 206), also by Siegel, has been achieved by printing two negatives on one positive; in this print, one negative carried the image of a girl and the other an image of a tree, shadows, and a gate. By combining the two, a new experience is afforded the observer, an experience beyond that which either would have called forth by itself. The loveliness of the girl, the grace of the tree, and the nostalgic character of the gate and shadow interact one with the other. The forms become altered and elusive yet highly evocative when fused in a new relationship. Thus the photographer like the painter is not limited to depicting the light reflected from one object or scene at a specific time but can integrate two or more impressions.

The time exposure of moving high lights on water (Figure 209) by Harry Callahan illustrates another experimental use of the camera. Here is a record, not of an instant, but of a period of time. Everyone has at some time watched with fascination the movement of light on water, but this is an experience all but impossible to capture in a conventional painting or photograph. By concentrating on one aspect of the subject and by overcoming the usual time limitation, the photographer has conveyed in a remarkable manner the restlessness and vitality of water in motion.

These are but a few of the techniques which experimental photographers have developed. Many such innovations eventually find their way into the plates of fashion magazines, travel brochures, motion pictures, and scientific research. In the second century of its life, photography is proving more than ever to be a field of great accomplishment and possibility.

MOTION PICTURES

Motion pictures combine the photographic arts with the dramatic arts. As we sit in the dark luxury of the movie theater our attention and thought are all for the unfolding of the narrative before our eyes. We seldom think of the photographic problems in a motion picture. It is good that we do not because, often, a needless preoccupation with technicalities disturbs our appreciation of the dramatic experience. Now, however, our problem is the photographic one.

Motion pictures do not move. What we see on the movie screen is a series of twenty-four still pictures each second, all made on the same theoretical basis as "The Doorway." Each picture is slightly different from the next, and the motion is really an optical illusion.

When you go to the movies, watch for the credit titles which appear at the beginning of the film and observe that usually the name that heads the list of collaborating artists—script writers, editors, scene and costume designers, musicians, etc.—is that of the chief photographer. He is a man who ranks high in his profession not only because of his surpassing knowledge of the techniques of photography but because of his ability to understand what effects the director wants and his ability to get these effects on the final movie screen through his many technical assistants. He does none of the actual shooting of the film. Assistants check on the lighting and report to him when the scene has the contrast he demands. He tells the camera operators how to frame the scene, what angles to shoot from, and what special lenses to use. When the scene is photographed and the exposed film is ready for processing ("in the can"), the chief photographer's work is done except, sometimes, for suggestions to the processing laboratories concerning the kinds of positive stock that might be used for the final positive print. (The positive that is run in your local theater is called a *print* in quite the same meaning as "The Doorway" is called a print.)

During the one hundred years of photographic history there have always been many people—photographers as well as other artists—who demand that, beyond routine negative processing and straightforward printing, no changes be made in the image after the shutter is released. Photography, like all arts, has its purists. They have their demand answered in motion picture photography because changes in composition and contrast in this kind of photography are almost impossible to make. The motion picture photographer puts all his eggs in the one basket of what happens when the shutter clicks on each of the rapid succession of exposures. Unlike the still photographer, he has little opportunity to exercise control over the print. The parallel here with certain forms of sculpture is striking. It is like the making of "Peace Memorial." Carl Milles left the final cutting to the quarry men and the stone workers. The motion picture photographer leaves the final processing to laboratory technicians.

COLOR PHOTOGRAPHY

The owner of a simple box camera is often surprised to learn that color photography is merely black and white photography carried several steps further in the final processing. In our brief discussion of filters it was mentioned that film emulsions, either with or without filters, responded to different colors in different ways. The astronomical photographer can, by means of his black and white negatives, actually determine the color of a remote star or planet. The color photographer can also get a record of the different colors within a scene. How these different records are made simultaneously, by means of filters or special emulsions or both, is information that belongs properly to the technical domain of photography, quite beyond the purposes of our present study. Books on contemporary chemistry and physics now contain special sections on this subject and the person who wishes to improve his color photography will find a study of these books valuable.

The color we see in a print or in a transparency is actually the dyed gelatin of the emulsion. In some color processes the original gelatin, which contained the light-sensitive silver halides, is utilized. In processes of this kind, the black metallic silver clusters are chemically removed and substituted with colored dyes. In most of the modern three-color systems the colors used are magenta, cyan, and yellow. From these come images representing in varying degrees of accuracy the colors seen in nature. The use of color transparencies projected onto a screen either as "stills" or as motion pictures has become fairly widespread in the past twenty years. Recently improvements in making color prints on paper have greatly increased their popularity. But color photography is still young, very much in the experimental stages, and only the future will tell us its full potentialities.

CONCLUSION

Photography is, then, one of the important arts. But it is more than that—it is also a people's art. Satisfaction in results can be had by the

361

small child with his dollar box, by the vigorous adult with his complex camera and many lenses, or by the retired oldster sitting in his sunny chair taking snaps of his grandchildren or of his flowers in bloom in the nearby garden. Photography has infinite flexibility. It is not a mechanical craft but an art since, as we have seen, it is not the camera but the person behind the camera and in the darkroom who imagines, composes, takes, develops, prints, and who thus creates art.

PHOTOGRAPHY AS A HOBBY

As a hobby, photography is most satisfactory when you do your own developing and printing. That it can become enormously complicated, we have already seen. Still, with practice in the field and in the darkroom and with some study of the many books about photography, the amateur can make expressive, well-designed, technically good photographs.

For a materials survey and for current prices, consult the catalogues of any general photographic supply house. Especially good is:

Photographic Catalog (Montgomery Ward and Co., published yearly, no charge).

For the beginner and inexperienced amateur: .

T. H. Miller and W. Brummitt: *This Is Photography* (Garden City, 1945).
A. Adams: *Camera & Lens* (Morgan and Lester, 1948).
A. Adams: *Negative: Exposure and Development* (Morgan and Lester, 1948)

For the more advanced photographer:

W. D. Morgan and H. M. Lester: *Graphic Graflex Photography* (Morgan and Lester, 1943).
W. Mortensen: *Mortensen on the Negative* (Simon and Schuster, 1941).
F. Bond: *Kodachrome and Kodacolor from All Angles* (Camera Craft, 1948).
Beaumont Newhall: *Photography: A Short Critical History* (Museum of Modern Art, 1938).

PART IV

Painting, Sculpture, and Architecture

CHAPTER 15

Painting

ONE night in London, the American painter James McNeill Whistler was invited to a friend's home for dinner. It was at the time he was doing his now famous series of paintings of London fogs. Shortly after arriving at his host's house another guest rushed up to him and exclaimed excitedly: "Mr. Whistler, I just crossed the Thames River, and it looked exactly like one of your paintings!" Whistler smiled and replied: "Thank you, madam. Nature is improving."

This anecdote raises some fundamental questions: Does the painter "hold a mirror up to nature" trying to make his picture an exact imitation of what he sees, or does he interpret his subjects and help observers to gain new insights into the world about them? Why are some pictures "natural" looking, others very unnatural? And there are other questions that might be raised. Why does an artist paint pictures? What should we look for when we are trying to "appreciate" a picture? How can paintings be judged?

An artist draws, paints, models or carves to clarify his own reactions, feelings, thoughts, attitudes and beliefs and to communicate them to those who look at his work. Whether or not he chooses to paint objects in a realistic manner will depend on what he is trying to express and communicate. Thus, as we have discussed in Part I and as we shall take up further in this section, the "form" of a work of art grows out of expression.

Painting and sculpture have often been referred to as the *Arts of Representation* because in many instances the work of painters and sculptors bears a marked resemblance to the persons, trees, skies and other objects of the natural world. Ofter the degree to which painting and sculpture approximate the appearance of nature is taken as a criterion of excellence, and many persons look only for realistic perspective, proportions and colors. If a picture or a statue looks "natural" or "real," it is good; if it does not, many observers assume that the artist was incompetent or careless. However, as the problems of painting and sculpture are investigated, it becomes evident that imitation or verisimilitude is seldom held as a goal by artists.

Although all plastic art expresses and communicates feelings and ideas, painting and sculpture, being less determined by utilitarian considerations than the other arts, admit greater freedom and intensity of expression. They appeal to man's sensibilities in a peculiarly direct way. Literature, for example, depends on words which are secondary symbols for things, and music, because of its abstract character, uses sounds only indirectly related to natural sounds. Sculpture and painting, however, run the gamut from photographic representation of objects and events through various degrees of modification, intensification, and distortion to complete independence of natural forms. With such broad range, these versatile arts are equal to the expression of almost any experience open to man.

In Part I we discussed the major life areas in which art is active and from which, consequently, much painting and sculpture are generated. Thus, paintings are used to enrich the walls of our living quarters (page 8), and also to preserve likenesses of members of our families (page 13). Similarly, paintings are used to commemorate events of social importance and to embellish public buildings. Religion, the most generous sponsor that painting and sculpture have enjoyed, has led to many significant expressions (pages 98, 212 and 234). Commerce and industry, in producing and marketing various commodities, have likewise called on the commercial artist and designer to produce advertisements (pages 139 and 211). In such cases, painting and sculpture are not produced primarily to be enjoyed as ends in themselves any more than is that music composed for religious or military purposes. Their basic aim is to arouse, exhort or educate, to lead the observer on to other things, to direct his thinking and sway his emotions on issues of one sort or another.

It is a readily observable fact, however, that not all art products are means to other ends: some of them are ends in themselves. The symphonies of Beethoven and Brahms, the preludes and fugues of Bach, were composed and are performed primarily for the esthetic pleasure that they afford the listener.

This is equally true of much painting and sculpture. Frequently, artists work without any specific "program" or "cause." Thus, the development of the principles of perspective occupied the energies of many painters during the fifteenth century as they explored new spatial concepts of their world; Cézanne (Figures 239 and 240) worked on portraying significant form carefully related to the flat picture surface. Important artists do not just paint objects; each painting is a new solution to some problem. It is a creative experience for the artist, not a repetitive one.

Looking at painting or sculpture should also result in growth on the part of the observer. The painter or sculptor through his work should enable the observer to grasp some new aspect of artistic reality, should open up or enlarge some new area of experience. Works that are "great" are so termed because they have continued to offer new experiences to those who see them. "Adam" (Figure 242), painted almost four hundred years ago, transcends any specific time or place because of the qualities with which Michelangelo has invested the figure. Through its simple expression of power we feel that we are witnessing the birth of the human race and from the hand of the Creator is passing the spark of life that set into motion the whole of human history. Michelangelo has made man a noble creature truly in the image of God, and we feel ennobled from studying it. The "Deposition from the Cross" (page 98) also has continued to be a "great" work of art because Giotto has conveyed in it an almost overpowering sense of grief that has meaning to anyone who has been moved by great misfortune and unhappiness.

All painters have some idea or message to convey. Of the many factors involved in the production of a painting, such as subject-matter, content, the personality of the artist, expression is foremost. Artists may call attention to aspects of nature not observed before, as fogs or sunsets (Wilde said that no one noticed sunsets before Turner painted them), or intensify types of experiences not commonly perceived in routine living (as was done by the Dutch painter Vermeer in his glowing paintings of interiors; see Figure 237). Sometimes painters reveal to us the vibrant color seen in sunlight on snow or grass, the subtle color nuances in haze and fog; sometimes they bring a new realization of the form and rhythm intrinsic in such prosaic things as apples and jugs; and sometimes they deal with abstract shapes to point out new concepts of space, color and texture relations. These have no practical value in the narrow sense because they concern the qualities of things and the qualities of experience. A still-life sketch may emphasize the roundness, roughness, and smoothness of fruits—not their flavor, keeping qualities or digestibility. A water color by John Marin (Figure 241) brings the vigor and surge of wind and water against trees and rocks without presenting a literal description. Although such expressions and experiences are not common

367

in everyday life, they are central to and distinctive of art as a field of human activity. They offer rare but vital insights into man's relation to his environment.

An important determinant of what the artist is trying to convey is the particular age or period in which he lives. Thus, a painter who in the fifteenth century would have painted religious or mythological scenes, might use factories, landscapes or abstractions as subject matter were he alive today. A visit to any show of painting, old or new, is ample evidence not only of the wealth of material which life offers as potential subject-matter but also of the range of taste and temperament of the artists.

In doing a painting, the artist must react deeply and intensely to his basic idea. It must inspire and stimulate him and he must convey the intensity of his emotions to the observer. If intensity is lacking, the painting is, more than likely, spiritless. Painters select subject-matter toward which they feel congenial and which offers them possibilities for portraying what they believe to be worth-while. Subject-matter is thus important because it gives many clues about the painter's personality and aims. For example, if a painter is concerned with the precision, speed, and regularity of the machine age, he may express his beliefs through factories, machines or geometric abstract forms; if he is interested in the phenomena of nature, he may paint landscapes or seascapes; or if he is inspired by the subtleties and complexities of people, he will undoubtedly use them as subject-matter.

The artist selects his subject-matter as a vehicle for expressing his ideas, and the treatment given a particular subject is of more importance than the original selection. Two painters may choose a dilapidated house as subject-matter: one may emphasize its picturesque, charming or quaint aspects; the other may make of it a social commentary on the conditions that produced such a dwelling. This brings us to the important distinction between *subject-matter* and *content*. In the example cited above, the *subject-matter* of both paintings is a dilapidated house, but the *content* is not at all the same. The content of the first painting is the charm of the quaint and picturesque; in the second, the unpleasant conditions under which some people live. In the paintings of Maria Lani (Figures 221 to 227) you can see how the identical subject-matter has been used to present such diversified content as healthy optimism, delicacy and reserve, gaiety and tragedy. In some cases, such as Miro's "Composition" and Pereira's "White Lines" (Figures 234 and 235), there is no subject

368

matter directly and specifically related to objects in the visible world. Rather, the painters have chosen to portray in a generalized, perhaps philosophic, way their thoughts and feelings about such abstract but basic concepts as order and regularity or the interrelations of organic forms. Whether the subject matter be realistic or not, the painter's first concern is to express his understanding of human experience.

The second problem is organizing the plastic elements with which he works to give order and intensity to his ideas. He thinks not merely of balance, rhythm, and emphasis, but of which kind of balance, which type of rhythm, which degree of emphasis will best convey his content. Finally, we should be aware of the tools and materials the painter uses. Almost any flat surface—paper, canvas, plaster, wood or metal—receives paint. And for each of these surfaces there is a pigment-bearing medium, a paint of some kind. The kind of paint, or the medium, with which a painter works determines to a marked degree not only what the finished product will look like but also its size and permanence, and in some instances the place where it will be used. These important factors—the matter of expression (and the related topic of the personality of the artist), organization and materials—will each be considered in this discussion. Note, too, that this repeats and applies to a specific field of art the three fundamental problems treated in Parts I, II, and III of this book.

First let us look closely at four paintings to see different kinds of expression and how the painters achieved their results.

FOUR PAINTINGS

Many people, in looking at a painting, are afraid to respond to it or to express an opinion. "Am I having the 'proper' reaction?" "Is this the way I am 'supposed' to feel when I look at this painting?" "This picture does not affect me, so I fear I have no esthetic sensibilities." These are typical reactions.

In many respects paintings are like people: they are richly varied, and each has a distinct personality. They can be serious, profound, trivial, humorous, sad, or any of a wide range of characteristics that could also be applied to people. In meeting an individual you react to his behavior traits, his speech, his clothes, his ideas, his responses to situations. On such bases you form your opinion: you like him; you dislike him; you are neutral; you wish to withhold judgment until you have seen him again. Sometimes on the basis of further acquaintance you reverse your opinion: a person toward whom you were neutral may become a valued friend as various aspects of his personality are slowly revealed; another who at first seemed to possess charm and graciousness may before long seem superficial and shallow.

Carrying the analogy of pictures and people further, we may state a few generalizations. First, the cultivation of people and pictures repays one in abundant measure because in the process new and richer aspects of both are revealed: a profound picture in a short space of time can no more reveal all that it has to offer than can a profound individual. In fact, the full depths of personality of either are never fully plumbed; hence, their continued appeal. Second, additional contact with and information about both give us greater understanding and appreciation. Although we can react to the sensuousness and glitter of Louis XVI court paintings, some knowledge of the manner in which people then lived will give us further insights into the art of the period. Likewise, knowing about the home life, the education, the hobbies and job of an individual will help in an understanding of him. Third, we have something in common with all people and with all pictures: the basis for an acquaintanceship with both exists. You may begin a conversation with an individual whom you have just met by talking about the weather; and you may react only to the color of an abstraction which you see for the first time. But both are starts, and further conversation and study will reveal more and more. And last, your reactions are your own: do not be afraid of them! Do not be afraid to modify them either, for only through a revision of attitudes and beliefs and understandings is true growth able to take place.

In looking at the four paintings (Figures 216 to 219), imagine that each is a person and you, on the basis of how this individual appears and what he says, are trying to arrive at some understanding of him. The situation is the same as that which we all face when we go to an art gallery or to a tea party and are confronted with many strangers. Our task becomes one of discovering what experiences we have in common with the people and with the pictures if the occasion is to offer us any more than mild stimulation. Pictures, and the study of them, can be a most rewarding activity because you are assured of meeting interesting and varied personalities. In looking at these pictures we will attempt to

370

answer such questions as What is the general effect of the picture? What is the artist trying to "say"? What means has he used in communicating his idea?

TWO LANDSCAPES

"Starry Night" (Figure 216) impresses us first of all by its tremendous sense of movement and vitality; a restless energy permeates every inch of the canvas. The universe is portrayed as a system of mighty and tremendous forces which make the works of man, typified by the church and houses, appear puny and static. It is the magnificence of nature, the natural laws that order the stars and that determine the forms of hills and the growth patterns of trees to which the artist is responding.

We have all experienced starry nights in which we feel something of the gigantic forces that produce them and ourselves as a tiny part of a universe which we cannot fully comprehend. It is this kind of a feeling that the Dutch artist, Vincent Van Gogh, tried to communicate, and the magic of a starlit night can no more be conveyed by a literal painting than by a literal photograph. To get across his idea he has used non-representational means; movements of light pattern the sky with all the energy and much of the form of nebulae; individual stars in their brilliance take on tremendous size (compare them with the buildings); the moon, not dominating the sky as is usual in night scenes, takes a lesser place in the firmament (as indeed it has). The cypress tree in the foreground partakes of this "universal" quality because the same nervous energy also pervades it as it writhes heavenward in ecstasy and in agony. "Starry Night" is a romantic subject, romantically portrayed, highly emotionalized both in its content and in the means used to convey its ideas. It is obviously the work of a passionately sensitive individual who feels deeply and intensely the wonder and the awesomeness of nature.

In looking at "Starry Night" one is also conscious of Van Gogh's technique because it is in large part responsible for the dynamic quality of the canvas. Every brush stroke is visible and each falls into place as part of a large moving pattern. Even more basic, however, are the composition and forms. The areas occupied by sky and ground are generally horizontal as are the lesser forms within them. Opposing these, both in direction and value, is the form of the cypress tree. Its startling darkness adds brilliance and luminosity to the sky; its verticality makes the earth forms appear more stable and placid. We have already commented on the tree's writh-

371

ing quality which serves as a link between it and the sky, giving the two a basis of unity even though in other respects—direction, hue, and value—they are drastically opposed. It is within the sky, and properly so, that the most compelling and unusual forms are found. Almost directly in the center are two large interlocking spiral forms (with a lesser one slightly below and to the right) which are part of a great movement entering the picture at the left and climaxing in the spirals. The spiral, with its constantly changing direction and speed, is an admirable form to give a sense of movement and energy. Filling the rest of the sky are the stars and the moon, each burning with a terrible intensity. These are all circular, and circles can be restless, mobile forms. The unstable forms hanging in the sky are in stunning contrast to the stable, rectangular solids of the buildings. The hills, with their gently rounded forms, serve as transition between ground and sky. In color the hot piercing yellow of the moon and stars contrasts violently with the cool greens and blues in the tree, land and sky.

Thus we see some of the means which Van Gogh used to get his effects: the impulsive technique, the rhythmic forms, the vibrant color, the dynamic contrasts. Study the picture closely and see what other devices he used to communicate his ideas to you.

In contrast to "Starry Night" let us observe another painting in which quite other goals are sought. The painting, "Stairs, Provincetown," by Charles Demuth (Figure 217) is a calm and reasoned, rather than an emotional and impassioned, work. Compare the subjects which the two men have chosen: Van Gogh has taken a great and impressive natural phenomenon; Demuth has used a simple, unpretentious, outdoor wooden stairway of the sort that abounds in all American towns and cities. Both have used commonly perceived subjects, but a radiant night of the sort interpreted by Van Gogh is compelling for its own intrinsic beauty and grandeur; an outdoor frame stairway is generally so ordinary and commonplace that we scarcely notice it. Both men have been faced with the necessity of drastic transformation: Van Gogh to capture within the confines of a small canvas the great energies and relationships that make a starlit night the impressive experience it is; Demuth to take an ordinary and unattractive subject and make of it a work of art.

We notice in "Stairs, Provincetown," a series of carefully contrived relationships. In general, the composition is triangular with the broad base at the bottom, the apex at the dark opening of the door. The eye level of the observer rises with the flight of steps, so that as one looks

372

at it from the bottom to the top (try it) one gets something of the effect of an elevator ride. The observer is not tied to one spot but is enabled to move about. Thus a dynamic effect and a sense of freedom are achieved.

The device of changing position makes the observer an active participant in the process of appreciation. This concept is of great importance in modern art and, if kept in mind, should be helpful in understanding what a great many painters are trying to do. It is logical, too, that this concept is being developed in an age of great mobility with the automobile and the airplane having become commonplace. True, the idea of the utilization of various eye levels is not new, having been used by artists centuries ago, but it has had to await the development of generally available fast transportation before it could be fully exploited.

Let us look more closely at Demuth's treatment of his subject in the expression of his idea. The most conspicuous aspect of a flight of stairs is the riser (the vertical part) as opposed to the tread (the part you step on). With only two minor exceptions, Demuth has chosen to show only the risers of the steps: he is interested in the concept of verticality and in heightening the impression of ascending. Had he shown the treads, their horizontal planes would have diminished the vertical movement.

Still another important point to observe in the Demuth is the feeling of interpenetration among the various elements. The hand rails "stop" at neither the bottom nor the top of the steps but continue into space through extended lines or planes. This gives a fluid and dynamic effect and a feeling of interrelationship among all parts of the picture. One of the greatest discoveries in physics is that the effect of any object does not stop at its physical boundaries, and this concept finds embodiment here. Making use of interpenetrations and interrelationships gives the composition a transparency which is further heightened by the medium—transparent water color. Although the effect of this painting in black and white is calm and reasoned, in color there is a great deal of warmth, since the predominant hue is red. The darks tend to be clustered about the stairway and thus throw into prominence the major element of the picture. Note, too, that the general impression of the dark and light areas is angular, sharp, and staccato in keeping with the essential nature of a stairway, which is a series of sharply defined rectangular solids. Demuth has allowed this angularity to permeate the entire composition (as Van Gogh did the feeling of flowing movement) and we see it appearing in the forms of windows, siding, and shadows.

These two paintings tell us much about modern art, even though the Van Gogh was done in 1889. One is a romantic conception, a passionate outpouring in response to an impressive aspect of nature; the other is classical in concept, carefully reasoned and constructed, intellectually controlled. Both painters have gone beyond surface appearances; both have heightened the effects of their subjects through transforming them.

TWO PAINTINGS OF PEOPLE

"American Gothic" (Figure 218) is a comforting picture to many people because Grant Wood left no doubt as to what he was painting. It is a portrait of an American farmer and his wife against their Gothic Revival farmhouse and one of their barns. It is a picture of two people (in actuality, Grant Wood's sister and an Iowa dentist) who, to the artist, typified Midwest American farm folk. The couple appears severe but not unkind, hard-working and thrifty, clean and unpretentious. Of pride in their well-kept farm there is much evidence: the farmer grasps his pitchfork as a king would hold a scepter, the expression of his wife implies a humorless pride in her neatly kept house as indicated by the thriving house plants, the shades in the living room drawn to keep the rug from fading, and the lace curtains in the bedroom.

Yet for all its apparent casualness the artist has done much to unify the composition. The two figures are held together, pictorially, by the gable and porch roof, and the composition is generally triangular with the resultant effect of stability. The area between the two heads is given importance by the dark windows (note that they, too, take on a triangular form). The pitchfork, serving as a symbol in the picture (its resemblance to a scepter has already been noted), appears significantly in many variations. Most obvious in the stitching in the overalls revealed by the open coat; in the hand of the man grasping the pitchfork handle; and, somewhat more modified, in the tracery of the windows and the joint lines of the sheet metal roofs. The pitchfork, in addition, strikes a note of thin verticality, echoed in the man's shirt and the vertical siding of the house and barn. These linear, angular, vertical forms are associated with the man. Opposed to these are the rounded forms found chiefly on the left, or woman's side, of the picture. Note the softly curved lines which delineate her dress and apron, the cameo pin and the pattern on the apron. In the background of the woman are several house plants, the leaves of the begonia repeating the shape of her cameo. It is interesting to observe the placement of the figures in relation to the background: the man stands in front of the barn, the woman in front of the kitchen sides of the house, and the living and bedroom areas are between them. The man standing slightly ahead of and dominating the woman is significant in what it tells us of their personal relationship.

Here is a highly competent portrayal of two persons, rendered with a high degree of reality and composed with some subtlety. It presents a specific situation, at a particular time, and a definite place.

In contrast, "Seated Woman" (Figure 219) is a generalized picture rather than a specific one. No one would hope to recognize the woman in the picture because, obviously, no one has ever looked like that. What then has the painter, Pablo Picasso, tried to do? Rather than give us a detailed portrait of a person or persons, as Grant Wood had done, Picasso has given us a universalized portrait; rather than work toward realism, he has used the human figure as a point of departure for his expressive efforts. This is a much more strongly organized composition than "American Gothic." Emphasis on plastic relationships of figure to background, of each part to all other parts, precludes naturalistic details. The elements in the composition can be recognized—the face, eyes, breasts, hands, dress—but they are reduced to essentials and stripped of all irrelevant details.

Picasso, in approaching the subject of a seated woman, observed, as has everyone, that there were many points of vantage (such as front and side view) from which a figure could be observed, and he has attempted to combine several views in the same picture. In attempting that problem, however, it can readily be seen that naturalistic drawing is unsuitable because no one can see two sides of a figure at once. Nevertheless, we know that there are many aspects of every figure even though we can see only one at a time, and the fact that we cannot see several does not mean that we cannot paint them. In that sense, this painting is a highly intellectualized interpretation somewhat in the same sense as is the Demuth.

Look now at the painting to discover some of the aspects of the seated figure revealed to us. In the head there are three rather easily discernible views: two profiles, one looking each way, and a full face view. None of them is in any sense photographic but each has all the elements to make a convincing, if simplified, face. Note that only one can be seen at a time, and that as one appears, the others disappear and that looking from one to the other gives an effect of movement. The breasts, torso and arms are also treated so that varied views and relationships are introduced.

375

Picasso explores these complex relationships through such means as the following: the forms range in value from very light to very dark; they overlap and penetrate; they take varied and ingenious shapes; they have rich and telling textures. Look at the vitality of all the shapes in the picture, how each has a unity and integrity of its own, yet how each fits into and is part of a larger form and of the entire composition. Certain of the areas (the crosshatched one, for example) appear in a number of different guises, sometimes as part of the figure, sometimes as part of the background; sometimes as a light value, sometimes as dark. Note further the relation that is achieved between the figure and the background by the continuity of the forms. Certain of the lines of the figure continue into the background even though the color, value, and texture may change. Thus unity between the various components of the composition is achieved.

Essentially, there are three major areas of the figure: the head, the torso, and the area occupied by the hands. Each is a convex form with a simplified edge: within each the area has been broken up into various component parts which relate to a major form or to the views depicted. As each element appears something different is told about it: hair texture appears in a highly simplified manner twice, once in a light area with dark lines, once in a dark area with light lines. Note the same kind of varied treatment of the breasts and hands. The latter are part of a larger generally oval form, and the observer feels a sense of movement which is a characteristic of hands; one can almost feel them move. One is light, one is dark. One hand is shown with the fingers extended, the other with the fingers drawn but with lines echoing and repeating the resulting form. These are not unlike the lines of a field of force which physicists diagram to show how the effect of a body extends beyond its physical limits. Note, too, how the pattern of the dress becomes altered as it passes through the field of force of the hands: the stripes become dashes.

Picasso, in "Seated Woman," has treated an aspect of experience in a manner not unlike a musician. As Bach and Stravinsky worked with musical symbols and developed majestic and meaningful relationships, so Picasso has worked with plastic symbols and relationships. This kind of art approaches music in its "purity."

"Seated Woman" and "American Gothic" were painted within three years of each other, in 1927 and 1930 respectively, and illustrate two divergent trends in contemporary painting. People are the *subject matter* in both paintings, but the *content* is markedly dissimilar. Wood's paint-

376

ing is a literal, factual document of two Midwestern farm folk in front of their house and barn. Picasso's painting is an imaginative expression of the essential qualities of many seated women; it is not a portrayal of one specific woman in one specific chair against one specific background. Perhaps the major difference is in the degree to which each painter has generalized his subject matter: "American Gothic" is specific, "Seated Woman" is general. Another way of saying this is referring to one as "realistic," to the other as "abstract." The mention of such categories may mislead you into thinking that there are two types of painting and that all of it can be placed into one or the other. This is not true. All painting is abstract to a degree—portraying three-dimensional forms on a two-dimensional surface necessitates some abstraction—and there can be no sharp dividing line. Some paintings are more abstract than others; there are innumerable steps from one extreme to the other.

THE MAN BEHIND THE EASEL

Look at the photograph and seven portrayals of Maria Lani in Figures 220 to 227. All are of the same person yet we cannot help being struck by the wide range of interpretations. In the manner of a scientific experiment, the subject of these pictures has been held constant, thus reducing by one the number of variables. What then is responsible for the fact that seven very different portraits have resulted? It is obviously due to the artists and to the mediums they used, and since in this case each artist chose the medium he wished, it all pretty much comes back to the artist himself.

Maria Lani, the subject of these portraits, is an actress of great talent and beauty. When these paintings were done (in the late 1920s) she was living in Paris and a number of artists of the Paris School either painted or modeled her remarkable head. Look at her photograph in Figure 220. There are several distinguishing characteristics: the lovely triangular shape of the face, the large lustrous eyes and heavy eyelids, the strong arched eyebrows, the wide, full mouth, the general fullness of form. All these combine to make a head that is beautiful and distinguished. Hers is a beauty of structure and form; it is not superficial or skin-deep.

We cannot help noticing that although all seven portraits are different they are at the same time very much alike: they all look like the subject.

Interestingly enough, five out of the seven have chosen a three-quarters view, only one a profile, and one a full-face view. All have taken note of the characteristic shape of her face; of the wide forehead tapering to the full chin; and of the heavy-lidded eyes.

Yet it is the differences which we note even more than the similarities. In Kramstyck's picture we see a lovely, healthy woman who gazes upon the world with assurance and equanimity. It is a literal portrait because her physical appearance has been set down with little change either in form or value. In the Rouault she is portrayed as tragic, her face a mask, the eyes still full but unseeing. In contrast, the Matisse is gay and alive with sparkle and vitality. Kisling has given great emphasis to her eyes. He has made them appear even larger by tilting the head downward, and the sketchy quality of the rest of the figure further centers attention on them. They are the troubled eyes of a woman, perhaps not sure of herself, who looks to others for assistance and assurance. The Soutine with its general aspect of somberness is somewhat allied to the Rouault, but the elongation and distortion of the forms give us a portrayal that is ascetic and neurotic. (Compare this with the El Greco, page 234.) In the Pascin there is a nervous sensitive quality which pervades the whole picture and the softness of the lines and shadows heightens the dreamy detached look of the figure. Of all the portraits, the one by Lurçat is the most depersonalized. He has seen her not so much as a woman but as a design with richly varied forms and strong contrasts. But even that tells us something about the effect of the model on the painter.

How can we explain all these varied interpretations? True, the model was a person of rich and varied personality as the wide range of interpretations testify. But the artists saw different things in the model, and they saw different things because they themselves were all different people with different backgrounds, experiences and goals. We cannot help concluding that Rouault has something of the somber and tragic in his personality, Matisse the gay and cheerful, Kramstyck the healthy and untroubled, Soutine the moody and introverted, Lurçat the intellectual and impersonal. A study of other works of these artists will bear out these generalizations because the characteristics exhibited in these portraits are found there. We conclude that artists interpret their subjects in terms of their interests and experiences. In this case they have done it with a living subject, but the same is true if they had painted a mountain or a bowl of fruit. Every aspect of our environment is capable of such varied interpretation as we have seen in the above portraits.

One might therefore ask: Where does reality lie? In subject or in the experience of the artist? The answer is that it lies in both. All of the pictures look like Miss Lani, yet each of them "looks" like the artist who painted her. The subject was one that possessed such rich possibilities of interpretation that each artist could find a reflection of his own interests and personality within the subject. And carrying this point one step further, it is equally true that you, the reader, see that work of art through your personality. The Lurçat portrait of Miss Lani (Figure 227) or the Giotto "Deposition" (page 98) or the Michelangelo "Adam" (page 408) look different to everyone who sees them depending upon his experiences and the kind of a person he is. An individual who has experienced inconsolable grief will bring a different understanding to the Giotto than one whom tragedy has not touched. The lovely pensive, sensitive quality of the Pascin portrait will be especially meaningful to a person of like characteristics. But the point must be repeated again that although we bring our own experiences to a picture, we find our experiences enriched by contact with a work of art. The seven artists who painted Miss Lani have interpreted aspects of her personality that would not be apparent to any single person.

Thus we see a new aspect of understanding in looking at a work of art—the artist. Out of the richness of life and nature the artist selects those aspects that have meaning for him and constructs his own artistic reality. In looking at a work of art, we are equally selective in seeing and reacting to those things that have meaning for us. But just as the artist can develop and grow in his study of a subject and his portrayal of it, so we can develop and grow in our study of art. Appreciation can be, in fact should be, if it is worthy of the name, an experience whereby our own lives are made richer and more meaningful.

ORGANIZING A PAINTING

Painting a picture, like designing a building or a stove, is an activity which involves much serious thought and hard work. Because the elements of which he composes his picture are readily controlled, still-life painting is one of the simplest problems which a painter faces and we can most readily gain a better understanding of the way in which a painter works by following step by step the production of a painting.

A still-life is arranged (Figure 228)—a well-composed organization of an amaryllis plant, a pineapple, two oranges, and a cloth all arranged upon a table. In the background is a sketch in lithograph crayon that adds interest to the upper part of the composition. All masses in the still-life are variations of spheres, cylinders, cones and cubes. Notice the similarity in form between the flower pot and the pineapple, the repetition of the circular forms in the abstraction on the wall. Notice, also, the pleasant variety of textures in the parts of the pineapple, the oranges, the flower pot and the textiles. All in all, this is a good photographic portrait of several handsome objects which look clean, appetizing, and a bit posed.

It is fairly possible that the painter may remember that he likes fresh pineapple, that orange juice is a refreshing breakfast drink, that an amaryllis is beautiful when in bloom. In short, he may distinctly think about these objects and his experiences with them. All this is permissible and downright enjoyable. But are these gastronomic and associative experiences central to the problem of painting?

Let us suppose that the painter carefully copied the textures, accurately imitated the forms, and rendered the lights and darks with fidelity. Then he has a picture which closely resembles the photograph (Figure 229) but lacks its sharpness of detail and finely portrayed textures. Suppose that he worked this sketch out in colors. The only thing that the painting would have that the photograph lacks is color. But color photography is here and hours would have been spent in trying to do what can be done in a much shorter time by the click of a camera shutter. Although imitative painting still finds a place, it is seldom significant. It is an attempt to compete with nature on her own ground which cannot be done successfully unless all that is wanted from a picture is a diluted portrayal of something to remind us of the real thing in nature. Painting can give us much more than that.

But the painter of this still-life has other ideas and experiments by walking around the still-life, studying the relationships among the various objects, looking at it from different viewpoints. He stands on a chair and looks down (Figure 231). Although nothing has been changed in the arrangement, from this angle it has a dramatic quality not present in the first view. The white fabric suggests movement and the form now showing on the top of the flower pot finds repetition in the forms of the oranges. Notice particularly what has happened to the table legs; the sharp perspective of this view makes them converge and results in a strong, dynamic effect. This view reveals a new series of relationships not seen in Figure 228.

The artist then may say: "Why, when I paint this still-life, must I limit myself to just what I see from one view at a particular time or with a particular light? Why can't the picture have in it some of the variety that I have observed from viewing the still-life from many angles?"

So the artist prepares a new sketch (Figure 230). Gone now are the tasty pineapple, the luscious oranges and the leafy amaryllis. The artist is not interested merely in *what* he paints; his concern is also *how* he paints it. Therefore he investigates the essentials of the objects in the arrangement. He becomes interested, first of all, in thinking of the still-life as large movements or directions suggested by the various objects. These movements appear as planes, and the one which passes through the flat leaves of the plant is the most conspicuous (notice how obvious it is in the photograph). Another demonstrates the inward thrust of the pineapple. Behind these two planes is another—the wall itself. The table on which the objects are resting makes a fourth. Thus four major planes or directions express the basic forces or tensions in the arrangement. On this kind of structural analysis depends the compositional success of a painting. This is not a new idea; great painters have always known it and used it.

Structurations like these are as delicately balanced as mathematical formulae, as carefully, if not as consciously, calculated as the stresses and strains in the steel frame of a skyscraper. But here lies a vast difference, too. The steel frame of a skyscraper is in three dimensions, but a painting has only two—length and breadth. Expressing the three-dimensional solidity and space of the real world on a two-dimensional surface is a complex matter.

There are other features in Figure 230. Notice the line that portrays the shape of the pineapple and then the series of lines which show its texture. Two aspects of the pineapple are shown separately in order to give each special meaning and emphasis. A similar device is used with the flower pot: one line indicates the texture; another the shape. Observe, incidentally, how the plane which passes through the leaves of the plant has affected the drawing of the flower pot.

Now another sketch (Figure 232). In this one the artist studies the roundness, solidity, and mass of the objects. Although this new sketch is closely related to the preceding one, it investigates an altogether different aspect of the still-life. Again, no attempt is made to draw the specific characteristics of the objects; but instead, the essential structure of the *whole composition* in a simplified form. The large mass of the plant is easily identified, and it clearly indicates the direction of the leaves. A variation—coming from the mind of the artist—occurs in the absorption of the general mass of the oranges with the mass of the plant and the flower pot. The relationship between these objects is so strong, particularly as seen in Figure 228, that this solution is quite natural. This location of the orange handsomely emphasizes the plane which was shown in the preceding sketch. It shows how the painter thinks in terms of larger wholes, rather than in terms of separate units. If we think of the objects in a still-life as dynamic, interacting elements which influence the objects that surround them and, in turn, are influenced by them, we shall begin to appreciate one of the things many modern painters aim for.

But now, as a result of these experiments, the artist makes a final sketch (Figure 233), this time incorporating some of the things learned through studying the different aspects of the still-life. Before you look at this sketch too long and before you decide whether you like it or not, compare it with the artist's first sketch (Figure 229). The last one is vigorous, dynamic, compelling; the first, static, reserved and quiet. The first is a pleasant copy of what the artist saw; the last is a reorganization of experiences—a process of making use of certain aspects of the objects in order to express certain relationships. The painter has indicated a three-dimensional grouping on a two-dimensional surface, a vital consideration not well handled in the first sketch. But by the time the final solution is reached the feeling of a two-dimensional surface is established by setting up a great number of planes which relate to the flat surface of the canvas and to the objects in the picture. They move in and out, but always in reference to the plane of the picture.

This, of course, is only one of the countless ways in which this still-life could have been portrayed. Some painters might have made the final painting closer to the appearance of the actual objects, while others might have made it more abstract. Some might have painted it with more vigor and movement, while others might have chosen to express great delicacy or refinement. The sketch illustrated here emphasizes organization of planes, textures and colors to express order. Each painter is concerned with that which is significant to him and thus brings to us new facets of experience.

An important point to remember, however, is that every painter must modify nature in doing a painting, no matter how interested he may be in getting the most realistic effects possible. In the first place, whereas any subject matter exists in three dimensions, the painter has only two in which to work. Second, the value range in nature is many times greater than can be achieved with pigments; the brightness of a sunny day cannot possibly be achieved by realistic means since white, the lightest pigment of the artist, is not light at all compared to sunlight. For example, a piece of white paper indoors is a lower value than a black car standing in the sun. (Try the comparison sometime.) Third, a scene looked at by an observer does not have any definite boundaries because the image on the retina of the eye is circular in shape and grows gradually less distinct as its distance from the center of the image increases; but a painting has a definite and, in most cases, rectangular boundary. Finally, there are always factors of change and movement when we look at actual objects. We almost invariably move our eyes and our heads, we may shift our bodily positions or walk around. This results in a total visual impression that is not static but is compounded of a series of slightly—or markedly—different images. Furthermore, the apparent character of the object is modified by the quantity, quality, and direction of the light falling on it. Although we may move while looking at a painting and the light may change, the resulting differences are far less marked than when we look at real objects.

Thus, the painter sees and moves through a changing three-dimensional world which has enormous range of color and no sharp visual boundaries. Beyond the purely visual aspects are the equally, or possibly more, important psychological factors giving greater importance to some objects than to others. Two trees, for example, may be of equal size, but one may be attractive in color, the other interesting in form and growth pattern; one may produce edible and salable fruit, the other may have no economic value; one may be part of a large orchard, lost among many other similar trees, the other may be silhouetted against the sea and sky above a stretch of lonely beach. Each has its own values, each its own significance. From these values the painter selects those which have meaning for him and subjects them to his own interpretation. His job is to transform the raw materials of life into artistic realities which will objectify his own significant experiences and which will have meaning for those individuals who will see his paintings. Since the beginning of man's history, painters have experimented with diverse approaches of expressing their concepts of space and form and each age has discovered new means of interpretation. There are, unfortunately, many people who would set limitations not only upon the subject matter of art but upon the artist's means of organizing his experiences. To apply narrow critical or creative criteria to painting would imply the rejection of much of the great art in the world and, if imposed on the artist, would restrict him from full expression. Below are listed and described briefly a number of the ways in which painters, now and in the past, have organized the plastic elements to transform their world of experience into new meanings.

Single Unit. Depicting one object alone, as in Rivera's drawing (page 187), is the simplest method. The one element stands by itself and the only spatial relationships are those within the object itself and those between the object and the edges of the picture. This method is effective in presenting one idea forcefully and clearly.

Size. When more than one object is portrayed, the larger ones have more importance and also appear to be nearer the spectator than do the smaller elements. In Poor's mural (Figure 243), the two central figures gain spatial prominence through their size (as well as through their forward position) and the other figures recede.

Vertical Location. The child's drawing, "It Is Slippery" (page 167), shows the representation of depth by vertical placement: the row of houses, higher in the composition, look further away. (Few, if any, of these examples employ only one of these methods—in the child's drawing the houses also recede because they are smaller. In this section, only one method will be pointed out for each picture mentioned, but let that not mislead you: painters combine all of these methods as the need arises.) Suggesting recession by vertical location has been employed by many painters, notably the Egyptian and Oriental.

Overlapping Forms. Because a form is obscured by another form in front of it, overlapping is one of the painter's chief means of indicating depth. In "American Gothic" (Figure 218), the farmer and his wife overlap their farm buildings and the farmer's right arm overlaps the figure of his wife, thus establishing a definite spatial organization.

Linear and Aerial Perspective. The representation of space by means of linear and aerial perspective is the method most widely used by American and European artists today. The laws of perspective were discovered in the fifteenth century and have been in widespread use in the western world since then. The camera also has tended to popularize this method of space depiction. *Linear perspective* concerns the arrangement of lines and forms as they fall on the retina of the eye, or on a photographic negative. Parallel lines, such as railroad tracks, appear to converge and distant objects appear smaller than those nearby. *Aerial perspective* concerns the representation of space by weakening hues and values, by lessening the contrasts among them and by softening the edges of objects in proportion to their distance from the observer. Through the discoveries of artists, and more lately, the development of photography, we have become very familiar with these devices of space organization.

Even though perspective is an "accurate" method of depicting space there is considerable psychological evidence to prove that we do not "see" according to the laws of perspective. Thus a round table, though its image as it falls on the retina is an ellipse, still appears round. In other words we see according to what we know. There have been many periods in which art of the highest excellence was produced without recourse to the laws of perspective. A great deal of Oriental art makes use of inverse perspective in which lines, instead of converging in the picture, diverge. Thus, instead of closing space in the picture in relation to the observer it is opened up and a sense of spatial freedom is achieved. This same treatment of space was also used in much art during the Classical and pre-Renaissance periods. Even since the discovery of the laws of perspective great artists have avoided their slavish use and have employed such devices as several vanishing points in a picture or several horizon lines to increase the sense of space. The limitation of linear perspective is that it freezes the position of the spectator in relation to the picture and may produce a static, lifeless effect. Present-day painters have spent much of their energies discovering new ways of depicting space in keeping with the dynamic principles of life and growth.

Interpenetration and Transparency. The methods discussed above have long been in use, but contemporary painters have also tried others. X-rays and fluoroscopes make us realize that opaque forms under certain conditions become transparent. Physicists and chemists are conscious of the manner in which physical and chemical forces interpenetrate solids, liquids, and gases; and psychologists and sociologists are well aware of the way in which human actions carry through and permeate their environment. Less concerned with outward appearances and enclosing surfaces than with inner forces and drives, some painters have treated their forms and colors so that they interweave and penetrate their surroundings (see Figures 217, 219, 233, 234, and 235).

385

For another example of what an artist does to organize space in a composition, compare the photograph of a landscape (Figure 238) in southern France and the oil painting (Figure 239) of that same scene by the French painter, Paul Cézanne. What are the differences and what are the similarities? Which one is easier to look at? Which do you prefer? What has been done to "nature" to transform it into "art"?

Perhaps the first thing you will notice is that the painting is easier to look at as a unit. The foliage and ground shapes have been changed from a more or less hit-and-miss pattern into an orderly arrangement; the sky, instead of being merely a light area, has become an integral part of the picture. The organization has been accomplished in somewhat the same way as in the still-life discussed above. Basically, it is a series of planes, the first being the light wall at the bottom of the picture, the second the mass of foliage extending across from extreme left to extreme right. Then follow a series of planes, delineated by horizontal lines, contrasts of dark and light, and trees and houses that lead our attention to the mountain, the dominant object. Whereas the photograph appears to be a jumbled mixture of many kinds of trees, the foliage in the painting has a pleasing rhythm due to the shapes of the foliage masses and the consistent brush strokes. Throughout the painting movements and forces have been organized in relation and opposition to one another: notice in the large tree at the left how the left-to-right direction of the tree trunk has been counterbalanced by the right-to-left direction of the brush strokes in the foliage, or how the left-to-right movement of the three tree trunks have been opposed by the strong right-to-left direction of the light wall in the foreground. These are only a few of the many and varied means which Cézanne has used to give his painting the organized, rhythmic vigor which he felt to be fundamental, though not always immediately apparent, in nature. His painting is not just a literal representation of what he saw, but is a reorganization of the essential features to make them more forceful and more pleasing.

Look through the plates on painting in the book and study the different methods that have been used by the artists to reorganize the appearance and relations of natural objects to give them new meanings. This is one of the chief problems in painting and it must be repeated once more—there are many ways of solving it. There is no more reason that an artist should be restricted in his method of composing space than that he should be limited in his choice of subject matter. Different expressions demand different organizations and the criterion of judgment should be the validity of the means of organization in terms of the expression and whether or not, through it, the painter has achieved an artistic unity.

SOME OTHER NEW AND OLD PAINTINGS

Figures 234 through 237 are reproductions of four paintings, two contemporary, two from previous periods in the history of art. Each represents a different approach to organization; each has its own distinctive expressive aspects. Both of the contemporary paintings are highly abstract: both of the old ones are readily recognizable in subject matter.

The Pereira "White Lines" (Figure 235) is constructed entirely of rectangular forms of varying proportions, sizes, values, textures and solidity. Some are opaque; others are transparent. As various of the forms overlay each other new and subordinate forms are brought into being. The eye in moving over the canvas makes constant discoveries of new rectangles and new relationships. Basically, the composition consists of a central low-value rectangle around which are grouped lighter value forms. Note that all of the forms in the painting are parallel to the plane of the picture but that whereas some advance, others recede. All the forms are two-dimensional and there are no diagonal movements into space in the painting, all movement is parallel to the picture plane. This is a calm and reasoned painting with all irrelevancies eliminated and with all forces in delicate, precise equilibrium. Its clarity and order are somewhat reminiscent of the exactness of a mathematical formula or the logic of a philosophic essay, but its sensitivity and purity remind one of the music of Bach and Mozart or the architecture of the Greeks. It is an attempt to deal with essences rather than with external manifestations and to express these essences so that they will stimulate the sensitive observer to renewed thinking and feeling. Aiming to go beyond the hurry and confusion of some aspects of contemporary living, this painting restates a belief in the basic regularity of life.

The Miro "Composition" (Figure 234) offers a striking contrast. Like the Pereira, one kind of form has been used throughout, but instead of being regular and geometric, these are irregular and organic, similar to those studied in biology. In fact, they are often referred to as *biomorphic*, or life, forms. The general effect is lively and active, heightened by the fact that none of the forms in the painting is anchored; they seem to move and float on a soft, slightly differentiated background. Also, as in the Pereira, they overlap and interpenetrate, are transparent and opaque. This results in new and intriguing forms which seem mysteriously to appear. In this picture, and others which he has done, Miro was investigating elemental life-forms, their plastic possibilities and organization. Rather than the mechanical forms of the machine age, he chose to experiment with the organic forms of life. If you look again at the Eames chairs on page 269, you will notice how similar their shapes are to those of Miro's painting. Here, again, the relationships among diverse art forms of one age become as explicit as they did in the photographs of the community of Williamsburg. "Composition" is a painting of compelling liveliness and vitality and an important work in a movement that has done much to redirect the attention of designers to organic forms and forces.

The paintings by old masters are in interesting contrast to the contemporary ones. Here the subject matter is readily identified, and the pictures are varying interpretations of nature, of people, or of their interrelationship. Pieter Breughel, the Elder, a sixteenth-century Dutch artist, painted "The Harvesters" (Figure 236), one of four paintings depicting the seasons. Under a tree, the hungry and weary peasants eat and rest before returning to their work. Although the people occupy only a minor place in the picture, their impress on the landscape is clear, from the simple beautifully composed forms of the uncut grain on the left to the stacked sheaves on the right. The landscape is controlled by the people for their livelihood. Man is integral with nature and this relationship has been given a monumental interpretation.

The Vermeer "Lady with Lute" (Figure 237) depicts a figure in a different kind of relationship. Seldom has light been so miraculously treated, for the room glows with rich clear color. The subject is in no sense profound, but the organization is carefully and sensitively contrived. In both these paintings one senses the great sympathy and concern of the artist for what he is painting. Neither of the subjects is particularly impressive by itself. Yet in both, through a profound conviction of the artist in seeing his subject not as an isolated aspect of life but as a part of all life, a moving and monumental product has been achieved. The raw material of life has been transformed and we, as observers, have had our lives made richer through the artists' interpretation.

Some may see little relation between the two historic and the two contemporary paintings discussed above, while others may sense at once the underlying similarities. The most obvious difference, of course, is that Breughel and Vermeer depicted objects more or less as they appear to the eye whereas Pereira and Miro transformed their visual impressions markedly. It is often said that the elimination of specifically recognizable objects, especially the human figure, signifies a lessened interest in "human" or "real life" concerns. This contention is difficult to support. Whereas Breughel gives a specific representation of people in relation to the land that supports them, Miro expresses the communality of all organic forms through generalized plastic symbols. Vermeer gives us a peaceful portrayal of a figure in relation to architectural forms, and Pereira generalizes many tranquil events to give a distillation of the basic elements in calm, reasoned life experiences. No, we cannot say that *one type* of painting is more concerned with human experience than is the other; we can only study each painting by itself to ascertain its value. Two of these four paintings have used specific subject matter (as did Grant Wood in "American Gothic") and two have used abstracted forms (as did Picasso in "Seated Woman"). Each of these painters has chosen to deal with certain aspects of human experience, for no painter can deal with them all simultaneously (look again at the portraits of Maria Lani). Thus, these paintings are bound together by their portrayal of life as interpreted by each painter, their sensitive organization of the plastic elements, and the clear mastery of the materials and processes employed to give form to idea.

PAINTING IN OIL

Painters turn to this medium because it lends itself readily to intensive, personalized exploration. Oil painting has an advantage over such mediums as water color and fresco in that it may be worked over for an almost indefinite period of time. Notice again the "Sistine Madonna" (page 98). This is no moment's fancy or whim captured and held in a medium quickly and spontaneously worked. Much study, thought and reflection—plus experience—went into that composition while it was being developed. Similarly, the sensitive, orchestrated balance of Cézanne's landscapes (Figures 239 and 240) was created as the pigments were painstakingly laid on the canvas and their effect on each other was diligently observed. Because oil paint dries slowly and because areas can be painted over several, even many, times there is no need to hurry, no need for quick decisions, and if an unwise decision is made, in most instances it can be changed.

In no other paint medium is it possible to get as wide a range of effects. The pigment may be applied in thick, opaque masses (Figure 235), in separate strokes (Figure 216) or in washes of almost water-color transparency (Figure 234). Variations and nuances of color, subtle modeling of form, are limited only by the painter's ingenuity and skill. Another characteristic is also of considerable importance. In water-color painting the painter begins with white paper to which he applies color, each color darkening the paper. Thus, unless opaque white pigment is added to water color, the painter necessarily works from light to dark. The same is true of fresco. In oil painting, however, it is possible to work either from light to dark or from dark to light because, as typically used, oil paint is opaque enough to cover what is beneath it. For example, in painting an apple it is possible first to cover the whole shape with a middle red, then to darken the shaded side with a darker red, and to lighten the opposite side with a lighter color. These two characteristics—being able to work on oil paintings over a period of time and being able to work from dark values to light as well as the reverse—make oil paint an amazingly responsive medium. In the hands of an experienced painter the pigments can be combined and shaded on the palette or on the canvas to an almost infinite variety of hues, values, intensities and textures.

In oil painting, an artist first needs a surface on which to paint—one that will receive oil paint freely and yet not soak it up, that will withstand temperature changes and not crack or warp the pigment on it. Canvas is the most widely used support, although at one time or another wood, paper, metal and stone have been used. Many of the great paintings up to the time of the Renaissance were painted on wood, but the lightness, cheapness, and flexibility of good hemp or linen canvas have made rare the practice of painting on wood. Because oil ordinarily makes canvas brittle it is customary to treat it with a sizing coat of casein or similar material. When thoroughly dried, the sized canvas is ready for the pigments.

Pigments come from many sources: minerals, vegetable matters, coal tars and other chemical combinations. These are ground by hand or machine until the grains are extremely fine, then mixed with oils—olive, linseed, copal or poppy seed—and sometimes with wax to bring them to suitable consistency. Their quality depends primarily on the source from which they were obtained and on their purity. They likewise vary markedly in permanence: some, such as Prussian blue, absorb colors mixed with them and turn black; others fade on exposure to light. Such facts the painter must know.

The oil painter's brushes are of two general classes: (1) sable brushes, round and soft, which are excellent for precise detail such as the face on the figure in Raphael's painting; and (2) flat, stiff, bristle brushes for larger, freer strokes as in "Starry Night." Some painters use the soft sable brushes sparingly; they fear to be cramped and pinched into tongue-biting, inhibited brush strokes which, in turn, may make their paintings dull and flat. Some artists have abandoned brushes altogether and use, instead, the palette knife. This is a thin, easy-to-clean metal blade which can pick up the pure colors from the palette and apply them to the canvas in all their individual purities, in small dots or large, heavy strokes.

It would be a mistake to think that brushes and palette knives are used only to convey color to the canvas. They serve also as a means of giving texture to a painting. Texture is eagerly sought by most contemporary painters, but the oil painters have the edge on all others. For different examples of texture look again at the Van Gogh and the Pereira. Oil paint can be smooth or rough, fine or coarse, thick or thin, depending upon the effect wanted in a particular place.

Modern oil painters follow many paths. Some glory in pure colors, others use muted tones. Some use one kind of brush only, others a variety. In general, however, the idea the painter is trying to get across is the governing factor in his choice of materials and his development of technique. There is no one approach, no single technique, no body of inviolable laws.

PAINTING IN WATER COLOR

"Maine Islands" (Figure 241), a water-color painting by John Marin, is a spontaneous, vibrant picture. It shows a typical Maine scene in transparent, brilliant colors: blue-green and grays, with reds and yellows. It would be impossible to get the effects Marin achieved in any other medium than a watered pigment applied freely on paper. Good water-color paintings are not easy to make, despite their impromptu appearance. The painter who decides to work in this medium must be sure of his techniques, else his idea will fail to materialize.

One of the first things he must do is find a suitable surface. Paper is commonly used and most painters like a paper that is rough in texture, not slick or oily to the glance and touch. The rich quality of a good, firm paper contrasts subtly with the swift or slow brush strokes that will appear on it and generously lends texture to the otherwise limpid paint used with it. The paper, too, must be well stretched or anchored on a board because the painter will have little time to contend with curling edges and bumpy surfaces.

The water-colorist's brushes are also carefully selected. Naturally, the idea he has in mind will largely govern his choice: if he wants an abandoned, carefree effect of great vigor and energy, he may select ones with fairly stiff bristles that will leave a brush mark somewhat like those broad, dark strokes used on the two sides of "Maine Islands." But usually the painter's supply of brushes will be made up of large red-sable brushes which come to a point when wet. These will carry the paint well and allow for a great variety of strokes without annoying pauses for reloading.

The most important part of the water-colorist's kit is his collection of pigments in tubes or cakes. These are soluble in water—which, of course, he must have at hand—and are prepared and combined on his palette. A glance at John Marin's palette shows what really a small number of colors an artist needs from which to work out his chief problem of color: *Blues*—French ultramarine, cerulean, cobalt; *Reds*—rose madder, light red, spectrum red; *Yellows*—aureolin, yellow ocher, cadmium; *Greens*—viridian, oxide of chromium; *Gray*—Payne's gray; *Black*—lampblack. And thus, with paper and brushes and palette, the painter is ready to begin.

"Maine Islands" shows all these materials at work. The paper works: its own handsome texture gives the unpainted areas the effect of distant water and sky or the reflection of light from a nearby evergreen, just as the painter desired. Brilliance is often achieved in water-color paintings as much through the areas of unpainted paper as those which are covered by pigment. The brushes and pigment, too, work well: the islands look distant, deep and mysterious because Marin guided his paint-laden brushes surely and quickly. The sky and the sea have a northern, watery appearance because Marin's brushes, intelligently handled, correctly chosen for their task, put it there.

It is easy to see that water-color painting can be more than a girls' seminary summer afternoon pastime; the artist must be in complete command of his medium to be able to give his work the strength and vitality of "Maine Islands." He cannot dawdle along, touching up here, repainting there. Water colors become muddy and dull when worked over too long. The original Marin water color is not large because this medium limits the size of paintings. We have no regrets that water colors cannot be made in more heroic proportions—simply because the medium is not heavy and grand enough for such subjects. The medium of water color is ideally suited to quick rendering of brilliant scenes or atmospheric effects.

It is fairly evident from Marin's water color that he approaches his work as a means of recording his understanding of natural and artificial forces active today. He is not concerned with literary, social, or imitative values. He tells no "story," fights for no cause. But he presents the coast of Maine and the streets of New York in a way which uniquely reveals their essential but often overlooked qualities. He offers the observer the possibility of an invigorating, intense experience. His comments are as dynamic and accented as his paintings.*

> For the worker to carry on, to express his today, with the old instruments, the old tools is inexcusable, unless he is thoroughly alive to the relationships of things and works in relationships. Then he can express his today in any material. . . .
>
> Consider the material side of today with its insistence: glass, metals, lights, buildings of all kinds for all kinds of purposes with all kinds of materials. Lights brilliant, noises startling and hard, pace setting in all directions, through-wires, people movements, much hard matter.
>
> The life of today so keyed up, so seen, so seemingly unreal yet so real and the eye with so much to see and the ear to hear. Things happening most weirdly upside down, that it's all— what is it? But the seeing eye and the hearing ear become attuned. Then comes expression:
>
> > taut, taut
> > Loose and taut
> > electric
> > staccato

---

* Printed with the permission of John Marin.

To get to my picture . . . I must for myself insist that when finished, that is when all the parts are in place and are working, that now it has become an object and will therefore have its boundaries as definite as that the prow, the stern, the sides and bottom bound a boat. . . . I am not to be destructive within. I can have things that clash. I can have a jolly good fight going on. There is always a fight going on where there are living things. But I must be able to control this fight at will with a Blessed Equilibrium.

Speaking of destruction, again, I feel that I am not to destroy this flat working surface . . . that exists for all workers in all mediums.

Too, it here comes to me with emphasis that all things within the picture should have a chance. A chance to play in their playground, as the dance should have a suitable playground as a setting for the dance.

Too it comes to me a something in which I am curiously interested. I refer to Weight Balances. As my body exerts a downward pressure on the floor, the floor in turn exerts an upward pressure on my body.

Too the pressure of the air against my body, my body against the air, all this I have to recognize when building the picture.

Seems to me the true artist must perforce go from time to time to the elemental big forms—Sky, Sea, Mountain, Plain,—and those things pertaining thereto, to sort of re-true himself up, to recharge the battery. For these big forms have everything. But to express these, you have to love these, to be a part of these in sympathy. One doesn't get very far without this love, this love to enfold too the relatively little things that grow on the mountain's back. Which if you don't recognize, you don't recognize the mountain.

And now, after looking over my scribblings on various pieces of paper, I think that what I have put down is about what I wanted to say, the gist of it anyway. My present-day creed, which may show different facets on the morrow.

Marin's comments merit serious consideration on many points. First, his explicit reference to expressing "his today" through "relationships of things" gives a direct clue to his reason for painting. Objects and things are less important to him than are the relationships existing among them; consequently, the identity of things is frequently disregarded in the interests of relationships. His reference to the material sides of today—"lights brilliant, noises startling and hard, pace setting in all directions"—demonstrates his sensitivity to the characteristic flavor of contemporary life. Second, his references to the organization of his work—to the definite boundaries enclosing a "jolly good fight" within a "Blessed Equilibrium," to "Weight Balances" and to giving all things in the picture "a chance" —show his interest in producing a lively design in which forces play against and with forces. His mention that he is not to destroy the flatness of the working surface shows genuine respect for the two-dimensional quality which distinguishes painting from sculpture or architecture. To him painting is not creating illusions of three-dimensional nature on paper or canvas, but rather re-creating the essential relationships on a plane surface. Finally, his sympathetic love and admiration for the "elemental big forms" reveal the source of his inspiration. He constantly returns to nature to "recharge the battery." From this constant, penetrating study of natural forms and forces comes much of the strength and freshness which mark his paintings as a landmark in American art.

We have chosen to discuss in detail a work by John Marin because more than most water-color painters he has grasped the possibilities and avoided the limitations of the medium, but there are many other good ways of handling water-soluble pigments. The Chinese have used water colors with great delicacy and softness, and with superb feeling for their liquid, transparent quality. The English school of water-color painters employ carefully graded washes of color to portray the atmospheric effects characteristic of the English countryside. Not a few contemporary painters prefer to use opaque water colors, an effect which can be produced by mixing Chinese white with water-color pigments, or by using gouache (opaque colors ground with water and mixed with a preparation of gum). When used in this way, water color loses its transparency, but the fluidity of the medium is largely retained. Good gouache paintings have a distinctive and unique quality. Painters often use opaque pigments to accent or touch up compositions done in water color. This practice is frowned upon by the purists but is not uncommon.

Any medium is used well when it serves the artist as a vehicle for expressing his ideas. Sometimes the color is put on paper (either wet or dry) and then blotted in some places to produce the sensitive, delicate effect secured by Demuth (Figure 217). Sometimes the color is in small strokes as the Cézanne (Figure 240), leaving blank white paper to carry most of the responsibility of the painting. Nearly any painting exhibition affords an opportunity to see many other uses of water color, or you can experiment by actually trying to find out what water color can be made to do. In either case you will find that the effects gained through water color are quite different from those possible with oil paint.

PAINTING IN FRESCO

The ceiling of the Sistine Chapel in Rome is magnificently decorated with paintings by Michelangelo, a tremendous project on which he worked for years. The figure of "Adam" (page 408), larger than life size, is but one small detail in a series of compositions. Today, three centuries later, this series of paintings is still, and will be until the ceiling falls, one of the finest examples of painting in fresco that we know. Michelangelo's problem was a difficult one: the surface was large; it was the ceiling of a chapel; and great permanence was desired. Michelangelo wanted a painting medium that would endure as long as the building itself. Besides, there was the fact that the surface was part of the building: would it be possible to use a paint which actually became part of the wall?

The answer was fresco. Fresco originally meant "fresh," but is now used to describe the process of painting on fresh, wet plaster. The medium is somewhat akin to water color: the pigments in both cases are mixed with water, and a glance at "Adam" shows that fresco has something of the transparent, fluid quality of water color. But here the similarity ends because fresco is a medium suited to monumental painting which becomes integral with the building.

Generally the process begins with preliminary sketches, later enlarged to full size cartoons which are transferred to rough plaster. The basic outlines of the compositions are done in red or black, and show rather accurately where everything goes. The fresco painter, faced with the problem of covering possibly hundreds of square feet while lying uncomfortably on his back on a scaffold precariously high, finds it more than a convenience to have his plan or organization well mapped out before he begins painting. Next he decides on an area which he is certain he can complete in one day or the length of time he will work at a

216. "The Starry Night" by Vincent Van Gogh is an excited and impassioned reaction to an impressive phenomenon of nature. The artist has taken great liberties with the subject in order to convey his feelings. Notice the "paint quality" of the entire picture and how it heightens the effect.

217. In contrast to the Van Gogh, this water color by Charles Demuth, "Stairs, Provincetown" is a more intellectualized approach to a man-made subject. Demuth also has taken liberties with his subject and the lack of a fixed viewpoint, such as occurs in most paintings and photographs, gives the observer a sense of flexibility and increases the "stairness" of the painting.

218. Grant Wood's "American Gothic" (1933) is typical of much of the American Scene painting which discovers and interprets for us many aspects of our country and our lives. Highly literal in its interpretation, it is a penetrating study of Midwest farm folk.

219. The highly generalized nature of "Seated Woman" by Pablo Picasso, done in 1927, is in striking contrast to the Wood. The artist avoided specific statement and has combined full-face and profile views in a highly ingenious manner which demand discovery and exploration by the observer.

A photograph of the French actress Maria Lani and seven portraits of her done by well-known artists. One is struck both by the similarities and dissimilarities in the portraits; the subject matter is the same in all but the content is varied—a striking example of the effect of the personality of the artist on his work.

(*Top row, left to right*)
220. Photograph
221. Romain Kramstyck
222. Jules Pascin
223. Chaim Soutine

(*Bottom row, left to right*)
224. Georges Rouault
225. Henri Matisse
226. Moise Kisling
227. Jean Lurçat

228. (*Upper left*) Photograph of a still-life arrangement. This is an example of the raw materials used by painters in building pictures.

229. (*Lower left*) An imitative charcoal drawing of still-life arrangement. Although drawing of this type serves many useful purposes, it affords little opportunity for an artist to express anything beyond the surface appearance of objects, something done much more efficiently by the camera.

230. (*Lower right*) Diagram of important planes in the still-life. Compare with the photograph above. All sketches of the still-life were done by Josephine Lutz.

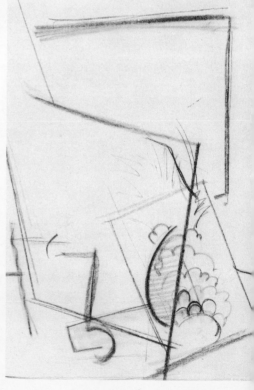

231. (*Upper right*) Photograph of still-life from above, showing new relationships not visible in Figure 223.

232. (*Lower left*) Diagram of significant masses and suggested movements emphasizing three-dimensional, plastic qualities and interrelatedness of objects.

233. (*Lower right*) Charcoal drawing, based on studies in Figures 225 and 227. Particular attention is given in this sketch on the relation of the objects to the two-dimensional surface on which they are drawn. This shows only one of the many ways in which this subject can be portrayed.

234. (*Upper*) Joan Miro. "Composition." An investigation of organic forms.

235. (*Lower*) I. Rice Pereira. "White Lines." A carefully contrived oil painting using only rectangular forms.

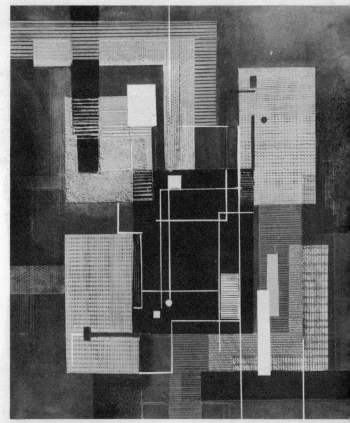

236. (*Upper*) "The Harvesters" by Pieter Breughel, the Elder, is a monumental treatment of a Dutch rural scene.

237. (*Lower*) Few painters have equaled Jan Vermeer in the treatment of light as in this picture "Lady with Lute."

238. (*Upper*) Photograph of a landscape in Southern France. Though a pleasant view it is in no sense an unusual or dramatic one.

239. (*Lower*) Oil painting of same scene by Paul Cézanne. Note how the landscape has been ordered and clarified and how cluttered the photograph looks in comparison with the painting. Observe, in particular, the treatment of the middle-ground and the effect of making the ground forms concave rather than convex. Cézanne has transformed an ordinary scene into a stunning organization.

240. (*Upper*) A water color sketch, also by Cézanne, of the same general view as in Figure 238. Here one is conscious of medium and yet, even though delicately treated, the feeling of scale and solidity of the mountain have been conveyed.

241. (*Lower*) The treatment in "Maine Islands" by John Marin is in striking contrast to that of Cézanne. The ruggedness of the Maine seacoast has been admirably portrayed and a number of non-realistic elements have been introduced to heighten the effect.

407

242. (*Upper*) "Adam," a portion of a larger composition on the creation of man done by Michelangelo on the ceiling of the Sistine Chapel in the Vatican, Rome. Primarily a sculptor, Michelangelo was one of the finest draughtsmen who ever lived.

243. (*Lower*) Central portion of mural painting at Pennsylvania State College done by Henry Varnum Poor. This is done in fresco.

stretch and covers it with fresh plaster. When the day's work of painting is done, he carefully cuts away the unused plaster. Because of the impossibility of matching colors perfectly, a line is formed where each day's work stops and the observer may often pick out this line because it is impossible to avoid. Several of these are discernible in the fresco by Poor (Figure 243). These lines are generally made to coincide with the edge of a figure or object so that they are not noticeable, but sometimes this is impossible. The Mexican painter, Rivera, once worked for a thirty-hour stretch without rest, so that a monumental figure which was the central element in the composition would not be marred by these tell-tale lines.

The coloring substance, of course, must be ready to use as soon as the plaster is put on the wall. It is prepared by mixing a pigment with water or water and lime; when this is applied to the wet plaster, the lime binds the pigment to the plaster and makes the painting actually part of the wall. A certain amount of touching up with tempera paint is often done. But colors applied to dry plaster lack the permanence of those bonded into the plaster, so that this touching up is avoided as much as possible.

Fresco painting has a long history. However, other than the fact that contemporary painters have at their command a wider range of colors than did earlier workers, the present-day methods of painting are similar to those used by Michelangelo and, in fact, by painters centuries before him. During the seventeenth, eighteenth and nineteenth centuries the interest in fresco painting declined, but the twentieth century has witnessed a renewed interest in mural paintings done in the fresco medium, an example of which was shown in Chapter 2. It was in Mexico that the art of fresco was revived as a way of painting permanently on the walls of schools, governmental offices, libraries and hospitals. Led by José Orozco and Diego Rivera, an active group of painters combined the well-known European methods with some used centuries ago by the Mexican Indians, and established a school of mural painting which became known throughout the world. Following the lead of the Mexicans and sponsored by government art projects, painters in the United States have risen to the challenge of enriching the walls of public buildings with frescoes of conspicuous merit. There are probably some in or near your own community which will repay a visit.

The work of Henry Varnum Poor, who is equally noted for his ceramics and easel paintings, is typical of such murals. In the following discussion he tells how he studied and solved the problems of portraying significant events in a fresco at the Pennsylvania State College * (Figure 243).

> First a mural must decorate a wall. Second, it should be a human document with real meaning to the people who use the place. From the architect's and purist's point of view, the first is more important. But there have been occasional instances of great human documents spread upon walls without much regard to the architecture, yet taking a certain grandeur and scale from their contact with building so that even the purists forgive them.
>
> Moreover, decoration pursued as a decoration is apt to be so shallow and limited, that an artist bent upon setting his symbols on a wall in paint or carving will probably give an infinitely richer wall than the decorator repeating his patterns.
>
> Still the ideal remains—the perfect harmony of the two; and for that ideal there must be a close union between architect and painter. For that union to be really fruitful, there must be a common understanding of symbols—all communication being by means of symbols. Purely realistic painting is not communication: it is just representation. There can be no eloquence, no stirring of the imagination, no quickening of all the senses through a certain stress put upon the one sense, such as does happen in communication through symbols—poetry, painting, music. . . .
>
> I think through a union with architecture, working in a common sympathy for and love of materials, more universality can be reached—something that makes sense without plodding realism and so contains the elements of fine decoration.
>
> This mural at State College, Pennsylvania, first had to be in terms of what is, as much as we have arrived at it, a universal pictorial language. It was not for a special group—it was to be on the most-seen interior wall in the main administration building of a big democratic state university, the first school established under the Morrill Land Grant Act signed by Abraham Lincoln during the Civil War. Started as the Farmers High School of Pennsylvania about 1855, it was the product of real vision and a real need on the part of agricultural and in-

---

* Printed with the permission of Henry Varnum Poor and the *Magazine of Art.*

dustrial workers for special training plus the classical education of the day. With its first main building stopped for lack of funds, the Land Grant Act gave it new life and it became Penn State College, the first in the series of great land grant colleges, which now include the Universities of Wisconsin, Iowa, Kansas, Michigan, Illinois, and many others. In education it is a most concrete expression of the American ideal of democracy, giving advanced specialized training to the sons and daughters of the average family. This is the rich human background that the mural had as subject matter.

Architecturally, the building, "Old Main," is in the classic tradition. The selected wall faces the main entrance across an open foyer some fifty feet square and two stories high. It is seen through four large columns set twelve feet forward from the wall. It starts above the low wide landing of the stairway where it is about sixteen feet high and diminishes with the rise of the stairs on each side to about five feet on the ends.

The columns, in relation to the mural, play two parts. First, since they are large and structural they give to the wall back of them the character of a screen setting the boundaries of the room, rather than that of a wall carrying the weight of upper walls. This makes it fitting, without any outrage to the structural fitness, to give to the wall great spatial extension, which would not be fitting for a "weight-carrying" wall.

Secondly, the columns become a shifting element in the design. In themselves they supply the main vertical masses of the design. They create empty spaces in an otherwise too crowded pattern, but the placing of these spaces changes with the movement of the spectator either forward or back, or from side to side. . . .

As to subject again. State College is in the geographic center of Pennsylvania where the rolling farm lands meet the high long ridges of the Alleghenies. The farm lands have developed, and kept, farms that are a delight to the eye, with barns like temples set in the most sightly places; with diversified and balanced farming that is serving as a model of agricultural life. The mining and industrial sections are even more uniquely rich and in their more somber way equally beautiful. So the panorama of the State itself I felt as the most compelling theme.

I wanted, no matter what grouping of figures I arrived at,

to make the whole wall unified in one light, under one skin, to give to the obviously improbable or impossible juxtapositions which formal composing demands, a sense of unity and probability, even of inevitability, through all the changes of scale and meaning in the groups. So I put the source of light, the sun itself, in the lunette at the top, keeping the center figures which, because of their position and scale, would be otherwise too dominant, in the heavy but vibrating neutrality of colors seen against the light.

On the left, the hills and fields are bathed in sun, while over the high ridges on the right falls a more misty and somber light. But at each end the color rises to its greatest intensity and the eye travels over the whole wall with no let-down at the ends.

As for wishing to have the whole under one skin, that skin is the sense of surface which comes from a love of your material for its own sake, not just a medium for representation; so your material, your surface, is always there and even though you represent depth and roundness, it is just a symbol of these qualities. This is the beauty of fresco. It is plaster; it belongs to and is part of the wall. The lime which holds your plaster and finds and gives depth and brilliance to all your color, is one of the fundamental earthy but miraculous mediums.

CONCLUSION

Briefly, a painting is a record of human experience expressed through organized color, form, line, texture and space on a flat surface.

The most important aspect of a painting is what the painter has to express. In looking at any painting we may ask such questions as: What is the painter trying to communicate? Is what he is attempting to say significant? Is the painting sincere and profound, or is it shallow and dishonest? Is it creatively original, or is it weak and imitative? Does it indicate that the painter was adventurous and courageous, or cowardly? Does the painting express something significant of the time in which it was painted? Does the painting give you a new experience, or does it merely tickle your memory?

Secondly, we may concentrate attention on the way in which color,

412

form, line, texture and space have been organized. Does the organization grow out of the expression? Do the forms and colors appear in a unified pattern? Is the painting interestingly varied, or does it seem monotonous? Have the forms been satisfactorily related one to another as well as to the picture plane?

Finally, we may examine the way in which the medium has been employed. Is the medium chosen well suited to the expression? Have the possibilities of the medium been investigated and used profitably? Have the limitations been observed?

Looking at all these aspects of paintings sympathetically yet critically, comparing and contrasting the work of different artists, studying these pictures in relation to the social setting in which they were produced, will help to enrich and increase your appreciation. Remember, if you find the ideas of many contemporary painters difficult to understand, it may be your shortcoming, rather than theirs. Give him a chance to enlarge your experience by being open-minded. A first thing to do is to look at as many original paintings as you can find; then look at some truly excellent modern color reproductions which convey much—but not all —of the vitality and beauty of the originals. Look at them, not once, but many times, studying, analyzing, interpreting. See how many different uses of oil and water color you can discover. Ask yourself whether each painter used his medium to best advantage to express and communicate his ideas. Make every attempt to be open-minded about new experiments, new techniques, new expressions. Give the painter the same encouragement accorded the experimental scientist: both have duties to open our eyes to new fields of knowledge and experience. Neither is here "to do what has been done before." And be equally open-minded and sympathetic toward historic paintings. Look at them in terms of your own experience and then try to see them as they were seen when first painted. Remember that the "old masters" of today were the "new masters" of their times.

Another activity which might well precede or be carried along with the above is that of actually trying to paint with as many mediums as you can lay hands on. See what the possibilities and limitations of each are; working with oil leads to effects not possible with water color, and the converse is equally true. Experiment freely as an aid to a better understanding of what professional artists are doing.

The third thing to do is to look at some of the many books on painting.

For historical discussions:

David Robb and J. J. Garrison: *Art in the Western World* (Harper, 1942). Includes a concise history of painting as well as of architecture and sculpture.

Frank Jewett Mather: *Western European Painting of the Renaissance* (Henry Holt, 1939). A more comprehensive history of one period of painting.

Holger Cahill and Alfred Barr: *Art in America* (Reynal and Hitchcock, 1935). A résumé of painting in America.

Thomas Craven: *A Treasury of Art Masterpieces* (Simon and Schuster, 1939) is profusely illustrated with superb color reproductions.

Suzanne La Follette: *Art in America* (Norton, 1939). An absorbing account of the development of the arts in the United States and their relation to other cultural manifestations.

Robert John Goldwater and Marco Treves: *Artists on Art, from the XIV to the XX Century* (Pantheon, 1945). Statements by artists on their approach to painting and sculpture.

Everard M. Upjohn, Paul S. Wingert and Jane Gaston Mahler: *History of World Art* (Oxford University Press, 1949) comprehensively covers the development of painting, sculpture and architecture.

For contemporary trends and appreciation:

Alfred H. Barr: *Cubism and Abstract Art* (Museum of Modern Art, 1939). A scholarly but readable statement on many of the various manifestations of cubist and abstract art.

Alfred H. Barr: *Picasso, Fifty Years of His Art* (Museum of Modern Art, 1946). A study of the development and works of the most influential and perhaps the greatest of living painters.

Alfred H. Barr, Jr.: *What Is Modern Painting?* (Museum of Modern Art, 1943). An exceptionally clear, brief statement on the aims of modern painting.

Roy Bethers: *Pictures, Painters, and You* (Pitman, 1948). A lively, popularized and well-illustrated book on painting, mostly contemporary.

Sheldon Cheney: *Expressionism in Art* (Liveright, 1934). A good account of how the contemporary painter organizes his visual materials.

Sheldon Cheney: *The Story of Modern Art* (Viking, 1942). A clear readable statement on the development of modern painting, sculpture and architecture.

414

Erle Loran: *Cézanne's Composition* (University of California Press, 1943). A significant, profusely illustrated study of the approach to composition followed by Cézanne and by many contemporary painters.

Ralph Pearson: *Experiencing Pictures* (Brewer, Warren & Putnam, 1932). An introduction to the study of plastic values in painting.

Lionello Venturi: *Painting and Painters—How to Look at a Picture* (Scribners, 1946). A stimulating, provocative, and somewhat abstruse analysis of what painters have tried to do.

On materials and processes:

Ralph Mayer: *The Artist's Handbook of Materials and Techniques* (Viking, 1940). Comprehensive reference book on techniques of painting in oil, tempera, fresco, and water color; pastel drawing; graphic arts; and sculpture.

The Encyclopaedia Britannica: Excellent semi-technical articles on Water Color, Fresco, and Oil Painting. Also good treatments of the history of painting and such special aspects as Landscape Painting, Portrait Painting, Mural Painting, Flower Painting, and Still-Life Painting.

CHAPTER 16 *Sculpture*

S CULPTURE and painting are two forms of expression that are invariably linked. Many similarities exist between the two: both spring from and are used in relation to architecture; both make use of kindred subject matter—although sculpture is more limited in this respect; both are concerned chiefly with expression and communication. Much that was discussed in the preceding chapter on painting concerning organization and communication applies equally well to sculpture, and much of the material in this chapter applies to painting.

The most obvious difference between the two lies in the fact that painting, with its materials of pigment and paper, canvas, or wall surface, is two-dimensional, whereas sculpture, with its materials of stone, wood, metal, and clay, is three-dimensional. Painting, because of its materials, relies heavily on color. Even though artists in the two fields may try to express much the same idea, the materials used will produce different results.

In the various periods of the history of art, painters and sculptors have worked on the same kinds of problems. Medieval painters and sculptors both used religious subjects, Victorian artists were preoccupied with realistic representation, many contemporary painters and sculptors are concerned with the development of new concepts of space. There exists an easily perceivable congruity among the works in these fields during any one period, and if a person is familiar with the characteristics of, say, early Flemish painting, he will have no difficulty recognizing sculpture done at the same time. Occasionally, as with Michelangelo or Picasso, an artist will both paint and carve, and in such cases the presence of a close relationship among his various products is easily understood. Such instances are not common, however, and even when they exist the artists usually identify themselves with one or the other field. Thus, Michelangelo considered himself primarily as a sculptor, though he has given us some of the most remarkable painting and architecture in the

416

world; Picasso considers himself primarily as a painter, but he has done considerable sculpture. It is the similarity of the basic drives, interests, and problems of artists who are contemporary one with another and the fact that they move in the same cultural milieu which accounts for the relationship among their products. The sculpture and painting of any particular period exhibits, of course, considerable diversity of expression. John Marin and Picasso are contemporaries and so are William Zorach and Henry Moore. But within any cultural period, painting and sculpture exhibit the same general range of expression.

Although some kinds of subject matter are equally suited to both fields such as figures, animals, and abstractions, sculpture is more limited in the kinds that can be treated. The reason is simple. Since the products of sculpture (not including relief sculpture for the moment) can be viewed from all sides, those subjects in which distance is involved—as landscapes, interiors, etc.—are not suitable for sculptural treatment. Although, from one point of view, this limits and simplifies the field, at the same time it makes it more difficult and complex, for the problems involved in organizing a figure that can be viewed with satisfaction from all sides (the problem of the sculptor) is much more difficult than presenting a figure from one viewpoint only (the problem of the painter). On the other hand, the sculptor, in dealing with a single figure, or even a group of figures, does not face the problems of relating them to the background or frame of the picture in the same manner as a painter.

As a means of clarifying some of the expressive problems of sculpture, let us look at two examples, widely separated in time of creation and in expression.

TWO SCULPTURES OF WOMEN

The "Hera of Samos" and "Walking" (Figures 244 and 245) were done almost twenty-five hundred years apart, the first by an unknown Greek sculptor in the sixth century B.C., the second by Alexander Archipenko, a twentieth-century American. About the only thing they have in common is the subject; both are figures of women; both artists have used the female form as a point of departure for expressing ideas in three-dimensional form. Past that, they have gone in different directions and have secured equally different results.

417

The matter of material is basic. Whereas "Hera" is of stone and was carved, "Walking" is of terra-cotta and was built up of small masses of clay. The figure of "Hera" seems static, composed, the parts subordinated to the generally cylindrical mass of the figure; in "Walking," the form seems to have grown from the inside—it has a living, organic, and dynamic quality. In keeping with the columnar form, the details of the figure of "Hera" are subordinated to it. The arms are held close to the body, the folds of the garment repeat the vertical line of the figure, the lower edge of the dress curves outward and serves as a transition to the base on which the figure stands, thus repeating the line of the feet. This gives the figure greater stability and contributes to the static quality mentioned above.

The forms in the terra-cotta sculpture are moving and sinuous in accord with their intent. We see the figure, not at one instant in the process of walking, but at many instants. Of particular interest are the varied forms which are used. Most of them are full, convex, positive: the portion in the center is concave and negative. The opposition of the concave and convex, of the positive and negative, gives the figure a great deal of its vitality. The texture is also excitingly varied, ranging from smooth to rough, the roughness of the texture increasing with its distance from the center of the figure. Note, also, that the texture is one that is natural to a material used in an additive manner.

There are other traits and characteristics of the two figures that could be pointed out. The "Hera," being the figure of a goddess, is heroic in its effect, calm, serene, majestic, belonging to a public world. "Walking" is an intimate figure of a more private world, feminine and introverted, sensuous and suggestive. But both are remarkable in that the materials have been given form in keeping with the idea to be expressed. Sculpture is capable of as varied interpretations as painting.

THREE SCULPTORS ON SCULPTURE

For first-hand information about sculpture and its problems, we turn now to statements by three sculptors, Richard Davis, Charles Rudy and Henry Moore. All have done distinguished work (Figures 246, 248 and 260); all are sensitively aware of the complexities of the field. They describe both their feelings about sculpture and their methods of working.

418

All work chiefly in stone, although many of Moore's most famous pieces are in wood. As you read the statement by each artist, study the figure by which he is represented in the book to see the relation between his utterances and his work. The first quotation is by Richard Davis, who did the black granite "Bison" (Figure 246), a sculpture which shows a feeling for sensitive line and strong form combined with a deep respect for the hardness of stone. Mr. Davis says: *

> I would define sculpture as the *art* of creating and organizing significant forms or shapes (representational or non-representational, natural or geometric), the goal being to enrich one's experience in regard to form and form relationships. By "significant forms" I mean those forms which, though they need not necessarily represent an object of nature, must in some way be meaningful or significant in regard to humanity or life. If someone will create a slop pail whose shape and form is of such beauty as to give *significance* to our life, or perhaps give some emotional reaction to one who sees it, I am willing to call him a sculptor. . . .
>
> Feeling sculpture to be the art of creating significant form, and believing sincerely that self-expression in this art must be in the dialect best suited, not only to the subject and the material, but also to the artist speaking, I have found that, for me, carving is the most satisfactory idiom. The harder the material and the greater its resistance, the easier it is for me to develop a pure shape. I feel about soft materials the way a woman must feel who wants to make balls out of soft butter.
>
> I have often been asked to justify "direct carving" as opposed to copying in a hard material a sketch or model conceived and executed with greater ease and freedom in clay. My defense is again based on my conception of sculpture as a language. If I wished to write poems to be read in Italy I would not, by choice, write them first in English. I would try to learn to speak, write, and understand Italian. If I were a composer and were able to play the violin, I would not compose a violin obbligato on the piano.
>
> I like to compare a sculptor's direct carving to a composer's recital of his own compositions. He has composed and memorized his concerto. He knows every passage and phrase, every climax and arpeggio, every note and liaison. And when he takes

* Printed with the permission of Richard Davis and the *Magazine of Art*.

his place at the concert piano, the whole composition is part of him, a unified entirety, a homogeneous, well-understood, and digested piece of music. The recital becomes a new experience for him and his listeners. He does not play from notes, echoing in empty tones his earlier creative effort. The recital is a new creative experience—fresh, vital, toned and tuned to the concert hall and the audience.

Before starting a "direct" carving one must have first attained a careful and complete knowledge of the subject being carved. Sometimes it is necessary first to work out a great many sketches on paper or in clay, to determine even the basic composition or, if the subject is a human being or an animal, to learn the anatomy and the character of the natural forms to be carved. But once these facts are well in mind, carving in the stone will establish the dialect and the idea will be translated into the idiom of the particular stone. It is by creating directly in the material that I can best maintain the genuine character and the personality of the medium. Each different piece of stone suggests new shapes and forms. Each carving becomes a new experience—an experience in form. To write or talk of "experiencing form" is almost futile. It is only in their creation and, for me, in carving them that I can get that sensation, both emotional and physical, which I refer to.

The method of cutting away rather than building up is such that one is forced to see the statue first as an entirety—to see the thing primarily as a combination of a few big, simple geometric shapes. One is forced to feel and to establish in the stone only the basic and essential masses, to see their relationship abstractly—to work out the desired rhythm between them.

It is obvious that all details, everything but the most all-encompassing masses, must be obliterated from the first steps of carving and therefore from the first vision of the statue. Facial features are details of a head, unneeded until the individual character of that particular "egg form" is determined. The whole statue is covered with a thick layer which, as the carving proceeds, becomes thinner and thinner until finally the most delicate details of modeling and sensitive vibration of planes and forms gradually work themselves into existence.

The very hardness of stone and relative slowness of carving permits and even forces the carver to concentrate on shape rather than meaning or idea. And the greatest carvings are those which have the most perfect marriage of the idea and the form, the most perfect relationship between the subject and the material.

We turn now to the statement by Charles Rudy for his comments on similar problems. His work is illustrated by "The Sisters" (Figure 248), an appealing and charming piece, yet one which cannot be dismissed with such adjectives, for in addition to or rather combined with its charm and appeal are notable strength and vigor. Mr. Rudy writes: *

A pencil feels less friendly to me than chisels, hammer, and stone. At work with these I believe I can find better a sculptor's way to tell, with gravity and zest, of that intimate need between me and the piece I am making. When each sculpture is in itself completed it becomes a part of the experience and intensified enthusiasm with which I can begin a new work in stone, in wood, in bronze, or whatever I will. So it seems hard for me to imagine any time in my life when the joy of this work, and that personal need to do it, was not or will not be with me; or any time that working in sculpture does not bring me a sense of discovery and of new-beginning.

Most of us begin early to build, to draw, to "make" things—and to absorb, unconsciously perhaps, the life of our localities, our country, and our respective families. So it was with me. After some years I am still "making" things—in sculpture. . . .

Art has a mutual profit in every astringent anger that rebels against chaos and falsehood—in every act of faith specifically expressed by each artist—just as all life has a mutual profit in art and its challenge of form. At this time—at any time—the sculptor, as artist, is not only charged with his share in the nourishment and growth of our culture, but, working as he is with this sculptural vernacular, he has always been propagandist of order and clarity, spontaneity and control. Here universality and individuality are not selective contradictions but a singular development. Just as the phases of working out a piece of sculpture do not contradict but explain their single identity with its conception. This is, in a sense, my credo; is, rather, the way I would express this belief, in words.

All of us who can live and do the work which is at once our need, our pleasure, and our excitement, must afford, if need be, only to live and *do* that work. There are few of us

---

* Printed with the permission of Charles Rudy and the *Magazine of Art*.

however who are not, at least for a time, unable to contrive both. While I was at school I had never carved wood or stone. In New York, desiring to afford some permanent materials for my work, I got a piece of stone from a dismantled building, some tools from a blacksmith and began scruffing my knuckles and learning to carve, attentive to the speech of the stone and to the forms which responded as the ensemble developed. This was an invaluable and constructive experience, for it demonstrated most clearly the artist's need for the cooperation of his material through sensitivity to its inherent qualities, whether it be stone, bronze, wood, terra cotta, or newly developed plastic. . . .

I find I am becoming more and more sympathetic to the variety of approach used in the creation of sculpture. Much of my own work is made without any preliminary sketches. In carving "The Sisters" for example, I began simply with the idea of doing two children. As I carved, the composition seemed to come naturally into the discipline of the stone—the form and feeling with it. I love working this way.

However, I often make small rough sketches of an idea, then adapt them into the final size and material. With some commissions I have sketched out the size and scale in rather exacting detail to use as a guide; then I begin work directly in the material, checking with a few points and measurements, changing where it seems essential. On the other hand, when designing certain pieces of sculpture for an architectural setting I make carefully studied scale models. Then the full size can be pointed quite faithfully from them. . . .

I do not feel dogmatic about the many methods and techniques. I do know I want to explore a great deal more and use any of them which will help me accomplish what I most desire to achieve in my work. Often in studying the construction of form in nature, I find myself bringing my interest in animals into some sculptural form. Not that I have the intention of concentrating on "animal sculpture" especially. But I think animals so often suggest themselves by the adaptability of their varied shapes to the advantage of certain compositions. Then, too, they move about so much I have to concentrate immediately on co-ordinating the essential masses in a simple manner. This makes me search at once for those masses which are the most telling, and leads me to a natural simplification which I like very much. I think, too, that its effect on my approach

to all other sculptural forms is a healthy one. It is a lot health-
ier, I believe, than simplification for its own sake.

Henry Moore, the author of the third statement, produces work which
bears a less easily discernible relationship to natural forms than either
Davis or Rudy: he is exploring other possibilities of expression. "Reclining Figure" (Figure 260) is one of his sculptures and, even though
mystified by the total figure, one cannot help reacting favorably toward
the bold and beautiful forms which compose it. In the following discussion,* Moore explains some of the sources from which he derives inspiration, and the manner in which he transforms that inspiration into
sculpture:

> It is a mistake for a sculptor or a painter to speak or write
> very often about his job. It releases tension needed for his
> work. By trying to express his aims with rounded-off logical
> exactness, he can easily become a theorist whose actual work
> is only a caged-in exposition of conceptions evolved in terms
> of logic and words.
>
> But though the non-logical, instinctive, subconscious part of
> the mind must play its part in his work, he also has a conscious
> mind which is not inactive. The artist works with a concen-
> tration of his whole personality, and the conscious part of it
> resolves conflicts, organizes memories, and prevents him from
> trying to walk in two directions at the same time. . . .
>
> This is what the sculptor must do. He must strive contin-
> ually to think of, and use, form in its full spatial completeness.
> He gets the solid shape, as it were, inside his head—he thinks
> of it, whatever its size, as if he were holding it completely en-
> closed in the hollow of his hand. He mentally visualizes a
> complex form *from all round itself*; he knows while he looks at
> one side what the other side is like; he identifies himself with
> its center of gravity, its mass, its weight; he realizes its volume,
> as the space that the shape displaces in the air.
>
> And the sensitive observer of sculpture must also learn to
> feel shape simply as shape, not as description or reminiscence.
> He must, for example, perceive an egg as a simple single solid
> shape, quite apart from its significance as food, or from the
> literary idea that it will become a bird. And so with solids such
> as a shell, a nut, a plum, a pear, a tadpole, a mushroom, a

---

* Printed with the permission of Penguin Books.

mountain peak, a kidney, a carrot, a treetrunk, a bird, a bud, a lark, a lady-bird, a bulrush, a bone. From these he can go on to appreciate more complex forms or combinations of several forms. . . .

Although it is the human figure which interests me most deeply, I have always paid great attention to natural forms, such as bones, shells, and pebbles, etc. Sometimes for several years running I have been to the same part of the sea-shore— but each year a new shape of pebble has caught my eye, which the year before, though it was there in hundreds, I never saw. Out of the millions of pebbles passed in walking along the shore, I choose out to see with excitement only those which fit in with my existing form-interest at the time. A different thing happens if I sit down and examine a handful one by one. I may then extend my form-experience more, by giving my mind time to become conditioned to a new shape. . . .

When first working direct in a hard and brittle material like stone, the lack of experience and great respect for the material, the fear of ill-treating it, too often result in relief surface carving, with no sculptural power.

But with more experience the completed work in stone can be kept within the limitations of its material, that is, not be weakened beyond its natural constructive build, and yet be turned from an inert mass into a composition which has a full form existence, with masses of varied sizes and sections working together in spatial relationship. . . .

As far as my own experience is concerned, I sometimes begin a drawing with no preconceived problem to solve, with only the desire to use pencil on paper and make lines, tones and shapes with no conscious aim; but as my mind takes in what is so produced, a point arrives where some idea becomes conscious and crystallizes, and then a control and ordering begin to take place.

Or sometimes I start with a set subject; or to solve, in a block of stone of known dimensions, a sculptural problem I've given myself, and then consciously attempt to build an ordered relationship of forms, which shall express my idea. But if the work is to be more than just a sculptural exercise, unexplainable jumps in the process of thought occur; and the imagination plays its part.

It might seem from what I have said of shape and form that I regard them as ends in themselves. Far from it. I am very

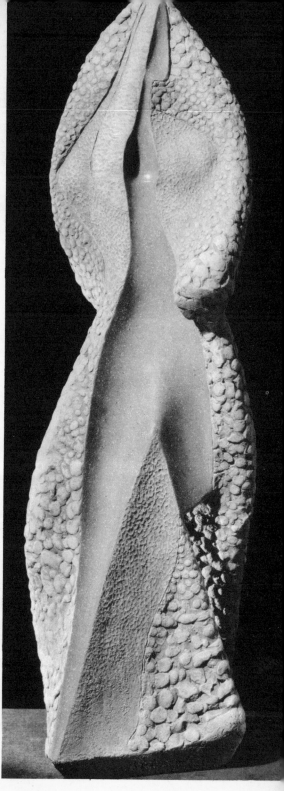

A contrast in treatment of the female figure.

244. (*Left*) "Hera of Samos," a Greek sixth-century B.C. formalized figure.

245. (*Right*) "Walking" by Archipenko, a twentieth-century American.

246. (*Upper*) Richard Davis. "Bison" in black granite. Notice the massive sculptural solidity, the contrast of textures.

247. (*Lower left*) William Zorach. "Child with Cat," an appealing, compact sculpture in Tennessee marble.

248. (*Lower right*) Charles Rudy. "The Sisters," a closely knit composition.

249. Oronzio Maldarelli. "Reclining Figure." This simple, sensitive, and beautifully modeled figure may be compared with the other female figures in Figures 243, 244, 257, and 259.

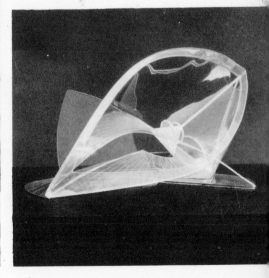

250. (*Left*) Concetta Scaravaglione working on heroic figure. Notice small model.

251. (*Right*) Naum Gabo. "Spiral Theme," a non-objective construction in plastic. Note how the light becomes an integral part of the forms.

252. Andrea del Verrocchio. "Madonna and Child" in terra cotta, by a master of
the Italian Renaissance, is a warm, human interpretation of one of the great
Christian themes in art.

253. Jacopo della Quercia. "Adam and Eve." A strong and vigorous relief carving done in the early fifteenth century when interest in the sculptural possibilities of the nude human figure were being discovered.

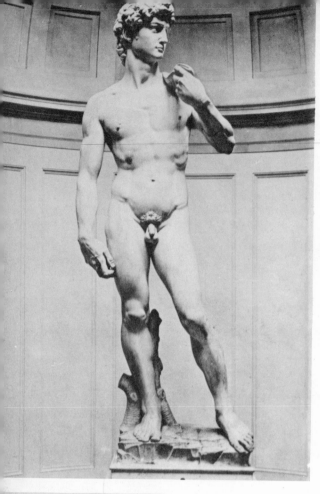

254. (*Left*) Michelangelo. "David." It is interesting to compare this remarkable figure with the work of this great artist in other fields, his "Adam" and the dome of St. Peter's.

255. (*Lower left*) Roman head in bronze of Agrippa. The aggressiveness and materialism of the Romans are both apparent in this striking head.

256. (*Lower right*) This stone Cambodian Bodhisattva from Angkor Thom with its Oriental serenity is an interesting contrast to the Roman head.

257. (*Right*) Emile
Bourdelle. "Hercules."
Sculptural forms well
suited to metal.

258. (*Lower left*) Jacob
Epstein. "Oriol Ross,"
a portrait bust in
bronze in which one is
conscious of the plastic
material from which
the casting was made.

259. (*Lower right*) Carl
Milles. "Europa and
the Bull." Contrast this
with the work of the
same sculptor in stone,
Figure 47.

260. (*Top*) Henry Moore. "Reclining Figure," a sculpture in elm wood.

261. (*Lower left*) William Steig. "Proud Woman," is amusingly expressive.

262. (*Lower right*) Carl Hallsthammar. "Venus in Red Cherry." Note how the grain of the wood emphasizes the modeling.

much aware that associational, psychological factors play a large part in sculpture. The meaning and significance of form itself probably depends on the countless associations of man's history. For example, rounded forms convey an idea of fruitfulness, maturity, probably because the earth, women's breasts, and most fruits are rounded, and these shapes are important because they have this background in our habits of perception. I think the humanist organic element will always be for me of fundamental importance in sculpture, giving sculpture its vitality. Each particular carving I make takes on in my mind a human, or occasionally animal, character and personality, and this personality controls its design and formal qualities, and makes me satisfied or dissatisfied with the work as it develops.

My own aim and direction seems to be consistent with these beliefs, though it does not depend upon them. My sculpture is becoming less representational, less an outward visual copy, and so what some people would call more abstract; but only because I believe that in this way I can present the human psychological content of my work with the greatest directness and intensity.

These artists have written eloquently about the problems of their craft. They see sculpture as an important aspect of a culture, as bringing "order and clarity" to life, as being "meaningful and significant in regard to humanity," for good sculpture can no more be divorced from life than can our methods of transportation. In the light of what they say, the relationship between painting and sculpture becomes even clearer. The aims and goals of the artists in the two areas are the same; the medium in which they work is different, as is the use to which the results of their labors are put.

Much of the great sculpture in the world has been developed as part of architecture. The figures on the portals of Chartres Cathedral (page 97) are integral with the structure, conceived and executed in relation to the building: they are columnar and assume an architectural form. On the other hand, there have been times during the development of art when sculpture and architecture were quite separate; when the work of sculptors was conceived apart from buildings. This characterizes the situation today. Its parallel in painting is the dominance of easel painting and the relative unimportance of mural painting. Whether or not this is a healthy situation for sculptors (or painters) is not clear. In both fields, this independence gives the artists greater freedom: on the other hand,

433

by being separated from architecture, they are deprived of a base of support and of a discipline that can give direction to development.

All three of the sculptors above frequently discuss their materials. Davis speaks of maintaining "the genuine character and personality of the medium," Rudy of "the discipline of the stone," Moore of the necessity of a "great respect for the material." Because of the importance of the material in the conception, development and execution of a piece of sculpture, the remainder of the chapter will be concerned with a discussion of the field in terms of the three most common media: stone, metal and wood.

SCULPTURE IN STONE

For the many centuries that man has been doing sculpture as a means of giving embodiment to his feelings and ideals, stone has been his most favored material. It has many admirable features as a medium, especially its availability and permanence. Not only does stone occur pretty generally throughout the world, but it is an extremely varied material in all respects—in color, in hardness, in texture. As a raw material, it offers an engaging array of possibilities. During the last century white marble was especially favored because its fine even grain made it possible to carve with great detail. Offsetting these advantages (which often led to dull excesses) is its lifeless and characterless color and texture. Contemporary sculptors are being more experimental and are using such other stones as granites, sandstones, and limestones with their diverse colors and textures.

The permanence of stone also makes it an attractive medium, for it is one of the most durable of all natural materials. Wood, another commonly used material, while more easily carved than stone, disintegrates more rapidly and is subject to limitations of size. It could almost be said that stone has no size limitations if we consider such gigantic undertakings as the Sphinx in Egypt (page 95) and the even larger projects in this country—Mount Rushmore in South Dakota and Stone Mountain in Georgia—where entire mountain sides are carved into portrait busts of famous American presidents.

Stone as a material, furthermore, has possibilities of monumentality possessed by no other material. This is partly due, no doubt, to the

434

resistance that the material itself offers to the sculptor, thus forcing upon him monumental conceptions. In contrast, wood, with its organic qualities and its relative softness, is an intimate material suited to less grandiose conceptions. And lastly, the fact that carving in stone is direct makes it especially attractive and satisfying in contrast to metal where preliminary models and molds are made before the final casting results.

Carving directly in stone, although at one time practiced by all sculptors, was rejected for the most part during the nineteenth century in favor of easier methods. It became the custom then merely to make a clay model at full or even reduced size, and hire skilled artisans to copy it in stone. Modeling in clay is a process of building up; carving in stone is a cutting away. Copying in stone forms which were originally designed in clay is more than likely to lead to a misuse of the medium, such as an excess of undercutting and fragile non-stone detail. When the sculptor works directly in stone with no more than a preliminary sketch in pencil, wax, or clay, there is little danger that he will forget the possibilities and limitations of his material. If, with chisel in hand, he faces a block of marble or granite, he will probably not think of carving delicate flowers, arms or legs extended far from the central mass of the body, draperies floating lightly in the wind; instead, as Rudy states, he will be "attentive to the discipline of the stone."

When sculpture assumes monumental proportions, such as Scaravaglione's statue (Figure 250), it becomes necessary to have a carefully studied small model made in some easily workable material which the sculptor can twist and change, add to or take off, until the work has taken the shape most suitable to express the idea he has in mind. Working directly in stone on sculpture of this magnitude is rarely possible. Although clay and wax have been widely used for this preliminary modeling, Plasticine (clay treated with oil so that it does not harden) allows the sculptor to work without fear of having the model harden before he is finished. The full size sculpture can then be made by stepping up the proportions of the small model, as in the large statue in Figure 250 which is being prepared for casting in another material.

A significant sculptural expression of community ideals—the "Peace" statue (page 58)—has already been mentioned, but a discussion of the process by which this statue came into final form will throw further light on the way in which sculptors tackle large commissions. Milles prepared small figures in a plastic material before beginning on the full scale model.

These he made small so that he could see in three dimensions his plans which then could be changed again and again until his basic idea had crystallized. This work on the preliminary model often takes as much time as the making of the full scale model; actually, of course, the artist is working out his most difficult problems: Milles did not begin on his large model until he was certain that he saw satisfactory solutions for his problems in the small figures.

Since the completed statue was to be about thirty-six feet high, the sculptor was then faced with the difficult problem of erecting a model which would hang together long enough to allow a plaster cast to be made from it. Because solid Plasticine would have collapsed from its own weight, besides being unnecessarily expensive, Milles prepared a framework or armature of metal and wood, and on this he applied the Plasticine. Then, with the various tools of modeling, paddles, cutting wires, and scoops, he began the thirty-six-foot model of the peace memorial. He bore in mind that the finished work was to be Mexican onyx instead of, say, a bronze cast. Because of this, he remembered always to consider how the particular surface or part of the statue he was working on would look in its final form.

When the original model was completed, the next step was to transport it from Cranbrook, Michigan, to St. Paul, Minnesota. But Plasticine sculpture can be transported only with great difficulty. So a safer method of getting a copy to St. Paul was used. The ordinary procedure of making a cast is one of making a mold, or negative, of the model; next, making a cast from the mold; finally, using the plaster cast as a guide in cutting the stone itself. It is apparent that the safest place in this scheme to make a change of locations is immediately after the mold is finished. Therefore, a mold of the full size model was prepared and shipped to the stonecutters in St. Paul.

In modern times, stone carving is a relatively simple task. Accuracy is made possible by a special device known as a pointing machine, and the drudgery of chiseling and polishing is lessened by power tools. Since Mexican onyx is not obtainable in very large pieces, the statue had to be built up from many separate chunks of stone (as you can readily see in the photograph). By using the pointing machine each piece of onyx was formed to correspond with one section of the statue. At first, the workers cut sharply into the onyx with automatic chisels, using the pointing machine only at intervals. But as they neared the surface of the statue, the pointing machine was used more frequently until finally it appeared as if the completed statue were actually there, but covered with a rough woolly coat of white material. The chisels were abandoned and special polishing materials were used which brought out the beautiful color and texture of the onyx.

Michelangelo, whose "David" appears in Figure 254, once said that it should be possible to roll a stone statue down a hill without breaking it. This drastic criterion of sculptural excellence emphasizes the sculptor's necessity of keeping in mind the solidity of both the mass of material with which he started and the finished product. Michelangelo worked chiefly with stone, and it is necessary to bear this in mind because his statement applies only to sculpture made of stone or similar brittle material. This "rolling-down-hill" criterion of good sculpture means simply that the basic structural properties of stone be respected, that the possibilities and limitations should be considered. This leads to the conclusion that stone is especially well suited to solid, compact forms, poorly suited to extended or widely separated shapes.

SCULPTURE IN METAL

Sculpture in metal is quite a different thing from sculpture in stone. Emile Bourdelle's "Hercules" (Figure 257) would have been impossible in marble, but in bronze * it becomes expressive of the great tensile strength of that material—the subject and the material are in harmonious relationship. Notice the openness of the composition—the thin bow, the extended legs and arms—in brilliant contrast to the compact stone forms seen above.

Two other examples will show further the possibilities of sculpture in metal. Carl Milles' "Europa and the Bull" (Figure 259) may well be compared with his treatment of stone (page 58) to see how differently the same sculptor works on different problems in contrasting materials. The general effect of "Europa and the Bull" is quite unlike that of "Peace." Whereas "Peace" is noble and restrained, worthy of its monumental setting in the St. Paul Court House, "Europa and the Bull" is carefree, playful, and entertaining. One might expect to find it in a

---

* See discussion of bronze in Chapter 10.

437

garden or a public park where its openness and sense of movement would make it harmonious with a background of trees and sky. In the onyx "Peace," you will look in vain for such extended parts as abound in "Europa and the Bull"—the tongue, ears, horns, and tail of the bull or the arms, legs, and draperies of Europa.

Metal is also a sympathetic medium for sculptural portraits, examples of which are illustrated in Epstein's "Oriol Ross" (Figure 258) and the Roman head of Agrippa (Figure 255). In the latter, metal seems well suited to the powerful masculinity of the head while in the Epstein, the same material has been given a much softer feminine effect. In the girl's portrait, also, the vigorous modeling of the hair, the varied textures of the muscles and skin, indicate that the sculptor worked in a material quickly and forcefully manipulated. In all of these bronzes the effect is greatly enhanced by the rich color of the metal.

The methods of working stone and bronze are radically different. In carving a statue in stone, the sculptor's problem is that of removing material, of chipping away the excess. In making a bronze statue, the sculptor builds up his forms from a plastic material, generally clay (or wax), then casts them in bronze. Although the sculptor works directly in clay, he must not lose sight of the fact that the finished statue will be in metal. When the statue is completed at full size in clay, it is ready for the process of casting. Thus, stone carving is a process of subtraction, clay modeling is primarily a process of addition.

There are two methods of casting in bronze: (1) the *sand process*, and (2) the *lost wax*, or *cire perdue*, *process*. In the *sand process*, a plaster cast is first made from the model furnished by the artist. This cast is placed in a heavy iron frame and a special French sand, composed of clay, silica, and alumina, is pounded and packed solidly around the cast until the sand mold bears the impression of the most minute details of the original statue. If the piece has any deep incisions, elaborate undercuts, or other difficult areas, it is necessary to make separate piece molds of these parts. The iron frame is usually in two parts, so perfectly constructed that when fitted together around the model and sand, the clamps and bolts hold every part rigidly.

After the plaster model is released from the sand each half of the frame contains a perfect reverse image of the original. These can be fitted together again, and any molten metal be poured into it. But such a process would involve an extravagant waste of material resulting in a statue

438

whose weight would be too great to be handled conveniently. Hence a core of the same French sand is prepared to fit inside the mold, leaving a space between itself and the mold to be filled by the liquid bronze. When this has been done and the sand has been thoroughly dried, liquid bronze, at a temperature of about 1900 degrees Fahrenheit, is poured into the space between the core and the mold. After the bronze has cooled, the sand is removed, the metal is cleaned with nitric acid, and the final operations of finishing the bronze are begun. Unwanted bits of metal are chiseled off, and the whole surface is polished by skillful workers.

The *lost wax* (or *cire perdue*) process is complex and entails constructing a model and coating it with wax to the thickness desired for the metal, the surface of the wax corresponding to the finished surface of the statue. Around this a sturdy outside mold is constructed. It is then heated to a point where the wax melts and runs out leaving a thin space all around the model into which the molten metal can be poured. This method requires less finishing than the sand process and for that reason is preferred for finer kinds of work.

In either process a statue is first a model which is then duplicated. Because both the original model and the final cast can show much intricate detail, bronze statues are apt to be more complex and detailed than those in stone. Another difference is that a reasonable number of replicas can be made in metal, whereas in stone there is only one "original."

So far we have seen examples of the two major classifications into which sculpture may be divided. The first, illustrated by Richard Davis' "Bison" (Figure 246), was *carved* or *cut-down* sculpture. Marble, limestone, granite, sandstone, jade, crystal, onyx, and wood, and many others are used as materials for sculpture of this classification. The second major classification is *modeled* or *built-up* sculpture, illustrated by Emile Bourdelle's "Hercules" (Figure 257). The original material may be anything which can be worked and modeled, such as wax and clay. If, from the original, a permanent copy is wanted, any material which can be made plastic and that will then solidify into a permanent hardness may be used for casting. Bronze is the material used most frequently, although there are others—steel, glass, aluminum, and various synthetics.

Both the Calder "Mobile" and "Hostess" (pages 232 and 188) have been discussed earlier. Of metal, these utilize space in a manner unique in the development of sculpture. "The Hostess," an entertaining and ingenious contrivance, is really a sculpture in line. The "Mobile," a much more significant work, is literally moving sculpture and depends on movement and on constantly changing spatial relationships for its effectiveness.

SCULPTURE IN WOOD

After everlasting materials like bronze and marble, wood as a sculptor's medium seems fragile, transitory, and subject to decay, and yet since time immemorial, wood has been carved into expressive shapes. Primitive men found it easier to handle than stone or metal and, as a consequence, used it freely. Much primitive wood sculpture, such as the African wooden sculpture (page 95), has now found its way into museums and galleries. Wood sculpture is still a widely practiced art, not only in primitive but in sophisticated societies.

Most commonly used woods are oak, yellow pine, and limewood. Many others are used, however, such as mahogany, walnut, chestnut, and (for small articles) ebony, boxwood, pearwood, and cherrywood, and the rare myrtle that grows only in two small areas in Palestine and along the Pacific coast. English oak is a favorite, for its texture is hard and close and its color beautiful.

Wood sculpture falls into the same classification as stone sculpture because the artist begins with a crude mass of material in which he visualizes his finished product. His chief tools are chisels and gouges of many kinds and shapes. He may also use an electric drill, much like a dentist's, and thereby hasten the otherwise slow process of gouging and chiseling. As in other types of sculpture, one of the great problems of the woodcarver is knowing his material. The grain of wood usually runs in one direction while the lines of the figure being carved may run in many. The carver learns to honor the grain and to treat wood not like clay or marble, but for what it is—yellow pine or oak or cherrywood. It is only recently that extensive use has been made of the grain as an integral part of the sculpture. In the medieval period, when wood was used extensively as a sculptural medium, the finished figures were invariably painted. Today, with a concern for natural materials and for the relation of form to materials, most wood sculpture is given a finish of oil or wax and the grain and texture are treated as basic elements.

Because of its organic nature, and because it is less formal in appearance than stone, wood sculpture is often used for expressions of an intimate, miniature, and sometimes even whimsical character. Monuments of wood do not endure unless they are heavily coated with preservative agents, oil and paint. It is true that some races of men, not adept in stone or metal, have used wood for monumental purposes. American Indian and Alaskan Eskimo totem-poles are examples. But today, we like best to see it used in a way that lets us feel its texture and see its soft colors and delicate veinings.

The three wood sculptures (Figures 260, 261, and 262) offer an interesting contrast. Like "Hera" and "Walking" that opened the chapter, these, too, are all female figures and are equally diverse in their expressive aspects. Note that in all three the grain of the wood has been used as a part of the design and has not been covered. In Hallsthammar's "Venus in Red Cherry" (Figure 262) one feels, in particular, the rich *woody* quality of the material. Notice how beautifully the grain has been used to emphasize the modeling of the breasts, abdomen, and hips. The forms are highly realistic but have been fused satisfactorily with the texture of the material. In Steig's "Proud Woman" (Figure 261), of pearwood, one is less conscious of the material but more conscious of the expressiveness of the forms that have been used. By simplification and exaggeration and by the use of full forms, Steig has made the figure the epitome of snobbishness. The Henry Moore "Reclining Figure" (Figure 260) in elmwood is the least realistic, yet one perceives at once that it is the most monumental. Like the Archipenko "Walking," he has used the female figure merely as a point of departure. The "femaleness" of the figure remains in the full sensuous modeling and in the subtlety of the forms. But he has given the figure a new kind of unity, sculptural rather than anatomical, and the continuity of the sculptural masses with their sensitive and yet powerful modeling make this a beautiful and impressive work.

SOME OTHER SCULPTURAL MATERIALS

Quite frequently, sculpture is made in cast stone, which is stone dust mixed with a binder. Like sculpture in metal, a mold is made from the original sculpture and in it castings are made. Unlike metal, the final product is solid rather than hollow and is comparatively fragile. Cast stone closely resembles stone both in appearance and physical characteristics. Being brittle and easily breakable, sculptures made from it must be compactly designed.

A great deal of clay sculpture of the "built-up" variety is not constructed for casting in other materials but is made as an end product. If large, these are generally referred to as terra cotta. "Walking" by Archipenko is such a figure as is the lovely "Madonna and Child" by Verrocchio, having been built up of clay and fired as a ceramic. In Chapter 11 ceramic sculpture is discussed briefly. When molds are made, as is done with commercial figurines, identical copies can be turned out in great quantities.

Such sculptures as "Spiral Theme" (Figure 251) and "Column" (page 190) by Naum Gabo, the Constructivist, also fall within the built-up category. These constructions, similar in intent and content to much nonobjective painting, are attempts to discover fundamental and basic plastic relationships that underlie our existence. Aspects of the visible world have been rejected as subject matter because of their illusory and transitory nature; basic and unchanging truths are being sought. The plastic materials of which they are made offer new sculptural possibilities; for, as can be seen, light becomes an integral part of the material itself.

SCULPTURE THAT LIVES

Stone and bronze and clay and wood live when they have been fashioned by the hand of man into forms that express significant human experience and ideals. Judgment and enjoyment of sculpture should not rest only on the cleverness and dexterity of the manipulation of the materials and processes; nor should they depend on the artfulness and ingenuity displayed in the forms, colors, textures, or spatial relationships: these are only means to an end. Sculpture that lives has behind it an idea based on a human need. That human need may be utilitarian or it may be (for want of a better word) esthetic. If appreciation begins with this concept, it opens a world rich in meaningful, vital experiences. We look upon sculpture not only as a handling of eye-pleasing forms and deftly guided chisels, but as something of and from the human mind or heart—call it what you will.

The three sculptors, Charles Rudy, Richard Davis, and Henry Moore, treat sculpture as "the art of creating and organizing significant forms."

as a language for the communication of ideas and experiences. The appreciation of sculpture is primarily a response to human experience expressed not in words as in literature, nor in two dimensions as in painting, but in three-dimensional materials. Although the source of their inspiration varies greatly, the sculptors' general aim is to record and communicate to others some aspect of human activity or nature that they believe to be significant.

Undoubtedly the most important generalization that can be drawn from this and the preceding chapter is that painters and sculptors hold a variety of specific goals, and, consequently, approach their work in many ways. In some cases they present a record of significant ideas, events or situations in the form of mural paintings on the walls of a building (Figures 43-46, 60 and 243), or in stone (Figure 59); in some cases they work with human and animal forms as sources of inspiration (Figures 242 and 246); and in other cases they select forms and build partially, or almost completely, abstract compositions (Figures 119, 233, 251 and 260) that represent no particular thing but the order and beauty fundamental to all things.

If the work is large—a mural or a monumental statue—countless sketches of details and total organization precede the actual painting or carving, and require much conscious intellectual effort. If the work is small and direct—a water color or a small, abstract sculpture—it may be done very quickly, without preliminary sketches and *apparently* without "thinking." That some art may be created in this way has led to the mistaken belief that art production is primarily an emotional, as opposed to an intellectual, activity. What actually happens is that in work quickly executed, the laborious thought processes are done beforehand, and the artist is no more conscious of intellectual effort *while creating* than the skilled pianist is conscious *during a concert* of making each finger move. Inspiration may come suddenly and carry an artist through a brief period of creativity, but inspiration is developed in large part from much keen observation and careful thinking as well as from esthetic sensitivity. Art is not born from thin air, or from contact with supernatural sources of inspiration, but from a directed and sensitive study of human experiences.

Further readings:

Bruno Adriano: *Problems of the Sculptor* (Nierendorf Gallery, 1943). This book is a good statement of just what the title promises.

H. S. Ede: *The Savage Messiah* (Knopf, 1931) which is an exciting account of the turbulent life of a modern sculptor.

443

Painting, Sculpture, and Architecture

G. H. Chase and C. Post: *History of Sculpture* (Harper, 1924) is a thorough, academic account of the development of the art.

Sheldon Cheney: *A Primer of Modern Art* (Liveright, 1929) in Chaps. XIII and XIV has a readable account of modern trends.

Malvina Hoffman: *Heads and Tales* (Scribner, 1936) is a friendly, interesting account of sculpture by a talented sculptress.

Malvina Hoffman: *Sculpture Inside and Out* (W. W. Norton, 1939) takes the reader along with the sculptor in creating a work of art.

R. H. Wilenski: *The Meaning of Modern Sculpture* (Stokes, 1933) is a scholarly approach to the problem of modern work.

W. R. Valentiner: *Origins of Modern Sculpture* (Wittenborn, 1946). Good statement of the relation of modern sculpture to contemporary life.

If you should feel the urge to try some whittling yourself, read:

Alan L. Durst: *Wood Carving* (Studio, 1938).
Lester Gaba: *On Soap Sculpture* (Holt, 1935).
W. B. Hunt: *Ben Hunt's Whittling Book* (Bruce, 1945).
Paul McPharlin: *Paper Sculpture* (Marquardi & Co., Inc., 1944).
C. M. Sayers: *Book of Wood Carving* (Caston Printers, 1942).

CHAPTER 17

Architecture

ANCIENT Egypt's rulers thought chiefly of building for eternity. This purpose drove the earlier Pharaohs to build massive stone pyramids in which their dead bodies would be stored and preserved against decay, until that time when, according to their religion, their souls would once more return to their bodies. The Great Pyramid of Khufu has already been illustrated and discussed in Chapter 3. Estimated to weigh 5,750,000 tons, it is the heaviest structure ever built, yet for all its size, 760 feet square and 482 feet high, it contains only three small rooms, two of which are burial chambers. The one for the Pharaoh is only 34 feet 6 inches long, 17 feet wide and 19 feet high; the other two are smaller. The remainder is solid masonry. How it was constructed is still largely a mystery. Without crane, block and tackle, wheel or wagon, nearly six million tons of stone were quarried, carried by raft across the Nile and put in place. In return for its cost in materials, transportation, and human toil and sweat, it gave little in the way of usefulness, and judged by that standard it is probably the most extravagant building ever constructed.

In striking contrast, the buildings of Rockefeller Center in New York City (Figure 264)—thin shells of steel, concrete, and stone—house theaters, offices, stores, restaurants and broadcasting studios. Compare the size of the two developments in Figure 263. Many thousands of people work in the buildings, thousands more enter them every day. They were built to be used, not by mummies waiting for eternity, but by radio stars, executives, secretaries, janitors, office boys, and by you and me. Thus the human needs, which these two buildings were constructed to meet, are vastly different. But the concern in this chapter is not only with human needs but with consideration of more technical architectural problems such as materials and methods of construction and how they relate to and are integral parts of the design and appearance of buildings.

Man's problem in architecture has always been one of enclosing usable space. Almost always, too, he has the desire (and the necessity) to use materials more economically, more efficiently, and with less labor. Progress in most fields of art is difficult, if not impossible, to point to directly. Thus, one would not say that the work of modern painters is more significant than that of earlier men. Change we are certain of; but progress is not easy to determine. In architectural *construction*, however, one can state with certainty that there has been definite progress in the use of materials, that today man is able to enclose more space with less material than ever before. The diagram shown below which compares the Pyramid

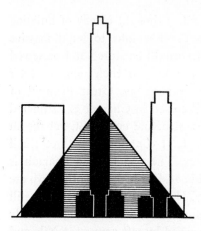

263. Size comparison of Rockefeller Center and the Great Pyramid of Khufu.

of Khufu and the central buildings in Rockefeller Center portrays this dramatically. The development of construction from the massive, ponderous buildings of Egypt to the light, flexible, steel-skeletoned structures such as Rockefeller Center, the Bauhaus (Chapter 4), and the Philadelphia Savings Fund Society Building (Figure 267), demonstrates a line of evolution as exciting as that in the animal kingdom.

THREE SKYSCRAPERS

Americans are proud of their skyscrapers. Representing new conquests of space and materials, these "poems in steel" have added a new beauty to the urban scene. At the same time they are expressive, in their domination over the rest of the community, of the place which commerce and industry occupy in contemporary life. In the medieval period, the cathedral occupied the cultural and visual center of community life; in twentieth-century America, the "cathedrals of commerce" tower above all else.

Although exciting when seen from a distance or from the air, our tall buildings have their less pleasant aspects. In the struggle for light, air, and space, streets and offices below are often left dark and sunless; in the concentration of peoples and facilities in a small space, serious and almost insoluble problems of congestion have been created; in the erection of expensive buildings on small plots of ground, speculative practices, detrimental to the best development of a community, have been encouraged. It is highly probable that the great age of skyscraper building (in terms of numbers) has passed because these structures have created more problems than they have solved. With present forces tending toward decentralization, we probably shall be more concerned with spreading out than going up. But skyscrapers will undoubtedly continue to be built, and with some heed to our earlier errors and excesses. Rockefeller Center is notable in that it is a large group of commercial buildings designed as a unit.

Perhaps because of pride and our materialistic outlook, our admiration of skyscrapers tends to be unthinking. A building of forty stories is assumed to be better than one of thirty. We confuse size with excellence and numbers with quality. What should a skyscraper "look" like? What are valid criteria of judgment? Does the architect, like the painter, have problems of expression? What are the forces, the new materials, the techniques which should be given visual expression? These are problems which have occupied the attention of architects since the development of steel construction and the invention of elevators first made tall buildings possible. Let us look at two examples.

The tower of the Chicago Tribune Building (Figure 266) impresses us with its verticality. The observer, however, can well wonder why the building is Gothic in style, why a twentieth-century structure has been given a sixteenth-century cloak. The prototype of this building is the Tour de Beurre, or Butter Tower, of Rouen Cathedral in France, which is an excellent example of late French Gothic architecture. Built of stone, it employed the Gothic system of construction of piers, arches, and buttresses, the forms being outgrowths of a method of building which was integrally related to medieval life. Essentially a vertical style, the Gothic imparts a feeling of aspiration entirely in keeping with the religious preoccupations of the period.

Perhaps it was the common factor of verticality between a medieval tower and a modern skyscraper that led architect Raymond Hood to use the Butter Tower as a model. But, obviously, he had to make many concessions and changes. For example, the Tribune Tower was taller than its

447

model and, because of its height and to meet the demands of space and economy, was built primarily of steel. Still he decided that it should look like a Gothic tower so that, even though everyone knows the shell of a modern building is hung on a steel frame, the stonework is designed to look like masonry construction. Yet the slender piers of stone could not possibly support themselves, were they built apart from the steel frame. Near the top of the tower where the first set-back occurs, the designer (following the model) has introduced a series of flying buttresses which, in the original, resisted the thrust of the arches in the center. Here again the forms are false; there is no reason for flying buttresses in skyscraper construction. They were put there, presumably, for "artistic" reasons, a far cry from the hard-headed functionalism which is supposed to characterize American business.

The building, however, does possess a degree of attractiveness. One could apply to it, with generally favorable results, all the principles of design. It was clearly conceived by an individual of taste and discrimination. Yet, as a twentieth-century American product, it is not a good building because it is neither honestly expressive of the times which produced it nor of the methods whereby it was built. While making use of present-day technology, the Tribune Tower attempts to conceal all such evidence: while housing the complex of activities which go into the production of a newspaper for a large American city, it takes on the appearance of an architectural style long outmoded. The thinking that prompts such expressions is difficult to understand; yet it is the same as that which still impels many people to buy imitation eighteenth-century furniture and to build Colonial houses.

Compare the Chicago Tribune Tower with the Wainwright Building (Figure 265). Even though the St. Louis structure was built many years earlier, in 1891, it appears to be, and is, the more "modern" of the two. It was designed by Louis Sullivan, one of America's great architects, who was the first to realize that the skeletal frame of a skyscraper should be reflected in the design; that a tall office building should look like what it is, and not like a Greek temple or a Gothic cathedral. Sullivan's sensible and revolutionary ideas were temporarily rejected in the stifling wave of eclecticism which the more "correct" architects were using as the basis of their work and he died a heart-broken and disillusioned man, his great contribution largely unappreciated. As we look at the picture of the Wainwright Building we cannot help being impressed with the great clarity with which Sullivan saw the problems of tall building design. The line

264. Rockefeller Center, New York City. An outstanding architectural development in that it represents unified planning of a group of office buildings. At the same time it creates an area of overcrowded density.

265. (*Upper left*) St. Louis, Missouri. Wainwright Building. Louis Sullivan, architect. In this and several other buildings which he designed, Sullivan formulated the bases of modern skyscraper design.

266. (*Upper right*) Chicago, Illinois. The Tribune Tower. Raymond Hood, architect. An attempt to make a twentieth-century skyscraper look like a medieval cathedral tower.

267. (*Lower*) Philadelphia, Pennsylvania. Philadelphia Savings Fund Society Building. George Howe and William Lescaze, architects. Perhaps the best designed American skyscraper. Notice the unbroken horizontals, expressive of cantilever construction.

PEDIMENT

CORNICE

FRIEZE — ENTABLATURE

ARCHITRAVE

CAPITAL

SHAFT — COLUMN

STYLOBATE

268. (*Upper*) Model showing the restoration of the Parthenon, Athens, Greece. Often referred to as the most beautiful building in the world, it is a marvel of subtlety and refinement.

269. (*Lower*) Roman Aqueduct at Segovia, Spain. The characteristics of arch construction are clearly visible in this plate. Compare the restlessness of the arch form with the repose of the post and lintel construction below.

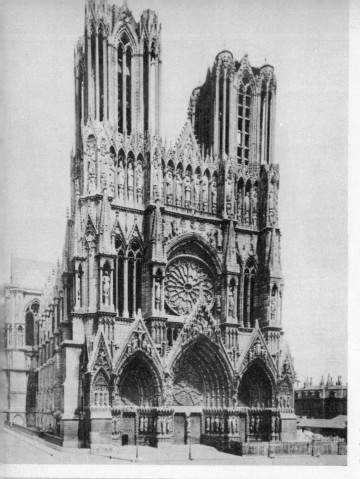

270. (*Upper*) Rheims, France. Façade of Cathedral, 1212-1241. This is one of the finest of the French Gothic cathedrals.

271. (*Lower*) Rheims, France. Lateral view of the Cathedral. Notice the flying buttresses, especially clear around the apse, which support the interior vaulting.

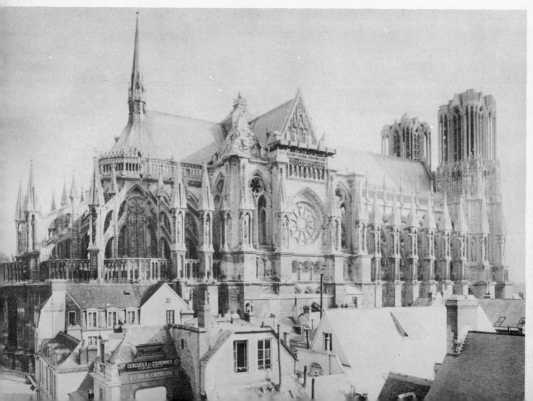

272. Rheims, France. Interior of Cathedral looking up nave toward choir, showing the sense of openness and flexibility possible in Gothic construction. Notice also the organic nature of the construction and the continuity of the structural forms.

273. (*Upper*) Milan, Italy, Basilica of San Ambrogio. Interior view. Compare the heavy massive interior with the later Gothic vaulting in Figure 272.

274. (*Lower*) Rome, Italy. St. Peter's. The impressive dome by Michelangelo dominates this tremendous edifice. Notice the great plaza which serves as a setting and approach.

275. (*Upper*) Orly, France. Hangar for dirigible. Eugène Freysinet, designer. The arch form interpreted in new materials for new needs.

276. (*Lower left*) Reinforced concrete construction. This method, in common use today, involves the encasing of the steel skeleton with concrete.

277. (*Lower right*) Rome, Italy. Arches of the Basilica of Constantine. A monolithic structure of concrete. The octagonal coffers are characteristically Roman. 455

278. (*Upper*) Maricopa Mesa, Paradise Valley, Arizona. Frank Lloyd Wright. Taliesin West. No matter what the materials, Wright uses them in fresh and ingenious forms. Here wood is used impressively and dramatically.

280. (*Lower right*) North Bergen, New Jersey. Ramp approach to Lincoln Tunnel. Three-directional rigid frames make this a handsome as well as efficient structure.

279. (*Lower left*) U. S. Army Regimental Chapel constructed with glue-laminated arches. These continuous structural members are extremely strong in relation to the material used.

281. (*Upper*) Detroit, Michigan. DeSoto Plant, Chrysler Corporation. Albert Kahn, architect. Shows directness and integrity.

282. (*Middle*) Cleveland, Ohio. Lincoln Electric Co. The Austin Co. Interior with "tree-form" welded frames.

283. (*Lower*) Baton Rouge, Louisiana. Welded stressed-skin Hortonspheres are the most efficient structures ever built.

457

284. (*Upper*) Dome
and vault forms,
quite different from
earlier ones in
masonry are readily
fashioned from steel
as in this structure
by William Lescaze.

285. (*Lower*) Rio de
Janeiro, Brazil. Min-
istry of Education
and Health. Costa,
Niemeyer, Reidy,
Leao, Moreira and
Vasconcelos, archi-
tects. In order that
the brilliant sunlight
might be controlled
in the offices, the
entire north side of
this building is made
up of movable
louvres.

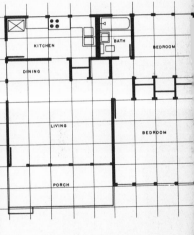

286. (*Upper*) General Panels Home, an industrialized house designed by Konrad Wachsmann and Walter Gropius, utilizing a quickly and easily assembled panel system.

287. (*Lower right*) Plan of the General Panels Home. Note module lines corresponding to panels.

288. (*Lower left*) Four steps in the erection of a prefabricated wood house. 459

289. (*Upper*) Bear Run, Pennsylvania. Kaufmann house, designed by Frank Lloyd Wright, combines an organic relationship to its site with the freedom and daring possible with steel and concrete.

290. (*Lower*) Portland, Oregon. Equitable Savings and Loan Building. Pietro Belluschi, architect. This brilliantly designed "crystal and metal tower" is the frankest and most direct statement yet made in a multi-story building.

of descent from Sullivan's structures to Rockefeller Center is easy to perceive: the details have been simplified, the forms perhaps refined, but the design theory is the same.

Another building which is in the Sullivan lineage is that of the Philadelphia Savings Fund Society (Figure 267). This, too, is a frankly designed building of steel and concrete encased with granite and limestone below, with gray brick above. A striking development is the use of cantilever beginning a few stories above street level, in which the screen wall of the building has been set out beyond the vertical steel supports thus making possible an unbroken expanse of windows across each floor. The outer wall becomes more frankly a curtain hung on the framework and the design is an acknowledgment that a tall building is made up of many horizontal floors occurring one on top of the other and that movement within the building is primarily horizontal.

The building of the Philadelphia Savings Fund Society is probably the best designed skyscraper in the United States. Structurally, it, too, is little advanced over the early buildings of Louis Sullivan. Yet it represents a development of his ideas in its greater acceptance of the implications of steel cage construction, the frankness with which the outer shell of the building is treated as a skin covering, its dependence upon direct statement without taking refuge in the forms and details of other periods.

Rockefeller Center, the Tribune Tower, and the Philadelphia Savings Fund Society Building exemplify the enormous complexity of modern architecture expressing and contributing to the high degree of specialization in contemporary life. In almost any structure built today, provision is made for a variety of special activities and facilities scarcely hinted at in historic work. We demand in our architecture increasing control over our environment. Air-conditioning systems and insulation control temperature, moisture content, and purity of air; elaborate systems of illumination, natural and artificial, control light; acoustical treatment of interiors controls sound. This intensive effort to control our environment profoundly affects building practices.

Traditionally, the basic requirements of architecture are few: an efficient plan; solid construction; attractive appearance. These requirements still exist but each has become complicated. Our large buildings are used not by a few persons but by many thousands: elevators and escalators as well as halls and stairs are needed; air-conditioning and artificial illumination as well as windows are necessities; precise information on construction materials and processes are requisite to safe, economical building. Thus the expertness of a host of specialists is needed in any large building enterprise. Each contributes his share and each determines in his way the form of the building.

The factor of precise control is the key to most recent architectural developments. Through heating and cooling systems our tasks need not be subject to the seasons; through artificial illumination we can carry on our activities by night as well as by day. For some activities, such as radio broadcasting and scientific research, a high degree of environmental control is basic. In fact, a large portion of the world's work of the twentieth century is possible only because we can regulate the temperature, humidity, light, and sound in our surroundings.

Such environmental control demands two things: first, precise analysis of human needs; second, great mastery of architectural materials and processes. For the first time in history the human being has been studied by physiologists and psychologists to determine optimal conditions for his productivity and welfare. And for the first time in history, the major phases of construction have become an exact science: mathematics has superseded observation. It is now possible to compute the kinds and amount of loads to which a given building will be subjected, and then to provide adequate structure. The precision of measurement now available to architects and engineers has not only given them specific information on historic materials and structural systems but has opened the door to an era of experimentation probably unequaled in the world's history.

Such knowledge has made possible the skyscraper and it has also made possible the modern factory, probably the best example of contemporary development in architecture. Factory design has been relatively unhampered by sentimental considerations which frequently restrain progress in the design of homes and community buildings. Factories have incorporated the technical innovations of scientist and engineer with inevitable naturalness because the factory is a huge precision instrument in which control of environment is vital to efficient production. Look at the recently constructed factories by Albert Kahn and The Austin Company (Figures 281 and 282).

Significant architecture, however, not only meets the physical needs of its occupants but expresses their social and political philosophy, their spiritual aspirations, their desire for beauty. In Part I we analyzed human needs in relation to domestic, communal, religious, industrial, and commercial architecture and saw how forms were developed to meet these needs. In Part II, examples of architecture were discussed from the point of view of design. In the remainder of this chapter we will look more closely at what man has done in architectural construction with the major building materials—stone, concrete, wood, and steel—to control his environment and to express his ideals. Bear in mind that materials and processes are only means through which man seeks to develop a completely satisfying way of life.

PROBLEMS AND SYSTEMS OF CONSTRUCTION

All architecture is a struggle between natural forces—gravity, wind, and earthquakes—which pull things down or out of shape and man's ingenuity in finding materials and methods for holding buildings in shape. As building technology developed, it became clear that architecture has three components directly comparable to the human body: the *skeleton* or frame which supports the building; the *skin* which encloses it; and the *equipment* or "vital organs" through which air, light, sound, and sanitation are controlled. In early architecture little distinction was made between skeleton and skin, minimum thought was given to equipment; today each component has been the subject of careful study to increase building efficiency.

Historic systems of architectural construction are generally classified in four categories:

1. *Post-and-lintel* in which horizontal beams are laid across the spaces between upright supports (see Figure 291); if the upright support is a continuous wall instead of separate posts, the system is more aptly called *wall-and-lintel*.
2. *Arch* in which small pieces of material, usually wedge-shaped, are placed with joints at right angles to the curve (see Figure 292). This defines the *true* or *radial* arch, but the term has come to describe any structure with curved elements.
3. *Cantilever* in which load-carrying beams are supported only at one end (see Figure 299).
4. *Truss* in which beams, bars, etc., are assembled into a rigid triangulaı framework (see Figure 296).

463

Useful as these categories are in studying historic work, they are completely inadequate in studying contemporary practice. Today architects and engineers usually divide buildings into two major categories:

1. *Bearing wall construction* in which the wall supports not only itself but the floors and roof as well: skeleton and skin are one and the same thing. For example in a log cabin or solid masonry building the walls *are* the structure. Two specialized variants deserve mention.

> *Monolithic construction* in which the material is continuous (that is, not jointed or pieced together) as in the concrete Basilica of Constantine (Figure 277).

> *Structural skin construction* in which sheet materials (such as plywood or sheets of metal) are placed and held under stress to assume a structural form. Skin and skeleton are one, but they are more or less continuous thin, sheet materials rather than "chunks" and their shape exploits their potential strength. Typical examples are the shell of an egg or turtle; a gas-filled balloon; and silos, grain elevators, and oil storage tanks of wood, concrete, or metal as the Hortonsperes (Figure 283). This is also called *stressed skin, shape engineering,* and, in the airplane industry where it is used for wings and fuselages, *monocoque.*

2. *Skeleton frame construction* in which a framework supports the building, and the walls (or skin) are merely fastened to it (Figure 276). Called balloon framing in wooden-house construction and steel-cage in skyscraper construction, with this method the enclosing walls are merely fastened to the structural skeleton of wood, steel, or concrete. Two specialized types of skeleton frame construction merit attention.

> *Suspension construction* in which the structure is suspended from a tower mast, as in suspension bridges (see the George Washington Bridge, page 271 and Figure 298) and in experimental "mast" buildings as the Hall of Transportation in the New York World's Fair.

> *Cantilever construction* as explained above.

Each of these systems will be discussed in greater detail in relation to specific materials and buildings in the following sections.

BUILDING IN STONE

Most of the world's architecture regarded as great is in stone because until recently it was the material used in practically all buildings where monumentality and permanence were desired. Thus the stone tradition has permeated much of our architectural thinking and has determined much of our taste and judgment.

To say that the history of architecture is embraced entirely in stone structures is not accurate, for this neglects the remarkable work of the Romans in concrete and many structures of wood and brick throughout the world. Nevertheless, the architectural tradition of western Europe, our major source of knowledge and ideals, is a tradition of stone, and it is probably safe to venture that the structural and esthetic possibilities of stone have been more completely developed than have those of any other material.

In this country there is not, and never has been, a genuine stone tradition. In the early days, the need for quick shelter led the colonists to use wood creatively. By the time brick became common, colonial architecture was a reflection of English work, and stone was not used extensively until our thinking had been stultified by revivals of Greek, Roman, Gothic, and Romanesque forms. True, there are many buildings in this country in which stone and brick play an important role, but their use has been traditional, derivative, or false. It is only natural, therefore, that the examples chosen for this section should be historic and non-American. Removed as they are from us in time and space, they have great relevance not only because of their intrinsic merit but because in a large percentage of our buildings European forms have been used derivatively or adapted eclectically. Churches with Gothic ornament and banks with classical detail are commonplace in the American scene. By becoming aware of their link with architectural history we can appreciate their strengths and weaknesses.

•

POST AND LINTEL: AN EXAMPLE FROM THE GOLDEN AGE OF GREECE

Perhaps the most famous building in the world is the Parthenon in Athens, Greece. Built about twenty-five hundred years ago (454-438 B.C.)

465

as a temple to the goddess Athena Parthenos, it has become synonymous with perfection in art in the minds of many people. The illustration (Figure 268) of a model gives a better idea of the original effect of the temple than do the usual photographs of the ruins, even though the model lacks the Parthenon's magnificent setting. It has suffered an unusual number of vicissitudes (including an explosion when it was used as an arsenal by the Turks), and today only a few columns remain standing and most of the sculpture has been carted away.

First, however, a word about the Greeks and the country in which they lived. To the south and west a multitude of islands create scenic beauty which has been a joy and pleasure the thousands of years that men have lived or visited there. Inland, the mountainous country provides the excitement of jutting cliffs and plunging waterfalls. This thrilling scenery is matched by a brilliant climate. There is none of the parching midsummer heat of our western deserts; there is little of the dank fog and gray skies of some of our coastal regions, or of England or northern France. The Greek's religious ideals and practices, unlike those of the Egyptians, belonged to the people. Theirs was a democratic religion, serving and influencing a democratic people.

The Parthenon represents the culmination of several centuries of architectural development. Like any great flowering, it did not emerge fullblown. Preceding it were several centuries of building similar stone temples and before that a considerable period of experimentation with wood. In each of them, there are new developments and refinements. That the Parthenon had a wooden parentage can be observed from a study of the building itself. Columns, such as those which surround the building, are a natural form in wood for a single tree will provide a column. Their translation into stone is less natural because they are built up of a number of separate pieces, or drums. The triglyphs—those rectangular forms that appear directly above the columns in the frieze—are undoubtedly modified beam ends. But the Greeks turned to stone because it was a more durable material and because Greece itself is blessed with some of the finest marbles in the world. The Parthenon is constructed of Pentelic marble which develops a rich glowing yellow as it ages.

The Parthenon is built on the *post* and *lintel* system of construction (Figure 291). The simplest system of construction, it consists merely of upright posts supporting horizontal beams (or lintels), and can be readily demonstrated by standing two books on end and bridging the gap with a third. Yet through its use builders and architects have given us some of the most distinguished buildings in the world. The Parthenon, however, reveals one of the major limitations of post and lintel construction when stone is used. Notice that the columns (posts) are set relatively close together, not necessarily because the designers, Ictinus and Callicrates, wanted them that way but because stone lintels of great length are not safe. As a building material, stone is enormously strong in compression (that is, when squeezed) but it is weak in tension (that is, when stretched or strained). As shown in Figure 291, stone posts can be high because the weight above merely compresses them. Lintels, however, are another matter: the upper half is in compression, but the lower half is in tension.

 291. Diagram of post and lintel construction.

Therefore the tensile strength of the material used is a determinant of the design—lintels of wood or steel can be much longer than those of stone.

A brief description of the parts of a classical building such as the Parthenon is pertinent at this time because the forms themselves have been in recurrent use ever since they were developed and especially because we are surrounded in this country by so many derivative classical buildings. The temple rests on a sturdy base of three high steps, called the *stylobate*. Above this rise the *columns*, simple *shafts* surmounted by a simple but delicately curved *capital*; the columns are channeled to make them seem more slender, and the capital forms an admirable transition between the vertical column and the horizontal *entablature*. The *architrave*, adorned with bronze shields, acts as a good foil for the sculptured panels in the *frieze*, above which is the *cornice*. Architrave, frieze, and cornice make up the entablature just as the shaft and capital make up the column. Surmounting all is the *pediment* filled with sculpture pleasantly adapted to the triangular space. The Parthenon is built in the Doric Order (order in architecture signifying a column and the entablature which it supports), the simplest of the three Greek orders. The Ionic Order is distinguished chiefly by more slender columns resting on a base and capitals adorned with volutes or scrolls. The Corinthian Order has

467

even more slender columns and capitals richly ornamented with acanthus leaves. The Romans made extensive use of all three (with some modifications) and added two of their own, the Tuscan and the Composite, thus making up the Five Orders of Classical Architecture.

To attempt to describe and explain the beauty of the Parthenon is a task which offers little or no hope of satisfactory achievement, for the factors on which this beauty depends are enormously complex and subtle to the point of defying analysis. To be sure, the proportions were exquisite; the glistening Pentelic marble of which the temple was built is one of the world's finest building stones; and the sculpture in the pediment and frieze, originally enriched with vibrant color, added interest and variety. Yet none of these goes far toward explaining why the Parthenon has become a symbol of the beautiful. It is, nevertheless, safe to say that every part of the Parthenon appears to be inextricably related to the whole design. Beauty is often considered as a matter of harmonious, functional relationships, of adjusting each part to its neighbors through careful refinements, and the Parthenon shows so many refinements that years of detailed study have been devoted to analyzing them.

Of the many ingenious devices employed by the architects only one type can be mentioned: those concerned with correcting optical illusions. Although we are not generally aware of it, forms and lines do not always appear to the human eye as we know them to be. For example, long horizontal lines seem slightly concave; identical spaces do not always appear equal. Unless compensated for, such illusions interfere with the appearance of structural soundness. Through several centuries Greek builders observed these phenomena in their temples and developed means of overcoming them. In a remarkably sensitive and inventive manner the architects of the Parthenon used a number of refinements to help give the building a vibrant, living quality which accounts, in part, for its enduring reputation. Some of the major ones are listed below; the optical illusions are in one column and the refinements used to overcome them in the other.

Optical Illusion	*How It Was Corrected*
Long horizontal lines in a building appear to sag.	All the long horizontals such as the steps and the cornice are bowed up in the center. The amount of this correction across the front is about two and one-half inches.

Optical Illusion	*How It Was Corrected*
Columns with straight sides appear concave.	Columns are given a slight bulge or swell, called entasis.
A building rising straight from the ground often appears to be leaning forward.	The whole front of the Parthenon is tilted backwards slightly (about two and one-half inches).
Equal spaces between columns in a colonnaded front do not appear equal.	Distances between columns are different to make them all appear equal. The one in the center is the largest and they get progressively smaller towards the sides.
Columns silhouetted against the sky appear slenderer than when seen against a darker background.	The corner columns, often seen against the sky, are heavier than the other columns in the colonnade.

The peculiarly satisfying contrast of the vertical columns, fluted to emphasize their dominant direction, with the horizontal lines in the base and portion above the columns; the rhythmic contrast of sculptural forms against architectural rectangularity; and the beauty of the creamy marble and richly colored ornament made this a building worthy of veneration and a source of inspiration to those sensitive to remarkable subtlety in architecture.

THE ARCH

The aqueduct at Segovia (Figure 269) built by the Romans shows clearly the characteristics of arch construction. Unlike the Parthenon, in which each opening was spanned by a single beam or piece of material, each opening in arch construction (Figure 292) is spanned by a number of pieces of material. The advantages of arch construction are immediately apparent: an opening is not limited by the length of a beam; by the use of relatively small pieces of material, areas of great dimension can be spanned. Although the Greeks knew the principle of the arch, they made little use of it. It was the Romans, their immediate followers in the march of architecture, who first saw the possibilities in the arch and began to develop it. Indeed, it was the development of the arch in its varied forms that was one of the chief concerns of builders for about two thousand years.

The difference in effect between post and lintel and arch construction is apparent if you compare the Parthenon with the Basilica of Constantine and the aqueduct at Segovia. Whereas the former with its balanced verticality and horizontality is static and reposed, the last two suggest movement and easy continuity from one form to another.

The development of the arch was intimately related to the development of the Romans as a people. We know that they were more aggressive and materialistic than the Greeks. Their commercial activities, big public meetings, fabulous banquets, and renowned trials demanded buildings with larger, more flexible interiors. To meet such needs, the Romans

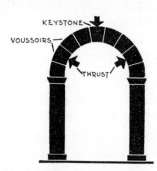

292. Diagram of round arch.

found it necessary to span greater openings than was possible with post and lintel construction. The arch provided the solution for such buildings, but they found other uses for the arch as well. Monumental triumphal arches commemorated the conquests of victorious leaders. Vast amphitheaters permitted multitudes to enjoy circuses and pageants. Arched bridges over rivers, together with good roads, enabled armies to march swiftly. And arched aqueducts, built so well that some are still standing, brought water great distances to key cities. Thus, the arch was a dominant motive in Roman architecture.

We pause for re-definition: an arch is an architectural form of wedge-shaped pieces of materials (voussoirs) with joints at right angles to the curve (see Figures 292 and 293). Stone is a material uniquely suited to arch construction because all material in an arch is in compression. Stone can stand great pressure and, of course, is extremely durable.

Builders have learned many facts about the arch. First, large openings may be spanned with small pieces of materials. In post and lintel construction, openings are limited by the length of available lintels and their tensile strength. Although the longest stone beams ever used were about twenty feet, the majority were much shorter. But with small pieces of stone, Michelangelo, in the dome of St. Peter's Cathedral, was able to span almost one hundred and forty feet of unobstructed space! That marked progress in building.

Second, builders have learned of the weaknesses of the arch. The major limitation, called lateral thrust or spreading, has brought into existence braces and buttresses for counteracting it. Lateral thrust may be easily demonstrated: arch a piece of paper, and then slowly bring the weight of your hand to bear on top of it. The arch, besides dropping in the center, shows a tendency to spread at the sides. These movements, indicated by the arrows in Figures 292 and 293, are characteristic of all arches. Further experiments with paper will reveal that the flatter the arch, the greater the tendency to spread. Tall, pointed, or parabolic arches show less spreading tendency and therefore need less support. To counteract this lateral thrust, arches need to be supported or braced at this point of weakness. This is generally done with a solid wall, another arch or a buttress.

Third, the Romans and succeeding builders who used the arch learned that the rounded forms could be developed, expanded, varied and decorated to produce an architecture vastly different in effect from the rectangularity of post and lintel. The interior of the Basilica of San Ambrogio, Milan, Italy (Figure 273), built chiefly in the twelfth century, is clear evidence of the manner in which the arch may lead to flexible, dynamic interiors. Notice the way in which the decoration is concentrated at important structural points: the bases of the piers, the points at which arches begin to spring from columns, the arches themselves and the horizontal lintels. Not only does the decoration occur at the important structural points, but it invariably emphasizes the basic forms or directions. As discussed in Part II, good decoration follows and expresses the underlying structure. Notice, too, how these Italian builders counteracted the lateral thrust of the great arches in the nave. They literally tied the sides of the arches together with iron bars to keep them from spreading. This is not an architecturally distinguished manner of handling the thrust of an arch, and the Northern European builders developed a different method, as we will discuss shortly.

THE VAULT AND THE DOME

The principle of the arch gave rise to vaults which are arched coverings in masonry. The simplest form of vaulting, merely the projection of a simple arch, is called a barrel vault and the name is an apt one since in appearance it looks like a barrel cut lengthwise. The barrel vault has the characteristics of the simple, round arch. There is the same tendency to spread, the same need for support at the place where the lateral thrust makes for weakness. In the Basilica of Constantine (Figure 277) you can observe a short barrel vault, in this case made of concrete.

The Romans carried the development of the vault much further, but let us skip over the centuries to San Ambrogio in Milan (Figure 273) to look at a more complex type than the barrel vault built late in the eleventh century. We will confine our discussion to that portion of vaulting at the top center of the picture. Here four massive piers define a square area (or bay), the piers occurring at the corners of the square. These piers are connected with each other by arches. Four arches define the limits of the bay, two are sprung diagonally across the square. The triangular areas which remain are filled with masonry and the result is a vaulted ceiling. It appears simple, but many centuries were required to reach this level of complexity. This, however, is only an intermediary step in the development of considerably more involved forms. Look at the plate of the interior of Rheims Cathedral (Figure 272), built over two hundred years later, where pointed arches are used.

The dome is another extension of the principle of the arch. This can be demonstrated by observing half an orange, and noting that it is but a multitude of arches so arranged that all the bases rest on a circle and the tops all cross at a common point. In the dome all the characteristic weak points of the arch remain and, consequently, it requires support at the points of lateral thrust. Usually, but not always, this is taken care of by properly designed buttresses which in turn become decorative features on the exterior.

The type developed in Italy during the fifteenth and sixteenth centuries, culminating in Michelangelo's magnificent dome for St. Peter's in Rome (Figure 274), is best known in this country inasmuch as it is the prototype for the dome on the nation's Capitol in Washington, D. C., as well as for many state capitols. In order that it be a spectacularly dominant element in the building, its mass towers high above the church proper. To counteract the spread of this enormous dome Michelangelo placed sixteen buttresses at its base which also serve as transitional elements to the main mass of the building. Even these have not proved sufficient to counteract the thrust of the masonry for at various times ten encircling chains have been placed in the dome to keep it from spreading. The dome itself, including the lantern, is 450 feet high, and is constructed of an outer and inner shell, the latter 137 feet 6 inches across. The base of the dome is nearly 250 feet above the floor of the cathedral, the distance from the floor to the internal cupola, 335 feet, a height greater than a thirty-story building. The dome, as might be imagined, is an engineering marvel and one of the most impressive architectural monuments in the world.

Domes invariably give a dominating effect, which accounts largely for their wide use on important public buildings. We get from the exterior a feeling of power, a sense of crowning achievement. The interior gives an impression of spaciousness because no supports interfere with the vision or bodily movement. A strong feeling of centrality is also produced—the place immediately beneath the center of the dome becoming the point of focus.

Few, if any, domes today are constructed on the true arch principle. The Capitol dome in Washington is of cast iron; most of them nowadays have a steel frame and are encased in stone. This is a justifiable procedure if it is frankly accepted in the appearance of the dome. Often, however, the steel construction is covered to make it imitate a true stone structure which, in the light of what has been said before, is obviously a violation of honest, sincere building. As an architectural form, however, domes will continue to be constructed, but of modern materials and with modern methods. The basically simple, geometrically satisfying form of a dome lends itself to contemporary architectural treatment.

THE POINTED ARCH

Scarcely any record of man's accomplishments is more interesting than the development of the Gothic cathedrals, of which Rheims Cathedral is an important example. Like the Parthenon, the cathedral at Rheims (Figures 270, 271, 272, 294, 295) is the result of many factors—of climate and geography; of the thoughts, actions, dreams and aspirations of mankind; of the knowledge of architectural construction of a particular period. As we look at Rheims Cathedral, we are impressed chiefly with its ascending, aspiring, uplifting character, the product of an intensely religious people who were eager, literally, to reach heavenward with their lofty houses of worship.

The social order which reared these Gothic cathedrals was a vigorous one. Fourteenth-century France was witnessing a great upsurge of religious feeling along with a tremendous growth in trade and a phenomenal development of cities. Men were coming to live in towns, to turn their attention to the higher pursuits of science and religion. Rivalry was intense among these growing cities and they competed with one another to produce cathedrals that would be truly expressive of their great faith in God and their community—and, also, a little bigger and better than their neighbors'.

The Gothic period was an intensely religious one with great interest in all matters having to do with the saving of the soul. In order that the

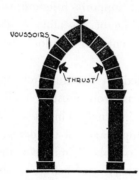

293. Diagram of pointed arch.

people, most of whom were illiterate, might know more of the life of Christ, of holy men and women, and that they might visualize and feel more the great glory of their God, Biblical incidents and stories from the lives of the saints were depicted in richly carved stone and glowing stained-glass windows. Thus these glass windows and stone images which are an integral part of the Gothic style are there, not as technical flourishes, but as direct answers to deeply rooted human interests and needs.

Still another factor affecting the construction and the appearance of Gothic cathedrals was climate. We saw how the Greeks did not have to build against the rigors of bitter winter weather, deep cracking cold and tons of snow bearing down on roofs; they took full advantage of their mild, temperate climate by erecting buildings with open porticoes and colonnades. But farther north the architects had to reckon with severe weather. Northern France has periods of cold, driving rains with long, dank, gloomy days. This coldness, wet, and gloom had to be kept out of the buildings, not only physically but psychologically, and architects made windows richly colored so that the dull light from the outside was transformed into warm, glowing tones.

474

In Rheims we do not find the rounded Roman arch but one which is pointed in form (Figure 270). As with the round arch, the actual time of its discovery is unknown. But from what we know of man's constant endeavor to enclose space with the minimum of materials and labor, and of his dogged attempt to make this space answer his needs and to express his whole nature, we may surmise that the pointed arch was called into use to answer new demands. The pointed arch is more aspiring, has greater lift than the rounded arch. Those builders, then, who sought to construct lofty, heavenward-reaching cathedrals used it naturally.

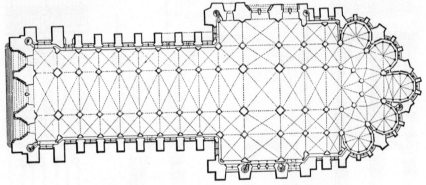

294. Rheims, France. Plan of Cathedral.

The use of the pointed arch is not, however, the sole characteristic of the Gothic cathedral. The photograph of the interior of the cathedral at Rheims (Figure 272) shows other features worthy of study. Especially, there is the high, vaulted ceiling; the continuity between all structural forms (i.e., piers and groins in the vaults); the large window areas; the exquisite proportions of all structural features; the carry-over of the structural forms into the purely decorative forms, i.e., the doors, windows, choir stalls and furniture use forms and shapes reflecting parts of the main building itself so that, for instance, the panels in the door repeat forms of windows. Note, too, that the sculpture shows a general inclination for emphasis on the vertical, heaven-seeking, rather than on the horizontal.

But the Gothic style, rather than being characterized by details, is primarily a system of construction. We mentioned earlier in this chapter that the development of the arch and its potentialities was one of the chief concerns of architects for a period of over two thousand years, and the Gothic cathedrals represent the culmination of a long period of varied

475

solutions to the arch problem. The ever-present difficulty of arch construction is how best to counteract that lateral thrust of the arches. The
Romans managed by using tremendously thick and heavy walls. The medieval Italian builders often "tied" the arches together with iron rods to
keep them from spreading (Figure 273). This was a makeshift solution

295. Rheims, France. (*Left*) Longitudinal section of the interior along the
nave. (*Center*) Transverse section through nave. Notice the manner in
which the buttresses support the vaulting at the weak points. (*Right*)
Elevation of portion of exterior along nave.

unacceptable to the French builders. Instead, they developed other devices. The pointed arch has less lateral thrust than the round arch, but
the force is still considerable. In a Gothic cathedral, the thrusts of the
great arches in the structure are met with counterthrusts from other
arches or buttresses on the exterior. Sometimes these buttresses spring
from piers that are free of the main mass of the building as shown in
the section in Figure 295, and are then known as flying buttresses. The
plan and longitudinal and transverse sections of Rheims Cathedral (compare with the plan) clarify the structural system and show how each force
is met with a counterforce, each thrust with a counterthrust, which has
led someone to say that Gothic architecture is less a style than a struggle.

476

This thrust-counter-thrust, existing in nearly every part of the building, means that Gothic cathedrals are in a delicate and amazingly complicated state of equilibrium. Theoretically, at least, the removal of one of the arches would mean the collapse of the whole building, because every part depends on every other part for support. Thus, Gothic cathedrals are almost as organic as the human body, and the term *organic* is often used to describe the Gothic style.

We have looked at the manner in which Roman, Romanesque and Renaissance architects used the round arch and Gothic builders used the pointed arch in stone buildings. Later we shall see how the Romans had, and contemporary architects have, developed arch forms in concrete, wood and steel. At this point an elementary principle of forces should be stated: namely, that forces, like water, tend to flow more easily around smooth bends than around sharp angles. Thus the arch, minimizing the break between vertical and horizontal elements, represents a great structural advance.

As has been stated, historic and stone architecture are practically synonymous. Yet for all its contribution to building history, stone is now outside the main stream of development because of its lack of plasticity, low tensile strength, great weight and difficulty of shaping. That it will continue to be used as *surfacing* material is obvious, for it is one of the most richly varied of natural materials. The high polish of marbles, the rich colors and patterns of granite, the coarse surfaces of sandstone and limestone still contribute handsomely to the appearance of modern buildings. After the enormous role of stone in the history of man, it has stepped aside as a structural material for concrete, wood and steel.

BUILDING IN CONCRETE

Concrete, often regarded as a new material, was well used by the Romans more than two thousand years ago for large, imposing structures. The Basilica of Constantine, a remaining portion of which is illustrated in Figure 277, is a concrete structure characteristic of much Roman work. It differs significantly from the stone buildings discussed in the previous section in that it is *monolithic* (the material is homogeneous and continuous) whereas in stone buildings relatively small pieces of stone are joined together. The round forms remind one of the arches in the Aqueduct at Segovia or the vaults in San Ambrogio. Their strength, however, comes primarily from the mass of concrete rather than from the small wedge-shaped pieces used in arch construction. Such monolithic arches have characteristics similar to those of stone arches. Notice the thickness of walls and piers and the general effect of heaviness. These are characteristic of early concrete construction, depending as it did on bulk and mass (rather than on precise knowledge of material and metal reinforcing) for structural strength. This heaviness has been lightened with recessed octagonal coffers in the vault which serve the double function of enriching the surface and saving material.

Concrete—an artificial conglomerate stone made by uniting cement and water with sand, broken stone, slag, cinders and the like—has characteristics both similar and dissimilar to those of stone. It may be well at this point to summarize the qualities of concrete.

Strength and Durability. Like stone, concrete withstands great compression, very little tension. And like stone, concrete does not rot or corrode, offers insects and vermin little opportunity to get a foothold, and is fire-resistant.

Plasticity. Concrete, starting its existence as a liquid, assumes the contours and textures of any "form" into which it is poured. It can be given the massiveness of the Basilica of Constantine or the Hiwassee Dam (page 50), the gracefulness of the Hangar at Orly (Figure 275), the slender rectangularity of cage construction (Figure 276), the continuous ribbons of our highways and sidewalks, or the small building blocks in common use. It has been well named, "the original plastic."

Appearance. In its typical form, concrete is a dull gray, nondescript material with relatively coarse, uninteresting texture. Unlike stone, wood or metal it has little inherent beauty and was accordingly treated for many years as an ugly duckling. But its appearance can be greatly enhanced by the type of cement and aggregate used or by adding colored pigment. Because of its plasticity the surface is subject to a high degree of control: it can be rough or smooth, regular or irregular, decorated with marble chips and the like, or cast into patterns.

Ferro-concrete (or reinforced concrete) has metal reinforcing embedded in the concrete so that the tensile strength of metal is united with the compressive strength of concrete. The extensive use of ferro-concrete has been made possible by the development of Portland Cement (the Romans used lime mortar as a binding material) and has retrieved concrete from the neglect into which it fell with the dissolution of the Roman Empire and has made possible much of our contemporary building. It is most commonly observed in buildings in which a steel *skeleton frame* is first erected and then enclosed in concrete. Notice that in Figure 276, the structural part of the building is complete; the walls will be fastened on later. Notice also that in addition to enclosing the metal skeleton, concrete (reinforced with metal bars) has been used for the floors. In addition to the combined tensile and compressive strength of ferro-concrete, the combination is far more resistant to fire than is an uncased metal frame (which may twist or melt).

As ferro-concrete technology has developed, there has been a notable tendency toward increased lightness and flexibility. Thus, some bridges use thin slabs of ferro-concrete shaped to become strong structural elements. Thin curved shells built with or without ribs have been found highly efficient for one-story structures with an unobstructed span. But perhaps the most startling experiment is that used in experimental small house construction in which the structural shell of the house is built by spraying concrete over inflated rubber forms. First a rubber form of the desired size and shape is inflated; second, a coat of concrete is sprayed over it; third, reinforcing material is put in place; fourth, another coat of concrete is sprayed on; fifth, the structure is waterproofed; and lastly, the rubber form is deflated leaving a thin strong shell. This is an example of *monolithic construction*—because the material is homogeneous and continuous—and it is related to *structural skin construction*—because the structural strength develops from the shape and nature of the skin. It appears that concrete, well used by the Romans but almost forgotten for centuries, has come into new importance.

BUILDING IN WOOD

The plentiful supply of wood in the United States has made it our most common building material, between 80 and 90 percent of our structures being of this material. Even though the increased use of steel and ferro-concrete is lessening its use, our building tradition is primarily in wood.

Most of us are familiar with the wood frame house in which a frame of studs and joists (a skeleton) is erected; the exterior (the skin) of wood, brick, or plaster is added; and the interior wall finish is applied. Called *balloon framing* or *light frame structure*, this is a type of *skeleton frame construction* developed in Chicago in the 1830s. Its invention was an important factor in the rapid development of the land beyond the Alleghenies, for it permitted much more rapid construction than did the older heavy frame structure. In contrast to masonry structure in which the wall is both load-bearing and surfacing, balloon framing is closely related to steel construction in its separation of structure and surfacing. Wood is also suited to *cantilever construction* (Figure 299), as in the eaves projecting beyond the walls of buildings; *trusses* (Figure 296), as

296. Common truss forms. (*Left*) Howe truss. (*Right*) Bowstring truss.

found in wooden barns and contemporary structures; and *structural skin construction* such as is found in the molded plywood chairs by Eames shown in Figure 150.

The characteristics of wood, discussed in Chapter 10, reveal its potentialities and limitations as a building material. It is easily worked and relatively durable; it has high tensile and compressive strength; it is attractive in appearance; and it lends itself to a variety of finishes. Yet it has limitations: moisture, insects, and fire weaken or destroy it; the strength of wood is more difficult to determine than is the strength of steel or concrete and necessitates a high factor of safety; and the size of individual pieces (until the development of lamination) was sharply limited. Such limitations, together with the rapid depletion of our forests and the development of other materials, have reduced the use which is made of wood.

At the same time, technological developments have given it a new life as a building material. Of greatest importance is plywood, already discussed in Chapter 10. Although veneer was known to the Egyptians and laminated plywood was manufactured in Russia in the 1880s, plywood still seems a new material. By placing the grain of thin sheets at right angles to each other, the structural potentialities of wood have been greatly increased and it has become, like steel, a precise material of enormous strength. Its use in large flat sheets is commonly known and has been illustrated in the interiors of the House of Ideas in Chapter 1.

When bonded with synthetic resins, plywood may be shaped permanently into many forms at low temperatures (in contrast to metals which require high temperatures). Fabrication is thereby greatly simplified. During the war, plywood was used structurally for the hulls of small boats and sometimes for airplanes. In relation to its weight, plywood is probably stronger than any known material. It can be a moldable "skin" material of considerable structural strength. Architecturally, molded plywood has not found wide application as yet—but it is a promising lead for *structural skin construction* in the future.

Plywood sheets are not the only new development in wood. Related to these are larger laminated structural members in wood, such as beams and trusses, of great size and strength. A *beam* is customarily regarded as a large single piece of wood (or metal) much longer than it is wide or thick and used horizontally to bridge the gap between upright supports; thus, it is the same as a *lintel*. Beams of single pieces of wood were limited in strength, length and predictability, but lamination has made possible beams of far greater efficiency. A *truss*, you will remember, is a rigid framework of beams, bars, rods, and the like (see Figure 296). Generally, a truss should be in the form of a triangle, or a series of triangles, because of all the geometric figures the triangle is the only one which cannot change shape without altering the length of one or more of its sides. Originally made of single pieces of timber, later of metal, trusses are now also made of laminated wood. Although the principle of the truss is remarkably simple, it has only been developed precisely within recent times.

In the small Army chapel (Figure 279) the laminated wooden structural members have a flowing, dynamic quality which is both visually satisfying and structurally efficient. It is unlike the kinds of structural wood forms to which we are accustomed: upright supports and horizontal beams or trusses. In load-bearing capacity it is superior to rectangular systems: engineers have long known (but architects have seldom used) the principle that forces travel more easily around smooth bends than around sharp corners. The structural members in the Army chapel, in which vertical and horizontal members literally flow into each other—a characteristic of arch construction—have far greater structural efficiency than those in which right angles abound.

The view of Taliesin West (Figure 278) is a striking example of wood used to give a monumental effect. The forms at the left are the ends of large trusses which extend over a work room. The organic texture of the wood is in handsome contrast to the brightly colored stone in the base below and the strong forms of both the wood and the masonry are suited admirably to the landscape. Like all of the work of Frank Lloyd Wright this is characterized by its adaptation to its site and by the vigor and ingenuity of the forms.

The developments mentioned above only touch the advances made with wood as a building material. As with many other materials, new possibilities have been discovered, previous limitations have been overcome. Science and art together are transforming and revitalizing an age-old building material.

BUILDING WITH STEEL

Steel has made possible our present industrial age. From tiny precision instruments to hundred-story buildings and mile-long bridges one sees the extent to which it and other metals have entered into and affected our lives. It is no accident that the steel industry is regarded as a barometer of American business which is largely dependent on it. The importance of steel in present-day life is all the more remarkable when we realize that its manufacture began just a few years before our Civil War. In the first half of the nineteenth century iron was used, but not widely, as a building material; but steel—finer and denser in structure and stronger in compression and tension than iron—was seized upon for widespread use as soon as it became available. Since then, it has been under constant study and development.

Logically, its use was first channeled into *steel cage construction* which we find in most of our tall buildings. This was natural because skeleton construction, typified by balloon framing, was in common use. Interestingly enough, steel-cage construction, like balloon framing, was also developed in Chicago—approximately half a century after balloon framing. At first called "Chicago construction," it received most of its early attention in that city. Not only were many buildings constructed with steel frame, but it was there that Louis Sullivan centered his early architectural activities. And it was he who, in a series of brilliantly designed buildings at the close of the century (look again at the picture of the

Wainwright Building), demonstrated that the steel frame of a skyscraper should be a determining principle in design; in other words, that "form should follow function" or more specifically "exterior design should follow construction." Although steel cage construction has since been used in all parts of the world and although Rockefeller Center represents the full flowering of the steel cage concept of building, its invention and early development centered in Chicago.

Steel, of course, made the skyscraper possible. When load-bearing walls of stone are laid up, the base must increase in thickness as the height of

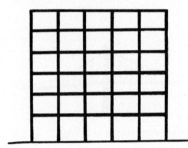

297. Diagram of steel-cage construction.

the wall increases. It is common to find stone buildings only two or three stories in height with walls several feet thick at the base. Were it possible to build a stone structure thirty stories high, most of the valuable space on the ground and lower floors would be taken up with walls and supports. With steel cage construction, the supports take surprisingly little space. And steel buildings resist the forces of wind and earthquakes with a resilience which stone structures do not have.

As in all skeleton frame construction, the separation of structure from surfacing material is characteristic of steel-cage construction. Yet architects after Louis Sullivan were slow in grasping the design implications of this fact as illustrated by the Chicago Tribune Tower. For many years they attempted to make steel skeleton buildings look as though they were solid masonry construction. However, a brilliant realization of the esthetic potentialities of steel structure has been realized in such buildings as the Philadelphia Savings Fund Society Building.

Throughout this book there are numerous plates that give evidence of the extensive use of steel in contemporary building, in community and commercial structures, in factories, and in schools. Figures 281 through 285 provide other examples of modern steel construction. In the viaduct in Figure 280, the steel plates are all riveted together to form a

483

rigid frame related structurally to the Army chapel shown in Figure 279. Similar, too, is the factory interior shown in Figure 282 where "tree-form" welded frames are used and post and lintel merge into one continuous member. Notice also the handling of the lighting. The exterior of the factory by Albert Kahn (Figure 281) is a dramatically simple solution to a large structure which houses many complex activities. Conditions in factories such as the two examples just mentioned must be carefully controlled to provide optimum working conditions for the employees and for the handling of the materials being manufactured. Modern technology is in fact being more fully utilized in factory construction and operation than in any other of our structures.

298. Diagram of steel suspension construction in a bridge.

The steel framework in Figure 284 shows the great flexibility that is possible with steel. Here vault and dome forms are combined with a lightness of structure not possible with masonry. The building of the Ministry of Education and Health in Rio de Janeiro, designed by a group of Brazilian architects with Le Corbusier as a consultant, is an ingenious solution to the problem of lighting in a country of brilliant sunshine. The entire northern side of the building is composed of louvers which can be moved to regulate the amount of light which enters. Besides having a real function, the louvers create a handsomely varied pattern.

Steel has great compressive strength as shown in the manner in which relatively small piers can support enormous superstructures, but its strength in tension is even greater. The possibilities of *tension construction* with steel were brilliantly demonstrated in the Brooklyn Bridge in the late 1900s but almost fifty years were allowed to elapse before further development was undertaken. There are now a number of magnificently exciting suspension bridges throughout the country which have exploited this potentiality of steel. Note Figure 298 and the photograph of George Washington Bridge (page 271). All the materials in the cables are in tension and their small size in relation to the load they carry make them miracles of strength. Construction in tension is thus directly opposed to

484

construction in compression, exemplified in uprights in post and lintel construction or the voussoirs in arch construction.

But bridges are not the only structures that offer possibilities for tension construction. At the New York World's Fair in 1939, the Hall of Transportation was constructed with the roof suspended from steel cables connected with uprights placed at the edges of the structure. A large area of uninterrupted floor space was thus provided. Buckminster-Fuller in his Dymaxion House, designed in 1933, hung the exterior walls on cables connected to a central mast. In general, however, architects have not been very imaginative in the use of steel tension construction. Here is a largely unexplored area of possibilities.

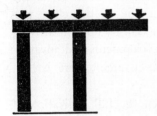

299. Diagram of cantilever construction. This system also requires material of great tensile strength.

The *cantilever* is another type of construction uniquely suited to steel. As can be seen in the diagram in Figure 299, cantilever (a load-carrying beam supported at only one end) can be used only with a material of high tensile strength. The Kaufmann house (Figure 289) is an exciting example of this type of construction. Here, Frank Lloyd Wright was asked to build a house near a waterfall because the owner expressed a fondness for rushing water. He designed the house to be built directly over Bear Run Creek by projecting the terraces dramatically free from the mass of the house. Cantilever, like steel tension construction, demonstrates the role of steel as a great liberating agent. Construction can be free and dynamic as never before.

Another development which already has had a great effect on building is electric arc welding. Through this process two steel members can be joined so that the joint is as strong as any portion of the members themselves. It can be seen that this is vastly superior to riveting where, in a sense, a joint was no stronger than the weakest rivet. Many of the recent skyscrapers have been arc-welded structures, but the potentialities thus far have been explored chiefly by the aeronautical engineer in airplane construction. Another common example of a welded structure, of the "stressed skin" type, are the Hortonspheres seen frequently around oil plants (Figure 283). Their structural strength in relation to the materials involved make these perhaps the most efficient constructions ever built. Here, again, new and largely unexplored possibilities have been revealed.

As stone was the great architectural material of the past, steel is the great material of the present—and presumably of the future.

INDUSTRIALIZING OUR ARCHITECTURE

The close relationship which should exist between the technology of a period and its architecture is both stated and implied in much of the foregoing. Exploring this relationship has been one of the chief preoccupations of architects during the past quarter century and, in arriving at solutions which took into consideration the developments and advancements of contemporary life, a virtual revolution in architecture has resulted.

Perhaps chief among those problems has been the full utilization of technological developments and fabrication methods. The effect of mass production and assembly line techniques on automobile manufacture has already been mentioned, and it is largely through our industrial production methods that we have achieved our present high standard of living. Many practices in the building field have been modified by industrial production and these become particularly evident if we compare the methods of building a house now and in Colonial times. Then all the parts of the house—the windows, doorways, stairs, cabinet work—were fabricated on the spot. To some extent, this helps to explain their design excellence, for the parts were all designed and constructed where their location and relationship to the rest of the house could be continuously studied. In contrast, many of the parts of a house built at present are made many miles away from the site. Windows and doors have for years been made in special plants where conditions of construction are more readily controlled and the products made more economically. An increasing number of parts of houses such as closets, stairs, cabinets, even whole bathrooms, are thus being prefabricated. Hastening this process is the fact that many items, such as metal window sash and bathroom fixtures, can be successfully fabricated only in large industrial plants.

486

But nonetheless, even though industrialization has affected to a considerable degree the building field, it, of all the large industries, remains the most backward technologically, and a high percentage of the construction operations (electric wiring and plumbing, to mention two) are still largely done by hand. As a result, modern building is exorbitantly expensive and falls far short of the efficiency that we demand of most of the products of present-day industry.

It is in home construction that this gap between potentiality and practice is particularly apparent. The *Architectural Forum* a few years ago reported that there were more than 30,000 items in a typical house which must be ordered as such (this does not count such items as nails, screws, etc.); that there were more than 500 operations such as sawing, hammering and planing; that 20 individual skills or trades, many of which take years to learn but are used for only a few hours on a house, are involved; that there are over 200 items of equipment, a figure which increases each year; that there may be 15 or more separate contracts resulting in overlapping, waste and duplication of overhead. It is small wonder that house construction has become prohibitively expensive for a large segment of the population.

One method of attack on this knotty problem has been the construction of large-scale developments. If five hundred homes are built at a time rather than one, certain obvious economies result. Materials can be purchased at lower rates and labor can be utilized with greater efficiency. Reduction of cost through this method is a matter of making present methods operate more efficiently; it makes no attack on the fundamental processes themselves.

A more promising development is the factory production, or *prefabrication*, of larger portions of the house, that is, having more of the house manufactured by machine, less by hand. *Prefabrication* is not a new idea; various architects, engineers and manufacturers have been at work on it for many years. Recently, the results of their experimentations, spurred on by the serious housing shortage, have been exceedingly promising. Two examples are shown here (Figures 286-288).

Notice first the plan of the General Panel home on which a grid pattern has been superimposed. As is indicated, each of these represents a three-foot, four-inch dimension. The important point to note is the fact that each of the strategic points on the plan—wall, partitions, windows—occurs on a grid line. Each of the grid elements is called a module and the use of modular elements is the basis of the plan and, indeed, the whole method of fabrication, for the house is constructed of standard-sized wood panels which can be swiftly assembled on the site. There is one type of panel for the floor, one for the roof, and a series for the walls which provides for any arrangement of doors, windows, and solid walls. These panels are put together with an ingenious connector and any of the panels interlocks with any of the others in either a horizontal or vertical plane. Wiring is built into the panels as they are fabricated at the factory. A prefabricated plumbing stack reduces much of the expensive hand work usually required to install plumbing fixtures and concentrates all plumbing fixtures in one area. The only tool needed in erection is a hammer, and thirty-eight man hours is all the labor required. With this panel system a great variety of designs can be built; the consumer is not limited to one design or style. Thus is overcome one of the most frequently voiced objections to prefabricated houses—that they would all look alike.

The photograph of the exterior repays study. This industrialized house is eminently straightforward and sensible, livable and attractive. It bears no superficial resemblance to Colonial or English half-timber houses in appearance—but there is a deep similarity with such architecture in integrity of structure and design. It shows the same honest use of materials that we find in all good building and it can be produced with twentieth-century efficiency. Industrializing our architecture need frighten us no more than does purchasing ready-made clothes (instead of individually designed, handmade garments of hand-woven fabrics) or than buying mass-produced dishes.

IN CONCLUSION

The last two plates in the book, the Kaufmann house (Figure 289), a residence by Frank Lloyd Wright, and the Equitable Savings and Loan Building (Figure 290), a commercial building by Pietro Belluschi, show both the possibilities and the range of expressions possible in contemporary construction. The Kaufmann house is almost as much a part of the landscape as the waterfall over which it is built. The major portion of the house is built of stone which seems to rise from the natural ledges of

488

rock below. From these stone walls, with an almost breath-taking audacity, spring two great cantilevered terraces which project themselves over the waterfall and become a part of it. These exciting forms are made possible by steel construction and could have been built at no other period in the development of architecture. Yet the house has a warmth and a feeling of relationship to the landscape that make it an inviting and restful place; it combines a feeling for the site from which it springs with the freedom and daring possible with steel and concrete.

The Belluschi building, one of the most brilliantly designed commercial buildings in the country, is in striking contrast to the Kaufmann house. Also frank and direct in design and material, it is the most logical statement yet made in steel-cage construction. No masonry whatever appears above the first floor, only aluminum and glass, obviously and clearly sheathing materials. The forms are clean and precise, the color lively and inviting. The simple masonry piers on the first floor are a rich red brown; the glittering aluminum above is in two finishes, with the lighter one covering the concrete and steel cage and the darker one the areas at the base of each of the windows; the windows are blue-green panels of heat-absorbing glass. Air conditioning and sound control are used throughout. Here is a structure which is related to the Kaufmann house in contemporaneity of statement yet divergent from it in what is being expressed. One is domestic, the other commercial. Both are valid expressions: both are art today.

As this book began with a discussion of architecture, so does it end, and in a sense, the presentation has run full circle. Architecture has been called, and justly so, the "mother of the arts" for most of the arts spring from or are related to it. Each of the many fields of art has its own importance and significance, each its own expression. Each too in its visible aspects speaks to us eloquently of the people who created them and use them; they reflect with infallible accuracy the heart and mind of the people and the times that brought them into being. As with all things, the basis of art is people. Art has as its special function, humanizing and giving meaning to a culture and this meaning is given to it by people, by the creators, the users, the appreciators—by the kinds of art forms they create and support. Our duties and responsibilities are clear.

While studying carefully the buildings in your community, some worthwhile books to read are:

Painting, Sculpture, and Architecture

Sheldon Cheney: *New World Architecture* (Tudor, 1936). A thoroughly readable account of new forms of building.

James Marston Fitch: *American Building—the forces that shape it* (Houghton Mifflin, 1948). In this remarkable book Mr. Fitch excitingly reviews the development of American architecture and establishes new critical standards for modern building.

Banister Fletcher: *History of Architecture* (Scribner, 1921). The standard history of architecture, full of photographs, sketches, and facts.

Siegfried Giedion: *Space, Time and Architecture; the Growth of a New Tradition* (Harvard University Press, 1941). One of the most important studies of architecture to appear in recent years.

Philip Lippincott Goodwin: *Brazil Builds* (Museum of Modern Art, 1943). A beautifully presented record of old and new Brazilian architecture. Especially significant since much of the best contemporary work is being built in South America.

Talbot Hamlin: *Architecture through the Ages* (Putnam, 1940). Remarkably readable treatment of the development of architecture in relation to social conditions.

Henry-Russell Hitchcock: *In the Nature of Materials* (Duell, Sloan and Pearce, 1942). A comprehensive, well-illustrated discussion of Frank Lloyd Wright's architecture.

H.-R. Hitchcock and Philip Johnson: *The International Style: Architecture since 1922* (Norton, 1932). A concise formulation of the principles and early examples of one type of modern architecture, well and critically illustrated.

William Lescaze: *On Being an Architect* (Putnam, 1942). Refreshing account of architectural training and practice by a leader in the field.

Margaret Miller: *What Is Modern Architecture?* (Museum of Modern Art, 1942). A brief and excellent statement of the various considerations that have shaped modern architecture illustrated with well-chosen examples.

Elizabeth Mock: *Built in USA: Since 1932* (Museum of Modern Art, 1944). This book is confirmation that exciting architecture suited to today's needs is being built in this country.

Lewis Mumford: *Architecture* (American Library Association, 1926). Probably the best short statement on architecture available.

Lewis Mumford: *Sticks and Stones* (Norton, 1933). A stimulating account of the development of architecture in America with emphasis on its human significance.

C. H. Whitaker: *Rameses to Rockefeller: the Story of Architecture* (Random House, 1934). A highly readable account of the development of architecture

Frank Lloyd Wright: *An Autobiography* (Duell, Sloan & Pearce, 1943).
The personalized story of the development of a great architect.

Frank Lloyd Wright: *Frank Lloyd Wright on Architecture: Selected Writings 1894-1940* (Duell, Sloan and Pearce, 1941). An excellent collection of the important statements of a great architect.

Glossary

ABSTRACT. Portraying essentials or fundamentals without imitating appearances. An abstract painting of a tree depicts the fundamental forces and organization in a tree, but does not look like an actual tree. (See *non-objective*.) See Figures 228 to 233, pages 402-403.

ACADEMIC. Art based on a more or less completely worked out theory and philosophy characterized by a crystallized approach; opposite of experimental.

AMERICAN SCENE PAINTERS. Those painters who are chiefly interested in recording and documenting the ordinary life and activities of America. They may be characterized as genre painters. Grant Wood and Thomas Benton are well-known American Scene painters.

ANALOGOUS. Related, or similar, in some way. Usually refers to color schemes; for example: yellow, yellow-green, and green are analogous colors because all have yellow in common.

APSE. A projecting part of a building, usually semi-circular or multiangular in plan, and usually at the rear of a church. See Figure 294, page 475.

ARCADE. A series of arches supported by columns or piers.

ARCH. An arch in the strict sense is a construction (usually curved) built up from wedge-shaped pieces of material with the joints between them radiating from the center, but any curved structure is often referred to as an arch even though not constructed on the true arch principle. See Figures 269 through 275, pages 451 through 455.

ARCHAIC. Referring to objects belonging to an early, conventionalized style; more advanced than primitive. See Figure 244, page 425.

ARCHITECTONIC. Having the nature, structure, or organization of architecture.

ARCHITRAVE. The lowest major division of the classical entablature resting directly on the capitals of the columns. See Figure 268, page 451.

ARMATURE. Framework or skeleton used to support clay or wax in modeling; usually made of wood or metal.

ART NOUVEAU. A style of art popular during the 1890s and extending into the twentieth century, characterized by flowing lines and free, loose

493

ornament. In applied decoration such flowers as wild roses and nasturtiums were widely used because of their flowing, sinuous character.

ASHLAR. Masonry of squared stones as distinguished from masonry of irregular or round stones.

ASYMMETRIC. Applied to that type of balance which is not symmetrical; generally much freer than formal balance. Also referred to as occult, active or informal.

AXIS. An imaginary line passing through a design, building, etc., around which different parts are balanced. In drawing or painting, an imaginary line expressing the dominant direction of any object in the composition.

BALLOON FRAMING. A type of construction in which the wood frame of a structure is first erected as an independent unit. The exterior and interior coverings and finishes, the roof, etc., are then added. This type of construction is used in most residential work.

BALUSTER. An upright support for a railing used in classical buildings and gardens; usually urn-shaped. A row of balusters and the railing on them is called a balustrade.

BAROQUE. A type of late Renaissance art which was a reaction from standardized classic forms in the direction of greater freedom. Baroque art is often characterized by strong contrasts, and elaborately twisted and curved forms.

BAS-RELIEF. Sculpture or carving in which the figures project less than one-half their true proportions from the surface on which they are carved. Bas-relief is frequently used in the ornamentation of buildings. The design on a coin is in bas-relief. See pages 428 and 429.

BATIK. A method of producing designs on textiles by covering part of the material with wax in a pattern and dyeing the parts left uncovered; the process is repeated for each color used. Also a fabric dyed in this same way.

BEN-DAY PROCESS. A mechanical method of putting stippled, or mottled, backgrounds on reproduced pictures. Often seen in colored comics.

BRAYER. Roller made of rubber or gelatin for rolling out and applying ink to plates or blocks for printing.

BURR. The rough ridge of metal thrown up beside each line on a dry-point plate.

BUST. Sculpture of the upper portion of the human figure down to and including more or less of the shoulders and breast.

BUTTRESS. A projection of masonry or wood to support or give stability to a wall or structure.

BYZANTINE. The style of art which became established about 500 A.D., developed in the eastern division of the Roman Empire. Byzantine

architecture is distinguished by the use of the round arch, dome on pendentives, cruciform plan, and rich mosaic ornamentation.

CAMPANILE. Bell tower or steeple, especially one free from the church. The Leaning Tower of Pisa is a campanile.

CANTILEVER. A construction device in which a non-vertical projecting member carries weight. See Figure 299, page 485.

CAPITAL. The uppermost or top member of a column distinguished from the shaft by some distinct architectural treatment. The orders of architecture can be distinguished by the treatment of the capital. See Figure 268, page 451.

CARTOON. An artist's drawing or study drawn on stout paper at full size to serve as a model or to be transferred and carried out in paint, tapestry, mosaic, stained glass, etc. Cartoons are frequently made for fresco paintings. Also a comic or satirical drawing.

CENTER OF INTEREST. The part of a work of art which has received special emphasis and around which the rest of the work is organized.

CERAMICS. Usually pertains to pottery, but also to any objects made from earth products and fired at high temperature.

CHANCEL. That portion of a church given over to choir and clergy.

CHIAROSCURO. The treatment of light and dark in a work of art, especially a painting or drawing.

CHINA. A term often applied to porcelain because porcelain was introduced to Europe from China.

CHIPPENDALE. Furniture with graceful, curved outlines designed by Thomas Chippendale, an English cabinetmaker, about 1750-1775. French Chippendale was influenced by elaborate French detail; Chinese Chippendale by the lattice and bamboo work of the Chinese; and Gothic Chippendale by the pointed arches and clustered columns of the Gothic style.

CHROMATIC. Pertaining to color or colors.

CLASSIC. Belonging to the culture and art of the ancient Greeks and Romans. Also refers to a system based on authoritative principles and methods used according to a coherent plan.

CLASSIC REVIVAL. Given its greatest impetus by the Chicago Fair of 1893, this style looks back to the Classic, chiefly Roman and Italian Renaissance, for its source material.

COLLOTYPE. An inexpensive yet highly satisfactory method of reproducing paintings, drawings, etc., in black and white or color by means of gelatin plates.

COLONNADE. A series of columns placed at regular intervals and usually united by other architectural members such as lintels, arches, etc.

495

COLOR, ADVANCING. A color which seems to be nearer to the observer than it actually is. Warm colors, such as red and orange, are advancing colors.

COLOR, RECEDING. A color which seems to be farther from the observer than it actually is; due chiefly to its hue. Cool colors are recessive.

COLUMN. A supporting member usually composed of a base, shaft, and capital. See Figure 268, page 451.

COMPLEMENTARY. A color or form which completes or fills out another.

COMPOSITION. That which is composed, planned, arranged, organized.

CONCOURSE. A large space for the gathering of crowds. Concourses are generally open areas in parks or in such buildings as railway stations.

CONCRETE. A synthetic stony material composed of broken stone, sand, etc., held together by a binder such as cement. Reinforced concrete is strengthened with metal.

CONGRUITY. Harmony of the various parts or elements with the whole; also agreement among the parts.

CONVENTIONAL. A stylized treatment of natural objects; also following rules or conventions rather than imitating nature.

CORINTHIAN. The lightest and most slender of the orders of architecture developed by the Greeks, and taken over and altered by the Romans. It is characterized by a bell-shaped capital covered with acanthus leaves.

CORNICE. The top and crowning portion of a classical entablature. In many instances it occurs without the frieze or architrave, or with these in highly modified form. See Figure 268, page 451.

COUNT OF CLOTH. The number of warp and filling threads in a square inch of fabric.

CUBISM. A movement in art which stresses significant form and specific esthetic sensations rather than the representation of appearances. The design is based on geometric forms which are often made transparent and intersecting, and lays emphasis on volume and space as well as mass. Cubism arose in France about 1905 in the work of Picasso and Braque but has had world-wide influence. See Figure 201, page 323.

CUL-DE-SAC. A passage or street with only one outlet. Cul-de-sacs, or dead-end streets, are used in many modern residential developments because they insure relative privacy and greatly reduce traffic in front of residences.

DECORATIVE. Intended to decorate the surface and to please by a harmonious organization of the plastic elements, rather than represent actual objects.

DELINEATION. Representation of an object or design, generally by means of lines rather than masses.

DESIGN. A planned or intended arrangement; an adaptation of means to a particular end.

DISTORTION. The twisting of an object out of its natural shape.

DOME. A type of roof developed as a form of arch construction, shaped generally like half a sphere, although there are many variations, such as stilted, squat, bulbous. See Figure 274, page 454.

DORIC. An order of architecture developed by the Greeks and used by them in the Parthenon and later adopted and altered by the Romans. The capital is characterized by its simplicity, being composed of a square block and a circular element which acts as a transition to the shaft. See Figure 268, page 451.

DORMER. A window protruding from a slanting roof.

DRYPOINT. A process of reproduction in which the design is scratched on the surface of a metal plate with a needle; the depressions made are filled with ink which is transferred to the paper in printing. See Figure 201, page 323.

DUNCAN PHYFE. A modified Empire style of furniture produced by a New York cabinetmaker of that name who lived from 1768-1854.

DYNAMIC. Giving an effect of movement, progression, energy.

DYNAMIC SYMMETRY. A theory of design which attempts to reduce all composition to a mathematical basis.

EARTHENWARE. Ceramic ware made from a clay which is finer than that used in stoneware yet coarser than that used in porcelain.

EAVES. The lower part of a roof which projects beyond the exterior wall of a building. Eaves protect the wall from the water that runs off the roof.

ECLECTIC. Selecting and combining from various doctrines, systems or styles that which is thought best. Most of our present-day houses are eclectic, borrowing from such historic examples as the Colonial, French provincial or Tudor. See Figure 266, page 450.

ELEVATION. A drawing, showing no perspective, of the front, side or rear of a building.

ELIZABETHAN. An early English Renaissance style of architecture and furniture (1558-1603) combining Tudor and Italian features and common in the country houses built during the reign of Elizabeth. The houses have large windows, long galleries, and tall decorated chimneys.

EMPHASIS. Dominance, accent, or principality of any portion of a design. Emphasis implies both dominance and subordination.

EMPIRE. A style of furniture developed under Napoleon I in the first French Empire (1804-1815). In character it is stiff, severe, and cold, making use of simple geometric forms, classic motifs, and an abundance of metal ornaments.

497

Glossary

ENGAGED COLUMN. A column which projects in part from a wall. An engaged column is round, whereas a pilaster is flat.

ENTABLATURE. In classical architecture that portion of the order which occurs between the capital of the column and the pediment; composed vertically of three major sections: architrave, frieze and cornice. See Figure 268, page 451.

ESTHETICS. Philosophy, theory, or science of beauty.

ETCHING. A graphic process in which the design is bitten (etched) into a metal plate with acid. These bitten lines are then filled with ink which is transferred to the paper in printing. See Figure 200, page 323.

EXPRESSIONISM. Art in which the emphasis is on inner emotions, sensations, or ideas rather than actual appearances.

FAÇADE. The front of a building.

FENESTRATION. The arrangement of windows in a building.

FILLING. The transverse threads in a woven fabric; those put in by the shuttle. Also called woof and weft.

FORMAL. Showing special attention to arrangement; also referring to work done according to definite rules, or that showing pronounced symmetry.

FOUR-COLOR PROCESS. A process of color printing in which four plates, similar to half-tone plates, are used. The four-color process is used to reproduce in color paintings, drawings, and photographs with shaded areas.

FOYER. A lobby or promenade in a theater, auditorium, or other public building.

FRESCO. Wall painting in which mineral colors mixed with water are applied to wet plaster.

FRIEZE. The middle portion of the classical entablature; also a band or strip of painted or sculptured decoration. See Figure 268, page 451.

FUTURISM. An art movement originating in Italy in the early twentieth century which aimed to portray the movement and change in objects rather than their appearance at any particular time.

GABLE. An end of a ridged roof, generally triangular in shape.

GARGOYLE. A projecting stone spout, usually grotesquely carved, used on medieval buildings to carry off rain water. Gargoyles are frequently carved with the heads of fantastic animals.

GENRE. A style, especially of painting, illustrative of the common life of a people.

GEORGIAN. An architectural style developed in England and in this country between 1700 and 1800 and named for the King Georges who were ruling at that time. See Figures 17, 18, 19, 24, and 25.

GLAZE. Thin, glassy coating put on pottery to make it waterproof, durable and attractive.

GOTHIC. A style of art prevalent in Western Europe from the thirteenth through the fifteenth centuries (period dates given as 1160-1530). Gothic architecture is based on a highly developed system of construction of weight centralized in piers by means of thrusts and counter thrusts. Its most easily distinguished characteristic is the pointed arch. See Figures 270-272, pages 452 and 453, and Figures 294 and 295, pages 475 and 476.

GOTHIC REVIVAL. The period in American art beginning about 1830 when the Gothic style was used as a model by American designers.

GOUACHE. Paints formed by grinding opaque pigments in water and mixing with honey and gum arabic to form a paste.

GRAPHIC. Pertaining to drawing or painting in any medium.

GRAPHIC PROCESSES. Those processes for printing or reproducing drawings, photographs, etc.

GREEK REVIVAL. A period in American art, roughly from 1820 to 1860, when the Greek influence was predominant, chiefly in architecture. Characterized by exterior Greek porticos and general severity and chastity of detail. The first of the major eclectic periods.

GROTESQUE. An unnatural but decorative combination of human and animal forms interwoven with plant forms; also applied to art forms which are awkward or incongruous.

GROUND. Wax or similar material used in etching to protect parts of the plate from the action of the mordant.

HALF-TIMBER. A type of architectural construction in which the main supporting members are wood timbers, and the spaces between are filled with masonry and sometimes plastered. The structural timbers form a conspicuous design on the exterior of the building.

HALF-TONE. A photoengraving process used for the reproduction of photographs, drawings, and painting in newspapers, magazines, and books in which different values are printed as dots of varying sizes.

HARMONY. Agreement among parts of a composition tending to produce unity.

HIGH-KEY. Color values above middle value. High-key colors are generally pale and delicate such as lavender and pink.

HIGH-LIGHT. A spot of bright light or high value on an object usually produced by a reflection of the source of light.

HUE. The name of a color; actually refers to warmth or coolness.

IDEALISM. Imaginative treatment rather than imitative; perfecting forms above existing ones. Idealism in art is opposed to realism.

IMPRESSIONISM. A movement in art, particularly painting, in which the aim was to record the effect (or impression) that one receives from the first glance at a scene. Impressionism is often associated with broken color, whereby complex colors are rendered by juxtaposed strokes of their component colors which blend in the eye of the observer.

INFORMAL. Irregular; emphasis on naturalism rather than studied organization.

INTAGLIO PRINTING. Done from an engraved or incised surface; the opposite of relief printing.

INTENSITY (OF COLOR). Purity or brightness of a color.

IONIC. An order of architecture with columns more slender than the Doric, and capitals decorated with volutes. Developed by the Greeks and adapted and altered by the Romans.

JACOBEAN. A continuation (1603-1625) of the Elizabethan style of architecture which made freer use of the classical orders.

KEYSTONE. The central stone of an arch, sometimes given a highly decorative treatment. See Figure 292, page 470.

KILN. A furnace or oven for drying, baking, or firing various products. Ceramic kilns are used in firing and glazing pottery.

LAYOUT. A term used in printing and in commercial art referring to the arrangement of pictures and words on the page.

LINE-CUT. A type of photoengraving in which only one value is reproduced. Comic strips are line-cuts.

LINTEL. Horizontal architectural member of wood, stone, etc., to span openings; supported at ends by piers or walls. See Figure 291, page 467.

LITHOGRAPHY. Method of surface printing from a plate of stone or metal and greasy ink. See Figure 202, page 324.

LOGGIA. A sheltered gallery running behind an open arcade or colonnade.

LOW-KEY. Color values below middle value. Low-key colors such as maroon and navy blue are rich and deep.

MADONNA. Italian word meaning "my lady," usually referring to the Virgin Mary.

MAJOLICA. A type of stoneware usually decorated profusely with large bold floral patterns. Most majolica comes from Italy but was introduced there from Spain by way of Majorca—hence the name.

MEDIUM. The material used to produce an art object. Also the liquid with which pigments are mixed to make them suitable for painting.

MEZZANINE. A story between two lofty ones. The mezzanine is usually a balcony between the main and second floors.

MOBILE. A term applied to sculpture, usually of metal, in which the parts move. See page 232.

MODELING. The representation of solid forms in either sculpture or painting. Modeling refers either to the actual shaping of clay, stone, or other materials in sculpture, or the use of colors and values to represent forms in painting.

MOLD. A concave form from which something takes its shape. Most commercial pottery is made in molds.

MOLDINGS. Ornamental projecting strips with varied contours.

MONOCHROMATIC. Using only one hue. An example of a monochromatic color scheme is one based on various tints and shades of green.

MONOPRINT. A type of surface printing in which a sketch is done on glass or metal with oil paint or ink and then transferred by contact to paper. Only one print can be made of each design.

MORDANT. In etching, any fluid, usually a strong acid, used to bite the lines into the plate; in dyeing, a substance used to fix the color.

MOSAIC. A type of inlaid decoration, either decorative or representative, composed of small pieces of stone or glass, generally used for the decoration of walls and floors.

MOTIF. A distinct principal idea or element of a design.

MULLION. A piece of material dividing window lights or panels. The stone mullions in Gothic cathedral windows are clearly shown in Figure 295, page 476.

NAVE. A term applied either to the long portion of a church leading to the choir, or to the central aisle as distinguished from the side aisles.

NICHE. A hollow recess in a wall generally intended for a statue or ornament.

NON-OBJECTIVE. Referring to painting and sculpture which are expressions in pure form and design showing no resemblance to natural objects.

OCCULT (see *asymmetric*).

ORDER. A term used in connection with classical architecture to signify a type of column with the entablature which it supports. The three Greek orders, Doric, Ionic, and Corinthian, were taken over and altered by the Romans, and two more, the Tuscan and Composite, were developed. See Figure 268, page 451.

ORGANIC. Having the character of living forms. Organic art, such as the houses of Frank Lloyd Wright, shows the vitality and unity found in animal and plant forms.

ORGANIZATION. The systematic relation of parts to each other and to the whole; design.

PALETTE. A flat thin piece of metal, wood, porcelain, or glass used by a painter for mixing colors.

PALETTE KNIFE. A thin flexible knife used by painters for mixing oil colors or applying them to the picture.

PARAPET. A portion of a wall, rising generally two to four feet high, at the edges of roofs, balconies, platforms, bridges, etc.

PATINA. A film produced on the surface of bronze or copper by oxidation; also applied to similar surfaces on other materials. Patina is usually green.

PEDIMENT. In classical architecture, the triangular area above the entablature forming the gable of a two-pitched roof; also similar areas on such things as doorways and furniture.

PERSPECTIVE—AERIAL. Representation of space by weakening hues and value contrasts and softening edges of objects in proportion to their distance from the observer. The apparent haziness of distant objects is an example of aerial perspective.

PERSPECTIVE—BIRD'S-EYE. The representation of a building or some scene as it would look if viewed from the air.

PHOTOGRAVURE. A method of printing pictures from intaglio plates made photomechanically. Rotogravure is a type of photogravure.

PHOTOMECHANICAL. Pertaining to a number of printing processes in which the plate is photographically prepared and the copies printed on mechanical presses.

PICTURESQUE. Striking or irregular beauty in which variety is more prominent than unity.

PIER. A support of metal or masonry, or both, occurring between openings, as supports for arches or lintels, at ends of bridges, as enlarged portions of a wall, etc. A column is a specialized type of pier.

PIGMENT. Any coloring material, but usually a dry earth mineral, or vegetable compound, which is mixed with a liquid to produce paint.

PILASTER. A pier in a building, rectangular in plan, a part of, but projecting slightly from, the wall and given the architectural treatment of a column. Pilasters generally mark the supporting part of a wall.

PILE. Loops of threads occurring above the regular cross threads in fabrics produced by a certain type of weaving. In velvet the piles are cut and trimmed, in terry cloth they are uncut.

PLASTER OF PARIS. A fine white powder which sets rapidly when mixed with water, and is generally used for making molds for pottery, etc. So called because it is made from rock found at Montmartre, Paris.

PLANOGRAPHIC OR SURFACE PRINTING. Printing done from a flat plate, the design being neither raised nor lowered. Lithography is a type of surface printing.

PLASTIC. Capable of being formed, molded, or modeled.

PLASTIC ELEMENTS. Line, form, space, color, and texture; the elements of which all products of the plastic and graphic arts are composed.

PLASTICINE. A clay material for modeling which has been mixed with oil so that it does not harden.

PLASTICS. A term applied to those materials or products made from various organic and inorganic substances which lend themselves to molding in various forms. Bakelite, Formica, Celluloid, Pliofilm, and Lucite are all trade names of various plastics.

POINTILLISM. A type of painting in which the paint is put on in little dots or points; a type of broken color.

POINTING. The mechanical measuring of an original piece of modeling or sculpture when reproducing it in some other material. Stone cutters make use of pointing in order to copy accurately the model supplied them by the sculptor. Also the filling and finishing with mortar of joints in masonry.

PORCELAIN. A ceramic product made from a fine even-grained clay and fired to a high temperature; a tough beautiful ware which is translucent when thin.

PORTAL. A door or gate; usually one that has been given architectural emphasis. See Figure 270, page 452.

PORTICO. A large scale porch; a colonnade occurring generally at the entrance to classical buildings.

POST AND LINTEL. A system of architectural construction based on upright columns or posts and horizontal beams or lintels. See Figure 291, page 467.

POST-IMPRESSIONISM. A movement in painting growing out of the Impressionist movement in France during the latter part of the nineteenth century. It differs from Impressionism chiefly by aiming to paint the forms of the objects rather than the effects of light only.

PRIMING. Covering a surface, especially wood or canvas, with a ground which prevents it from absorbing the paint. Priming a canvas is similar to sizing a plaster wall.

PROPORTION. The relation among parts and of parts to the whole; ratio among parts.

RADIATION. Divergence from a center.

REALISM. The representation of things as they are in life without idealizing them.

REGENCY. The English version of the French Empire style which developed in the early nineteenth century during the regency of George, Prince of Wales, later George III. Characterized by refined severity of line and decoration.

REGIONAL PLANNING. An extension of city planning to include a considerable area of land around cities. Sometimes whole counties, states, or geographic regions are planned as a whole.

REPEAT OR SURFACE REPEAT. A term used to denote one complete unit of a repeated design.

REPETITION. Using the same element or motif more than once in one or more directions. Repetition is a form of continuity.

RENAISSANCE OR RENASCENCE. The great revival in art and learning in Europe beginning in the fourteenth century in Italy. The Renaissance began in Italy but quickly spread to the other countries of Europe. Artistically it involved the rejection of the Gothic style and the revival of the classical Roman style and ideas.

RHYTHM. Generally used to describe the results produced by either repetition or sequence or both; continuity.

ROCOCO. A type of Renaissance ornament developed during the seventeenth and eighteenth centuries in which rocks and rock-like forms are combined with fantastic scrolls, shells, etc., to present a lavish but often confused display of decoration. In architecture this style was characterized by an abundance of florid and broken curves, in sculpture by figures with exaggerated poses.

ROMANESQUE. A style of art which flourished from about 775 to 1200 A.D., the architecture of which is characterized by round arches, heavy massive construction, rich, concentrated and free decoration, and the development of vaulting which led into the Gothic style.

ROMANESQUE REVIVAL. An American style, begun by H. H. Richardson and extending from about 1870-1900. This period produced many distinguished buildings marked by an integrity not often found in eclectic design. The buildings are generally of masonry, with richly ornamented stonework and sturdy round arches.

ROMANTIC. Emphasizing imagination, sentiment, and individual expression and opposing the restricting formality of classical standards.

ROSE WINDOW OR WHEEL WINDOW. A circular window filled with a design which radiates from the center like the spokes of a wheel. Rose windows are often found in Gothic cathedrals. See Figure 270, page 452.

SATIN. A type of weave in which there are a series of warp threads on the surface with a cross thread at intervals, giving the typical satin surface.

SASH. The frame in which the glass of a window is set.

SCALE. The size of the parts in relation to the whole object. Also the size relation of the representation of an object to the object itself. For example, architects draw plans in which the scale is one inch to four feet, eight feet, etc.

SECTION. The representation of the way anything would look if cut straight through and one portion removed. A section of a building shows the interior and its relation to the exterior along a given line. See Figure 295, page 476.

SEQUENCE. A succession showing orderly progression or change; a type of continuity.

504

SHED. The opening formed by the separation of the warp threads in weaving to allow for the passage of the shuttle carrying the filling thread.

SHERATON. A furniture style developed in England, chiefly by Thomas Sheraton, toward the end of the eighteenth century. It is characterized by a chaste appearance, straight lines, and inlay.

SIGNIFICANT FORM. A term applied to the total organization or any element of a work of art which is particularly expressive, meaningful, or vital.

SILK SCREEN. A method of color reproduction in which colors are forced through silk screens in those areas left permeable to pigments. See Figure 203, page 324.

SIZE. A glue-like or viscous wash used to prepare or prime walls, paper, or canvas for painting.

STATIC. At rest or in complete equilibrium; suggesting no movement; opposite of dynamic.

STEEL ENGRAVING. The process of engraving a design on a steel plate; or the print made from such a plate.

STILL LIFE. A painting of objects, such as fruits, flowers, vases, etc., as distinguished from those of landscapes or people.

STONEWARE. A heavy, porous type of ceramics used for inexpensive utilitarian ware, such as flower pots, jugs, etc.

STRUCTURAL. Of or pertaining to construction or structure as distinguished from decoration and accessories.

STYLE. The manner or mode of execution or presentation in art as distinguished from the content.

SURREALISM. A type of painting in which the artist paints the images from his subconscious self rather than what he sees about him. Surrealism is an attempt to go beyond actual observation, and paintings are likely to be full of symbolism.

SYMBOLIC. Representation by symbols rather than direct imitation.

SYMMETRY. A balancing of parts in which those on one side of the center are the exact reverse of those on the other. Symmetry is the most obvious form of balance.

TABBY. A type of weave in which the warp and weft threads are woven in simple alternation. Crash, muslin and gingham are examples of tabby weaves.

TACTILE VALUES. An expression used to describe the quality of a painting (or other work of art) which appeals to the sense of touch.

TEMPERA. An opaque paint in which the pigment is mixed with an albuminous substance, frequently white of egg rather than oil or water.

TENSION. Stretching, straining, or pulling as opposed to compression. Tensions in architecture are the actual straining forces in various members; tensions in painting are the representations of the pulling forces between forms.

TERRA COTTA. A ceramic product used both for construction and decoration in architecture. Also a color named from that which the clay assumes on being fired.

THREE-COLOR PROCESS. A photoengraving process in which unshaded areas are printed in colors.

THRUST. An outward force produced by an arch or vault. Thrusts in Gothic architecture are controlled by buttresses. See Figure 295, page 476.

TONALITY. The general quality of a painting produced by the color scheme. Generally, tonality is developed from the predominance of one hue or from closely related values.

TRABEATED. Pertaining to architecture characterized by the use of horizontal beams. Greek architecture is trabeated.

TRANSEPT. In churches with a cruciform plan that portion of the building which transverses the major dimension. Sometimes, as in most Gothic cathedrals, the transepts project conspicuously beyond the nave. See Figure 294, page 475.

TRANSITION. Getting from one thing to another without a definite break or change; a type of continuity.

TRIAD. A group of three colors generally forming an equilateral triangle on the color wheel. Red, blue, and yellow form a triad.

TRUSS. An architectural form in which beams, bars, etc., are combined into a rigid framework the shape of which cannot be altered without deformation of one or more of its members. Trusses are usually triangular or are made up of triangular forms because the triangle is the only polygonal form which cannot be altered without changing the length of one or more sides.

TWILL. A type of weave in which there is a diagonal rib running across the fabric. Herringbone cloth and gabardine are twill weaves.

TYPE FACE. The character, shape, or design of the type used in printing.

UNITY. Oneness; singleness; all means or elements adapted to a single purpose or end.

VALUE. The degree of light or dark. Values range from white to black.

VARIETY. Differences or variations.

VAULT. An arched covering in masonry over a building or room. Vaults are of many kinds: barrel, groined, ribbed, etc. See Figures 272 and 273, pages 453 and 454.

VICTORIAN PERIOD. Taking its name from Queen Victoria, this period includes most of the ornamental excesses of the nineteenth century. Designers used the Gothic style as a point of departure but were inventive in developing new forms and in a free use of vigorous if often crude detail.

VITREOUS. A term applied to high-fire ceramics which are dense, glassy, and nonporous, as opposed to stoneware which is granular and porous. China is a vitreous ceramic.

VOLUTE. The scroll or spiral occurring in Ionic capitals.

WAINSCOT. The paneling on the lower part of walls; usually of wood.

WARP. The lengthwise threads in a woven fabric. Warp threads are strung on the loom before the weaving begins. See Figure 183, page 310.

WEFT. The crosswise threads in a woven fabric; also called filling. Weft and warp threads are interlaced in weaving.

WOOD BLOCK. A block of wood in which the background is cut away and the remaining raised surface is used for printing; also a print made from such a block. See Figures 197 and 198, pages 321 and 322.

WOOD ENGRAVING. The process of engraving designs on the end grain of wood for printing; also a print made from this engraved surface. Wood engravings generally show finer detail than wood blocks.

ZONING. Restricting the uses of land areas in city planning.

Index

Index

518